CAR CRASH CULTURE

EDITED BY
MIKITA BROTTMAN

palgrave

For M. G.

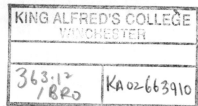

First published 2001 by PALGRAVE™
175 Fifth Avenue, New York, N.Y. 10010
Companies and representatives throughout the world.

PALGRAVE is the new global publishing imprint of St. Martin's Press LLC
Scholarly and Reference Division and Palgrave Publishers Ltd. (formerly
Macmillan Press Ltd.).

ISBN 0–312–24036–8 hardback
ISBN 0–312–24038–4 paperback

Library of Congress Cataloging-in-Publication Data
Car crash culture / edited by Mikita Brottman
    p. cm.
   Includes bibliographical references and index.
ISBN 0–312–24036–8— ISBN 0–312–24038–4 (alk. paper)
   1. Traffic accidents—Social aspects—History. 2. Automobiles—Social
aspects—History. 3. Celebrities—Death—History. I. Brottman,
Mikita, 1966-

HE5614.C368   2002
363.12'5'0973—dc21   2001036102

First PALGRAVE edition: January 2002
10 9 8 7 6 5 4 3 2 1
Design by Letra Libre, Inc.

Printed in the United States of America

She loved accidents: any mention of an animal run over, a man cut to pieces by a train, was bound to make her rush to the spot.

—Émile Zola, *La Bête Humaine,* 1890

CONTENTS

EDITOR'S ACKNOWLEDGMENTS

Thanks are gratefully extended to all contributors, and special thanks to Kenneth Anger, David Kerekes, Randy Malamud, Kristi Long, Thomas Jones, Adam Parfrey, and Joseph Rupp. Most of all, much gratitude is due to my friends at the Columbia Seminar on Cinema and Interdisciplinary Interpretation for their continued interest and encouragement, especially Krin Gabbard, Pamela Grace, Bill Luhr, Chris Sharrett, and David Sterritt.

INTRODUCTION

MIKITA BROTTMAN

I'VE HEARD IT SAID THAT EXPERIENCED RESCUE WORKERS CAN, from some distance, recognize the distinctive smell of an accident, just as many psychiatrists can recognize the smell of a schizophrenic in crisis. I wonder what an accident smells like. I wonder if there's any similarity between these two smells.

You're driving calmly along the freeway when, in the distance, you spot the red and blue flashing lights of a police car. Suddenly a blaring ambulance comes rushing past you down the hard shoulder. Ahead, the traffic slows to a crawl, people stopping to gaze in fascination at the wreckage by the side of the road. Trapped in the middle of a huge collision, a human body has just been transformed into something special— a man-machine centaur, an obscure roadside saint. For just a moment, death has infected your life; the corpse has encroached upon your day.

Memories of accidents plague our highways and haunt the paths of our journeys. Every bad stretch of freeway and blind corner has its ghosts, casualties of automotive carnage.

I've also heard it said that everybody has one major accident in their lives. If this is true, then I had mine in October 1992 on the Salamis Road in Turkish Cyprus. It was a Friday night and I'd been out for a drink with a friend. We'd shared a bottle of wine at a bar, and around midnight I'd dropped off my friend at her apartment and stopped in at another bar to see if some other people I knew were there and to check out the band. But my friends had already left, so after having a beer at the bar, at about one o'clock in the morning, I set off on the three- or four-mile drive back to my apartment.

In any European country, I would probably have been slightly over the limit for drunk driving. But this was Turkish Cyprus, and it was pretty much the usual practice for everybody on that side of the island to drive home if they'd been out drinking on Friday and Saturday nights. There were no laws against drunk driving, virtually no public transport, and no system of police road checks or breathalyzers. Perhaps more significantly, the only places to go in the evening were bars and nightclubs, and the only way to get to them was by car. The police all went home at five o'clock, which was also when the buses stopped running. In other words, everybody drove everywhere, no matter how much they'd had to drink. Even worse, the majority of the people on that side of the island were the kind of college students known as *magandas*—the none-too-clever, binge-drinking sons of wealthy Turkish families, away from home for the first time and behind the wheel of their first Mercedes. As a result, fatal car crashes were a weekly affair.

The road leading back to my apartment is also especially dangerous, and well known for its car accidents. There are no road lights and no center markings. I'm driving pretty fast on this particular night—probably around fifty or sixty—and, as usual, I'm not wearing my seat belt. I'm less than half a mile from my apartment building when another car turns into the road rather sharply, about two hundred yards in front of me, with its headlights on full. It turns into my side of the road and starts moving toward me, gaining speed. I'm blinded momentarily by its headlights, and I notice they're getting closer and closer, and the car still seems to be way over on my side of the road.

The next thing I know, I'm sitting up in my car seat and I realize that my engine seems to have stalled, because my car isn't moving. It's completely dark and silent, and there's no light at all outside. I turn the key in the ignition, but the engine seems to be totally dead. I can't understand what's happened. I try turning the key a second time, a third time, but nothing.

Then, gradually, I become aware that my car windshield is totally smashed up and—beyond that—that the hood is all crushed in. Then I realize that there's another car right in front of me whose hood is sort of embedded in mine. I don't know how I didn't notice it before—it's so close I could almost have reached out and touched it through the smashed glass of my windshield.

The next thought that comes into my head is the realization that I must have just had a major car accident. It's a thrilling thought. I'd never been in any kind of serious accident before in my life. And for some reason, the thought that I'm sitting there in the middle of a major car wreck—perhaps even a fatal one—suddenly seems terribly exciting to me.

The next thing I remember is noticing a blood-covered man looking in through my driver's side window. He stares at me for a while through the broken glass, then starts trying to pull the door open, but it's all smashed in and he can't open it. Then, behind him, I notice there are some other people, also covered in blood, walking aimlessly around into the mist. It's a very vivid scene, and reminds me a little bit of *Night of the Living Dead*. Until this point I haven't thought about my injuries at all, but now I think that if these people are all covered in blood, then maybe I am too. I reach up to the rearview mirror, twist it down toward me, and I'm right. My face is not my face anymore. All I can see is a mess of torn skin and blood, and my own eyes looking back at me through it.

Next, somebody is pulling me out of the wreck by my legs, which is unbelievably painful, but a pain that is quickly forgotten (isn't it curious how difficult it is to retain our memories of physical pain?). Later I learn that one of my hips has been dislocated, which is what makes extricating me from the car so painful—or perhaps the process of being pulled out of the wreckage has actually caused the dislocation. Nobody knows.

Then I'm being carried into a vehicle—I imagine it to be an ambulance, but later I learn it was actually a passing taxi; in fact, the hospital in Famagusta didn't even *own* any ambulances. Then somebody with a knife or pair of scissors is cutting up each leg of my favorite pair of jeans. These jeans are later mended perfectly and free of charge by a local tailor (who comes and sits by my hospital bed and reads me his abysmal epic poetry), and for a while I loved wearing them just to show everybody where they were stitched up after the accident.

The next morning I wake up in a hospital bed: an accident victim. They show me the damage. I'm covered in little cuts from glass splinters.

I.1   Northern Cyprus, October 1993.

My left wrist is fractured and my right hip dislocated—and soon becomes infected with thrombosis. Worst of all, however, my face is all
smashed up from where I crashed headfirst into the broken windshield;
my nose is crushed and split open all down the middle. Still, I'm pretty
lucky. The people in the other car, a Turkish family on their way back
from a wedding on the other side of the island, all have injuries far more
severe than mine.

I'm in the hospital for about six weeks: an ordeal that is dull, tedious, op-
pressive, and—from time to time—physically painful. What makes it worse
is the fact that I'm the passive victim of the hospital's only doctor—an arrogant despot who speaks to me in German because he doesn't know any
English. The fact that I don't speak German is somehow beside the point.
Friends tell me that he's well known on the local bar scene as a transves-
tite—something I find difficult to believe until, during one of his brusque
morning visits, I notice very faint traces of black eye makeup under his eyes.

But the most interesting part of the whole accident is that at no time,
either during the crash or afterwards, did I ever feel any trauma of any
kind. In fact, even when they were pulling my body out of the wreck, I
remember only feeling thrilled by the fact that I was in the middle of a

serious car accident and experiencing an unusually heightened sense of consciousness and a powerful feeling of vitality and well-being. And this led me to understand an important truth: that accidents can bring as much pleasure as pain.

And let's face it: we all feel a slight thrill at the thought of any serious accident.

Enormous amounts of money are invested every year by the car industry in the development of new safety features; in most Western countries, penalties for driving offenses such as speeding and driving under the influence are draconian. But it still seems perplexing to me not that there are so *many* car accidents on the road today but that there are so *few*. In the United States, the typical driver is involved in a road accident about once every twelve years. Also, ironically, two out of every five automobile-related deaths are caused by pedestrians making hazardous forays into the road. One recent study of the world's most dangerous places concluded that there is nowhere in the world more precarious than Atlanta, particularly if you are trying to cross the road.[1] In fact, by far the most dangerous form of transportation today is *walking*. Perhaps the best answer to the problem of road safety is to get more people off the sidewalks and behind the wheel.

As the chapters in this book illustrate, however, the car crash is the archetypal means of *celebrity* death—certainly the most memorable, and perhaps also the most appealing, forming an appropriately dramatic closure to a life lived in public. From motorcade and gold-plated Rolls to tour bus and stretch limousine, celebrities are particularly fond of their automobiles. Nothing makes a better tabloid headline than the celebrity car crash, especially if it involves drugs, alcohol, excessive speed, violence, or passengers who shouldn't have been there. Nothing ends a tale of beauty, wealth, and potential better than blood on the tracks. The celebrity car crash is a sacred moment in time, a magic ritual, an instant constellation of tragedy, sacrifice, mass fantasy, and monumental comeuppance.

The youngest celebrity ever to have been killed by a car was the infant Pauline Flood, better known as silent-movie star Baby Sunshine. Flood was run over by a truck in Los Angeles when she was only one year old. Seven other minor celebrities were killed in car accidents between 1910 and 1920, and seven more in the following ten years. These included the great dancer Isadora Duncan, who was killed at the age of forty-nine in September 1927, on the French Riviera. It was around ten in the evening, and Duncan was heading back from a walk along the Promenade des Anglais in Nice, beautifully dressed as usual in three or four immense iridescent scarves that streamed around her neck and body. On the way back to her hotel, she found a vacant taxi—a convertible—and got into the back seat, not realizing that the loose end of one of her scarves had fallen outside the car and was caught in the rear wheel. As the taxi reached full speed, the scarf wound itself round the wheel and the strong silk began to strangle Duncan, finally dragging her bodily out of the car and throwing her down on the cobblestone street. She was dragged several yards behind the cab before the driver was alerted to the accident by the cries and shouts of passersby. Duncan was strangled and killed instantly. Interestingly, two of her children had also been killed in a freak car accident in 1913, when they were left unattended in a vehicle that rolled down a hill and plunged over a bridge into the Seine.

In the decade that followed, the number of celebrity car accidents increased significantly, partly due to the expansion of the motion-picture industry but also due to the enormous increase in traffic on the roads and the sudden expansion of the freeway system around Los Angeles. The most colorful celebrity car crash of the 1930s was probably that which involved F. W. Murnau, the German-born director of *Faust* and *Nosferatu,* who was killed on March 11, 1931, in Santa Barbara, at the age of forty-two. When Murnau's car came off the road on a stretch of Californian coastline, it was determined that the driver was not the film director but his fourteen-year-old Filipino houseboy, Garcia Stevenson. The rumor that Murnau was going down on his servant at the time, spread by Kenneth Anger in the book *Hollywood Babylon*—and recalled by both Anger and Howard Lake in this volume—has never been "officially" confirmed, although it's clear the boy was one of Murnau's lovers.

Between 1940 and 1950, the number of celebrity car accidents was somewhat lower, perhaps as a result of increases in road and traffic safety. Notable crash victims included cowboy film star Tom Mix, who was killed in 1940 after breaking his neck when his car overturned in Florence, Arizona (in chapter 1, Kenneth Anger relives his childhood memories of this thrilling trauma: a shocking index of the loss of innocence). Author Nathanael West and his wife, Eileen McKenney, were killed in El Centro, California, on December 21, 1940, in the same week that saw the death of West's literary hero, F. Scott Fitzgerald. Other car-related fatalities during the decade included the especially interesting case of Charles Butterworth, a character actor who starred in a string of comedy classics throughout the 1930s. His death in a car crash in 1946 was registered as an accident, but since he was reportedly distraught at the time, many believe his death should have been classed as a suicide. (See chapters 9 and 10 in this volume for the difficulties in classifying single-car auto accidents.)

The mother of all celebrity crashes took place at 5:59 P.M. on September 30, 1955, at the intersection of routes 41 and 466 near Pasa Robles, California. A week after completing shooting on *Giant*, James Dean, the enfant terrible of car crash culture, was, as everybody who cares knows, on his way to a sports car rally in Salinas in his silver Porsche Spyder, the "Little Bastard." A few hours earlier, in Bakersfield, Dean had been issued a speeding ticket and warned to slow down, but when his car crashed head-on into an oncoming vehicle, he was reportedly driving at a speed of at least 86 mph. His last words—to passenger Rolf Weutherich—were apparently "he's got to see us." Dean's head was nearly severed from his body by the crash; Weutherich suffered a broken leg and head injuries, and the driver of the other vehicle, Donald Turnupseed, was only slightly injured.

A compulsive and reckless personality, Dean had been invited during the last month of his life to take part in a traffic safety commercial on behalf of the National Highways Committee. During Dean's sequence, he is interviewed by actor Gig Young, who starts off by saying to him "Jimmy, we probably have a great many young people watching us tonight, and, for their benefit, I'd like your opinion about fast driving on the highway. Do you think it's a good idea?" In response, the guilty speed freak looks directly at the camera, grins sexily, and warns the film's teenage viewers to "Remember, drive safely—because the next life you save may be mine." After Dean's death, his wrecked Porsche was used as

I.2   1949 Mercury from *Rebel Without a Cause*.

a safe driving exhibit in a nationwide tour to discourage his teenage fans
from similar feats of daredevil driving.[2]

"The Curse of James Dean's Car" gathered momentum over the years,
resulting in a total of twelve documented fatalities in which the "haunted
car" was allegedly involved. Celebrity car customizer George Barris
bought the mangled wreck of the "Little Bastard" to sell off some of the
undamaged parts. Barris claims that Dean's car was "wild-looking, evil-
looking," and gave him the creeps. He says he always had a "bad feeling"
about the Porsche—which lacked the safety features of similar models—
and apparently had warned Jimmy many times about the car. When the
smashed vehicle was delivered to Barris's yard, it allegedly rolled off the
back of the delivery truck and broke a mechanic's legs. A Beverly Hills
doctor, Troy McHenry, who also raced cars, bought the engine from the
"Little Bastard," transferred it to another car, and was killed the first time
he drove it. A fellow doctor who bought the transmission put it in his
own car and was then seriously injured in a crash, and a man in New
York who bought two of the Porsche's tires spent weeks in hospital when
they both "mysteriously" blew out at the same time. A year later the curse
claimed another victim, when the remaining shell of the car was being

transported to a public road-safety exhibition in Salinas and the driver of the transporter was killed as the truck skidded and crashed. After that, the remains of the wrecked Porsche disappeared in the Florida Keys— and have not been heard of since—although individual relics occasionally crop up from time to time, like pieces of Christ's "true cross," as Julian Darius explains in chapter 26. Indeed, in chapter 1, Kenneth Anger confesses to owning a piece of Dean's death car, which he bought for the bargain price of $300.

Is it possible that the highly charged panic and emotion of a violent death can stay with the parts of a wrecked car? Can accident sites somehow retain the ghosts, the memories, the smells of an accident? This common superstition is the basis of "The Death Car," one of the many urban legends involving automobiles chronicled by the popular folklorist Jan-Harold Brunvand.[3] In the most frequently recounted version, explains Brunvand, a friend of a friend picks up a flashy sports car for an inexplicably cheap price. The reason for the reduced price, it turns out, is because somebody has died in the car. One version of the story—recounted briefly here in chapter 28 by Gregory Ulmer—has the car sitting in the middle of the Mojave desert for a week with a dead body in it. Another has someone committing suicide inside the vehicle and the body being left to rot for months. In every version of the tale, however, the fundamental point is the same: The vehicle is almost always described as new, a model deemed to be highly desirable at the time of the story's telling (Model A, Buick, Cadillac, Corvette, Jaguar, and so on), and the smell of death can't be eliminated. No amount of washing or scrubbing can make it go away.

According to Brunvand, folklorist Richard M. Dorson thought that he had traced "The Death Car" back to a 1938 suicide in the small town of Mecosta, Michigan, but later study turned up prototypical elements earlier in Europe. Other folklorists have speculated that the car's offensive smell is perhaps not only the smell of death but that of filthy lucre. The prestigious sports car can be obtained by working class people only if it is defective—in other words, if it stinks. In this narrative, as in so many similar tales, the accident-scarred automobile becomes a forcefield of trouble, terminally hexed by the ghost of *one previous owner.*

Everyone knows that his car crash was the best career move Dean ever made. Parallels are often drawn between his death and the "chicken run" scene in *Rebel Without a Cause* (1955), in which Jim Stark (Dean) and another boy are driving two hot-wired cars toward the edge of a cliff. The first one to jump out is a chicken. Jim rolls free at the last second, but the other boy's coat sleeve is caught in the door handle of his car, and he rolls over a cliff to his death. In the aftermath comes Dean's anguished voice crying "a boy was killed!"

The 1960s were a fashionable decade for celebrity car crashes; twelve well-known personalities were killed in automobile-related incidents between 1960 and 1970, not including what Vaughan in J. G. Ballard's novel *Crash* memorably describes as the "special kind of car crash" experienced by John F. Kennedy on November 22, 1963, analyzed in detail here in chapter 16 by Pamela McElwain-Brown. The year 1960 saw the death of author and philosopher Albert Camus, at the age of forty-six, in a car driven by his publisher in Le Sens, France—a crash whose cultural significance is examined in this volume in chapter 25 by Derek Parker Royal. That same year rock-and-roll singer Eddie Cochran was killed at the age of twenty-one in a taxi crash in Bath, England; two years later comedian Ernie Kovacs was killed in a terrible accident at the age of forty-two. The defining car crash of the 1960s, however, is the midnight collision that took the life of actress Jayne Mansfield in 1967.

After standing in at a nightclub engagement in Biloxi, Mississippi, as a replacement for Mamie Van Doren, the thirty-five-year-old Mansfield was being driven to New Orleans in the early hours of June 29 to be interviewed on a local television show. She was traveling with her current boyfriend (San Francisco attorney Samuel S. Brody), three of her five children, and four pet Chihuahuas. The 1966 Buick Electra was being driven by Ronnie Harrison, a college student who was working as a chauffeur for the summer. The party set off from Biloxi at about 2:30 in the morning. About twenty miles outside New Orleans on windy U.S. Highway 90—often known as the Spanish Trail—the Buick smashed straight into the back of a trailer that had stopped suddenly behind a city truck spraying the swamps with anti-mosquito insecticide.

The crash was so forceful that the impact sheared off the top of the Buick, which apparently "crumpled like piece of tinfoil after a cookout"[4]—in fact, crash investigators first assumed the hardtop was a convertible. Jayne, Brody, and Harrison were killed instantly, their bodies thrown out of the wreckage and on to the road. The three children, who were sleeping in the back of the car, received only minor bruises.[5] Most accounts of the crash—including Kenneth Anger's, in chapter 1—describe Mansfield as being decapitated; Anger recalls seeing a photograph of the actress's severed head mounted on the front of her wrecked car, "surrealistically transformed into a bloody hood ornament." Other, less lurid reports claim that Mansfield wasn't in fact decapitated but scalped by the car's roof, her blonde wig thrown forward on to the hood of the Buick. However, in the clearest photograph of the wreck, Mansfield's body, covered with a tarp, lies in the foreground, and it's clear to see that there is nothing where her head should be. No one, however, will debate the fact that two innocent young Chihuahuas also lost their lives in tragic circumstances.

The 1970s saw a significant increase in the number of celebrity car crash deaths. The decade's casualties include former child actor Brandon de Wilde, who was driving through Denver, Colorado, on July 6, 1972, when his car hit a flatbed truck, killing him instantly. In Britain, the world of pop music was shaken by the untimely death of Marc Bolan, amphetamine sage and lead vocalist of the group T-Rex, who was killed in the early hours of September 16, 1977, when he and his girlfriend, Gloria Jones, were returning from a nightclub. Gloria was at the wheel; Bolan, despite a lifetime's fascination with cars, had never learned to drive. (See Howard Lake's creepy chapter 6 in this volume for an investigation of the role of the passenger in car crashes.) The Bolan crash took place in Barnes Common, North London; Jones, having just driven over a humpbacked bridge, took a sharp curve and lost control of the car, which came off the road at high speed and crashed into a tree; Gloria Jones survived, but the twenty-nine-year-old Bolan was killed on impact.

Bolan's car crash, like many later accidents, provoked a considerable media-based frenzy of mourning. The day after the fatal crash, which made front-page news, crazed fans broke into Bolan's home and stole almost everything they could get their hands on; a hospital worker even tried to sell the blood-splattered clothes the eccentric star had been wearing the night of the crash. The funeral was a circus of grieving fans, and even now the "death tree" on Barnes Common remains a roadside shrine for tender messages and other sentimental ornaments of tribute and grief.[6]

I.3   Grace Kelly and Cary Grant in *To Catch a Thief.* © Photofest

"Adult" motion picture actors—a community not generally known for their precautionary lifestyle—are particularly frequent victims of the automotive exit. Recent death crash porn stars include among their illustrious ranks Veronica Blue (2000), Krysti Lynn (1995), Tommy Wilde (1994), Leo Ford (1991), and Tom Farrell (1993), who was killed by a hit-and-run driver while urinating by the side of the freeway. The archetypal instance of the genre took place on October 3, 1979, when "vivacious 29-year-old *Playboy* playmate" Claudia Jennings was involved in a fatal accident on the Pacific Coast Highway. This is a stretch of road notorious for its car crashes as well as for its ghost sightings. According to popular superstition, spirits are drawn to the water, and the Pacific Coast Highway is the road at the end of the earth. If accident sites are haunted by their casualties, then this must be an especially resonant site. Perhaps the smell of death is buried in the surface of the road, just as accident scars are buried in the flesh.

The number of celebrity car crashes stabilized during the 1980s and 1990s to about twenty-five to thirty per decade. Increases in the security and safety of celebrity transportation since the 1980s have meant that such instances of vehicular mayhem, when they do happen, make even more tawdry headlines for the tabloids. One especially compelling accident happened on September 13, 1982, at approximately 9:30 A.M., when former movie actress Grace Kelly was driving from Roc Agel along a hazardous road on the Moyenne Corniche, toward Monaco (coincidentally, the same snaking road she traveled in a thrilling ride with Cary Grant in the 1955 film *To Catch a Thief*). While passing through the town of Mentone, the car failed to negotiate a curve and flew off the road, rolling down the side of a steep cliff. Grace's daughter Stephanie survived the crash, but the princess drifted into a coma. At six the following morning she was pronounced brain dead. After her husband, Prince Rainier, terminated her artificial life support system at noon, she died that evening, at 10:35.

The autopsy apparently suggested that the princess suffered a minor stroke while driving, leading her to lose control of the vehicle. And while the exact circumstances of her death remain ambiguous, the accident is hardly shrouded in mystery; the road from Roc Agel to Monaco is dangerously steep, and everyone who knew her agreed that Grace was a terrible driver. Nevertheless, like all similar accidents, the Monaco crash has been the source of much speculation, rumor, and fetish-filled reveries involving Princess Stephanie, Prince Rainier, and a shady character named Joseph di Mambro, the magus allegedly responsible for initiating Grace into a religious cult related to the Order of the Solar Temple.[7]

Similar rumors, gossip, voyeuristic fantasies, private nightmares, conspiracy theories, and allegations of cryptic skullduggery surround most of the celebrity accidents analyzed in this volume. Compelled by an elemental fear of powerlessness, the human mind seems unwilling to contemplate the idea of the pure accident—especially one whose victim is young, popular, beautiful, talented, and protected by the necessary security that accompanies wealth, fame, and all the other trappings we have come to associate with "success." As this volume testifies, many of us are haunted by the compulsion to apply categories and schema to all notions of randomness, to forge a science out of chaos and a taxonomy out of probability. We regularly feel driven to discern that sense of rhythm and proportion that we are convinced—often despite ourselves—must lie behind all purportedly accidental events. In fact, a number of somber philosophers, including Sigmund Freud, have observed that it is humanly impossible to come to terms with the enormous influence that chances and accidents have on our lives.

This insatiable impulse to make order of chaos seems to drive our obsession with the most spellbinding car crash of the 1990s—the death of Princess Diana beneath the Pont d'Alma in Paris on August 31, 1997. As we all know, the princess was returning home in the early hours of the morning after dinner at the Ritz, when she, her companion Dodi Fayed, and driver Henri Paul were killed when Fayed's Mercedes hit a pillar under the tunnel and went into a deathly roll (see chapter 6 for a blow-by-blow account of this crash). Initially the princess's death was blamed on the scurvy antics of paparazzi pursuers so rabid for a picture they were accused of opening the door of the crashed car—not to assist, but to rearrange the bodies for a more powerful shot. Later a second scapegoat was found in the figure of the car's driver, Henri Paul, especially after it was discovered he was over twice the legal limit for drunk driving and under the influence of psychotropic medication.

Still, conflicting early reports of the accident have left enough questions unanswered to breed plenty of puzzling rumors. Initial news broadcasts stated only that Diana had a concussion, a broken arm, and cuts to her thighs; how could this diagnosis have been so seriously wrong? Why did the ambulance carrying the princess take so long to travel the six miles to the hospital? How was it possible for a photographer to open the door of the car in order to take Diana's pulse when rescue workers claimed she had to be cut from the vehicle? Did the doctor on the scene really administer oxygen to the princess without recognizing her, as he claims? These and other questions will always be compelling because merely to ask them evokes the possibility, however remote, that Diana's death was part of a narrative with purpose, order, and motive, not without precedent, not without order, and, most of all, not without meaning.

If an accident is something more than an accident, then what else might it be? How tempting and exciting it is to see the celebrity car crash as iconic—as ritual sacrifice, perhaps, or obscure triumph; an exercise in hermetic synchronicity or harbinger of a new age. When the automobile suddenly becomes a coffin, how befitting it is to see a cryptic revelation reflected in the shattered windshield. Are wrecked cars hieroglyphs, transitional objects that forge a link between the sensible world of logic and the unknowable realm of the occult? Or are they just chunks of bloodied metal littering the road for a while?

There are three periods during which accident victims die: the so-called golden hour (the first sixty minutes after the crash), within hours of the crash (sometimes because the wrong treatment was given at the scene), and over the following few weeks. Numbers in the first two categories have fallen radically over the last thirty years, partly because of improvements in car safety and partly due to a better understanding of emergency medicine. It is important to understand that most crash injuries are caused not by the first collision (between the car and an external object), nor by the second collision (between the victim's body and the interior of the vehicle), but by the third collision: between the internal organs and the walls of the body—injuries that often can be reduced by the use of a safety belt.[8]

According to Dr. Howard Burgess of the Cowley Shock Trauma Unit in Baltimore, the patterns of car crash injuries are very predictable, generally bearing the imprint of a rigid surface encountered at high speed, with special impact to the legs and lower torso. ("Many patients look like somebody would look if they tried to commit suicide or jumped from a burning house."[9]) Medical understanding of such injuries has increased rapidly since the development of the crash test dummy—although, to occasional press outrage, some scandalous European researchers still prefer to get as close as possible to the real thing in their crash tests and continue to use human corpses.[10]

Despite substantial improvements in emergency medicine and in the understanding of crash injuries, however, the hazard of any form of accident is an increasingly significant concern to people in the West now that most of us are pretty much guaranteed seven or eight decades of life. "The Accident has become a paradox of necessity," writes the Mexican poet, author, and essayist Octavio Paz. "It possesses the fatality of necessity and at the same time the indetermination of freedom."[11] In other words, the accident is a necessary property of any given system—of progress, movement, technology, and speed. In his essay on J. G. Ballard's novel *Crash,* French philosopher Jean Baudrillard explains how the accident is simply another form of order, like the order of the neurotic, the order of residue, and the order of transgression.[12] But at the same time, the accident is outside any form of human control, a fact that compels us to shroud it in superstition and taboo. As Paz explains, "[a]ccidents are part of our daily life and their shadow peoples our dreams as the evil eye keeps shepherds awake at night in the little hamlets of Afghanistan."[13]

In contemporary American culture, however, the nature of any form of "accident" is particularly ambiguous because the term is so inextricably bound up with the discourse of tort law and the jiggery-pokery of insurance policy. "Accidents" in the legal sense always involve a civil wrong. Indeed, in terms of the law, the "accident" is defined as "negligence and causation for which one party is held responsible and liable for damages incurred"[14]—a definition heavily invested with notions of blame and accountability that has application only within the strictures of a capitalist economy. In one sense, however, the law is right: Most car "accidents" are actually the result of bad driving, alcohol, or faulty mechanics, and could easily be avoided. But unlike the phrase "car crash," the term "car accident" does not generally include a sense of blame, evoking instead a metaphysical paradigm to describe the kind of random event that is popularly attributable only to the caprice of destiny.

What term, then, should we use to describe the "accident" that turns out to be something else entirely—something more akin to theatrics, initiations, strange occult ceremonies, or lethal skullduggery? On April 19, 1998, the *New York Times* carried the story of two men who admitted a painstaking history of staging serious car crashes on interstate highways to win insurance payoffs. The men's activities came to light only after they "accidentally" caused a crash that led to the violent death of a family of three. Investigators said one of the defendants, driving a Mercury Cougar, purposely slammed on the brakes so a truck would crash into it on the freeway in 1996. The truck hit the Mercury, forcing a station wagon carrying Juan and Maria Lopez and their two-year-old daughter to stop behind it. A truck behind the family wagon could not stop in time and crushed the Lopez vehicle, killing the whole family immediately.

In this age of multimillion-dollar liability insurance, who knows how many similar car crashes are deliberately staged? Researchers in the field of accident causation spend a great deal of time trying to work out how many crashes are due to accident insurance, which can be a very significant *cause* of accidents as well as a source of accident prevention. And now that most cars come fitted with CD players, cell phones, and other enticing forms of electronic folderol, including the VCRs that are standard in many of the new-model sports utility vehicles, accidents caused by in-car distractions are also on the increase. In September 1999 a case was reported in London where a woman heard her ex-husband crash his car and die while they were in the middle of a nasty argument via mobile phone.[15] Such an incident is probably far from unique.

As French media theorist Paul Virilio explains, "every time that a new technology has been invented, a new energy harnessed, a new product made, one also invents a new negativity, a new accident."[16] A good example of this is the variety of new brands of fatal accidents made readily available by exciting new safety features like airbags (a quick way to suffocate your kids or inflict chemical burns), steering wheel locks like "The Club" (handy cudgels when a fit of road rage strikes), and power windows (lethal traps for children's arms and necks). Automatic locking systems also can prove nasty. A number of recent cases have been reported of children climbing into the trunks of new cars and suffocating when the automatic latch lock is released. Four children trapped in the trunk of their mother's car died in a recent case in New Mexico, and in Salt Lake City, five little girls suffocated when they all climbed into the trunk of a car that a hysterical mother, searching for the missing kids, proceeded to drive round for hours in the midday heat.

And on July 22, 1997, in Maryland, an eighty-eight-year-old woman died in a 1995 sedan due to malfunctioning electric locks on the doors and windows. The woman was found dead in the driveway of her home with the words "Help Me" scrawled all over the car windows in lipstick. (Had she recently been watching *The Exorcist?*) Investigators were unclear how long the car had been parked in the driveway, but the outside temperatures were in the mid-80s and the woman had clearly suffocated.[17]

Again this was probably not an isolated incident; in 1999 a product liability suit was filed against the Ford Motor Company for failing to install
a cooling device in its cars.[18]

And consider the number of road "accidents" that turn out to be very
clearly attributable to faulty vehicle manufacturing. Internal documents
generated within the Ford Motor Company—and leaked to the press in
the 1970s—made the shocking argument that it was cheaper to let accident victims die from burn injuries (at $200,000 value of compensation
per burn death) than to make improvements in the dangerous fuel tank
system of the infamous Ford Pinto. Even knowing all the dangers of the
fuel tank placement, Ford lobbied against a federal safety requirement
that would have forced it to redesign the car.[19] Similar cases are reported
on a regular basis by the media. Most recently, forty-six deaths and
eighty injuries have been attributed to a design defect in Firestone's 16-
inch tires that causes the tread to separate from the tire, sometimes at
high speed, causing blowouts and rollovers. Ironically, these particular
tires are installed mostly on fashionable sports utility vehicles—which
themselves are more prone to rollover than other vehicles because of their
higher centers of gravity.

Such scandals probably have done much to fuel the number of conspiracy theories and contemporary legends that involve vehicle manufacturers and automobile design. These include the tale of the auto worker
who steals parts of a Cadillac bit by bit until he has the whole car, the
story that gas engines pollute as much as diesel (diesel just smells worse),
and the persistent rumor that the Volkswagen Beetle was designed by
Hitler (the people's car may have been the Führer's idea, but it was actually designed by Ferdinand Porsche). All these stories reflect an increasing
sense of individual isolation in the face of the enormous size, wealth, and
power of gigantic corporations like Ford and General Motors.

Other automobile-based urban legends seem to bespeak our fears
about the anonymity of the driver and the difficulty in tracking down
the faceless perpetrator of the hit-and-run. These fears have increased
since the easy availability of the car has made certain kinds of crimes
much easier to commit, especially kidnapping, rape, and abduction. In
addition, a murder is much more difficult to solve when the body is concealed in the car and then dumped some distance from the scene of the

crime. For those who prey on hitchhikers, the car itself may become the crime scene, as it was for coed killer Ed Kemper, whose morbid story is told by Michael Newton in chapter 12. For criminals like Kemper, the car is especially convenient, since it can later be cleaned up and re-upholstered (as in the case of SS-100-X, the Kennedy Lincoln) or pushed gingerly into the swamp (like Marion Crane's Ford Fairlane in *Psycho*).

Consequently, most of these stories involve satanic cults or gangs whose members drive around at night without headlights, and—in a dangerous ritual of initiation—will follow and kill any thoughtful motorist who flashes them. In some of the best-known urban legends involving vehicles, the car conceals a killer or becomes the site of murder, often not long after being the site of sexual activity—as always in such stories, premature or extramarital coupling has nightmarish consequences. If the car provides a secret haven for horny teenagers, it also contains a hiding place for serial killers. In "The Hook," a psycho's phallic hand/hook is left hanging from the car door, broken off just in time when the girl insists that her boyfriend drive away. In "Don't Look Back," the abandoned girlfriend who can't resist turns around, like Lot's wife, to discover a madman crouched on the roof of the car beating on the metal with her boyfriend's severed head. Other, similar stories feature killers who conceal themselves in the backseat of a woman's car, hairy-handed hitchhikers, and ankle-tendon slashers who lie in wait under parked vehicles.

The car also crops up in a number of similar contemporary legends in which the consequences of inappropriate behavior in the automobile are unforgiving. Most of these stories tell of bizarre accidents, such as the story of the schoolkid who sticks his head out of the bus window and is beheaded by a road sign. And the man who crashes into a toll booth while getting a blow job from his girlfriend, like the man who is shunted from behind while picking his nose at a traffic light, is crippled for life by brain damage, not to mention abject humiliation.

Car crashes may be the most common link between death and the automobile, but there are many others. Vehicular death can take a variety of forms, and one of the designs of this volume is to see what happens when the concept of the "crash" or "accident" is taken beyond its usual limits to embrace the many other kinds of deaths that have been enabled by the invention of the automobile. For example, the media-fashioned fad of "road rage"—an oblique reaction to increased traffic congestion over the last ten years—is statistically proven to be on the increase, and can be seen as a new kind of "car crash."

One particularly violent case of road rage was reported in the *L.A. Times* on January 15, 1998, when a mother and daughter became infuriated with the driver of a truck ahead of them. The two women chased the truck down the Golden State Freeway in Sylmer, taunting the driver with obscene gestures and tailgating his vehicle, then chased it to the end of an off-ramp and swung round in a U-turn to spray it with mud. But in turning to sideswipe their target, the women's car skidded and crashed, causing the truck to stop abruptly and topple over on its side, landing on top of the women's car and cutting it in half. The two women were killed instantly, as engine and body parts were strewn all over the road. "I don't want to remember it," said the uninjured truck driver, revealing a stoicism well suited to a lifetime in the slow lane. "I just want to go on with my life like nothing happened."

Unsurprisingly, road rage is most fashionable on American multilane freeways, which have always been the most dangerous places to drive. The first such motorways were built in Germany in the 1930s under the direction of the recently installed dictator, Adolf Hitler. On the very first stretch of motorway, on the very first day it was opened, a German motorist, Bernd Rosemayer, was killed in a car crash. In the former East Germany, many of the original *autobahnen* still survive, many of them old, poorly engineered, and dangerous to use. The safety record of U.S. freeways is hardly much of an improvement, but then, it got off to a very bad start. In December 1940 the first U.S. freeway was completed in Los Angeles, and the opening ceremony accidentally included a near-fatal crash involving three carloads of officials.

Can we ever hope to understand what goes through the mind of the fatal car crash victim? Interestingly enough, investigators have speculated that a certain percentage of the single-vehicle car crashes that happen every year may in fact be deliberate suicides, disguised as accidents either because of the social stigma frequently attached to suicide or in order to let surviving relatives claim substantial insurance policies. Clearly, given the absence of a suicide note or verbal declaration of suicidal intent, es-

tablishing the single-vehicle car accident as a deliberate method of suicide is a difficult empirical exercise. (See chapter 10.) Most vehicular suicides, of course, are a lot less ambiguous. In Pennsylvania in July 1991,
the press reported a case of a very determined gent who, having failed to
kill himself by crashing his car, climbed out of the wreck and went door
to door around the local houses asking for matches. He then returned to
his vehicle, set fire to it, and died as a result of smoke inhalation and carbon monoxide poisoning.[20]

Other would-be suicides elect more inventive uses for their vehicles. In
Anchorage, Alaska, in July 1999, an exhibitionistic twenty-six-year-old
murdered his mother, then committed suicide by rigging his car seat belt
around his neck and around a parking post and stepping on the gas, thereby
decapitating himself very efficiently.[21] But forensic investigators also believe
that a number of less transparent suicides occur each year in the guise of
single-vehicle automobile accidents, especially among younger adult
males—generally the most self-destructive element of any population.[22]

Such "accidents" are therefore not accidents at all, but a positive affirmation of voluntary death, like the carnage orchestrated by Robert
Vaughan, "the nightmare angel of the highways" in J. G. Ballard's *Crash*.
Vaughan is a master of catastrophic ceremonies who charts connections
between famous crash victims, explains events, and stages their ritual
observances. Baudrillard describes such events as the "residual bricolage
of the death drive for the new leisure classes."[23] These are the kinds of
"accidents" that, instead of being the exception to a triumphant rationalism, show this rationalism for the manipulative façade it really is.
Perhaps it's no coincidence that Cadillac, the leading manufacturer of
speedy convertibles in the 1940s and 1950s, was also the leading manufacturer of hearses.

And how "accidental" was the lethal design of so many of the other
cars at this time? Many of those beautiful, extravagant automobiles
built in the 1940s and 1950s had huge windshields that broke easily
and could sever jugular veins, upright metal steering columns ready to
penetrate thoraxes, enormous steering wheels that could crush chests,
protruding radio knobs that could enter skulls, and crazy suicide
doors that could spring open, spilling helpless bodies on to the concrete. In one survey, two eminent doctors concluded that "if one were

to attempt to produce a pedestrian-injuring mechanism, one of the most theoretically efficient designs which might be developed would closely approach that of the front end of some present-day automobiles."[24] In his famous review of public-interest activist and corporate critic Ralph Nader's radical critique of the auto industry *Unsafe at Any Speed*, urban researcher Lewis Mumford wrote that "The [American] car has been the result of a secret collaboration between the beautician and the mortician; and, according to sales and accident statistics, both have reason to be satisfied."[25]

Significantly, if the design of a car can be unconsciously lethal, so too, according to psychiatrists, can the designs of its driver. Crash investigators have described the ominous notion of "unconscious motivation to suicide," which apparently seems chiefly prevalent in relation to car crashes, because "more conventional modes of suicide do not offer as dramatic an opportunity for the gratification of destructive and aggressive impulses"[26] (perhaps one way of explaining the disproportionate number of traffic deaths among drivers of red sports cars). In *The Atrocity Exhibition*, J. G. Ballard notes that "[t]ests on a wide range of subjects indicate that the automobile . . . provides a focus for the conceptualizing of a wide range of impulses involving the elements of psychopathology, sexuality, and self-sacrifice."[27] In those cases where a suicidal motive is suspected, psychiatrists investigating the accident sometimes carry out what is known as a "psychological autopsy" to help determine the victim's state of mind at the time of the crash. One investigation concludes that "unconscious self-destructive impulses . . . are a major although covert factor in the etiology of certain automobile accidents,"[28] again, mainly those involving younger adult males.

To claim that fatal car crashes can be brought about unconsciously is to seriously question the ontology of the accident. Cultural theorist Marq Smith[29] has pointed out that Freud first begins considering the nature of the accident in 1886—only two years after the invention of the first automobile by German engineer Karl Benz. In America, the first recorded car accident took place on September 13, 1888, when a man alighting from a trolley stepped right into the path of an overtaking car. Freud, however, came to believe that there is really no such thing as an "accident." In *The Psychopathology of Everyday Life,* he makes the case that all accidents are the result of unconscious impulses or manifestations of the death drive, whose forceful effect made him rethink his theory of the pleasure principle. According to Freud, the death drive is the urge that compels us to lean too hard against the stair rail we forgot was broken, to get in the way of oncoming traffic, to stand right underneath a shaky light fixture, to take a bend too fast. In other words, we are all responsible, albeit perhaps unconsciously, for the "accidents" that happen to us.

Freud's theory suggests there are no such things as fortuitous collisions, mishaps, or lapses of attention, only the forceful will of the death drive working in a deliberate way to a very definite end. "Certain performances which are apparently unintentional," writes Freud, "prove to be well motivated when subjected to the psychoanalytic investigation, and are determined through the consciousness of unknown motives."[30] "The conscious motivation does not extend over all our motor resolutions,"[31] and the errors of judgment, sudden impulses, unforeseen expressions, and symptomatic actions that lead to accidents, *actes gratuites,* and other fortuitous events are, in effect, the "wishes and phantoms"[32] of the unconscious. J. G. Ballard agrees. "Deep assignments run through all our lives," he writes. "There are no coincidences."[33]

Looking at my own accident in retrospect, I must admit that there are a couple of seconds that don't really fit the time frame. There was definitely a moment or two when I realized what was happening, when I saw the other car coming right at me at high speed. The police investigating the tire tracks concluded that the other driver was responsible for the crash but were curious why I hadn't at least attempted to swerve over to the hard shoulder. I didn't have an answer. Was it the alcohol slowing down my reaction time, or was there some more subtle reason? Was there a possibility—however remote and unconscious—that I drove deliberately into those oncoming headlights? Did I, for some unknown reason, *need* this accident to take place?

Now consider what would happen if the law were to take Freud's reading of "accidents" on board. Blame could not be attributed to anyone except the accident victim, for unconsciously causing the accident to happen. There would no longer be such a thing as compensation—or, if there were, it would have to be paid by "victims" to "perpetrators" (the driver of the oncoming car or train, for example), for putting them through the trauma of the accident. Perhaps, instead of saying that accidents "happen to" people, we should say that they "happen by" people. After all, if there were no victims, there would be no accidents. If Freud is right, then we are all responsible for our own destiny, even if we end up wrapped around the guardrail.

This is something that's not very easy to contemplate, particularly in today's ideological climate, where the most powerful position in society is that of the victim, and when non-Jewish minority groups have been "diagnosed" by sociohistorians as suffering from a condition known as Holocaust inferiority syndrome or, more plainly, Holocaust envy. Who wants to be responsible for their own actions when they could be a victim of someone else's—a victim of inadequate parenting, or emotional abuse[34]? How would the victims of My Lai or Hiroshima feel about the notion that they themselves were responsible for the atrocities that "happened to" them?

On the other hand, of course, accidents can be "explained" in various ways, generally involving the laws of science, physics, nature, and "chance." Accidents also happen to creatures that don't have consciousness so can't possibly have an unconscious; cattle panic and trample one another to death; crocodiles accidentally swallow their young. Still, there might be other kinds of laws guiding the path of our accidents—principles unknown to existing systems of logic and rationalism. It has been suggested that there may be a connection between the accident and the creative impulse, between the "random" path of the chance event and the structure of the work of art, whose understanding, like that of the accident, also depends on the accumulating effect of clues, allusions, and the progressive growth of that sense of anticipation we have come to call "meaning." Philosopher, scientist, and conspiracy theorist Robert Anton Wilson sees accidents in occult terms. To others, such as psychiatrist Jan Ehrenwald in *New Dimensions of Deep Analysis,* accidents are governed by definite laws, but laws that are not identifiable to the limits of science, consciousness, and nature. These are the same laws that apply to the structure of the dream, to the neurosis, and to unconscious processes in general.

And if accidents can have motivations that are hidden to conscious reasoning, then crash victims may be closely connected, pileups may be linked, and deaths on the road may be subtly orchestrated. This is the premise of J. G. Ballard's *Crash*. In this apocalyptic novel, Vaughan understands that what seem to be random accidents actually work in harmony and stand in a very significant relationship to one another. Cars plowing in to one another on the same road, crashes taking place at the same time or in the same place, have their own form of synchronicity, without being causally connected. (Ballard charts a parallel between road intersections and astrological signs.) Vaughan shows us how road accidents, particularly those involving celebrities, have their own chaotic orderedness. Instead of being random accidents, celebrity car crashes are revealed as deeply meaningful arrangements connected by a pattern of correspondence beyond space and time—a very special class of events orchestrated by the choreography of contingency.

On the subject of contingency, a couple of weeks after coming out of the hospital after my crash, I was involved in another road accident, although one that was rather less serious than the first. While I was in the hospital, my university-appointed lawyer, a shady and lecherous gentleman named Mr. Bayram, had been visiting me regularly to discuss my insurance claim—which, incidentally, he never settled. Mr. Bayram kept promising that as soon as I was out of the hospital, he'd take me out for a celebratory round of gin and tonics. One Friday night not long after I had started walking again without the aid of crutches, this gentleman called for me at my apartment and took me to a small seafood restaurant about five miles from town, on the same road where I'd had my crash.

After a huge meal of fried squid, he cracked open the much-discussed Gordon's, and it soon became clear that it was not just my legal case that interested him. A bottle of gin later, and I was helping him back to his car and trying to persuade him not to take his "special romantic route" back into town. Not surprisingly, he was far too drunk to be able to keep the car in a straight line, and before we were even halfway home we'd come straight off the road and were careering headfirst into a steep mud ditch. Was this the "romantic route" I'd heard so much about?

When the truck finally arrived to tow us out, Mr. Bayram suddenly became terrified that his wife would get to hear about his little "romantic adventure" and persuaded me to squat down in the back of his car while he handed out fistfuls of cash to keep the tow-truck guys quiet. By the time he'd had a sheepish piss in the ditch and was back behind the wheel, it was pretty clear there would be no further discussion of accidents and even less talk of romance.

In the West, the car has become a symbol of democracy, of individual freedom, and of the increasing independence enjoyed by the mass of the population of the industrialized world. In the United States in particular—historically, a restless, mobile society—the automobile has always been the most obvious index of individual prosperity and personal control. But America's wonder and worship at the glory of the automobile as a totem of change, speed, and technological progress has a grim underside. No other civilian invention has such an enormous degree of carnage associated with its everyday use. Unlike Europe, much of the United States was constructed with the automobile in mind. Consequently, the car has become as iconic to U.S. culture as the gun. If the automobile signifies wealth, movement, progress, and all that is venerated in America, then vehicular death embodies its counterpart—that violent rage toward destruction that lies beneath the surface of the proverbial "pioneer spirit." If the car is the symbol of America, then the car wreck is the nation's bloodstained sarcophagus.

The traditional kind of car crash, however, is only one of the many different kinds of deaths associated with automobiles. This collection of chapters has been compiled to investigate that bloodstained ground of contemplation that opens up whenever the automobile is the cause, or the site, of a human death. As a result, the notion of the "crash" has been opened up to help us understand how cars can be vehicles for destruction in all kinds of different ways, both accidental and deliberate. As well as the traditional kind of car crash, this collection includes cases of suicide from carbon monoxide poisoning, car bombings, drive-by shoot-ings, hit-and-run incidents, freeway murders, road rage killings, drag-ging deaths, and vehicular homicide.

"Something dead in the street commands more measured units of vi-sual investigation than 100 Mona Lisas!" affirms artist Robert Williams in his *Rubberneck Manifesto*. And he's right, as this volume amply testi-fies. Whatever their preferred form of conveyance, it's clear that neither princess, president, nor pope is immune from the hazards of vehicular transportation. This collection pays homage to the way in which our ob-session with death and the automobile manifests itself in an enormous variety of cultural contexts, from the popularity of demolition derbies and drag races to police high-speed chase videos and "reality TV" shows like *Pile-Up!* In community life, the car crash victim has become a style of saint, especially the child killed by a drunk driver, and commemorated by worshippers at a kitschy roadside shrine. In literature and film, crash culture finds its apotheosis in David Cronenberg's dolorous adaptation of J. G. Ballard's *Crash*. Ballard's own exhibition of crashed cars fore-grounded the possibilities of the accident site as art form: Car crashes are among the favorite subjects of artists Andy Warhol, Robert Williams, and Richard Hamilton.[35]

Interestingly enough, each collision in what Ballard describes as "the pantheon of auto-disaster victims," while reprising the archetypal pat-tern of premature ending and violent sacrifice, has its own unique style and tone. Every accident has a different disposition, a special mood. James Dean's fatal epiphany on the road to Salinas feels passionate, cul-tic, and legendary; the death of Albert Camus is slick, stylish, and in-evitably existential. Suicidal excess and hysteria surround Jayne Mansfield's terminal collision, while John F. Kennedy's deathly proces-sion through the Dealey Plaza is full of enormous foreboding. Grace Kelly's famous accident has left the road between Monaco and Roc Agel surrounded in mystery and scandal, and that other princess, in her Paris underpass, was transformed by a passionate and illustrious martyrdom.

Consequently, one especially fascinating dimension—partly because it is unanticipated—of this collection is the compelling variety of voices it contains. Since death by automobile takes such a wide variety of forms and can be approached from so many different perspectives, each car accident detailed in this volume is the object of a very different kind of fascination. Among the authors of the following chapters are doctors, pathologists, forensic scientists, film scholars, artists, coroners, cultural theorists, a poet, a lawyer, a psychiatrist, a criminal anthropologist, an urban ethnographer, a crime writer, and a passenger who can't drive. As a result, each chapter takes a surprisingly different approach to its own particular case of vehicular destruction.

For me, it is these variations in style and approach that make the following collection of chapters so fascinating. To most people, the car accident seems such a morbid and gruesome subject that the only acceptable way of approaching it is through the imperial voice of medicine or forensic science or the detached, rhetorical games of postmodern cultural theory. This volume contains examples of both these styles, but also includes many others, from the lyrical, philosophical, and self-reflective to the overtly lascivious and voyeuristic. This unsettling mixture of voices forces us to question the culturally accepted ways in which we have become accustomed to discussing the car crash. Why, for example, do we feel so much more comfortable with medical or forensic accounts of car accidents, even when they are full of rather gruesome and explicit details, as in most of the scientific chapters in this book? Why are we so uncomfortable with accounts that are gleeful, probing, and frankly lubricious? If there is a particular rhetorical tone that has become more or less appropriate for the discussion of the car crash, then I hope this book avoids it—or, at the very least, calls it into question.

Many people may find the subject matter of this book rather disturbing. It is very important to remember, however, that the fascination with car crashes to which this volume attests—ghoulish though it may seem—is essentially an attempt to confront some very deep-seated fears and anxieties. I believe there is a quasi-spiritual component to this compulsion to immerse ourselves in the etiology of the car crash and the rituals of sacrifice surrounding it—a compulsion that is resonant of some very archaic religious practices, including the worship of magic talismans and the collecting of relics. If nothing else, the need to give the accident some kind of order—to make art out of violent death—is itself perhaps no more than a superstitious need to assert (or to feign) control over the uncontrollable. I would also venture that most of the authors of the chapters in this collection are more conscious, more anxious, and more fearful of violence than most people, which is one way of understanding their engagement with it.

In the first section of this book, "Car Crash Contemplations," a group of writers and critics indulge in a series of ghoulish reminiscences and apocalyptic premonitions about particular deaths by automobile they have experienced, witnessed, or imagined. In chapter 1, "Kar Krash Karma," the filmmaker and occultist Kenneth Anger presents a wonderfully voyeuristic and lascivious account of Hollywood crashes. As he explains here, Anger has a particular fascination with cars and car crashes. His sensual and romantic three-minute drag-racing movie *Kustom Kar Kommandos* (1965)—a fragment of a much longer film—was made with a $10,000 grant from the Ford Foundation. *Kommandos* exemplifies Anger's interest in exploring fetishes—both his subjects' and his own—including the bodies of customized cars, as well as those of their customizers.[36] In this brief but mesmerizing film, images of car wheels function as mandalas, archetypal symbols intended to disturb customary modes of perception. The movie is also a celebration of the homoerotic world of drag racing and its relationship to Hollywood history as well as to gangster and cowboy mythologies. (Witness Anger's fascination with the cult of James Dean, the original cowboy drag racer.[37]) In chapter 2, poet A. Loudermilk indulges in a quiet, lyrical meditation on a spectacularly beautiful photograph that appeared in *LIFE* magazine in 1947; in chapter 3 Adam Parfrey recalls a life-changing crash, and in chapter 4 urban ethnographer Eric Laurier considers the role played by the mangled remains of crashed cars in the social and cultural landscape. In chapter 5, Willam Luhr relives a terrifying midnight accident, and in chapter 6, writer Howard Lake gives us the view from the back seat.

The chapters in the next section, "Car Crash Crimes," are reproduced mainly from scientific and medical journals, such as *Life Threatening Behavior* and the *Journal of Forensic Sciences*. As a result, these articles adopt the requisite tone of neutral objectivity even when reporting the most grotesque and outlandish events, their authors' glee betrayed only in the occasional apt turn of phrase or playful title ("The Love Bug," "A Case with Bear Facts"). In chapter 7, two pathologists discuss an unusual example of a dragging death, and in chapter 8, Dr. Joseph Rupp gives us a

brief glance into the strange world of sexual relationships between drivers and their automobiles. Chapters 9 and 10 include a collection of
compelling case studies involving examples of homicide and suicide by
automobile, and in chapter 11, a forensic anthropologist and a coroner
explain why you should never go into the woods alone. In chapter 12,
the final chapter in this section, Michael Newton brings the hard-boiled
style of the true crime writer to bear on the life of California's Freeway
Killer, Ed Kemper.

The third section of the book, "Car Crash Conspiracies," features
four very different studies. Philip L. Simpson, in chapter 13, is particularly interested in the politics and poetics that connect the deaths of
Princess Diana and Mary Jo Kopechne. In chapter 14, Jerry Glover uses
Paul McCartney's "notional" car crash as the springboard for an adven-
turous jaunt into the Beatle-based mythopoeia of the 1960s and 1970s.
Headpress editor David Kerekes considers the history of the "papal conveyance" in chapter 15, and in chapter 16, Pamela McElwain-Brown
takes a very close look at the history of SS-100-X, John F. Kennedy's fateful presidential limousine.

The fourth section, "Car Crash Cinema," is devoted to car accidents
that appear on film, both fictional and, in some cases, real. In chapter
17, psychiatrist Harvey Roy Greenberg provides a close analysis of David
Cronenberg's controversial movie *Crash*. This is followed in chapter 18
by a rather more apocalyptic reading of the movie by me and Christopher Sharrett; in chapter 19, Tony Williams reconsiders *Heart Like a
Wheel*, a critically neglected drag-racing movie, and in chapter 20 David
Sterritt presents a close, thoughtful reading of one particularly fascinating car crash scene in Godard's *Contempt*. Chapter 21 reconsiders those
much-missed Highway Safety documentaries that thrilled and terrified
high school kids in the 1950s and 1960s—films with titles like *Red Pavement, Highways of Blood,* and (my personal favorite) *Signal 30*, which I
discuss at some length.

The book's final section is entitled "The Death Drive." Jeff Ferrell, in
chapter 22, investigates the strange cult of roadside shrines, and in chapter 23 Jack Sargeant looks at the role of the car crash in a selection of pop
hits from the 1960s. Two very different investigations into the nature of
our obsession with celebrity death follow. In chapter 24 Steven Jay

Schneider writes about the crash that took the life of artist Jackson Pollock, and in chapter 25 Derek Parker Royal reconsiders the critical reputation of Albert Camus in light of his premature death. For Julian Darius in chapter 26, the wrecked car becomes a central conceit in a ludic piece that expertly juggles the two disparate events of celebrity accidents and crucifixion, and in chapter 27 Christopher Sharrett locates the car crash as the center of a whole historical tradition of American blood ritual. Finally, in chapter 28 Gregory Ulmer proposes a new kind of MEmorial project commemorating the roadside dead. This proposal helps us to recognize that whether we drive regularly ourselves or just travel as passengers or are mere pedestrians, all of us, both celebrity and civilian, are potential victims of that most democratic, that most compellingly familiar instrument of execution: the automobile.

NOTES

1. Robert Young Pelton et al., *The World's Most Dangerous Places* (HarperInformation, New York: 1997), 172.

2. The exhibition of famous people's cars—especially "death cars"—is a phenomenon worthy of further investigation, as are the ubiquitous urban legends involving jinxed or haunted cars whose former owners committed suicide. The car that once belonged to Ed Gein, the "Wisconsin Ghoul," was exhibited around the Midwestern United States for a number of years during the 1950s.

3. See, for example, Jan-Harold Brunvand, *The Vanishing Hitchhiker: American Urban Legends and Their Meanings* (New York: Norton, 1981).

4. At least, according to a representative of the Tragedy in U.S. History Museum in St. Augustine, Florida, which auctioned off the remains of the car (and failed to find a buyer) when the museum closed down on April 4, 1998. Other items in the sale included a bullet-ridden 1930 Ford said to have belonged to Bonnie and Clyde, which sold for $1,900.

5. One of these three children, Mariska Hargitay, is now a well-respected actress in her own right. She apparently remembers very little about the crash.

6. Steve Currie, another member of T-Rex, died in a far less widely publicized car crash in 1981, while vacationing in Portugal.

7. For full details of these allegations, see *Secret Lives: Grace Kelly* (Channel 4, U.K. December 21, 1997); also David Carr-Brown and David Cohen, "The Mystery of Princess Grace and the Temple of Doom," *New York Post*, December 28, 1997, 43. None of these allegations has been substantiated. Carr-Brown and Cohen claim that the cult into which Grace was initiated was the OTS, but the OTS was not established until 1984, and Princess Grace died in 1982. The authors seem to be confusing the OTS with a

French esoteric order with a similar name, the Sovereign Order of the Solar Temple (OSTS), whose Grand Master, Jean-Louis Marson, was, in fact, a Monaco socialite and friend of Prince Rainier.

8. See John D. Graham, *Autosafety* (Dover, Mass: Auburn House, 1989), 179.

9. Cited in Nicholas Faith, *Crash: The Limits of Car Safety* (London: Macmillan, 1997), 79.

10. See, for example, Mike Gardner, "University Defends Its Use of Corpses," *Times Higher Education Supplement*, March 12, 1993, 6.

11. Octavio Paz, *Conjunctions and Disjunctions*, trans. Helen R. Lowe (New York: Viking, 1969), 112.

12. Jean Baudrillard, *Simulacra and Simulation* (Paris: Edition Galilée, 1981), 168.

13. Paz, 111.

14. Denis Peck and Kenneth Warner, "Accident or Suicide? Single-Vehicle Car Accidents and the Intent Hypothesis," *Adolescence*, 30, 18 (1995): 463.

15. *London Evening Standard*, September 14, 1999. In a somewhat different but not unrelated incident, Geraldo Rivera, when he still fronted his voyeuristic talk show, screened the murder of a police officer caught on a new in-car police video camera (with the grieving widow shown in the corner of the screen, so that audiences could watch her reaction as she witnessed the murder of her husband for the first time). See David Kerekes and David Slater, eds., *Killing for Culture* (London: Creation, 1995), 128.

16. Paul Virilio, interviewed by Virginia Masden, "Critical Mass," *World Art*, no. 1 (1995), 81.

17. *Associated Press*, July 22, 1997.

18. Ben Schmitt, "Negligence Case Posits Novel Theory," *National Law Journal*, no. 8 (1999), 9.

19. Ralph Nader, *Unsafe at Any Speed* (New York: Grossman, 1972).

20. *Philadelphia Inquirer*, July 3, 1991.

21. The victim was Jonathan Kyakwok, and the case was reported on MSNBC.com on July 8, 1999.

22. See Peck and Warner; Carol Huffine, M.A., "Equivocal Single-Auto Traffic Fatalities," *Life-Threatening Behavior*, no. 2 (1971), 83–95; A. Porterfield, "Traffic Fatalities, Suicide and Homicide," *American Sociological Review* 25 (1960), 897–901; Chester W. Schmidt Jr., M.D., John W. Shaffer, Ph.D, Howard I. Zlotowitz, and Russell S. Fisher, M.D., "Suicide by Vehicular Crash," *American Journal of Psychiatry*, no. 2 (1977), 175–178; Melvin L. Selzer and Charles E. Payne, "Automobile Accidents, Suicide and Unconscious Motivation," *American Journal of Psychiatry*, no. 119 (1962), 237–240.

23. Baudrillard, 168.

24. Cited in Faith, 35.

25. Cited in Faith, 39.

26. "The automobile may also constitute a special enticement to the aggressive and vengeful feelings present in many would-be suicides. In an accident, not only is the automobile damaged or destroyed, but so is any object struck by the automobile, human or otherwise" (Selzer and Payne, 240).

27. J. G. Ballard, "The Atrocity Exhibition," *Love and Napalm* (New York: Grove, 1969). See also *Crash* (New York: Farrar, Strauss and Giroux, 1994).
28. Seltzer and Payne, 240.
29. Marq Smith, "Wound Envy: Touching Cronenberg's *Crash,*" *Screen* 40:2 (1999), 196.
30. Sigmund Freud, *The Psychopathology of Everyday Life,* trans. A. A. Brill (New York: Macmillan, 1955), 149.
31. Ibid., 165.
32. Ibid.
33. J. G. Ballard, footnote to Chris Petit's novel *Robinson* (London: Cape, 1993), 14.
34. For a further discussion of this point, see Philip Rieff, *The Triumph of the Therapeutic: Uses of Faith after Freud* (New York: Harper & Row, 1966).
35. Warhol's "White Burning Car III" (1963) and "Ambulance Disaster" (1963) both contain repeated images of car accidents, the former prominently featuring a crash victim impaled dead on a nearby telephone pole. Richard Hamilton's obsession with the automobile finds its apotheosis in his devotional painting *Homage à Chrysler Corp.* See also, by way of example, John Minton's *Composition: The Death of James Dean* (1957), Jim Dine, *Car Crash* (1935), Carlos Almaraz, *Car Crash* (1979), Robert Williams, *Brodyin on Feces* (1988).
36. See Dennis Conroy, "Kustom Kenneth Kommando," *Release Print,* November 2000, 22–40.
37. During the making of *Kustom Kar Kommandos,* Anger managed to come by one of his own most treasured fetishes—a T-shirt that allegedly belonged to a kid who'd died in a car wreck. Apparently there was a time in the late 1960s when Anger often wore this oily, blood-covered talisman to all his social engagements.

CAR CRASH CONTEMPLATIONS

ONE

KAR KRASH KARMA

KENNETH ANGER

SOMETIMES LIFE IS NOT PRETTY. It was a shock for me when my boyhood Saturday movie matinee Western idol, Tom Mix, died in a car crash when I was ten—in 1940—and idol Tom, after a long career in the saddle of wonder horse Tony, was a still swinging sixty. In my hometown Holly-wood I loved Tom's brash vulgarity. He was the only movie star to light up the night sky—outshining the multi-bulbed HOLLYWOODLAND sign—with a billboard-size white neon autograph spelling out TOM MIX beaconing over the tiled roof of his fantasy Spanish Hacienda in the Hollywood hills.

After I caught the news bulletin on my bedroom Mickey Mouse radio of hero Tom's shocking death, I rushed down North Alpine Drive, block after block, to buy the first *Examiner EXTRA! Edition* with the blazing headline "TOM MIX DEAD!" I still have that yellowed Hearst front page glued in my first scrapbook. The all-night newsstand was manned by Angelo, alumnus of *Freaks,* and we both bawled like babies as we mourned the loss of our silver screen Saddle Pal.

I took home the precious *EXTRA!* edition of the reviled tabloid, Hearst's lowbrow *Los Angeles Examiner,* sneaking it into my bedroom, breaking the No Hearst Papers! rule of my puritanical Presbyterian par-ents. (For kids, the Key to Joy is Disobedience). My Republican parents subscribed to the dull and sober-sided *Los Angeles Times.*

My bedroom door locked, I savored the forbidden tabloid. A *big* photo of Tom's smashed favorite car hogged first page. Then the luscious, purple porno prose of the Hearst copywriters took over, painting in lurid, well-chosen words the sickening state of the late star's mangled body, down to the gaping mouth and staring, bulging eyes. Boy, did I eat it up!

Yet doubt set in. Was my hero, my silver screen and radio pal Tom Mix, really dead? All I had to do was wait for the appointed, early-evening, child-friendly hour, switch on my Mickey Mouse radio, and— *don't touch that dial!*—there was Tom, alive as all get out, vocally swaggering over the desert wilderness of my boy's mind. What a downer when I found out years later it wasn't Tom Mix at all, but a radio actor impersonating the dead "real thing." The radio sponsors never tipped off the legion of loyal kid fans of *The Tom Mix Show* that their Saddle Pal had died. And this deception ran on the airwaves until 1950, fooling kids well into the debut of the rival television era. Tom Mix's career began with rodeos in 1905; his signature horse, the charismatic Tony, seemed as immortal to us kids as Tom Mix himself. Yet truth was, he was killed off not by a fall from the superhorse Tony—that would have been *unthinkable*—but by that mechanical monster thing: the custom-made, horrendously expensive, awesome racing car, with horns on its elongated hood. As I found out a few years later—the Age of Disillusionment—my hero had died enjoying his swank roadster at a speedometer-confirmed hot hundred per on a lawless stretch of Wild West Highway.

I confess to a love/hate relationship with the *car:* the essential tool of the late twentieth century and no doubt of the debuting twenty-first century as well. Gas-guzzling monsters swilling down huge quantities of fossil fuel like there's no tomorrow, we in the West always call them *cars* though we may still carry cards marked "Automobile Association" or the inescapable "Department of Motor Vehicles." As a kid growing up in the environs of Hollywood, I was awed by personal sightings of Gary Cooper's lengthy powerful Deusenberg and Joe Von Sternberg's swank streamlined Cord. Garbo's woven-wicker paneled Rolls: Who could forget it? Lust and owner-envy of these Tinseltown Dream Cars filled my waking thoughts and fevered dreams. These cars were as sleek as sharks and also potentially as deadly.

The deadly nature of luxury cars—or of *any* car for that matter—started in my mind with the snuff of Tom Mix and the wild wanton death of genius director Freddy Murnau. His limo was speeding to Santa Barbara with his newly appointed boyfriend-chauffeur at the wheel—a prudent choice, NOT! The coppertoned, purple-uniformed beaner beauty was distracted by Murnau's wandering hand, then by his salivating mouth. The resulting smashup was predictable. Sex while speeding down the open highway qualifies as an "extreme sport." I tried to read between the lines of the Hearstian broadly hinting salacious descriptions, and as soon as I watched *Tabu,* Murnau's Paramount Release, smothered in appropriate added "symphonic" sound, I wondered whether this German genius, recently imported from the defeated Fatherland, was really an old chickenhawk. Years later I confirmed it all was true.

The association of death with the car in the Tinseltown firmament was enhanced a few years later by the death of my favorite blonde, the "Ice Cream Blonde," in fact—the succulent and appetizing Thelma Todd. Todd died in a *parked* car in her own garage—a deadly gas chamber filled with monoxide fumes—when her drunken, pissed-off lover (genius director Roland West) petulantly locked her in, with the car motor purring like a killer pussycat. Naturally, this unsolved Hollywood crime story filled many pages of my expanding scrapbook, since the fan magazines were now covering these tragedies with sob sister abandon.

Remember that these car crashes all took place BSB—Before Seat Belts. Would these nagging nanny harnesses have made any damn difference? *No.* Seat belts—decidedly unmanly, to say the least (does James Bond buckle up?)—may save some mayhem in low-speed crashes, but the death tolls on the road roll on, despite dreary seat belts or the alarming and unreliable ABs—airbags that just *may* kill your kid.

Since as a child I literally worshipped Busby Berkeley, not missing a single one of his delicious Depression-defying movies, the lethal car crash of that American genius who worked the handicapped Hollywood track—and came out a winner every time—concentrated my developing boy's mind. Busby's grisly late-night post–wrap party crash, with drunk Buzz asleep at the wheel and swerving into oncoming traffic on coastal Roosevelt Highway, killed three women and bashed up Berkeley pretty badly in the blind bargain. Buzz was obviously guilty of DUI, but—miracle of what money can do to Old Blind Lady Justice—attorney-to-the-stars Jerry Geisler got him off with a ton of Warner Brothers' pressure and money.

But poor guilt-ridden Buzz did not get off scot-free. He suffered mightily from delayed stress syndrome *for years,* and a later bloody suicide attempt and wrist-and-throat-slashing that slopped up his tasteful posh Beverly Hills bathroom was a theatrical happening when the deadly car crash nightmares would not stop.

My scrapbooks numbered a baker's dozen, all pregnant with Tinseltown horror, when my new heartthrob Jimmy (James) Dean slammed headlong into legend. Yes, I was one of the many gay guys who was all torn up over this decidedly wrong career move, but I was one of the *select few* who had gotten into Jimmy's Aquarian pants (proving that two Aquarian buddies can hit it off).

Votive lights glowed in front of my very best James Dean photo, autographed—eat your heart out, Marlon—to *me,* and I carried my car-death compulsion to the point of actually acquiring—for three hundred bucks—a twisted shard of Jimmy's beloved Porsche. It is safe to say that Jimmy never loved a dude or chick as much as he was totally taken with the romance of that new Porsche. At twenty-four, Jimmy went out with a CRRUUNCH-BBAANNGG!!! and died doing what he loved doing, sliding directly into legend.

Five hundred bucks, slipped under the counter, procured for me the ultimate: JAMES DEAN BUCK NAKED BEAUTIFUL AND VERY DEAD ON THE SLAB. Eat your heart out *again,* fat old slob Marlon Brando—*your* buck-naked cadaver, long overdue, would make me puke.

After the Everest achievement of prime James Dean collectibles I have lucked on to—I have his neon red nylon jacket from *Rebel Without a Cause* (currently on loan to the Cinémathèque Française in Paris)—as well as a vivid memory of one horny Hoosier, I can always make Jimmy live again by slipping on a midnight cassette.

I have minor car crash photo treasures, such as the police accident investigation unit's document of Ernie Kovacs's fatal crash, his limp body sprawled broken doll-like from the unhinged door of his smashed sedan. Then there is the Jayne Mansfield Louisiana police accident investigation unit's thorough photographic coverage, from Jayne's ripped-off dead

1.1 Speeding ticket issued to James Dean just hours before his crash.

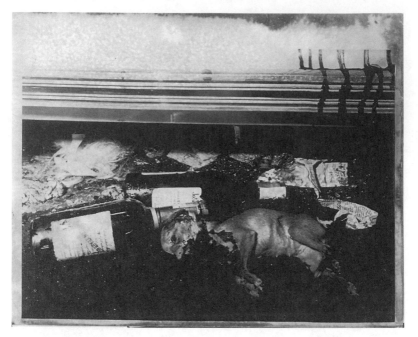

1.2   Jayne Mansfield crash. © Photofest

head surrealistically transformed into a bloody hood ornament, to a tough-and-tender ultra close-up of the pathetic carcass of Jaynie's itsy-bitsy Chihuahua doggy, dead as a doornail and artily surrounded by broken glass.

Then there are the photographs of Monty Clift's near-death experience after he was DUI leaving another Hollywood wrap party, and his pretty though mixed up and neurotic mug was turned into raw bloody hamburger. A panicked Liz Taylor hovers terrified over her broken-doll bloody Monty, her talented queer pal who would never be the same. The LaLaLand medics did their darndest, and then the team of top-dollar plastic surgeons took over for weeks and agonizing weeks, but this Humpty Dumpty could not be put back together again.

Let me wind up this tale of Kar Krash Karma with a visit to the obvious last stop: the graveyard—in this case, Hollywood Forever Cemetery. No, this time I'm not going to pay my respects to the shade of the Sheik, Rudy Valentino. I'm going to pay my respects to a man who made

me laugh—Mel Blanc. You know, the Man of a Thousand Voices—
among them, Bugs Bunny and Porky Pig. Mel just barely pulled through
a horrendous smashup on Deadman's Curve on Sunset Boulevard—the
winding section near where the fictitious Norma Desmond buried her
pet monkey and groped eager-beaver aspiring gigolo William Holden.
Sunset Boulevard—my old pal Billy Wilder really hit it off when he
named his great movie of Tinseltown's decline and fall!

Poor Mel Blanc *almost* didn't make it, so badly was he smashed up.
We almost heard the last of *What's up, doc?* as the medics labored to save
his life by head-to-toe plastercasting. *Pain?* Forget about it. Mel suffered
the agonies of the damned for months. And then—*resurrection!* "Hollywood endings" do occur, rarely, sometimes in real life. Mel Blanc returned to work at Termite Terrace, the Warner lot cartoon factory, to
Jack Benny and Rochester on the airwaves, and to one special fan, the
devoted and grateful Kenneth Anger.

Mel Blanc—the voiceover genius, the Man of a Thousand Voices—
lies at rest in the Jewish section, along with villainous Harry Cohn of
Columbia. And Mel has the best tombstone epitaph in the whole world,
the epitaph of a feisty survivor of Kar Krash Hell:

THAT'S ALL, FOLKS!

You, readers, have heard that before—or you're *truly* asleep at the
wheel.

As I take leave of the Hollywood Forever Cemetery, having deposited
one fresh yellow rose at the base of Mel Blanc's funniest tombstone, I take
a last look at Tinseltown's Kar Krash Karma in the rearview mirror . . .

TWO

CLUTCHING PEARLS

SPECULATIONS ON A TWENTIETH-CENTURY SUICIDE

A. LOUDERMILK

An act like this is prepared within the silence of the heart, as is a great
work of art. The man himself is ignorant of it. One evening he just
pulls the trigger, or jumps.

—Albert Camus, *The Myth of Sisyphus* (1940)

SHE FELL AS IF SHE HAD AN APPOINTMENT TO FALL. From the eighty-
sixth-floor observatory of the Empire State Building to West Thirty-
third below, she threw her own body down, down, down, eighty-six
times. Passing which floor did she clutch her pearls and never let go?

This photograph has haunted me since my angst-red days in high
school (when suicide was always a note away, when I thought *I'll shock
the world with my poignant corpse and they'll be sorry*). *The Best of LIFE*
(1974), an oversize book I underpaid a yardsale dollar for, includes, in a
section called "The Variety of *LIFE*," this photo by Robert C. Wiles. "An
illuminating look at the manners and morals of a nation in transition,"
or so the text claims, introducing an array of photographed situations
(birth, fireside chat by the radio, fox-whacking in Ohio, marijuana and

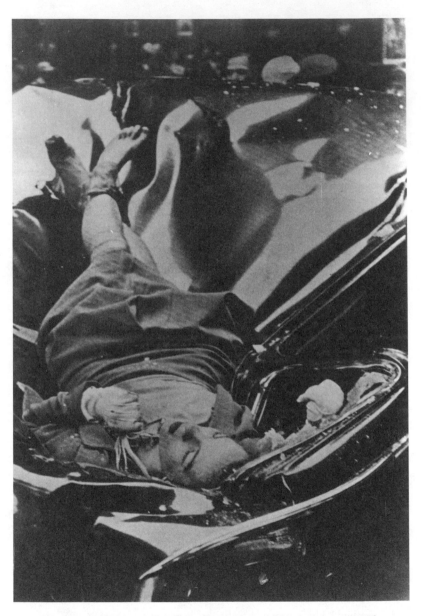

2.1   "Death at an Early Age," *LIFE* magazine, May 1947. © Robert C. Wiles

commune dwelling, the singles' scene). Juxtaposed against a photo titled "Still Kicking at 72," this morbid street scene is titled "Death at an Early Age" and accompanying text gives the reader no sense whatsoever of the "reason" behind her suicide: "After plunging 86 floors from the observation deck of the Empire State Building, an attractive 23-year-old lies peacefully atop the crumpled sedan she struck on West 33rd Street."

The text gives no reason, and neither does it *overtly* moralize, raising questions without the judgmental tone that one would expect from *LIFE*. The juxtaposition of the two photos does demand a reading of suicide as defeat, but the tricksterism of "sleeping" death and "peaceful" violence, and the who-and-why mystery of public suicide perpetuated by the immortalizing camera certainly eclipse any hint of defeat. She is intentional death caught in an accidental pose. Hasn't *she* defeated *LIFE*? She has fallen into an iconography that includes the automobile, the skyscraper, and the camera, each an implied presence in Wiles's photo and all emblematic of social forces in the twentieth century.

If the leap is symbolic of flight, then crashing down on to some ground-hugging car is ironic, not romantic. Turning to *LIFE*, its earliest representations of the automobile in popular culture are bolder than I anticipated. Margaret Bourke-White, one of the magazine's four original staff photographers, helped it attain its reputation for social insight with photographs like "Louisville, February 1937." Taking up more than the top half of the frame, a billboard claims "There's No Way Like the American Way," with smiling white parents and two kids framed in the front window of their family car, dad at the wheel. Though contradicted by a bread line of black Americans in the shadow of this street-side billboard, its topside banner cruelly boasts "World's Highest Standard of Living." The car was again central to a socially ironic photo in 1939, with United Auto Workers overturning the car of a nonstriker. Other *LIFE* photos involving the automobile fall into two categories: the automobile bringing the famous to the common and the automobile taking the common to famous places.

Bringing the famous to the common: Ticker tape or not, a line of cars makes a parade, especially when from car number one a president like Truman or Nixon is reaching his hand out to shake the hands of voters. In *LIFE,* Wendell Wilkie waves to potential voters from his car (but loses). Presidents Truman and Nixon wave from their cars (and win). The pope waves a saintly hand from his "papal conveyance."[1] Tax evader Spiro Agnew peeks out from his limo and is booed. JFK is paraded through Dallas and . . . As for bringing the common to famous places: The automobile took thousands of families down Route 66. It took millions of kids to school. Many of these kids as teens were taken to new heights *in the backseat.* Between the 1940s and the 1960s, the auto redefined the small-city downtown on Saturday nights into *the main drag.* When originally published, those who saw Wiles's photo probably did not read the destruction of a car by a falling career girl as an ironic or subversive component of this scene. But I did. The question is, did Wiles?

Mobility, agency, access to culture . . . these are not so difficult for the pedestrian nowadays. So if the car no longer brings the famous to the common (too risky, as Zapruder's film proved), or if we don't go to drive-ins or lovers' lanes, it's still okay. Between the VCR and the 'net, fame and heavy petting are virtualized. Anyway, teens don't do scenes from *Rebel Without a Cause* anymore, as drunk-driving hysteria has dampened thrills like drag racing and chicken-at-the-wheel.

It was obvious that the novelty of the automobile was wearing off with movies like *The Absent-Minded Professor* (1961) and *Chitty Chitty Bang Bang* (1968) in which drivers would rather be aerially navigating, *the envy of all they survey!* Also, the Volkswagen Bug altered the car from status/family symbol into one more suitable for counterculture. In Ed Clark's *LIFE* photo "Family Outing, 1956," he captures a timely phenomenon: A family, at such an event, would have commonly included the car in their group photos, as if the car—shiny or trashed—were a member of the family. When I was a kid in the 1980s, however, no one in my family wanted to be *seen* in our rustbucket, let alone pose with it for posterity. Traffic jams, carjacking, exhausts, seat belts and capitalism . . . no wonder punk icon Wendy O. Williams, another suicide, became famous for detonating cars—on stage and on talk shows—during her performances. As much as our cars are an extension of our ecological selves[2] (which is why we say "he ran into *me*" when we mean "he ran into my car"), they are a necessary evil, often a financial burden, and always considered safer than they actually are. They are us.

So when I checked out the *LIFE-TIME* photo site, it made sense that the gallery titled "popular culture" featured *only* photos of cars and traffic, even though to get to the gallery I had to click on the Statue of Liberty's head. In the fiftieth anniversary issue of *LIFE*, there are four times as many advertisements for cars than photos including cars.[3] I counted twenty-four car ads in total, eight of which were double-pagers. In the photo gallery, one photo was of a traffic scene in Tucson, another of an old couple in a truck dozing at dawn on Interstate 15, another of a clover leaf, and one from a helicopter entitled "Traffic Reporter." Also included is Ed Clark's "Family Outing, 1956." Both the first and fiftieth anniversary issues of *LIFE* opened with a car ad, the fiftieth opening obnoxiously into a five-page spread for THE UNBELIEVABLE AMERICAN, the Plymouth Sundance.

The Empire State Building is to New Yorkers what the Eiffel Tower is to Parisians, both symbols of modernity. According to art historian and critic Robert Hughes,[4] both are pivotal in human consciousness, allowing us to see the city from high above for the first time, predicting the sensation of seeing the earth from the moon—further evidence of man's need to dominate nature, according to feminist theory. In the documentary *The Cruise*, New York City tour guide Timothy Speed announces to his double-decker bus full of tourists, "If architecture is the history of all phallic emotion, the Empire State Building is utter catharsis." The Empire State Building, more available as a symbol than its parapets are as leaping points, lends itself with ease to any New Yorker's suicidal imagination. Heights in and of themselves make all of us visualize *falling*, but the Empire State Building is a specific height. A symbol of New York City and big-time capitalism, to *throw oneself* from the top of the building is, perhaps, arrogance.

"There lies New York before you—spectacular, arrogant, and splendid," plugged a story dispatched to Midwesterners, indulging and undermining their little-fish contempt for the big pond.[5] To stand atop

New York, city of all cities, to look down on it from a godlike height—this is a Babylonian thrill not only for corporate royalty in top-floor suites city wide but for tourists who comprise 90 percent of the Empire State Building's daytime observatory visitors. Between 1931 and 1947, fifteen "leapers" chose the Empire State Building to leap from—nine from the tower and six from offices on various floors.[6] The first *attempted* suicide from the eighty-sixth floor may have created a trend of cool-headed deception by leapers, as one Mr. Lawley "calmly removed his topcoat, put it and a note on the tower floor, climbed out on to the parapet, and jumped off, all in the twinkling of an eye and without a moment's hesitation."[7]

The first *successful* suicide from the eighty-sixth floor, in 1935, was a "moody Manhattanite," or so reasoned *TIME*, and according to *The Mirror* she "LEAPED—FOR LOVE! FROM THE WORLD'S HIGHEST BUILDING." She "asked the guard questions and seemed interested in his answers, but she also nodded absent-mindedly." And quick as a myth she was "swaying in the howling wind . . . sailing out into space like a huge bird." Might Irma P. Eberhardt, twenty-two, be Wiles's suicidal beauty? No, she landed on a marquee 1,029 feet below. In fact, architectural deterrence for leapers included the eighty-fourth floor ledge that "saved" Mr. Lawley, this 60-foot wide terrace that sheltered Fifth Avenue from Miss Eberhardt, and other such hardware.[8] It would take a certain determination, including an unruffled performance as a typical observatory visitor, to make it past the guards to the parapet, let alone to impel one's body out far enough to surpass ledges and marquees. According to the building's historian, suicide "seems to happen at a coolly determined pace. . . . There seemed to be few second thoughts on the part of the leapers."[9] Our career girl was no *pseudocide*, no mere attempter. She fell as if she had an appointment to fall

and fall she did, on the dot. I have never been to the Empire State Building, but I have heard of visitors getting nosebleeds, or "skysickness," or being completely disoriented as to the east and west of the landscape before them. I have also heard that according to a virtual collimator, the building does not sway as rumored. I imagine lightning, that flirt, would strike the building's tower with familiarity. Supposedly the eighty-first floor offers a better view of New York City, with visibility from the eighty-sixth inhibited by clouds. Did she break through clouds upon takeoff? Did the wind take her shoes?

Her face. Why should the beautiful want to die? Not central but fore-grounded, her face—to us upside-down—could be that of a Hitch cocked actress, martyred in the limelight after so much torment behind the scenes. In Wiles's composition, the suicide's face is isolated so that the sleep-soundness of her expression tricks us, at first, into the feeling that we are invading her privacy. Faceup in makeup, her eyes are closed; our gaze seems sadistic. We note her white-gloved hands: One grasps her necklace, the other grasps nothing. And blood hides behind her back like a liar's crossed fingers. Miss Suicide possesses a napper's countenance, a "career girl"[10] playing possum; only a torn stocking tells on her fated tableau as a scene of violence. The window of the sedan, bent free of glass, serves to frame her face; her chin is a prim pointer down her body to a naked foot, the most vulgar aspect of the photo (even with her an-kles crossed ladylike). Light exaggerates the sheen of collapsed metal into a gentler bed. This is a perverse Camille, however, as her pulse yaws the dirty breeze between skyscrapers. Her corpse is witnessed by the street, by those men in hats hidden beyond the car, peering.

This is not a private place.

I return to her face. When did she shut her eyes, or were they shut by a priest or by the photographer? She landed on her back: Did she dare to look, up, at the sky she fell from? Her mouth is not agape with scream. How is it that her pearls—in a hand that I imagine flailing against the fall—did not break?

As a suicidal teen in the early 1980s, personally and culturally, I could not help but see her death in the 1940s as glamorous. She denied death its realism—the split face of the rifle-to-chin suicide, the rot and bloat of the drowned, the blood splatter of the headfirst. Her portrait was death's glamour shot, a memento mori sealed with a lipstick kiss. She informed my idealization of suicide as a symbolically loaded act, even if she killed herself for reasons related to a "radically particularized" symbology I can-not fathom. She defied my acrophobia and though her anguish was heavy enough to crush a car, sending someone home in a taxi, her face (her identity, especially since I did not know her name) "survived" the brutality of her act. That, I thought, is *celebrity.*

Now an adult and writer, I am more compelled by the photo's penultimate narrative, one in which the details of the scene might be caressed into a suicide's logic. I know, for instance, that the elevator in the Empire State Building goes only to the eighty-fourth floor. Imagine her taking those last two flights in an echo-ridden stairwell. Did she take hold of the railing as she climbed? Did she nervously straighten her skirt's pleats, her pearls? Are they pearls from her mother, a lover, or are they even pearls? Did she fancy flight or crave the sickness of the drop? Did she force herself to think of nothing else or to think of anything else? As a suicidal fifteen-year-old I sainted her, so I can't help wondering how any knowledge of leapers before her shaped her image of herself during those last steps to the eighty-sixth floor.

After all my research into "Death at an Early Age," I failed to uncover the name of its subject, the year of her death, her hometown, her relationship to the person who identified her body. Most recent research shows that each suicide intimately affects six other people,[11] at least one of whom is probably a real bastard. Who were the six people intimately affected by this particular suicide? I know I cannot solve her suicidal logic, nor can I insist that the symbology I find in her act is relative to the symbology she particularized for herself upon her willing exit from the order of selves.[12] I wanted to deconstruct her methodology and found myself engrossed in self-revolving speculation. Speculation about suicide—like suicide—is at least one part arrogance. Decoding the suicide's mythology, whether to console yourself or to soothe death phobia, is to experiment with death in (exclusion of) an immediate world full of symbols. In trying to fathom why I find this death so provocative, I must admit that of the three elements I link to its "star"—the Empire State Building, the auto, and the camera—the last two could not have been "arranged" for or even anticipated by the suicidal woman. "Caught" by *LIFE* in a chance triangulation of icons, the suicide's pain is lost, and only her body as public spectacle, as career girl interrupted—one element among several in a photographic composition—is available for us to make significant in narrative terms.

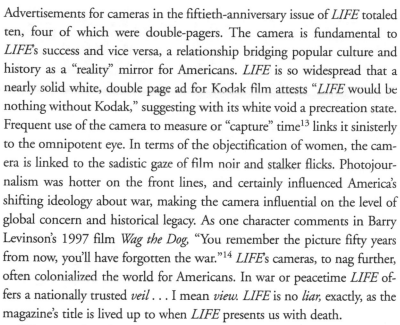

Advertisements for cameras in the fiftieth-anniversary issue of *LIFE* totaled ten, four of which were double-pagers. The camera is fundamental to *LIFE*'s success and vice versa, a relationship bridging popular culture and history as a "reality" mirror for Americans. *LIFE* is so widespread that a nearly solid white, double page ad for Kodak film attests "*LIFE* would be nothing without Kodak," suggesting with its white void a precreation state. Frequent use of the camera to measure or "capture" time[13] links it sinisterly to the omnipotent eye. In terms of the objectification of women, the camera is linked to the sadistic gaze of film noir and stalker flicks. Photojournalism was hotter on the front lines, and certainly influenced America's shifting ideology about war, making the camera influential on the level of global concern and historical legacy. As one character comments in Barry Levinson's 1997 film *Wag the Dog*, "You remember the picture fifty years from now, you'll have forgotten the war."[14] *LIFE*'s cameras, to nag further, often colonialized the world for Americans. In war or peacetime *LIFE* offers a nationally trusted *veil . . .* I mean *view. LIFE* is no *liar,* exactly, as the magazine's title is lived up to when *LIFE* presents us with death.

"Photographs of corpses were some of the most important images produced when photography made its debut," according to John Pultz in his enlightening book *The Body and the Lens.*[15] Not only did images of battlefield corpses bring home the realities of war, reality inside the home was simultaneously faced and denied when parents paid photographers to photograph the corpses of their little ones. "In order to have visual records of dead children, . . . sometimes parents would go so far as to carry their child's body to a photographer's studio for a post-mortem portrait."[16] The photographic image, though in and of itself *dead,* proved that one existed, that one was, or is, alive. Group photos unite individuals, public and domestic photos relate individuals, and portraits stress individuality. The ultimate result of such technology: Society locates identity in the exterior image, in one's tie or pearls, rather than in character or accomplishment. In "Death at an Early Age," the camera is present only in that what we are looking at is a photograph. Dwell on the image, however, and this "hidden" camera unnerves, like the men in hats peering over the wreckage.

Like love at first sight, I was immediately seduced by "Death at an Early Age," the photo's composition leading my eye from beauty to horror. This spontaneous process involved isolating the image from all else (including the photo on the opposite page) as if it were a crime scene ripe with *evidence*. We have only a few details with which to make sense of this lost *LIFE:* the career girl's suit, the necklace, the gloves, the penciled eyebrows, and the public spectacle of it all.

Yet like a work of art she begs symbolizing, not solving. Returning to the image over the years, I forsake physical evidence for symbolic evidence by "reading" the image purposely juxtaposed against its opposite page, and haphazardly juxtaposed against a backdrop of iconography, social reality (hers *and* mine), and psychological theory. We are, after all, reading not just an image but an artist's vision, a woman's body, the public's spectacle, and *LIFE*'s representation of twentieth-century American *LIFE* in typified "variety."

I think in gender terms how this career girl has been "caught," how the leading representation of women is still: Ambitious grit okay as long as she shows some *winsome vulnerability*. This photograph represents the career girl in such a way that when viewers see her, how can they not project on to her the other stories they read in *LIFE* about pretty young women in secretarial attire? Those men in hats and the other pedestrians gawking at this New York street scene—did many of them assume that the poor thing couldn't keep her man? When I was fifteen wanting to die and I saw her in *LIFE,* to me she was a victor. When I was her age and a front-desk receptionist, I wanted the time clock to die, so then, to me, she was a martyr. I never ascribed to her the narrative of being unable to keep her man, even though similar backlash narratives were epidemic in 1980s cinema. I assumed she was lonely like I was lonely. She wanted out. I wanted out.

She didn't want to die, she just wanted to force a change, to escape agony. She condemned herself to such flight, yet square on her back she crashed into the roof of a sedan car, black metal crumpling around her shiny as death-dressing satin. She hurled herself from an observation deck into clouds and intruded upon a crowded city street, on display for cameras. Posthumously she is immortalized. In *LIFE.* What is her name? Something pretty and French sounding? Anomie? Or something all-American like Jane Doe?

A few more details about the story behind this seductive photograph were given when it was originally published in *LIFE* magazine on May 12, 1947. The suicidal beauty was twenty-three-year-old Evelyn McHale, who plunged to her death on May Day, after leaving her fiancé. She left a note that read, in part, "He is much better off without me. . . . I wouldn't make a good wife for anybody"—then she crossed out everything she had written. The magazine pointed out that her suicidal leap must have been characterized by a "desperate determination" in order for her to fall wide of "the setbacks" (the ledges, parapets, and marquees described by Loudermilk). The car she landed on was a United Nations limousine parked at the curb. Robert Wiles was a photography student who was passing on the other side of the street when he heard an explosive crash. "Just four minutes after McHale's death," we are told, "Wiles got this picture of death's violence and its composure."

NOTES

1. See David Kerekes's chapter in this volume (15) for more thoughts about this wonderful vehicle.
2. See Ulrich Neisser's "Five Kinds of Self-Knowledge," *Philosophical Psychology*, 1.1 1988, 28–42. Niesser explains that "self-knowledge is based on various forms of information, so distinct that each one essentially establishes a different 'self.' The ecological self is the self as directly perceived with respect to the immediate physical environment" (35). He later addresses the vehicle and the body: "Any controllable object that moves together with the point of observation can become part of the ecological self. This principle even applies to automobiles" (35).
3. *LIFE—The First 50 Years 1936 - 1986*, (New York: Little, Brown & Co., 1986).
4. Hughes himself was the victim of a controversial car crash; see chapter 4 by Eric Laurier in this volume.
5. John Taurunac, *The Empire State Building* (New York: Scribner, 1995), 270.
6. Ibid., 333.
7. Ibid., 241–242.
8. "'How many suicides are deterred by this disappointment we can only guess, but we know it plays a factor,' said observatory manager Joe Bolton in 1924" (Taurunac, 241). But by 1947, "a seven-foot high stainless steel fence laced by diamond shaped mesh . . . topped with sickles curving inward thwart[ed] climbing up and over" (ibid., 334).
9. Ibid., 241.
10. In a 1948 photo-essay, in typical postwar backlash, *LIFE* worries about the career girl's perennial problem, that she will "jeopardize her chance [for marriage] by trying to close her eyes to everything but her career." The career girl featured looks remarkably like the suicide in Wiles's photo.
11. See Dr. John McIntosh's website, "USA Suicide Summary: 1998 Official Final Data," at www.iusb.edu/—jmcintos/USA98Summary.htm.

12. See Mitch Zeftel, "Disaffected Selves: Madness as Symbolic Experience," at www.edgmag.com/vol2.doc2/suicide.html (website no longer available). Zeftel's twenty-five page essay addresses such issues as suicide as public spectacle, psuedocide and suicide, outsider versus insider modes, constructing commitment to suicide, reconciliation with the other, and so on.

13. In 1937, *LIFE* featured a series of six photos called "Mr. Chadwick's Little Girl Grows Up," one taken every two years and each the same in pose and setting. Cameras proved to Americans early on that they had the power to freeze time, to mark it like miles on a road, to use it as evidence that an aging actress has had a facelift since her last movie or lost twenty-five pounds on the Slim-Fast plan (the *before-and-after* phenomenon). The movement of the moon eclipsing the sun, a process that occurs over time not unlike growing, through the technology of photography can be "reduced" to a single image. (See *LIFE: The First 50 Years,* 389.) Nature is humble before the lens, as multiple exposure, like God's eye, sees it all).

14. Robert de Niro as the president's spinmeister in *Wag the Dog* (dir. Levinson, 1997). He has turned to blockbuster producer Dustin Hoffman to "produce" a war that will distract the public from a presidential sex scandal.

15. John Pultz, *The Body and the Lens; Photography 1839 to the Present* (New York: Calmann and King Ltd., 1995), 33.

16. Ibid.

EXISTENTIAL REALITY ON POWELL BOULEVARD

ADAM PARFREY

IF THE CHOICE HAD BEEN MINE, the antagonist would have possessed more character.

A thirty-three-year-old salesman embodying the essence of the pejorative word "yuppie," tie sloppily attached to his short-sleeved shirt beneath his midnight-drunk face, careens his upscale BMW past a side street stop sign into my all-white half-ton pickup, halting its swift and witless progress down this major Portland boulevard, hurtling my body through its windshield, emptying me scarred face nose down on the red, yellow, and clear plastic lens–littered asphalt.

The crash delays the yuppie's homeward, barmaid-fucking progress. This twit, who has no deliberate, maleficent cast, makes out with hardly a scratch or a thought.

The spectacle deters a woman driving from the opposing direction, who stops her car and begins directing traffic around my shattered, feeling-free body. And there I float, watching the scene beneath me. The fog, the distant sounds. A person shakes me, whom I answer with my annoyed mind ten feet above them, "Let me sleep."

Awakening from a coma some hours later, my first sight is a cop, pen and notebook in hand. He tells me that I'm lucky. Lucky is the word he uses. Had I worn a seat belt, I would have been crushed by the engine and no doubt killed. Shortly after I leave the hospital I find the name of the woman who directed traffic around my bleeding head on the wall of an antique store, a bad patron publicly humiliated for leaving a rubber check. Two years later I'm arrested for not wearing a safety belt.

The crash changes me, alters me. And I search for lessons constantly, and unsuccessfully. All I know is that the severity was arbitrary and mindless.

And that is its spectacular essence.

THIS WRECKLESS LANDSCAPE

ERIC LAURIER

Allegory is in the realm of thought what ruins are in the realm of things

—Walter Benjamin,
The Origins of the German of Mourning (1928)[1]

Severed—this usually applies to wiring harnesses trapped or cut through by damaged metalwork

—D. Griffiths,
Automobile Assessing (1983)[2]

ON SOME CHEAP LAND LEASED FROM A RAILWAY COMPANY they are stacked up to ten high, headlights plucked out, strands of wiring trailing. Carrion for breakers, brokers, and the drivers of bangers. There might be the odd stolen car hidden after dismantling, its undamaged parts reassembling an insurance write-off for illegal profit, creating a "ringer." These are the road's ruins, crumbling faster than buildings; they are the rusting record of metallic modernity, an intimate architecture of vehicle fashions. Some still wearable, others exotic, historic, nostalgic. Modern men's discarded wardrobe. Mobile machines immobilized. An archaeological record of the just past.

Near the bottom of the dump, in among the confusion of metal, paint, and rubber are preserved industrial messages—the lost badges of car manufacturers. The spinning "L" of British Leyland—the badges of failed state intervention in industry. There are the stars of Chrysler cars, which in their later models are silver Ts for Talbot before the badge disappears altogether in a further "streamlining" operation by Peugeot, who in turn merged with Citroën. Somewhere down deep there are still lions and chevrons forming a dwindling continuity.

My father, when he was still belted into the stability of middle management in the early 1980s, brought home his company-provided Talbot Alpine to show off to our family. And I knew I was being given privileged treatment as the oldest child, aged fourteen, when I was taken for a drive, to see "what the car could do." To test out the all-important car stereo I brought my cheap pop compilation tape, and we sped down to the sea front to cruise along between the suburban coastal houses and the water. The car was a space of patriarchal intimacy, or perhaps the wish of fast fatherhood when children seem so much quicker. More than that, for my dad and me, the car was a vehicle for a proffered pleasure, much as mythical fishing trips and Saturday afternoons at football grounds were for other boys.

Every two years at the end of the summer the car was replaced as the registration letters changed. I can still measure significant periods of my life as much by the letters of car alphabets as by pop songs. My mother meanwhile drove her canary yellow Renault 5 until it collapsed, then a succession of elderly secondhand run-arounds, Citroëns with dodgy plumbing, 1970s Datsuns spotted and crumbling with poor-quality steel.

During some corporation downsizing my father had to hand back the keys to his office and his company car. In the bourgeois town where we lived it was a conspicuous kind of repossession, a middle-class resettlement of older men. Unable to find an equivalent job, he took to taxi driving, which did, after all, still offer a company car. My mother divorced him and not long after bought a nippy silver Fiat with a sunroof. He never wrote off a car, although he once drove over a policeman's foot.

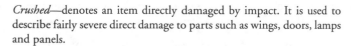

Crushed—denotes an item directly damaged by impact. It is used to describe fairly severe direct damage to parts such as wings, doors, lamps and panels.

—D. Griffiths, *Automobile Assessing* (1983)

One summer my then girlfriend's brother, James, was sitting in the passenger seat of his friend's Mini when they collided with a big silver saloon car on their side of a narrow country road. They were struck a glancing blow that pushed them over the edge of an adjacent slope. Their little car rolled, bounced off the top of a low hedge, and came to rest upside down in a field. Inside the boys were suspended, dangling and shoulder-twisted by their seat belts. Having a received a blow on his forehead, James slipped in and out of consciousness. During one of those half-waking moments he heard cries of pain, saw that his friend was trapped by his foot, and tried to start freeing him. In doing so the lack of movement in his upper arm and a steady ache brought to his attention the fact that it was almost certainly broken and definitely useless. He said he laughed a little before drifting back into a haze. Beside him, his friend continued to cry out, having shattered several ribs, broken his leg, and had his foot crushed by one of the car control pedals. Or that's how I remember the details as they were told to me by James as we drove back from the hospital several long hours later. His story of the crash was interrupted by his intermittent yelps each time our car went over a bump in the road.

The scene that I was witness to, and the one that I'm curious about, was when we went to see the wreck of the car a couple of days afterward— James with his broken arm in a sling and me with a camera that he had asked me to bring along. The crumpled Mini had been lifted from the field and taken to a small yard where auto wrecks were stored behind an ice cream parlor. It was one of those hidden places in the town that I would never have seen were it not for my being drawn into this postcrash process. Possible write-offs, like crumpled paper packaging, were left there for insurance companies to inspect them and decide on their futures.

There was a moment of perceptible shock as James spotted the car. He stood still, inhaled sharply, let out a little nervous laugh and then a bigger one. The curve of the car roof was inverted but the real deformation was at the front, where the front wing was folded to one side, pushing the wheel into permanent evasion. We walked up to it, James letting out a little whistle, saying "Well, what do you make of that!"

It had been reverted to an upright position. Impossibly parked at an even distance from the other wrecks on the gravel, as if owners might still get in these mangled, splayed, or flattened vehicles and drive them away. We walked around it a little before taking a look inside. James suggested some of the positions he wanted photographs taken from at a distance. While I was taking the photos, he recalled that there had been a lot of blood dripping from both him and his friend as they hung tangled upside down. And looking inside the car now, he noted with disappointment that it had merely left what resembled a mottled brown rust stain on the fabric of the car's interior roof. By way of contrast we agreed that the dashboard's position, jutting forward over the front seats, was impressive. In fact, we wondered how this could have happened without someone losing, at the very least, a leg.

His friend, the driver, was still in the hospital in traction, and with several more pins through his bones than James. They had a mean teasing sense of humor with each other. James had asked me to take photos so that he could bring them to the hospital for his friend's bedside table.

"Oh, and there's one other thing I promised him," said James, reaching around under the collapsed dashboard. "I can't get it out, though. Here, you try."

Just visible under the dashboard was a leather deck shoe still pinned under the accelerator pedal. Apparently the greatest pain for his friend had been having his pedal-pincered foot pulled from his shoe. To the wonderment of the ambulance crew who eased his foot out of his shoe, though swollen, purple-yellow, and sore, none of its multitude of small bones had been broken. With the professional unconcern of emergency teams for items of clothing, they left the driver's shoe behind. With good reason, I thought, since despite my pulling, twisting, and tugging the shoe wouldn't come out from under the pedal. I probably wasn't the first to try and pry it loose, since there were no other personal effects left in the car. So there it remained: a trace of flesh on steel and plastic bones otherwise picked clean in the few days between the crash and the detainment in this wrecked vehicle pound.

Lozenged and misaligned—used for chassis frames, door apertures and body shells.

—D. Griffiths, *Automobile Assessing* (1983)

The nineteenth century witnessed a fascination with ruined buildings, leading to the careful grooming of crumbled churches and castles to make them picturesque, to recapture the threat of decay by preserving it and perhaps reorganizing the passing of time. Between the abandonment of buildings to gravity, wind, rain, and vine and their restoration to a copy of what they once had been, the logic of the ruin is neither about the unstoppable loss to the passing of time nor the invisible repair of massive damage. Ruins commemorate as they commiserate, reinstate as they relegate. They do not quite renovate nor do they obliterate. They promise a recovery even as they refuse it.

Car shells dilapidate so much faster than stone buildings. They need repair more often than just about any other object ever manufactured. They are the feeblest of built environments. And yet they now have a central part in human activity that is a match for clothes, ships, houses, and places of religious devotion. How might they be preserved as ruins? How might we blend them into a landscape and mark them on maps as historical sites worth visiting?

In farmers' fields in the poorer regions of Britain, and even in the not so poor, you can find abandoned vehicles that might just about qualify as new ruins. There are tractors with footrests that now grow grass to be nibbled by sheep, black PVC seats half mummy-bandaged with black repair tape that have acquired a comfortable layer of bright green moss through not being sat upon. In the midst of the rusting ruin, protected by safety glass, immaculate instruments register just how many miles led to this final nonpassing of the vehicle. Not only tractors lie in the corners of these fields. I have seen small cars, delivery vans, and trucks all gradually returning their iron to the earth.

Where once these mobile machines had a clear gap between their carriage and the ground, they have blended with the earth either through its rising up to meet them or their sinking down to lie upon it. From their resting places, there is little sense of them having met a sudden end. Rather, they have just been abandoned and forgotten—a driverless crash into the soil occurring slower than the human eye could register.

Cracked—this is used for such items as cylinder heads, blocks and also glassware in appropriate cases

—D. Griffiths, *Automobile Assessing* (1983)

As part of Western culture's rites and legal definitions of maturity, a child is accepted into the realms of adulthood through being offered access to the world of driving for the first time. A shared anecdote from Western childhood (more likely boyhood than girlhood) is the first attempt to drive the car, normally at an early age, when it ends up reversed into a tree, lamppost, gate, or neighbor's car. At an older age, the gap between father and son is successfully traversed when the son takes the car out without his father's supervision. My recollection of childhood and car crashes involves a later and more serious tale of punishment for crossing this road.

At the age of fifteen, Donald decided to drive his parents' car while they were on holiday, his father having shown him the basics of driving. His disobedience was made all the more tempting because, as in all the best film plots, his father's car was a treasured Jaguar. The big oak-paneled saloon was a mechanical manifestation of his father's successful career, his role as head of the family, his absence from the home, his conservatism, and his office. As a father and a serious businessman, he drove it calmly and carefully. Donald—a rebel without a license—went joyriding in it, and he took two of our friends to see his girlfriend who lived farther up the loch.

On the first night, they drove to her house and back without any problem, even though they were fairly drunk. Then they did the trip again the next night. This time, on the way home, drunk again, they hit the high curb on the recently upgraded "A" road and flipped the car. Lyle, the shyest of the three, sitting in the backseat, was killed as the roof crumpled onto his head. Donald and his front-seat friend, only slightly bruised, got out of the car and ran away into the night. The oak-paneled saloon was winched upright in the early hours of the morning, once the police had finished recording the scene, and towed away to be hidden from sight at the back of a local garage. A year and a half later, when he was seventeen, Donald was banned from learning to drive for six months.

This story had a particular moral purpose. It was told and retold by my friends and our parents. It was not just an event, it was a lesson; it was a jury decision on the proper accession to our adult lives. For the first time, I dealt with the death of a friend and the death of a friend by the actions of another, even if not deliberate. Apparently an accident, it became part of our teenage arguments over alcohol, friendship, cars, fathers, death, and guilt. For Donald, it meant a ban from such discussions for more than six months.

I wonder where the Jaguar saloon went to, since—although being involved in a fatal accident and thus for some time the property of the law courts—it was a valuable car, not damaged beyond repair. Are the deadly histories of such cars airbrushed away like the faces of Russian ministers in group photos who fell afoul of Stalin? Where automobiles are concerned, this airbrushing takes the form of the careful valeting of interior trim to remove blood and tissue, the meticulous coachwork that puts the car roof back in place and takes the dents out of the bumper, and the mechanics that true the wheels misaligned by impact with the curb. For its next owner, there is barely a trace left of motoring misadventure.

Lacerated—this denotes light cutting of tyres and items of trim

—D. Griffiths, *Automobile Assessing* (1983)

Walking down a red earth road in the middle of a West African rain forest I came across a 1960s-style Volkswagen camper van. Earlier I had been looking at some spiny, brightly colored land crabs for sale. A village boy had collected them on a stick to sell them from the verge of the road. Not really fancying eating any of the crabs, I had paid him to allow me to take a photograph. Farther up the road from his selling point, there was a bridge built out of thick tropical tree trunks. Cars crossing it would get their wheels stuck between the still-cylindrical trunks and be forced to drive in the rut until they reached the other side. There was something laughable about the way they appeared to buck and struggle with the direction forced upon them by the trunks' tram-lining, like animals straining on a leash.

As I crossed the bridge on the edge that was set aside with small wooden rails for pedestrians (of which there were many more than vehicles), I glanced down river. Seemingly frozen midleap there was the VW camper van, its nose jutting out into the air and its rear firmly in the grip of vines and branches. Judging by its thick layers of red dust, it might well have actually been there since the end of the 1960s. Of course, I stopped to take some photos. While snapping and winding I fantasized about a group of acid-hazed hippies on a magic bus tour around Africa who were so trippy they couldn't stay on the road. After taking the photos I asked around to find out if anyone knew the story of how the van came to be abandoned there. There were jokes made about the driver having had too much palm wine, but no one knew for sure. Most likely it had once been a taxi that eventually had become so far beyond repair that it had been rolled toward the river and got stuck halfway on the route to its muddy-watered grave.

How often do we see cars, VW vans, articulated trucks, and yellow school buses jackknife and explode into flames in films and on television, while we almost never see sights such as this in our real landscape. They are tidied away, their remains removed for assessors' autopsies. A crashed car is seldom left to rust. Instead, all we ever see is a ribbon tied around a tree, a bent lamppost, wall, or railing with flowers strewn beneath as a sign that a fatal automobile accident has occurred in *this* place.

Buckled—describes rippling of panels, general distortion, also road wheels running out of true

—D. Griffiths, *Automobile Assessing* (1983)

Robert Hughes, the Australian art critic, in the opening to a series of television programs about contemporary Australian society, stands staring at the wreck of a car. It is his car, and it is part of the record of a crash that almost killed him. In the previous clip he stood on the Great Northern Highway near the spot where, two years earlier, his Nissan Pulsar collided head on with a Holden Commodore. There is a poetry of coincidence to this scene that is not lost on Hughes. The accident occurred when he was starting the filming for the series to which this confrontation with the wreck now provides a prologue. According to the production notes for the program, the filming of this scene was carried out as Hughes encountered the wreck for the very first time.[3] As a television audience, we witness the learned cultural critic, historian, and writer as he first sees and is shocked by the Nissan's crush. Quite where his bulky body could have been sitting inside the collapsed Nissan is an impossible mystery—there is simply no space for it. Instead, the shifting metal reshaped his body to fit by snapping and pulverizing his bones. A year later Hughes has made an incredible recovery, yet his shattered skeleton will never regain the strength he once had.

In the television scene, he rubs his head and stares in amazement; he still has no memory of the collision. What memory might have been reconstructed by the occupants of the other car he collided with has been rendered untrustworthy. Almost a year after the crash, Hughes was taken to court and during the case the eyewitnesses were charged with conspiracy to pervert the course of justice. The judge concluded that the witnesses were untrustworthy, unreliable, and willing to give perjured evidence to benefit financially from the trial. (They had in fact tried to extort money for their version of how the crash occurred.) The only reliable evidence was the remains of the two cars, and all that could be discerned from them was that they had met headlight to headlight and not quite head-on. Their off-shouldered impact was one of the reasons why Hughes survived.

After spending the morning fishing with Hughes, his friend Danny O'Sullivan was having a drink in a bar at Echo Beach when he had heard rumors there'd been a serious accident on the highway—becoming alarmed, he drove to the crash site. Here he found the bodies of three people lying in the road, and discovered Hughes trapped upside down in his car. It was several hours before the art critic could be cut out, during which time he was mostly conscious. Gasoline was leaking out of the car engine after the crash and, aware of this, Hughes had asked Danny to shoot him dead should the car catch fire. Danny is there as they walk around the tortured remains of the Nissan. As they circle the car, they repeat the sentences they exchanged while Hughes was trapped. Fishing around inside the collapsed passenger compartment, Hughes finds a pair of his spectacles. One lens is shattered and its counterpart's leg is bent. Looking simultaneously comical and fragile, Hughes puts on his lost glasses. They won't sit right. He doesn't quite stand right either. After a moment he makes a joke about the high cost of these spectacles and how he's going to take them to be repaired. It's hard to say why the idea of having the glasses repaired seems funny. In one sense, the joke relies on the presence of the written-off vehicle, which Hughes will, by implication, not bother trying to repair.

Also, his almost recovered body stands and moves in juxtaposition to the wreckage of his vehicle. Just by standing beside his busted-up car, Hughes is consciously posing a figure of brave recovery and courage who is being presented with a reminder of his year of suffering. The half-shattered and buckled spectacles, donned by the "cultural critic," dissolve the distance between Hughes and the wreck, between the spirit of a man as a triumph over his mere matter and an ordinary bloke who still thinks about wasting a good pair of glasses.

What was broken can be shown, but not what was lost—except, perhaps, when the driver and the wreck are reunited. Some losses are regained—losses that are mementos (literally memory-objects), to be repaired or at least gratefully abandoned.

Around the time of the trial, stories circulated about the fate of a freshly caught bluefin tuna in the trunk of Hughes' car. Before the crash, he had been out fishing on the coast and kept a piece of his catch for making sushi. In one story told about Hughes, he accused the firefighters who had saved him of stealing the tuna. In another, he made a joke about the tuna at least not going to waste if he couldn't have it, and offering it to the firefighters if they wanted it. It may be that the carcass was simply chucked to the side of the road before it started rotting in the trunk of the car. Clearly, the tuna was of some importance to Hughes, since he's a keen fisherman, and the fish formed part of his recollections of a day spent in blissful beachside ignorance just before the crash.

From the newspaper reports given by the rescue team and from the court transcripts, the tuna's disappearance from the scene of the accident was an irrelevance, except for the purposes of constructing Hughes' character. And as a media star with a love-hate relationship with Australia, the description—on the basis of his tuna handling—of Hughes as either contemptuous of his fellow Australians or a matey joker was actively pursued. The flesh of the fish was left out of these arguments, and would have become an important object only had Hughes wished to claim for it on his insurance, in which case an assessor might well have been sent in search of the lost tuna, interviewed witnesses, inspected the trunk for material evidence, and evaluated the financial worth of the fish. Not enough has been written about the looting, inheriting, or gifting of the artifacts left inside wrecked cars.

Missing—used for parts lost at the scene of an accident, such as wheel discs, chrome mouldings, etc, and is also used for items stolen in theft cases.

—D. Griffiths, *Automobile Assessing* (1983)

If the car crash is the event during which we face oblivion—whether erotic oblivion of the kind depicted in J. G. Ballard's *Crash,* the desired oblivion of a suicide attempt, or just the sudden uninvited arrival of the end of life—then the wreck that remains afterward is the memory of the event. In its crushed, buckled, smashed, shattered, cracked, twisted, torn, bent, bowed, sheared off, creased, and lacerated forms, we find the possibility of remembrance. For the protagonist of Proust's *Remembrance of Things Past,* it is the consumption of a delicate cake that triggers the return of lost time—or, rather, sets in motion an unmotivated recall, a form of remembering that is distinctive because it makes itself the subject for which our self is the object: It remembers through us. In the case of the car wreck, however, there is a sculptural rendering of some brief moments—moments of the near or actual loss of consciousness and, perhaps, of life.

First to visit the wreck are professionals in the production of a public record of memory—the fire brigade, ambulance crew, police, the assessors and lawyers and their assistants. Then, sometimes, family and friends will go to see what more intimate and private details can be retrieved from the towed-away vehicle. Depending on whether the car is to be repaired, kept, or dismantled, it may next be sent to a garage for repair, or auto-salvage experts may move in to break it up into pieces for donation to other cars. Among all these people coming and going, the driver and occupants, if they survived, may make an appearance. The profundity of their encounter with the car will depend on how closely the crash brought them to oblivion. Most of the time, crashes are only knocks. The car escapes its immobilization as a wreck, and its occupants get away with a little shock and some whiplash. Every year, auto safety is in some small way improved, though this has no necessary correlation with the number or severity of car crashes recorded. The goods news for car wreck visitors is that their numbers are steadily increasing. More and more of us can carry out the shocking or sentimental journeys described herein.

> *Details of Damage*—Such details should be as concise and descriptive as possible. They should assist the assessor to formulate a mental picture of the damaged vehicle long after the inspection. Notes made at the time should be legible, because it is possible that the assessor may be required by a judge to produce his original notes. Damaged parts should be detailed in a set order progressing from front to rear, side to side, or rear to front as the case may be. Items should be listed under headings, e.g., doors, lamps, bumpers, etc. The assessor should use a variety of terms to describe damage and he should use these at his discretion. The term "damaged" is too vague and should not be used.
>
> —D. Griffiths, *Automobile Assessing* (1983)

It is said often enough: We all make mistakes. Do not forget that each and every car is destined, with or without our errors, inattentiveness, or misjudgments, to be left wrecked one day in some way or other.

NOTES

1. Walter Benjamin, *Origin of the German of Mourning* (Ernst Rowohlt: Berlin, 1928). Reprinted in *Selected Writings*, volume 2 (1927–1934), ed. Marcus Bullock and Michael W. Jennings (Cambridge, MA: Belknap Press, 1983).

2. D. Griffith, *Automobile Assessing* (MacFarland: London, 1983). All references following this citation will be from the same source.

3. Although Hughes had never seen the wreck "in the flesh" (so to speak), it would seem unlikely that he had not encountered photos of the car smash in the year afterward, let alone descriptions from people who had visited the crash site.

STRANGERS IN THE NIGHT

A MEMORY

WILLIAM LUHR

"I felt like an amputated leg."

—Raymond Chandler, *Farewell, My Lovely*

I HEARD A CRASH.

It was past midnight and I was sitting up alone. You hear strange things in the night, things that catch you by surprise. After you've heard them, you aren't quite sure what you've heard; you start to sort out options as to what, if anything, happened out there. But I didn't have to sort out options.

I heard a second crash.

I lived on the service road of a sunken expressway in New York; the expressway was perhaps twenty or thirty feet below street level. The crashes had come from there. I rushed outside and crossed an overpass to the expressway so I could get down on to it by means of an exit ramp. As I did, a desperate screaming stunned me—a screaming that began and stopped abruptly. No traffic came by; the expressway was desolate and silent again.

An eighteen-wheeler was parked on the shoulder and a car sat diagonally, precariously blocking a lane. Nothing else. I felt entirely alone.

Screaming again consumed the night. I ran toward the car and saw two people in the front seat, but they weren't moving. The screaming came from the far side of the car and, again, it stopped abruptly. I walked around the car and found a man beside it, lying unconscious in a lot of blood. His leg was lying next to him.

Someone called down from the overpass that I had just crossed. I told him to call an ambulance and the police, that someone was badly hurt. He ran off to make the calls and it was quiet again.

Things then happened quickly and in confusion. The man's stump, which extended halfway to where his knee should have been, was bleeding badly. I tied my belt around it in an attempt at a tourniquet. A car sped past. I waved at it both to avoid being hit and to ask for help, but it did not stop. I was scared; I was way out of my depth. I covered the man with my jacket, then ran to the truck, found a blanket inside, and covered him with that also. I tried to make him comfortable. His severed leg just lay there.

I tried to talk to him. He woke up and started screaming. For a few minutes he seemed to understand me, seemed to be trying to respond, but I couldn't understand what he was saying. It was maddening; I couldn't help him. He was trapped in a terrifying cycle of blacking out from unbearable pain, then waking up and screaming, and then blacking out again. Twenty minutes had passed. Where was the ambulance? Where were the police? Where was anybody?

"Is he hurt?"

A banshee from the fifth century appearing suddenly and howling those words into my face could not have scared me more. But the question was asked quietly from behind me by a dazed and disheveled woman. She had come from the car. I hadn't heard her open the door.

"Is he hurt? He's lying, screaming, in quarts of his blood in the middle of an expressway with his leg next to him and you ask 'Is he hurt?'"

I didn't say that. She was dazed, shivering. Another car passed and did not stop. Bastards. Four or five people were coming down the exit ramp to see what was happening. I asked one of them to wave down, or wave off, oncoming cars. No police came, no help. I couldn't commu-

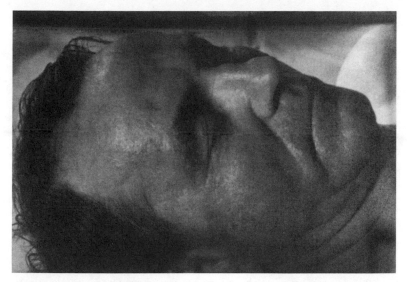

5.1   Car Crash Victim. © Feral House

nicate with the man. His bleeding seemed to have stopped but I couldn't really tell, given the raw mess of his stump, the volume of blood, and my fear of moving him. I rubbed his head and his arms, just to do something.

Finally, about forty minutes after it was called, an ambulance came. The crew shoved past me and went to work. The man started screaming again and stopped again.

I walked the woman to her car. She was shivering. She was about thirty. A man about her age had remained in the driver's seat, not hurt but dazed. He looked around but neither moved nor spoke. Probably on a date.

She sat in the car, held my hand, and told me the story.

They had been returning from somewhere and, on a curve, lost control of the car. It smacked a highway divider, spun, and settled to a stop. That was the first crash.

They must have both hit their heads on something—but not too badly, since no glass was shattered and they were not bleeding—and simply sat there, stunned. Not bright, sitting in a car blocking the fast lane of a dark expressway in the middle of the night on the wrong side of a curve. But who *is* bright under such circumstances?

As they sat there, dazed, a man knocked on her window. "Are you all right, lady?"

The voice was gentle, kindly. She said she was, and he said, "Good." He then walked around the rear of the car to check on the driver. He never made it. That was the second crash.

A second car had come firing around the curve and hit both the man and the first car simultaneously, shearing off his leg and sending the first car into another spin. Then, without stopping to either check or help, the second car sped away. It was gone. That's pretty much the whole story.

She kept repeating "Are you all right, lady?" Had that nice man not stopped his truck to help her, she kept telling me, he would still be all right. He would probably be home and in a warm bed by now. She kept telling me how gentle his voice was, how gentle his manner.

No more than ten people ever came by and the police never appeared. I helped the medics place the man on a stretcher. Then I picked up his leg and placed it beside him. The shoe was on the foot, the laces neatly tied. Then everyone left. The couple and their car were towed away, and it was over. It was quiet again and I was alone, so I went home. The next day the truck was gone.

I never knew their names. I never learned whether the man lived or died. The next morning traffic moved briskly on the expressway and the blood was gone. It was as if the entire thing had never happened. I called local hospitals but no one could tell me anything. I doubt the woman ever learned anything about the stranger's fate either, and not because she didn't care. Things happen that way in urban areas. The driver of the second car quite possibly hit the man and first car with no initial comprehension of what was happening. Rather than find out, help out, or assume responsibility, the driver simply got out of there as quickly as possible and never looked back.

We were all strangers and we still are. We briefly came together and shared fragments of an intense and intimate experience, a primal experience, one we will neither forget nor outlive.

Car crashes are confidential and anonymous. No one plans them; they blast into normal existence and reorder everything. They abruptly make intimates out of strangers. You're going about your normal activities one moment and the next moment transforms your life, instantly, like an apocalypse. You find yourself suddenly, intimately intertwined—sometimes literally, carnally—with someone you don't know and maybe never will. Life doesn't get any more intense.

Your life may be changed irrevocably, or maybe not. This happened a long time ago and my life has gone on.

NOTES

Special thanks to David Luhr for editorial assistance.

"JUMP ON IN, YOU'RE IN SAFE HANDS"

FLASH-FRAMES FROM THE AUTOMOBILE CARGO BAY EXPERIENCE

HOWARD LAKE

NEAR-DEATH EXPERIENCE #1   LYON 1989

EVERYONE IN THE CAR—A RENAULT, NATURALLY—was majorly twisted, a combo of Algerian red, amphetamine, and weird over-the-counter French fuckyerheads called "Nuocodeine." Four passengers and a female driver the total, barreling from Place des Terraux down to Bellecoeur at 2:30 A.M. to collect fresh supplies from the all-night liquor store by the underground car park. I'm seated behind the front passenger seat and only too aware, in that distanced-paranoia drug way, that she could easily kill us all, yet thrilling to the existential anarchy of the moment. (Sartre and Iggy Pop were our philosophical mentors then.)

And I knew it would happen; blast of prescience thirty seconds ahead of time as we lurched into the narrow side street lined on either side with parked cars. Somewhere up ahead the glint of metal signaled another vehicle doing exactly the same, triggering the subconscious calculus that somehow

*makes skilled telematrists of us all when impact beckons, a complex of data
processed and decoded in nanoseconds yet ultimately redundant. The only
party of any significance here is the driver and she's reacted already, a panicked swerve that throws the Renault through 90 degrees with brakes locked
(maybe, I can't truthfully say) and tires dead set against obeying her frantic
yanking at the wheel. Our car travels perhaps forty feet along the street sideways, neatly parallel front and rear to the cars lined up along each curb. We
jolt to a sudden stop a safe twenty feet or so from the oncoming vehicle, which
presumably braked upon seeing us lose control.*

*The laughter of relief and release inevitably follows. With more difficulty
than she had in almost crashing us, our driver stop-start reverses us out of the
column of parked cars and the journey continues.*

To enter any vehicle as a passenger is to relinquish control of your own
destiny and entrust your complete existence to another. It is an act of
faith from the second the driver turns their key in the ignition, whether
they are someone close to you or a complete stranger—the taxi driver,
the chauffeur, the trucker who pulls to the curb in response to the
hitcher's leveled thumb.

Once a vehicle is in motion, the passenger becomes little more than
baggage. The role they play in the ensuing journey is a passive one. They
may read maps or provide company for the driver, but essentially they are
a cargo of flesh and blood that the driver transports from one point to another. Quite literally, the passenger is just along for the ride. Only one person matters here: the driver. In the vehicular microverse, the driver is god.
The passenger's fate is entirely reliant upon the judgment, ability, and disposition of the person to whom they have entrusted their physical being.

Just take a look at any prime-time automobile commercial: Cars are
not designed with passengers in mind. All automobile advertising is
geared toward the driver. The assumption seems to be that people buy
cars because they want a machine to possess and master, one that will afford them profound sensual, spiritual, and emotional satisfaction: the
"driving experience," "the drive of your life," and so on, ad nauseum. In
every car commercial, the driver is depicted as a Supreme Being, one
whom, by dint of having selected the right car, is now able to cope easily with the stresses of everyday life. More often than not, among these

bugbears will be those who require ferrying from one place to another: the passengers. Passengers in car ads are regularly portrayed as burdens who must be transported by the driver: kids to be dropped off at school; spouses whose shopping requires portage; friends and teammates to be taken to social or sporting events. These are all chores the drivers can now accomplish with ease, ultimately leaving them at liberty to enjoy the spiritual capacities of their vehicle—commonly expressed by means of that curious metaphysical construct known as the "open road."

This notion of the driver as higher entity persists even within the construction of the car itself. There's no egalitarianism in car design; any item or function that plays a role in operating the vehicle is placed in easy reach of the driver, from air-conditioning to CD player to storage space. While this is plainly down to basic ergonomics—manufacturers have no truck whatsoever with car-pooling and the like (fewer drivers means less sales)—such design absolutes reinforce the notion of the driver-as-god. The driver's seat is a throne, its occupant ruler of all that is surveyed, with total power over the vehicular microverse at his or her fingertips. In car advertising, words like "comfort," "ease," "power," "freedom," and "control" all allude to the act of driving as a transcendental process toward existential perfection, with body and machine operating in a techno-physiological harmony that reaches far beyond the mere sublime.

And once driver and machine are enmeshed in such synergy, there is no room left for the passenger. Even vehicles targeted specifically at those requiring maximum carriage space—the "family" car, for example—are still sold to the *driver* first and foremost. Passengers are baggage at best, encumbrances at worst. In advertising, passengers exist as ciphers for that which either detracts from the existential driving experience or enhances it to the realm of fantasy. But whether screaming kids in the backseat or pneumatic blonde riding up front, neither is fundamentally necessary to the business of driving itself.

Doubtless, motor merchandisers would deem such thinking overly cynical, preferring to stress how the modern car has "evolved" to become a safer and more secure environment, a device in which the people or things most precious to you can be transported in total security and comfort. Yet as any putative passenger knows, the pitch of the ad men is directed exclusively at the driver. When the safety card is played in vehicle marketing, it is to provide assurance to drivers that this particular model will adequately protect those in their charge should the unthinkable occur. Airbags, rear seat belts, central locking, crumple zones, and roll cages are buzzwords freely bandied about in car commercials, flourished as semantic talismans guaranteed to ward off the evil eye. Likewise, the drivers who appear in such commercials are all thoroughly responsible road users, even those for whom a quick spin in the latest Peugeot is mere foreplay to carnal escapades on some exotic littoral. And when the vehicle is sold as strictly functional, it still has to exude a frisson of derring-do or sensuality, or—a recent device, this—confer superior intelligence upon the owner.

By buying a vehicle, they tell us, you are making a statement about the kind of person you are, about your belief system and the social and moral codes by which you live your life. This is the motor-marketing credo and one that, by and large, the majority of car-owners accept and embrace. They do so without regard to anybody else who might travel in their vehicle of choice. These people do not matter, and it is highly unlikely they will understand or identify with the driver's self-image to such an extent that their bond with the car is anywhere near as strong. Sure, they may appreciate the vehicle and the convenience it affords them; they may even enthuse over its styling and find the prospect of a journey in it an exciting or privileged event, but for all that the facts remain: It is not their car. This environment of metal, chrome, and vinyl is not their domain, and all control and authority rests with the driver. Once the vehicle is moving they are utterly powerless. They are mere cargo, no more than baggage, and their destiny lies in the hands of their pilot. Even those who exert enormous influence on the world outside the automobile microverse are completely stripped of all power once they accept the status of passenger.

Or so it might seem. But the passenger is not entirely without influence. Control of the automobile interior may well be the driver's domain but, as in all religious or quasi-religious interactions, the extent of the deity's power depends entirely on faith given voluntarily, fearfully, or even blindly. It is this faith that propels the dynamic between driver and passenger. And when, as often happens, the fragile structures underpinning and facilitating this faith are disturbed, then the dynamic can be shattered—and with catastrophic consequences.

NEAR-DEATH EXPERIENCF #2
DUDDINGTON BYPASS, SUMMER 1982

Like a stillborn sitcom sketch: there's a red Fiat Panda, five inside, all of us schoolmates headed for Heacham, Norfolk, the last summer before the college and university diaspora severed the hometown bonds. Sean's at the wheel, so tall he's hunched over comically as the rest of us, friends forever (or so we think), pass a glowing chillum along the backseat, where I am (right-hand side window seat, behind the driver) and to the front. It happens so suddenly, so gently and unexpectedly I don't actually notice what's going on until the alarmed shout of another passenger alerts me. By then it's too late for me to react. I can see the boot of the fawn Austin Maxi just inches from the Panda's bumper and can guess what's happened. Glancing through the window, we're on the feeder lane that funnels into the bypass proper, grassy slopes either side, traffic-planner anonymity. Toked, yes, but not really stoned. Even so, you've got to giggle when Sean gets out to check on the driver he's just rear-ended and there's a five-foot nun angrily confronting this Irish six-footer. If we hadn't slowed down moments ago when a haulage truck cut us off on the inside lane we'd have struck the nun's car at a good 40 mph faster than we did. As things stood, damage was minor, no urgent repairs were required, and after addresses are exchanged (false on his part, if memory serves), we continued to Heacham, arriving around midafternoon.

Car safety is big business. There is an extensive literature dealing with ways of ensuring maximum protection for car travel. Research into ever more sophisticated and elaborate safety devices is a process without end. Manufacturers invest enormous amounts in developing refinements designed to protect the purchasers and users of their products from any harm they may encounter on the world's highways and byways. Scientists pore endlessly over potential impact scenarios, imagining infinite collision permutations, from every imaginable angle, at every conceivable terminal velocity. The ultimate goal is to engineer a transportation device capable of withstanding any violent encounter with minimal injury risk to the driver or occupant.

It doesn't take Sigmund Freud to understand what this obsessive quest is really about. What these manufacturers are trying to achieve is a four-

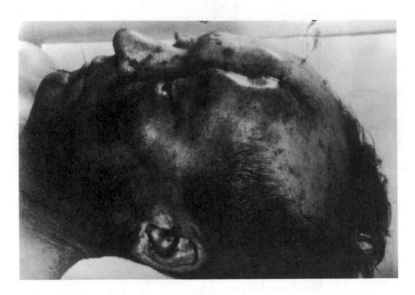

6.1   Car Crash Victim. © Feral House

wheeled womb, a hermetically sealed environment incapable of violation in which the car's occupants can relax and make their journey free from anxiety and danger. As with so much marketing strategy, the play on our memories of infantile cosseting is constantly reinforced. Many car ads push this angle zealously, with images intended to engage our subconscious desire to revert to a childlike state free from responsibility and protected from danger at all times. No family car ad is complete without an image of the classical family unit—handsome, assured father, content, fulfilled mother, and a rear seat adorned with trio of smiling offspring— heading off down the open road without a care in the world. Inside the vehicle, says the ad, we are as secure as in the home. Nothing can threaten us here; we are protected from all evil.

And evil is, of course, another crucial construct underpinning the auto business. In any discussion of car safety, it won't take long before we encounter the archetype of the "Other Guy." Over the years, this concept has achieved such common currency its authenticity is hardly ever given a second thought. However good and careful a driver you might be, they tell us, there's always a minority of road users who recklessly disregard the principles of proper driving and who will, through their intemperance, intoxication, or just sheer lunacy, endanger even those of us who stick to the codes of sensible driving. These Other Guys are, of course, inherently evil, and it's in order to protect ourselves from such madmen that we must surround ourselves by every safety device available. And, naturally, we have to pay a high price for the malevolence of others.

In recent times, this threat of evil waiting out there for us on the road has grown even greater. The concept of "road rage" has added another highway bogeyman to the list that already includes the drunk driver, the speed freak, and the manic tailgater. The highway is, or so popular folk-lore has it, a domain crammed with countless Other Guys hell-bent on our destruction. Regardless of whether our roads actually are teeming with motorized psychos intent on crashing into us—with all the risk and expense to themselves this would entail—fear of them is endemic, and continues to grow with every sensationalized incident. As an extension of the home territory, the vehicle is sacrosanct. It is considered justifiable to defend your car as you would your home, and the growth of the car protection and safety industry has very closely paralleled that of the home security business. The psychotic crackhead who invades the home to slice and dice your wife and kids has his vehicular counterpart in the gun or knife-toting White Van Man who cuts you off at the intersection and dares you to call him on it.

Yes, these are dangerous times for the all-powerful driver. Although in full control of his machine and all its assorted technology, although as-sured his preferred vehicle can protect him against all but the most cata-strophic of circumstances, he is now at the mercy of a nameless menace that could come from anywhere, at any time. Under such strain, the in-car dynamic assumes even greater importance, with the driver's dominant status requiring even further enhancement for him to be able to perform the multitude of functions now expected of him. Conversely, the role of the passenger must be further diminished so this dynamic can be main-tained in suitable harmony. What is increasingly expected of the passen-ger is nothing more than regression to a state of passive infantilism.

This is perfectly illustrated by legislation making the use of rear seat belts mandatory. Prior to their introduction, the back passenger seat was very much a zone of freedom within the car. It was the area where children or adult passengers were seated, and it afforded them license to behave with relative impunity compared to those seated in the front. With no role to play in the vehicle's operation, they were free to climb around or lie in whatever position they found most comfortable or relaxing. They had no obligation to consider the driving process at all. But there is a downside to granting such freedom to a passenger. In any crash scenario, there is always the possibility that backseat passengers may be thrown forward and into the front area, injuring themselves and perhaps the front seat occupants as well.

Children, due to their size and weight, are seen as carrying a higher risk of injuring those in the front. A 1999 public service commercial in the United Kingdom illustrated this danger in a scene where a mother making the daily school run is killed when, after she's forced to brake suddenly, her teenage son is thrown into the rear of the driver's seat, crushing his mother against the steering wheel. "She knew her killer," the somber voiceover intones. "After killing her, her son sat back down." This commercial is meant to show the importance of employing rear seat belts and is intriguing not only because its shock tactics demonstrate the gravity of the threat as perceived by safety campaigners but also because it presents the destruction of the family unit as a consequence of ignoring car safety. Viewers are expected to take on board the hideous irony of the near-oedipal subtext in the slaying of a mother by her son (a teenage daughter is also present but is unaffected by the crash). By disobeying the rules of car safety, we are told, we can destroy all we hold dear and close to our hearts.

Extrapolating further, we can assume the son shuns the rear safety belt for the very reason those responsible for the ad are urging its use. The son is reluctant to assume the passive infantile position of restraint, and, as a consequence, the family is devastated. Being a near adult, he sees no reason to be subjected to the kind of harness a young child would be forced into. And this is not overstating the issue. Car safety advocates never fail to stress the importance of corralling infants in the vehicle, as the following parental advice illustrates:

> You also must be patient, firm and consistent, letting your child know that the car doesn't go unless he is in his seat. Do not start the car until he settles down, and stop at a safe spot along the roadside if he gets out when the car is underway. Positive reinforcement is also crucial, such as small re-

wards for good behavior; short "training" trips to favorite spots; and dramatic play in which he buckles up a favorite doll or stuffed animal for a real or "pretend" car ride. You must be prepared to enforce your rules on every trip in the car. Allowing a child to do it his way "just this once" makes it that much harder to get him to do it your way the next time.[1]

In a society where fears for infant safety have reached hysterical proportions, such a neurotic, almost totalitarian approach to car safety is perhaps not so surprising. Ours is a paranoid world where the need for protection has become paramount, and the utopian ideal is to locate oneself in a place of sanctuary with the forces of evil held firmly at bay. In attempting to achieve this ideal, we inexorably regress to a dream of protected childhood or even further back, to the immurement of the womb itself. The modern automobile has been developed as a total immersion environment, a self-contained zone of absolute safety. And the dynamic between driver and passenger is thereby even further refined, the driver playing the part of protective parent to an infantile human cargo. Cosseted in the womblike safety zone of the backseat, the passenger has nothing to fear . . . or so we are encouraged to believe.

NEAR-DEATH EXPERIENCE #3
STOCKWELL, 1988

It was one of those kinds of nights. To the Scala cinema with flatmate John to catch a mammoth bill ending at 7:00 A.M. Then to the McDonald's in Warren Street where John picks up some junkie from out in Surrey somewhere (the guy's a compulsive skirt-chaser). She's got a red secondhand Mini, is going our way, and, sure, she'll give us a lift. We go via Soho, ejected from Maison Bertaux for being drunk at nine in the morning, then drive down to SE25 via Vauxhall, Kennington. John and the junkie in front, me in the back. There's a creeping paranoia about the whole thing viewed through my cheap speed comedown and drunkenness as it's plain the two are getting sexual as she's driving. His hand's in her jeans frotting you-know-what as the Mini's hemmed in either side by double-decker buses too cumbersome to respond to any sudden swerve on our part. He brings her off, leaning across from the front passenger seat, and she loses her grip on the wheel just as a 158 Brixton-Thornton Heath bus pulls away from the curb. The looming dirty red of the bus is just inches from the bumper as I shout a warning and her feet jam down hard on the brake pedals. Exhalation, relief... That would've taken some explaining to the cops, guys.

Pammy and Tommy Lee are in a private dreamworld filled with L.O.V.E. "We are so fuckin' outta here!" enthuses Tommy, as Pammy films him settling into the driver's seat of the SUV. They are heading for Lake Mead on vacation, eager to celebrate their abundant passion for each other. And they are eager to record that passion with an accompanying camcorder that will enshrine their most intimate moments for posterity.[2]

Make no mistake about it, their ardor is heartfelt and unrestrained by inhibition. Both are sexual creatures: she currently the focus of millions of erotic fantasies worldwide, her partner a walking definition of the rock-n-roll satyr. Whether they express it verbally or physically, their love is—at this point in their relationship—impossible to contain.

As they drive toward Nevada, this becomes evident. Tommy is feeling horny and demonstrates it by letting his oversized erection jut out from his shorts. Pammy can't resist grabbing it—she makes no secret of her delight—and the tape starts to roll as she leans across Tommy's lap to fellate him. Tommy's still driving in heavy rain, and although he glances up at the road from time to time, he's more engrossed in trying to capture Pammy's antics on videotape—at one point he moves her blonde tresses aside to get a better shot of the details. Watching, one gets the impression this is where things ended, or at least for a while. Pammy does not persevere with her oral ministrations; she does not fellate her husband to climax as he's driving. A remark from Tommy about having to pull off the road suggests that if this was an immediate prelude to sex, then they did not engage in it while the SUV was in motion.

This footage is perhaps the only genuine recording of any couple having in-car sex while the vehicle is on the road. This is not to say that the Lees are the only couple ever to have done this or even to have been filmed doing it. There are certainly many instances of porn films where sex acts have been filmed in moving cars. I can think of several myself but can't recall an example where one of the participants is sexually involved while also in control of the vehicle. It's not uncommon for makers of sex films to try to give the impression this is happening, but given the practical requirements of moviemaking, it's highly unlikely that this popular scenario is ever played out for real.

Danger is one very obvious reason why not. Driving requires a certain degree of concentration from the person at the wheel. As described earlier, the driver has total control of the vehicle and is responsible for the safety of the passengers. This is a fundamental tenet of the automobile creed. To permit oneself to be distracted while driving is an offense not to be taken lightly. Under U.K. law, the charge of failing to practice due care and attention while driving extends to using a mobile phone, changing a CD, and even drinking a bottle of mineral water in a car.[3] If activities such as these are considered sufficient distraction to cause unsafe driving, then any kind of vehicular sexual dalliance must surely be the ultimate form of automotive folly. And unless the sex act is masturbation, then the passenger has to be an active participant, thereby utterly transgressing the established codes of appropriate interaction between driver and passenger.

Pammy and Tommy's fun and games don't result in either of them coming to any harm—or harming any other road user, for that matter. The sex act never becomes so involved or intense that Tommy's driving becomes dangerous. The implication that they stopped the vehicle shortly afterward to finish what they had started suggests one or both of them realized it was unsafe to continue at that point. Imagine if they had decided *not* to call a halt and if, while in the throes of orgasm, Tommy had abandoned control of the SUV with fatal consequences to the couple or perhaps to another road user. In the pantheon of automobile fatalities, this would surely rank among the most spectacular and salaciously bizarre celebrity crash deaths of all time. It would not, however, be without precedent.

Today, F. W. Murnau is remembered by cinéastes primarily as the director of the original *Nosferatu* (1922). Following the success of this film, Hollywood beckoned, and Murnau was not slow to grasp the opportunity to exhibit his talents on a wider stage. He quickly found a niche in California and settled into the Tinseltown lifestyle with ease. His homosexuality was tacitly tolerated there, and his future seemed assured until his life was suddenly cut short in 1931, at the age of forty-two, when his Packard veered off the road in mysterious circumstances. Murnau died of head injuries, ostensibly caused by his skull being cracked against a telegraph pole. The true circumstances of the crash will perhaps never be known, but what details *were* revealed gave the rumor mill reason to grind. Kenneth Anger diligently recorded these rumors in *Hollywood Babylon:* "Murnau had hired as valet a handsome fourteen-year-old Filipino boy named Garcia Stevenson. The boy was at the wheel of the Packard when the fatal accident occurred. The Hollywood *méchantes langues* reported that Murnau was going down on Garcia when the car leaped off the road. Only eleven brave souls (Garbo was there) showed up for the funeral. . . ."[4]

The relationship between sex and the automobile in Western culture is so vast a subject it would require a volume in itself. There can be no doubt that this relationship is enormously varied and wide ranging, nor can the role of the car in our erotic activities, either actual or fantasized, be understated. Many different studies have analyzed the importance in our culture of the automobile as a site of sexual liaison. A high percentage of people report that their first sexual encounter took place in a car. In U.S. society especially, for the man, driving or owning a car has become a virtual totem of sexual maturity, a symbolic indicator of the fully functioning adult libido. Not for nothing do John Travolta and pals in Randal Keiser's movie *Grease* (1978) refer to their hotrod Greased Lightning as a "pussy wagon."

And, naturally, this sexualized vision of the automobile always favors the driver. When sexual congress of any kind takes place in a car, the instigator is always assumed to be the driver. Whether it's a hooker servicing a john or teenage virgins going through their rituals of sexual initiation, the passenger is always assumed to have a passive, even subservient role. Although often derided by those who see the correlation between cars and sexuality as ridiculously obvious—the automobile as simple "phallic symbol"—this implicit correlation persists and is subtly reinforced through any number of advertisements, movies, and television shows.

For many young males, having a "good car" is seen as an essential prerequisite to attracting the opposite sex. The psychology behind such thinking seems rooted in the male assumption that potential partners will be more receptive to sexual overtures if they are offered comfort and surroundings that flatter them in some way. If a girl is impressed by the size or strength of the car, then the esteem in which she holds it will be transferred to the driver—or, at least, that's the idea. A man's car is also assumed to represent many of his character attributes, such as style and taste, but mostly it reveals his power. Sometimes this potency can be further boosted by the way the car is driven, be it high-speed driving or the flaunting of stunt skills. What the driver is really showing the passenger is his ability to take total charge, his capacity to be dominant in a given situation, and to successfully take on challenges, even risks. What such displays of machismo indicate is evident to even the most casual anthropologist: In our culture, driving performance has become one of the most common methods of male sexual display.

And it has to be assumed this display is effective, given the enduring relationship between men and their cars—a relationship that began in the 1950s and continues to this day. Auto advertisers are never shy to exploit the sexual dimensions of their product, though today's commercials are less overt in their pitch—the days of muscle cars are over, after all, and today's cars are, well, a lot less sexy than their predecessors. Which is not to say the attractive blonde has totally vanished from the passenger seat. It's just that, these days, she's generally presented as the driver's wife instead of the comely roadside pickup. But she's still crucially hot to trot once her man has shown her his in-car CD player and hi-tech airbags.

NEAR-DEATH EXPERIENCE #4
KENTISH TOWN, 1986

The club ended around 3:00 A.M. but everyone was still up for it. We headed to our mates' place in Tufnell Park. A night bus would have taken us there, but a taxi was less hassle and less delay. With a four-passenger maximum and us a party of seven, we ask the minicab tout in Windmill Street to summon two. I get into the second car to arrive, a Granada, with Andrea and Drig. By the time we clear Piccadilly Circus, anxious glances are being exchanged. The Nigerian driver is so wired his eyeballs are genuinely bulging. He likes us, though, and is happy to detail his life story in between—and during— vehicle maneuvers carried out at approximately 60 mph on York Way. Unmarked police cars are a particular bane of his life, he says, throttling up to

80. And there's one of the bastards! His finger jabs in front, indicating a non-descript Rover maybe two hundred yards ahead. But, defiantly, he refuses to slow down until the last necessary moment, then casually stamps his foot on the brake pedal. Surface water? An oil patch? Whatever, the skid sends us into the adjacent lane where a haulage truck is idling at a set of lights. Andrea screamed a warning, if memory served, maybe Drig too. I was still looking for the unmarked cop car. I transferred my attention just in time to see the haulage company name writ large through the windshield and a plume of diesel emissions billowing from an exhaust as the Nigerian flicks the wheel right, almost contemptuous that anyone could doubt his ability to avoid calamity. I was wrong, they wasn't cops, he remarks, foot on the accelerator once more. What was that address you wanted again?

A chauffeured limousine is an environment comprised of contradictions. As a pedestrian making your way along the dirty, crowded pavements of any major city—London, Paris, New York—the sight of a limo headed through traffic immediately excites certain thoughts. These are conveyances designed to confer status on their occupants. They are an exercise in grandiosity, from the gleaming high-polished exterior to the ostentatiously oversize dimensions of the vehicle itself. Tinted, even mirrored windows may shield the passenger from view, further emphasizing that those within are not of our world. They may need to travel among us, but such is their status that they can avoid the stresses of actually mingling with their fellow man. Instead, the limo becomes a space that exists simultaneously among the bustling milieu of the real world and yet is as detached from this world as possible.

Other signifiers reinforce this notion. The passenger compartment itself often differs greatly from the kinds most of us know. Often these areas are custom-built to resemble a luxurious home or mobile penthouse suite, with everything from TV sets to cocktail bars to office equipment, installed to hammer home the fact that this is a space *exclusively* for passengers. No one who travels in such style is expected to participate to any extent in the actual process of driving, which would be beneath them and would be an insult to the special status they deserve. These passengers' power or celebrity means they can abrogate any responsibility for the actual driving process from the moment they enter the limo to the moment they step out of it—door held open, perhaps, by an obsequious uniformed lackey—at the end of their journey.

The task of actually driving the vehicle falls, of course, to the chauffeur. The word itself is significant, elevating the driver far above the level of being merely a *driver.* A chauffeur is a driver-plus, a superdriver, somehow better than any other. The fact that he usually wears livery or a cap further reinforces his status. The chauffeur's uniform signals his role as a guardian assigned not only to ferry his celebrity charge but to defend them as well. The passenger in a chauffeured limousine is the motorized equivalent of a Caesar parading in triumph through Rome flanked by his Praetorian Guard or a British monarch's horse-drawn carriage surrounded by Household Cavalry in full ceremonial regalia. It is a show, pure and simple, and a show that becomes more or less elaborate depending on the status of the passenger. Think of a U.S. presidential motorcade, where the display is embellished by a phalanx of motorcycle outriders and secret service agents attending the most powerful man on the planet. Additional deference is ensured by the closure to other traffic of the path along which the chieftain is to be driven, a somewhat paradoxical gesture—with the boulevards and avenues cleared of other road users, why drive at all?—but one that affirms the symbolic magnitude of this particular style of procession, one that has been especially eloquent since the events of November 1963 in Dallas.

In the case of the chauffeured chieftain, the notion of infantile regression is heightened to almost absurd proportions. There is certainly something strange in the idea that the greater a man's power and importance, the more extreme his cosseting becomes. The presidential limousine moves so slowly that a crash is highly unlikely, while the threat from other road users is eliminated entirely. This is hyperprotection, every potential risk to the passenger's safe conduct analyzed and anticipated; those charged with driving or otherwise ensuring the passenger's protection are presumed to be skilled operatives in their field, persons ready to lay down their lives rather than see the security of their charges compromised. For example, Trevor Rees-Jones, bodyguard to Dodi Fayed, referred to his boss and his companion very deliberately as "the passengers."[5] It was clear he felt his bodyguard status placed him apart from the ordinary category of passenger, even though he was as helpless to prevent the crash as Dodi or Diana themselves.

6.2   Jayne Mansfield. © Photofest

And accidents in which these passengers come to fatal harm have a far greater symbolic resonance than "ordinary" car accidents. The public attitude toward such crashes is liable to involve far more sympathy for the passenger-victim than the driver-victim. We can all share a shudder of grotesquerie at the notion of being "driven toward our doom." Despite the limo signifying in no uncertain terms the passenger's separation from

6.3 Jayne Mansfield crash. © Photofest

his fellow men, such crashes lead us to fixate with instant empathy on those whose terminal moments entail the kind of abject helplessness that anyone who has ever been a passenger can understand. Think of the Di-Dodi accident, especially the detailed newspaper reports that told us how the bodies were slammed into sundry parts of the car's interior, and at what terminal velocity and in what contorted postures they were found by those rushing to their aid. Think of the JFK assassination, especially the constant media recreations of the president's stricken body as it slumps in the limousine seat, endlessly replayed and mismatched to the entry path of the fatal bullet. Think of the Jayne Mansfield crash, in which a sleeping icon suffers the terminal indignity of near decapitation by a steel pipe smashing through the windshield of her Buick.

An interesting case of the disparity between the death of a driver and the death of a passenger is to be found by comparing Mansfield's death crash with James Dean's. When Dean crumpled his Porsche Spyder by the roadside he was a star in his prime, with a stellar future ahead. The image upon which his success was constructed was marked by recklessness, rebellion, and nonconformity. That such traits were contributory factors in his death makes his crash somehow less shocking. It was not an entirely unanticipated event, perhaps even one that fulfilled a destiny Dean had himself created. His role as death-crash driver magnifies his reputation as wild, defiant, and sexily self-destructive.

Mansfield, by contrast, was characterized by her passivity and the way she allowed herself to be controlled by the men in her life, especially husbands Matt Cimber and Mickey Hargitay. In contrast to James Dean, Mansfield was a fading star whose career had long ago peaked, one from whom the public expected little more than a shabby cabaret act and some tawdry scandal. Had her driver on that fateful Mississippi night managed to avoid the accident, then she probably would be remembered today as nothing more than a former 1950s bombshell, perhaps a suitable name for the "Dead . . . or Alive?" filler in *Star* magazine.[6] But the manner of her death changes everything. A sudden end colors all that precedes it, especially an end in which death comes swiftly, savagely, and out of the night.

Her role as helpless death-crash passenger amplifies Mansfield's reputation as a passive victim, making her image as celebrity sacrifice seem all the more appropriate. The hunger for attention, the notoriety, even the shamelessly exploited sexuality upon which she had so effectively traded can now be analyzed as in some way logically charting a course to a demise so bizarre and gruesomely compelling it's almost as if it couldn't have happened any other way. It's a ridiculous assertion, of course, but a lingering death from cancer would not have suited her style. We want our crash-and-burn blondes to do the decent thing and exit our lives in as ravishingly stylish a manner as they inhabited it, like Monroe, Mansfield, and Diana Windsor. Even better if we can recognize the hand of fate pointing the way to their death—Henri Paul and the paparazzi in Mrs. Windsor's case; the Kennedys and the FBI in Marilyn's; and, for poor Jayne Mansfield, a Faustian pact of fame: the Devil's deal paid by blood sacrifice.[7]

NEAR-DEATH EXPERIENCE #5
PONT D'ALMA, PARIS 8/31/97

I'll always regret it. Being a creature of habit, I rarely hit the hay immediately after coming in from a night out, but this particular night I was feel-

ing pretty wiped out after getting back from Tony and Donna's. Instead of doing what I normally do and winding down in front of the TV news before bed, I just crashed out. Had I stuck with my routine, I would have switched on Sky News at about 2:45 A.M., just as the first reports were coming in, way before she was even confirmed as dead. I would have been there as it happened and would have had to rouse Charlotte to share this incredible moment of proximity to the biggest media moment of if not my life, then certainly of hers. We can only fantasize about what excitement we would have had in those compelling hours and the intoxication of living the multichannel moments while everyone else slumbered unawares. God knows, we could have even caught on videotape the precise moment her death was confirmed to the world. Not a replay, but the actual moment itself. We would have had the raw, unedited, untampered footage to pore over for evidence of conspiracy; the unsanitized, blood-spattered media chaos where information comes in spasms of truth and untruth, rumor and conjecture.

Tony didn't make the mistake I did. Flicking through the channels after we left, he saw the twisted wreckage inert in the sodium haze, the LIVE tag beneath the station ident, and the on-screen words that prefaced all the madness. He was closer to the moment than I was, closer to it than most Britons. In the days and months that followed, I lived it again and again, along with everyone else, but sleeping through the initial flurry of reports will always rankle.

We were woken around 9 A.M. by the phone ringing. Charlotte answered her mother cheerily. "I suppose you haven't heard, then," her mother said grimly. "The princess is dead."

"Turn on the TV!" Charlotte yelled. I was actually doing so as she shouted. There was the shot: the wreckage in the tunnel, the gendarmes staring at it in appalled fascination, and an eerie absence of commentary, which conveyed the gravity of what the picture represented. I was there instantly, involved and absorbed and so close it felt as if I could touch the bloodstained leather interior. I was at the crash scene now but had missed the actual moment of impact. I was just another rubbernecker gawking at the aftermath of something ghastly.

When terrible car crashes like this one happen to celebrity passengers, we often have a peculiar compulsion to discover the precise circumstances of the disaster—almost a need to place ourselves beside them in the passenger seat. Is this part of our pathological desire to merge with the celebrity, to the point where we vicariously experience even their deaths? Or could it be that in the car wreck, the truth is suddenly revealed, the veil torn aside, the magic dispelled? Perhaps it is only in the celebrity car wreck that the pampered limousine passenger is shown in their human form, powerless, pathetic, and exposed—in other words, one of us.

The case of Princess Diana is perhaps the most archetypal case of the celebrity passenger being "driven to their doom." In this case, the helplessness of the backseat passenger is considerably reinforced by the fact that this is a figure perhaps most readily identified in her role as defenseless victim, constantly exploited by the media, the public, the British government, and, most obviously, the House of Windsor. And while we can never know precisely what happened in the passenger compartment of Dodi's Mercedes on that fateful night, we do have the next best thing—the computer simulation.

The computer simulation is, we are told, as faithful a reconstruction of how it actually happened as can be achieved with current technology. Using eyewitness descriptions and the findings of accident investigators, the computer generated reenactment shows a Mercedes S280 as it crests the dip in the road ahead of the tunnel entrance at high speed and veers to the right, striking the underpass wall and ricocheting across the carriageway. It smashes into a support pillar, then spins through 360 degrees and comes to a halt near the right-hand wall, its crumpled front end facing the way it has just come. The crash is then shown again, this time from the opposite angle and in slow mo. Now it is shown again in "real time," so we can understand the tremendous energies unleashed in the primary impact with the tunnel support, an impact that killed three of the car's four occupants.

With computer generated imagery, we are able to watch the crash from any perspective we want. It is even possible to experience it from inside the car, to see what would have been seen by the driver, or by the person sitting next to him, or even, should we want to, by the passengers sitting in the backseat. And this is as close as we can get, for we have no way of knowing precisely how those seconds were experienced. In the sensual blitzkrieg of the high-speed crash, things often happen far too quickly for the eye and brain to register, decode, and analyze. By rewinding and replaying the computer-generated simulation, and by studying the images it presents, we can understand what the victims might have seen from their positions in the passenger seat of the car. We can imagine vistas of naked white concrete as the car sideswipes the wall near the tunnel mouth, then perhaps another blur of concrete, then asphalt, sodium lamps, steel guardrails, and the tiled surface of the opposite wall. Then everything would be compressed together into a brutal collage as the car hurtles toward the pillar.

We live in a visual culture, where seeing truly is believing, where vicarious experience is nothing out of the ordinary, and where virtually every one of us can participate in any number of events "as though we were there." Placing ourselves in the backseat of a Mercedes traveling at over 100 mph isn't a difficult task for anyone who's experienced the view from the cockpit of an F1 racer or an F1–11 jet fighter on television, at the cinema, or on the screen of a game console. The camera's eye is now an extension of the brainstem, its lens an optional retina through which events can be experienced and images interpreted. These days, the ability to live through other people's experiences is something even a child can enjoy.

We now need to add our own soundtrack to go with these first-person images we have summoned into being. Perhaps we hear the jarring cadence of metal on concrete as the first impact takes place, followed by the screech of tires as the brakes are applied. Then, perhaps, comes the sense-swamping explosion-implosion of the fatal impact with the tunnel support, when the world outside violently enters the car interior and the dimensions surrounding us are remodeled and redesigned hundreds of times a nanosecond. The metals and fabrics of the Mercedes, sculpted to the implacable diktat of physics, now lie crumpled. All the calculations, modifications, and evaluations of the car's manufacturer have proven useless against the immutable absolutes of mass, energy, and inertia brought to bear on the vehicle and its occupants as it crashes into the thirteenth pillar.

Extra sounds may be added according to taste and inclination. Can we hear shouts of warning? Astonished curses from our copassengers? Screams of fear? The hubbub of shocked panic? The sounds we choose to accompany the computer generated reenactment depend on our capacity for empathy, morbid speculation, and groundless conjecture.

Though our mental capacities are mutating along with technological advances, this camera's-eye visualization is only the most basic cerebral add-on so far. We are still many years away from being able to reproduce sensual and emotional reenactments of a particular event. The thoughts and feelings of those whose experience we choose to revisit remain, at present, way beyond our grasp. No theme-park thrill ride has yet been constructed that would submit its users to the catastrophic emotional trauma involved in a high-speed car smash; not even the most sophisticated aircraft flight simulator can tell us how it feels to crash into the ground after a vertical descent from thirty thousand feet.

If we want to extrapolate our personal reenactment of the crash any further, we can do so only with recourse to what we have learned from similar experiences of our own—real car crashes we have had or chanced to witness. The details to hand, including the minutiae of the accident investigation and the sworn statements of those at the scene, can all be brought together to form a personal reenactment. We know this account of the crash to be "true" in that it faithfully reproduces the sequence of events from the moment the driver loses control to the moment the car comes to a stop; the rest, however, is speculation.

In the days, months, and years following the passion that unfolded inside the Alma bridge underpass, there can be few who have not had an opportunity to take that ride, to be there in person as the S280 plows into the concrete. Not since Dealey Plaza in 1963 has society's attention been so intently directed at a particular sequence of events transpiring in such a brief space of time and in such a tightly defined space. In the immediate aftermath of the crash, our camera's-eye gaze was fixed unswervingly on that wrecked Mercedes, its grotesquely twisted condition requiring no expert diagnosis for us to imagine the violence its occupants had undergone. In the ensuing investigation we were taken closer, as the "true picture" was revealed in words and images that eventually became so detailed that the journey under the bridge is now an experience available to us all. We too can play the part of hapless passenger ferried to oblivion by our drunken chauffeur. Just as NASA scientists use thousands of individual images to create an "authentic" picture of a planet's topography, the media collated hour on hour of videotape, including reconstruction footage, camera drive-throughs of the crash site, closed-circuit TV film from the Ritz, and static overviews of the death scene. As a result, any one of us can take our assigned seat in the back of Dodi's Merc for those terrible few seconds in hell. Are your seat belts fastened?

Staring from the rear window of the Mercedes, we begin our midnight journey through the darkened streets of Paris. Moving off from the Ritz Hotel, we turn left along the Rue Cambon and into Place de la Concorde. Halted momentarily by a traffic signal, we pick up speed after jumping the red to escape a motorcycle-riding photographer, and continue to accelerate along the Cours Albert Premier dual carriageway alongside the Seine. At 110 mph we pass through one underpass and, maintaining speed, negotiate the sudden dip that takes us into another beneath Place d'Alma and . . .

This is the moment where *The People's Princess*[8]—the first film dramatization of Diana's life and death—freeze-frames and fades to black. In this depiction, the icon and her recently acquired lover are shown huddled, trapped in the rear seat of the Mercedes, the lover with a protective arm thrown around the princess. The actor's expression is intended to convey grim resentment of their predicament; the actress playing Diana wears a more fearful expression, as if her character always knew it would end this way. Freeze-frame and fade. We are spared the anguish and horror of those bloody, twisted seconds of motorized carnage when our heroes' expressions turn to sheer terror, when famous faces are battered hideously by the impact, when lives are snuffed out before our very eyes. The filmmaker spares us this nightmare, but what film recreation could ever match the emotions we have already experienced inside that underpass as we drove with the icon on her fatal journey the first time, or the second, or the third? Or the feelings we had when we read how callous paparazzi snapped images of the dying celebrity? Or when we read that these images showed her lying on the floor of the passenger compartment "with her legs crumpled beneath her and her back hard up against the rear of the passenger seat"?

Or maybe we just don't care. Many commentators have pontificated that this crash, the "tragedy," was a collective experience, one a whole nation—perhaps even a whole planet—suffered together. Of course, this is an oversimplistic, highly sentimental interpretation that disregards the fact that a sizable proportion of the population of

Britain—let alone the world—was indifferent to the "tragedy" and repulsed by the subsequent media-fomented hysteria. For the crash and its aftermath was, first and foremost, a media event. And since it involved the violent death of the supreme media icon of the time, contagious outbreaks of hysteria, genuine or not, were guaranteed, since those to whom our culture accords the ambiguous status of celebrity exist and have meaning for us almost exclusively through their image. Indeed, many were quick to point out the irony of the fact that the accident may have been caused in part by the icon's need to escape those seeking to reproduce her image. But her image became the crux of the crash and our experience of it, although there was no live footage. It was almost as if we had somehow been cheated because the crash wasn't caught on tape by some sleepless Gallic Zapruder.

And in the days following the crash, enormous speculation revolved around whether pictures of the victims lying dead or mortally wounded in the debris had been taken, and, if so, who'd be so vile as to publish them? And when? And how could we see them?

And why do we have this need to obsess perpetually about the details of certain car accidents when there are so many of them happening all the time? Somewhere, right now, a vehicle is being destroyed beyond recognition. Somewhere, a car's occupants are but seconds from death. In the relentless cacophony that soundtracks the nightmare of modern civilization, the scream of cars in collision is mixed high. And for the most part, unless we are directly involved, we ignore these thousands of crashes taking place all around us every day, simply accepting that road accidents happen all the time in a culture so heavily reliant on the automobile. But right now, somewhere on earth, a car is crashing.

NOTES

1. Adapted by the University of Carolina Highway Safety Research Center from the American Academy of Pediatrics' *Safe Ride News* insert, fall 1989.
2. See *Pammy & Tommy Lee: Hardcore & Uncensored,* I. E. G. Entertainment, 1998.
3. Linda Smart, twenty-seven, an accountant from Chippenham, Wiltshire, was fined twenty pounds by a police officer who saw her sipping from a bottle of mineral water while her car was stationary at traffic lights. She vowed

to go to court if necessary to challenge the citation. *Times* (London) February 6, 2000.

4. Kenneth Anger, *Hollywood Babylon* (New York: Dell, 1975), 172.

5. Interviewed on ITV's *Tonight with Trevor Macdonald,* February 9, 2000 (U.K.).

6. A tabloid pop quiz that invites the reader to guess the mortal status—dead or alive?—of various celebrities long-vanished from the limelight.

7. In the mythology surrounding Mansfield, much is made of her brief flirtation with Anton LaVey's Church of Satan. As especially persistent story has her fatal crash as a result of a curse relating specifically to automobiles and decapitation placed on her lover, Sam Brody, by Anton LaVey.

8. L!VE TV, 1998 (U.K.).

CAR CRASH CRIMES

SEVEN

DRAGGING DEATHS

A CASE IN POINT

JAY D. DIX AND
STEPHEN BOLESTA

THE ACCIDENT

AT APPROXIMATELY 12:45 A.M., A SIXTEEN-YEAR-OLD BOY was riding his bicycle home after working in a fast food restaurant. While crossing the road, his bicycle was struck in the rear by a three-quarter-ton truck. A witness to the accident saw and heard the truck hit the bicycle; however, he never saw or heard anything from the victim. After the witness saw the truck drive away, he saw the bicycle and then called the police. Fifteen minutes later the boy's body was found on the side of the road 2.6 miles (4.2 km) from the scene of the accident.

The boy was found on his back. His shirt was pulled up high around the chest and his jeans were down around his ankles. He was not wearing either an undershirt or underpants. It was evident to the medical examiner who went to the scene that there were significant dragging injuries to the right side of the body.

Approximately two hours after the accident, the truck was located in a nearby trailer park less than a mile from the body. The man driving the truck said that he remembered hitting the boy's bicycle but did not remember hitting the boy. It was obvious to the police that the driver was intoxicated. (A blood alcohol content measured eight hours later revealed a blood alcohol level of 0.09mg/dL.) There was also evidence that the driver had tried to wash out blood from some of the clothing he was wearing at the time of the accident.

There was a passenger in the truck at the time of the accident who later confessed that both he and the driver had seen the boy. They also realized, after driving at least a mile or more from the accident site, that the boy was being dragged. They pulled off the side of the road after exiting the highway, stopped the truck, and saw the body under the truck. The driver then backed up the truck and manually dislodged the boy's body.

The truck was found to have a dent in the middle of the hood. This dent was thought to be from the body impact because the bicycle was lower to the ground. Examination of the truck's underbody revealed no hair, blood, or tissue. The only significant finding was a worn shininess to the inside of the right front tire caused by a recent rubbing action. None of the other tires was similarly worn.

Examination of the scene during daylight hours revealed a 5-inch- (12.7 cm-) wide continuous streak of blood track on the road surface beginning approximately 250 yards (230 m) from the scene of initial impact to the body. The amount and distribution of the blood at the body location confirmed the passenger's statement that the truck stopped and then backed up to dislodge the body.

AUTOPSY

At autopsy, the body was found to be a normally developed white sixteen-year-old boy. He was 5 ft $8^1/_2$ in. (174 cm) in length and weighed approximately 120 lbs. (54 kg). There was a $24^1/_2$-by-6 inch- (62- by 15-cm-) deep abraded injury to the right lateral flank which extended from midchest to midthigh. The tenth and eleventh ribs were ground down and the liver was exposed and abraded. The skin and soft tissues of the thigh were worn away, exposing the femur. Over the upper back were multiple areas of confluent abrasions. One of these areas was stained black. There were multiple abrasions over the mid- and lateral aspects of the back, which extended to the buttocks. Over the remainder of the body trunk and extremities were superficial abrasions of the forehead and the face.

The internal examination revealed the extent of the liver abrasion and an $8^1/_2$ in. (21.5 cm) in diameter defect of the overlying diaphragm. There was hemorrhage in the right perinepheric fat. Significantly, there were no fractures, subluxations, or disarticulations of any of the bones and joints, and there were no internal injuries or natural diseases to the organs. There was focal edema of the brain and a solitary focus of subscalpular hemorrhage that corresponded to the described contusion on the forehead.

A sample of blood was submitted for a drug screen, and no alcohol or other drugs were detected.

DISCUSSION

The question of time of death became important when determining the degree of driver negligence. Other than the injuries as a result of dragging, there were no other signs of significant trauma. Difficult to dispute would be the possibility of a fatal concussion. The only support for this diagnosis were the statements made by the driver, passenger, and witness who all stated the victim made no sounds after the initial impact. At the very least, it is possible to state that the victim was probably rendered unconscious.

The probability that seems most likely is the boy died either while being dragged or after he was left on the side of the road. Although there is no good method to estimate or measure the quantity of blood on the $2^1/_2$-mile (4-km) trail on the pavement, there must have been a considerable amount. There was also a significant volume of blood at the end of the trail where he was found. Could this amount of blood be deposited in such quantities without the heart still pumping? Unlikely.

The medical literature is replete with descriptions of injuries and causes of death in traffic and pedestrian accidents; however, there are no separate discussions of dragging deaths. Questions focusing on time of death are commonly asked and answered with ease by most forensic pathologists. In this particular case, the answers could not be given with any degree of medical certainty. Maybe these types of deaths will be more clearly understood when more are reported.

EDITOR'S NOTE

This dragging death is unusual because of the long distance the body was dragged, but less protracted dragging deaths are actually fairly common (as in the case of Isadora Duncan, described in the introduction to this volume). Another interesting dragging death was reported by the Associated Press on June 8, 1991, when a trash hauler was dragged to death by his own truck in Allentown, Pennsylvania. The victim, a thirty-one-year-old male, was playing with some sixth-grade children as his partner was driving the truck slowly along their route. The victim, joking with the children, apparently failed to notice that the truck had approached him from behind. His foot got caught in the double rear set of wheels, and according to the coroner, he died of multiple injuries after being dragged along the ground behind the truck.

THE LOVE BUG

J. C. RUPP

A RECENTLY PUBLISHED BOOK ENTITLED *Is Your Volkswagen a Sex Symbol?* by Jean Rosenbaum recalled this case to mind and provided the impetus needed to sit down and write it up for publication.

In the majority of cases handled by the Medical Examiner's Office, the scene is the most important aspect of a death investigation. In this particular case, the scene is everything; and once again, we have graphically illustrated the fact that we know very little about some aspects of human behavior.

CASE REPORT

On his day off, this forty-year-old airline pilot left home about 6:00 A.M. and told his wife he was going pistol shooting in a rural area of the country.

The subject was an air force veteran who had been a pilot during the Korean War. He was married and the father of two small children. There was no known psychiatric history and no known deviate behavior.

At about 7:30 A.M., a fisherman happened upon the scene of death. (See figures 8.1 and 8.2.) The police were summoned to the scene, and they, in turn, called the medical examiner who arrived at approximately 9:00 A.M.

8.1   View of the scene with concentric tire tracks. Courtesy J. C. Rupp

The subject was found apparently crushed against the left rear fender of a 1968 Volkswagen sedan. The car was at the end of a secluded road where there was a large turnaround area. The left front door of the car was open, the ignition on and the motor running. The car had an automatic transmission, which was in low gear; however, the car was not moving. The steering wheel was securely lashed in the extreme counterclockwise direction and secured by the subject's belt, which was connected from the steering wheel to the passenger's handle on the right side of the dashboard. On the right front seat was the subject's watch and cigarettes. His .22 caliber pistol was found underneath the driver's seat. Tire tracks in the loose gravel indicated the car had been moving in concentric circles. (See figure 8.1.)

The trunk of the car contained the subject's clothing, as well as a plastic zipper pouch containing locks, bolts, a length of chain, and wrenches. A padlock and key were found on the ground beside the body, and another padlock was found on the ground 20 feet from the body.

The body was in full rigor when first examined and was securely held against the left rear fender of the car by heavy link chain. The body was

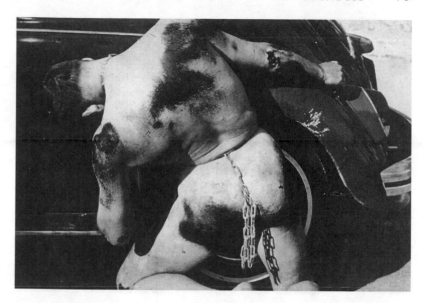

8.2   View of the body showing chain harness and chain attached to car bumper. Courtesy J. C. Rupp

completely nude except for a chain harness and was covered with large discrete and confluent skid-type abrasions.

The harness worn by the subject was constructed of link chain. There was a moderately tight loop around the neck bolted in front, the chain passed down across the sternum and abdomen, then passed around the waist to form a second loop. From the chain around the waist, strands of chain passed through each inguinal area, passed into the gluteal fold, and were secured to the chain around the waist in the midline of the back. (See figure 8.2.) The harness was very similar in construction to a parachute harness.

Anteriorly from the waist was attached a 10-foot length of chain, which was secured to the rear bumper of the Volkswagen. The chain attached to the car bumper was wound around the left rear axle of the car five times (see figure 8.3), and it was by this length of chain that the subject was held firmly against the left rear fender.

The autopsy revealed findings consistent with an asphyxial death, and there was a negative blood alcohol.

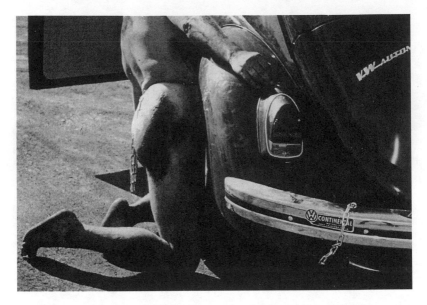

8.3   Figure 3: Chain attached to bumper and rear axle. Courtesy J. C. Rupp

Reconstruction of the events leading to the subject's death indicated that after removing his clothing and donning the chain harness, he attached himself to the back bumper of the Volkswagen by the 10-foot of chain. Then with the car in low gear and the steering wheel in a fixed counterclockwise position, the car ran slowly in concentric circles. It is not known whether the subject simply jogged after the moving automobile or allowed himself to be dragged. However, the tire tracks in the loose gravel were not significantly obliterated as one might expect if he had been dragged for a long distance by the moving car.

When the subject tired of this form of exercise, he apparently approached the car with the intent of taking it out of gear or turning off the ignition. At this point, there was a serious "pilot error," for he neglected to detach himself from the chain on the bumper of the Volkswagen before he approached the car. As he approached the car, the chain attaching him to the bumper became slack and the back wheel of the car rolled over the chain. The chain then began revolving onto the back axle. The subject must have realized his plight almost immediately and possibly sustained many of his abrasions fighting for his life against the ever-shortening chain. Ultimately, however, the chain wound completely around the axle and the subject was asphyxiated against the rear fender of the Volkswagen.

Background investigation revealed that the subject's wife knew about the chain harness, which had been custom made and recently acquired; however, she did not know for what use it was intended and had never inquired.

EDITOR'S NOTE

Two other cases of asphyxiation during unusual autoerotic activity with automobiles were reported by the Associated Press on June 19, 1999. Significantly, both these cases involved hydroelectric shovels on tractors.

In one case, a forty-two-year-old Asian man was found hanging by his neck, suspended by a rope attached to the raised shovel of his John Deere Model 410 diesel-powered backhoe tractor. The victim was last seen alive by his parents at 10:30 the previous night, when he left their shared rural home. Shortly thereafter, they heard the tractor engine start, as on prior occasions, but did not investigate further. The following morning the victim's father noticed that his son's bed had not been slept in and heard the tractor engine idling. Outside he found the body of his son, dead and cold. The victim was suspended in a semi-sitting position by a cloth safety-harness strap wrapped around his neck and clipped to a rope that was hooked on the raised shovel of the backhoe tractor. He had used a ligature to achieve partial autoerotic asphyxiation. Investigators hypothesized that he had lost consciousness and accidentally hanged himself.

Two years before his death, the victim had purchased his tractor as a Christmas gift to himself and named it "Stone." He used the tractor in occasional ditch-digging jobs and wrote about it in a Christmas newsletter to his friends, in which he enclosed Stone's picture. He also wrote about his tractor in a long poem alluding to "flying high in the sky" with his friend Stone.

The second case involved a sixty-two-year-old white man who was found dead in a barn pinned under the hydraulic scoop of his John Deere 1520 Model 145 tractor. A neighbor found the victim lying on the ground with the scoop of the tractor on his back. The engine was no longer running, but the ignition was in the "on" position. The victim was nude except for a pair of red women's shoes with 8-inch heels, a pair of knee-high nylon stockings, and duct tape around his ankles. The victim's ankles were taped to a 4-foot long segment of pipe, and his legs were spread. A yoke was attached to the center of this pipe. This yoke was attached to the front loader bucket by a chain. Two ropes led from the victim to the tractor's control lever for raising and tilting the bucket. Fully raising the bucket would have caused the complete suspension of the victim's inverted body by the ankles.

These unusual cases all emphasize how little we really know about people's relationships with their vehicles.

VEHICULAR SUICIDES

ELEVEN CASE STUDIES

COMPILED BY ALEX D. POKORNY, JAMES P. SMITH, JOHN R. FINCH, AND TAKESHI IMAJO

CASE 1

A THIRTY-SEVEN-YEAR-OLD MAN DIED ON EASTER SUNDAY of blunt trunk trauma following a single automobile crash in which he was the driver and sole occupant. Seven fresh superficial stab wounds on the lower chest and three incised wounds on the left palm were noted as well as several linear scars in the epigastrium, left antecubital fossa, and left wrist. Toxicological studies were negative for alcohol and psychotropic drugs. The above unusual injuries prompted a further investigation. The incident took place in the early evening with good driving conditions on a straight portion of an interstate throughway. The victim's vehicle left the roadway and traveled 480 ft (146.30 m) in a straight line before colliding into a concrete pillar of an overpass. The decedent had had a problem with alcohol, difficulty keeping a job, and disabling ankylosing spondylitis. Two weeks before the fatal crash he had been taken to a hospital by ambulance because of multiple self-inflicted superficial stab and incised wounds of the epigastrium and left arm. He admitted his suicidal intention at that time.

In this case, the stab and incised wounds and scars aroused the suspicion of suicide. Through enthusiastic police cooperation, information about the victim's sociopsychological history was obtained that helped to determine the manner of the death. Apparently the decedent failed in his attempt to stab himself to death and subsequently used his vehicle to destroy himself.

CASE 2

A thirty-two-year-old married woman drowned herself and her eleven-year-old son by driving her auto into Lake Erie. Before the fatal plunge she had been seen smoking a cigarette in her auto, which was parked near a pier directly across from a broken portion of a fence. She drove through the damaged fence and off the pier at a high rate of speed. When the vehicle was briefly afloat, she refused to be rescued by several men who jumped into the water, locking the rear door on the driver side. Her eight-year-old daughter who was also in the car was rescued after escaping through a window with the help of her brother inside. Toxicological analyses on the driver were negative for alcohol or psychotropic drugs. She had been under treatment for paranoid schizophrenia and had two past bizarre suicide attempts.

CASE 3

A thirty-three-year-old woman drowned herself and her three children (ages four, eight, and ten) in her two-door sedan submerged in Lake Erie. Their car had been standing with its lights on in a marina parking lot facing the lake. She was seen to drive to the edge of the water, back up, and finally proceed forward at a high rate of speed into the lake. The driver's blood ethanol concentration was 100mg/dL. The vehicle was in good operating condition. The ignition was in the "on" position and the other key was in the passenger side door, locking it from the outside. Her husband had lost his job two months previously because he had been charged with grand theft, thus depriving the family of financial resources. The decedent had been despondent over the financial situation and had left home in the car with the children after a debt collector's visit.

CASE 4

A twenty-five-year-old divorced man drowned in his own auto after it plunged into Lake Erie. He had been seen stopping his vehicle by the water and then driving into the lake at a high rate of speed. Despite the fact that the auto floated for a few minutes, the driver did not attempt to escape. Postmortem toxicological studies were negative for alcohol or common drugs. He was suspected of slaying his twenty-two-year-old girlfriend who had been found stabbed to death in their home just before his immersion in the lake. The man also had a police record of juvenile manslaughter, traffic violations, and aggravated robbery.

Cases 2, 3, and 4 were simpler for the investigators because each incident was witnessed throughout almost its entire course. All three drivers stopped near the water before the final plunge. Each of them showed sufficient acute psychosocial or psychiatric perturbation or both to account for at least some of their deliberate self-destruction. Cases 2 and 3 were noteworthy because of simultaneous homicides and homicidal attempts by mothers involving their own children.

CASE 5

A twenty-four-year-old man died in an auto crash. A few hours before the incident he had revealed in a conversation with a young woman at a bar that he was intoxicated and despondent. He recounted his recent loss of job, a pending marital separation, and ongoing doctor's care for a "serious illness." Before leaving the bar, he stated that he was going to "roll his car" and that she should come to "watch him die." She left the establishment in her auto shortly before he did, and then he passed her at a high rate of speed. Other witnesses saw him driving his car recklessly. He ran into an embankment and the auto rolled over several times, finally resting on the ejected victim. His fatal injuries were blunt impacts to head and trunk. The blood alcohol concentration was 230 mg/dL.

This case is unique because an account of the imminent suicidal intent and method had just been related to a female drinking companion by the suicide immediately before the fatal act. Without this woman's testimony, this case might have been called an accidental death, especially in view of his high blood alcohol level.

CASE 6

Mr. M was a middle-aged man who had a long history of antisocial acts. He had three divorces, each occasioned by his infidelity and physical brutality; he paid child support to none of his wives. He had numerous traffic offenses and two felonies on his record, and seemed to have no friendship or loyalty to anyone. During his fourth marriage he had become enraged because one of his ex-wives had related some of his previous acts of cruelty to one of his friends. He had always felt very insecure with women and seemed desperate to gain the approval of each one. On the night before his crash his brother informed him that he had seen this ex-wife talking to a boyfriend, making joking references about him. He discussed this angrily with some friends at his apartment and appeared to become increasingly enraged. He drank heavily throughout that night. At 6:30 the next morning he went to the apartment of his ex-wife. When she answered the door he began to abuse her verbally and physically, awaking several neighbors. When she refused to strike back, his rage increased and he walked away from her to his car saying "I have made a sorry mess out of everything and I wish I were dead." Approximately three minutes later he ran through an intersection at a speed of about 90 miles per hour and struck another vehicle. Both he and the driver of the other vehicle died in the crash.

CASE 7

This subject was a seaman who was considered by everyone as "the most easygoing man around." However, he was said by his wife to pace the floor endlessly after any disagreement with practically total inability to talk through any such discord. When walking did not seem to suffice, he would characteristically get into his car and "speed it off" until he had "gotten it out of his system." He had been raised by parents who discouraged any expression of negative or hostile feelings. During his depressed periods he would eat poorly. His wife typically would function as the peacemaker. His death occurred after he had asked his wife to buy him a book while she was downtown. She replied that she didn't have time, whereupon he promptly became mute and sullen. He then went to the kitchen and wrote a note stating "You'll be sorry when I'm dead!" He drove his wife downtown and left her at her destination, roared away, and was dead within two minutes, having struck a tree off the highway. "It looked like he pointed it into the tree," according to the police accident report.

CASE 8

This young, professional man had a hobby of dissecting rats in his own home, which had caused much discord between him and his wife. He had been treated intermittently for schizophrenia, paranoid type, for several years, receiving drugs and psychotherapy. He had on several occasions told his therapist of his fantasies of cutting up other people and himself as well as his rats. Legal separation from his wife was followed by improved functioning on his job, but the time spent on his dissections of rats increased. On the day of his death, he called his estranged wife and said to her, "It's up," and hung up the phone. In therapy, "It's up" had meant that the patient contemplated killing himself, blaming his chaotic life and his fantasies of killing others. Later that day he was found dead after his car had hit a bridge abutment at an estimated speed of 60 to 70 miles per hour. At autopsy it was found that he had also made a superficial knife cut on his chest over his heart before the crash.

CASE 9

This young, married female was the next to youngest of four siblings in a highly religious family. She was overindulged by her parents. In many situations there were no demands for performance, and she received almost instant gratification. She acted out sexually and married at age fifteen because of pregnancy. This marriage did not last, and her second marriage was "arranged by the family." This was equally unhappy for her, and she sought relief from her anxious and depressed periods through psychotherapy with her general physician, by use of lithium, and by occasional visits to a psychiatrist. She had told this psychiatrist several times that she frequently had suicidal ideas, especially when things did not go well with her husband. One of her customary methods of getting over depressed feelings was to drive, often for hours. After one fight with her second husband, she consulted a brother and talked about how useless and ineffective she felt. After this talk with her brother, she drove off the road into a concrete culvert in an area of clear visibility, without a seat belt on, and died in the crash.

CASE 10

This fifty-nine-year-old male was a supervisor with a construction company. He was illiterate, which led to problems in reading signs, especially on freeways. Nine months prior to his own death he had overturned his car in a one-car crash, killing his wife of thirty-six years. He blamed himself severely for this and developed early-morning awakening, loss of weight, and loss of interest in all activities around him. This so worried the son that he was moved into the son's house for the next several weeks. His moderate depression continued for nine months. He rarely drank alcohol, but on the infrequent occasions when he did drink, "it was to the bottom of the bottle." It appears that the combination of moderate depression, a 248mg/dL alcohol blood level, and his illiteracy and known difficulty in reading traffic signs all contributed to the fatal outcome. Early one morning he ran head-on into a car while entering an exit lane of a freeway.

CASE 11

This middle-age barber was having increased difficulty in operating his business because of chronic cystinuria, which caused chronic pyelonephritis, renal calculi, and left hydronephrosis. He had had several admissions to the local Veterans Administration Hospital for these problems. He had taken many medications but had also been told by one of his many physicians that alcohol could give him some relief from pain. He had subsequently used alcohol regularly; it is of interest that at autopsy, vacuolation of many liver cells was present. On many occasions he had told his wife and physicians how depressed he felt about his health and financial condition. He had consulted several physicians during the three months prior to his death, and none had given him encouragement about his physical condition, so that his depression appeared to deepen. Furthermore, his business was beginning to lose money during this same period of time, primarily due to his increased absences. He died when he struck a utility pole, driving with a blood level of 300 mg/dL of alcohol.

NOTES

An earlier version of the paper by Pokorny, Smith and Finch was read at the annual meeting of the American Psychiatric Association, San Francisco, California, May 1970. Their work was supported by contract with the United States Department of Transportation, National Highway Safety Bureau nos. FH-11–6603, FH-11–7254, and FH-11–7401.

SUICIDE AND HOMICIDE BY AUTOMOBILE

JOHN M. MACDONALD

DEATH BY AUTOMOBILE OFFERS SPECIAL OPPORTUNITY for concealment of suicide and homicide. The person who plans to take his own life may wish to prevent discovery of his suicide to protect his family from disgrace or to ensure payment of his life insurance. The person intent on homicide decreases the likelihood of detection and punishment by simulating the accidental death of his victim. Most crimes are reported to the police by the victims, but the victims of homicide seldom have the opportunity to exercise this privilege.

Official statistics may not reveal the extent of deliberate death on the highway. In a three-month period in Colorado, no suicides by motor vehicle were recorded, but sixty-two drivers were blamed for accidents causing either their own death or the death of others. Three of these drivers were former patients of the Colorado Psychiatric Hospital, and all three died under circumstances that suggested suicide:

- A middle-aged man was killed when his car was struck by a freight train at a railroad crossing. Despite excellent road conditions, flashing red light, warning bell, and repeated whistle blasts, he drove at 10 miles per hour into the path of the train. A postmortem blood alcohol test showed no evidence of alcoholic intoxication. One year earlier he had been admitted to hospital with a diagnosis of paranoid schizophrenia. He believed that planes flying overhead were searching for him, and he claimed that people were accusing him of being a sex offender and dope peddler.

- A young woman was killed when her car left the highway and overturned. There were no skid marks, and the circumstances of the accident raised the question of suicide. The police searched in vain for a suicide note. A few days before her death she applied for psychiatric treatment. As she was in a very distraught, discouraged state, every effort was made to persuade her to enter the hospital, but she kept postponing the day of admission. She had previously received psychiatric treatment following suicide attempts with drugs and with a knife. Her diagnosis was hysterical character disorder with passive aggressive features.

- A middle-aged woman while driving down a highway suddenly swerved her car into the path of a large semi-trailer truck and was killed. There were no skid marks, and she had made no effort to avoid collision. She had been treated four months earlier for psychotic depression with paranoid features. It is of interest that she had delusions that her husband intended to kill her by driving recklessly.

During this three-month period, one in every 17,765 drivers with a Colorado license was considered to be responsible for a fatal auto accident. The three former patients were among 1,725 patients admitted to Colorado Psychopathic Hospital in a nineteen-month period. The incidence of fatal accident drivers in this hospital population is over thirty times greater than expected. The probability of observing three such patients in the group of sixty-two drivers causing fatal accidents, strictly by chance, is less than one in a thousand.

The disproportionate representation of former psychiatric patients may be related to the greater risk of suicide in persons who have been in a psychiatric hospital. Temoche and others in a study of 1,457 suicides of Massachusetts's white residents found that the risk of suicide in former mental patients, in the first six months after leaving hospital, was thirty-four times greater than in the general population.[1]

Psychiatric examination of forty patients, of whom thirty attempted suicide, three homicide, and seven both suicide and homicide by automobile, may contribute to our knowledge of this problem. The majority were psychiatric patients who, either on initial interview or more often in psychotherapy, revealed information regarding such attempts. Three patients in surgical wards had been interviewed because police reports of their accidents aroused suspicion of deliberate intent, apart from a brain-injured patient with severe aphasia who had threatened suicide prior to his auto wreck, which was undoubtedly deliberate. Persons who ran in front of vehicles or inhaled exhaust fumes were not included.

All forty patients were driving at the time of the attempt with the exception of a passenger who seized the steering wheel and put his foot on the gas pedal. Three patients were killed and five were severely injured, including a man who suffered compound fractures in both legs, one thigh and one arm, as well as a serious head injury. Survival was sometimes remarkable even among those with trivial injuries. Thus a man who drove his car over a steep 90-foot hillside received only chest bruises and abrasions on his hands and feet. Twelve patients escaped with minor injuries despite major damage to their vehicles.

The sexes were equally represented. Their ages ranged from eighteen to fifty-five, and three or four patients were below thirty-six years of age. Significantly, a similar proportion had some form of character disorder. Hysterical, passive-aggressive, and sociopathic personality disorders each accounted for 25 percent of the cases. Depression, when also present in these patients, was often fleeting and seldom profound. Only six patients were psychotic. There were four schizophrenics, one patient with schizo-affective psychosis, and one with psychotic depression.

A striking feature was that half the patients made the attempt very impulsively following an argument with a lover, a marital partner, or less commonly with a neighbor or a superior at work. One young woman, when told by her boyfriend that he did not intend to marry her, drove off at high speed. She aimed her car at a brick wall but crashed into another car. Another woman, following an argument with her husband, jumped into her car and drove into a truck at the nearest intersection. "All of a sudden it came to me to ram into the truck and get it over with.

I didn't think about it 'till I saw the truck coming along the highway. I put on the gas and headed for the truck."

In three cases, argument or criticism occurred in the car and the attempt followed quickly. For example, a man who was driving his wife home reported, "I was just driving along. She said, "Now what have you started drinking for?" Right after that I did it. I felt no good, might as well end it all. I had the urge, I turned and ran right into a rock, a big rock cliff 75 feet high, all solid rock. I hadn't thought about it before. At the time it didn't enter my head I might have killed her."

In contrast, several patients gave considerable time and thought to se lection of a site for suicide. One man drove 160 miles to a location he had selected two years previously as particularly suitable for suicide. This was a section of mountain highway with no guardrail alongside a 75-foot drop. He drove past the spot twice and then spent several hours drinking in a nearby tavern before driving off the road at the location previously selected. Despite a punctured lung and ruptured kidney, he survived to face a summons for driving on the wrong side of the road. Twelve other patients had been drinking prior to their attempts.

Many patients, particularly those with hysterical character disorder, gave examples of previous suicide attempts in which drama was more evident than determination. Yet their subsequent attempts by automobile sometimes came close to success.

> A young girl with hysterical character disorder became depressed and for a week thought constantly of taking her life. She decided to poison herself but changed her mind. Instead she thought of asphyxiating herself by taping her mouth and nose, but dismissed this method as impractical. She resolved to cut her wrists but inflicted no more than a superficial laceration. She thought of driving off a cliff but could not find a place to drive off. One night her husband was awakened by the click of a rifle. He found his wife trying to shoot herself. Although he considered this a melodramatic gesture, the next morning he took all his guns to work. Two days later on returning home he found a note: "This is a suicide—don't blame anyone but me. I leave everything to my husband." That evening his wife drove her car at high speed into an approaching car. Although she sustained only minor injuries, the driver of the other car was seriously injured.

The suicidal driver is often a danger to other drivers; ten of these forty patients drove into other vehicles. For example, a young sociopath drove into the path of an oncoming car whose driver swerved into the wrong lane to avoid collision. This evasive action was not successful as the sociopath corrected his aim and both cars were badly damaged. The innocent driver had a smell of alcohol on his breath and the police disbelieved his account of the collision. He was charged with driving on the wrong side of the road and no action was taken against the sociopathic offender.

Passengers in the suicidal driver's car may also be injured. One passenger suffered a fractured thigh, and several passengers in other wrecks were less severely injured. Usually the driver denied any intent to harm his passengers, but two later threatened to kill passengers present at the suicide attempt. Eight of the forty patients had at some time made threats to kill others.

Twenty-five patients also attempted suicide by other means, and one later committed suicide with poison. The choice of an automobile rather than drugs, knife, or firearms as agent of death seemed frequently to be determined by the advantage of immediate availability. A majority of the nonpsychotic patients were unstable, immature persons who responded to rejection or other frustration by impulsive destructive behavior. Wrecking a car at high speed allows violent discharge of very great anger. The opportunity for concealment of suicide and homicide has been noted. Only one patient mentioned the attraction of double indemnity insurance payment for accidental death. The selection of a husband's prized, new, expensive sports car for suicidal purposes requires no comment.

Although these patients readily described their attempts, often there was little display of feeling and scant introspection. Intrapsychic conflicts found expression in action more readily than in fantasy. The symbolic significance of the automobile and its selection as an instrument of death device deserve further consideration than can be provided by this phenomenological study.

The role of homicidal impulses in the genesis of suicide was apparent in several cases.

One driver, whose attempt at suicide was frustrated by a guardrail on a mountain road, talked in group therapy about "putting away his mother" but showed little awareness of his murderous hostility toward her. Another patient wrecked his car and was critically injured shortly after learning that a friend, whom he had fought some days earlier, had lost an eye as a result of the fight. The role of guilt was apparent in a man who attempted suicide by automobile three times in ten years. He was preoccupied by the accidental death of his brother and visited his grave frequently. They had worked together on an oil rig and one day he suggested to his brother that they should exchange jobs on the rig. That day the rig collapsed and his brother was killed before his eyes.

In some suicide attempts an appeal for love and attention was evident:

- A young woman was informed by her city police officer boyfriend that he did not intend to see her again. She drove her car over an embankment at a location within his patrol assignment. After the suicide attempt he visited her daily.
- The influence of auditory hallucinations was seen in a thirty-two-year-old schizophrenic woman who, while driving with her husband and five children, deliberately crashed into the rear of another car at 80 miles an hour. She did this because voices told her to do so in order that the family could all be born again. Both cars overturned but fortunately no one was seriously injured and she was fined $10 for careless driving. Although her husband neglected to advise the police or court of her abnormal mental condition, he brought her to hospital for treatment three days later.

Psychiatric evaluation and treatment of persons who attempt to take life on the highway is desirable. However, these persons seldom seek help directly following such attempts. Early evaluation and treatment would be facilitated by recognition of deliberate intent in automobile wrecks. All police officers and hospital surgeons should be alert to this problem. Accidents should not be quickly dismissed as being due to alcohol, sleep, or loss of control at high speed.

Skid marks and the use of safety belts may mislead investigators. A young woman drove at a concrete overpass abutment at high speed. She was confident she would not survive despite use of her safety belt, which was worn to dispel any suspicion of suicide. Although her car flew through the air for 50 feet before striking the roadside again and was airborne for a further 25 feet before coming to rest, she survived serious bodily injury. In view of skid marks and use of safety belt, it is not surprising that the police officer did not consider the possibility of serious intent. A tire blowout may be the consequence rather than the cause of a car hitting a curb and crashing into a roadside tree.

Wheel marks at right angles to the direction of a mountain road should arouse question. In one such finding the suicidal driver survived because he drove directly down the mountain slope. Had he driven off the road at an oblique angle, his car would have overturned repeatedly with little prospect of survival. A driver found injured on a mountainside may report that his car skidded off the icy road. This explanation will not be questioned if snowfall has eliminated parallel straight wheel marks for some distance leading directly off the edge of the road at a curve without any evidence of breaking or skidding. Mechanical failure of the car may be falsely claimed or contrived to cause the wreck.

The progression of tire marks considered typical of a driver falling asleep at the wheel—marks on the gravel alongside the edge of the black-top followed by a sudden change of direction due to the driver awakening as his car runs on to the gravel and taking too sharp a compensatory turn of the steering wheel—may also be caused by the suicidal driver, who swerves the car slightly before overturning it with a sharp twist of the steering wheel. Such a sequence may be similar to the tentative superficial cuts found on the person who commits suicide by cutting his throat—preliminary efforts before the final plunge.

When police officers suspect deliberate suicidal intent, they are often handicapped in their investigation by their natural reluctance to press inquiries in the presence of serious injury and grieving relatives. The great emotional distress of the driver's wife at the scene of the wreck may not be due to a minor scalp wound but rather to awareness of her husband's homicidal and suicidal action. Such awareness may not be shared with solicitous police officers and hospital surgeons. Police officers are also handicapped by the natural reluctance of these drivers to reveal the true circumstances of the wreck.

Yet these drivers and their relatives will often freely reveal this information to physicians when encouraged to talk about the car wreck. Often indeed they are grateful for this opportunity, and sometimes there is considerable relief following recital of the true story and expression of long-suppressed emotion:

A thirty-six-year-old woman charged with reckless driving testified at her trial that because of a head injury she had sustained in the accident she could not recall what had happened. She was fined $100 for careless driving. Six months later following a suicide attempt, she freely volunteered full details of the "accident."

Her boyfriend had told her in a tavern that he was going with another girl. She became enraged, ran to the parking lot, and with her car she rammed the boyfriend's car three times. Then she caught sight of him on the sidewalk and tried to run him down. "I floorboarded the pedal and headed up the sidewalk after him. I hit a building and a tree. I fully intended to run him down." She had not revealed this to the police as she feared she would be charged with attempted murder. Her boyfriend, fearing publicity, was equally reticent.

COMMENT

Suicide and homicide by automobile are attempted more frequently than is generally recognized. Awareness of this problem on the part of police officers and hospital surgeons, who treat the victims of automobile wrecks, should aid in detection of such acts. This should facilitate early psychiatric evaluation and treatment of these persons who are a danger to themselves and often to other drivers on our highways.[2]

NOTES

1. A. Temoche et al., "Suicide Rates among Former and Current Mental Institution Patients," *Journal of Nervous and Mental Disorders*, 138 (2): 124–130, 1964.

2. Statistics and reports on suicides and accidents on the highways were made available through the courtesy of Colonel Gilbert R. Carrel, Chief of the Colorado State Patrol, and his officers. This paper was read at the 120th annual meeting of the American Psychiatric Association, Los Angeles, California, May 4–8, 1964.

A CASE WITH BEAR FACTS

TURHON A. MURAD
AND MARGIE H. BODDY

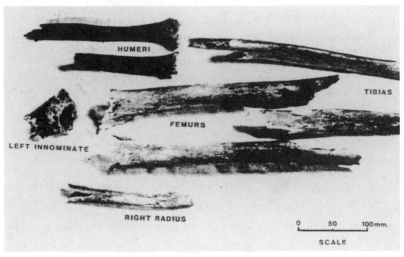

11.1   Bones left by the bear. © *Journal of Forensic Sciences*

ON JULY 9, 1985, A LAW ENFORCEMENT OFFICER was dispatched in Shasta County, California, to investigate the discovery of what was reported as human bones and a skull found along a logging road. There the deputy found a 1974 Oldsmobile with out-of-state plates. The automobile had been badly damaged by what the officer had determined to be a bear due to the dried muddy tracks on and around the vehicle. Furthermore, he reported extensive damage to the automobile's vinyl top and foam rubber from claw marks. Some windows were broken out, and the seats were described as having been badly torn by claws or teeth. The officer's report went on to state that clothing and various personal effects were recovered from within a radius of 70 yards (63 m) from the vehicle. Of particular interest to this report is the fact that animal feces were recovered from atop the hood and windshield of the automobile and in its vicinity. Within 65 yards (57 m) of the passenger side of the automobile and down an embankment, a major portion of a human calvarium and mandible as well as portions of the appendicular skeleton were discovered. Although numerous torn and tattered articles of clothing were found both inside and outside the vehicle, no human remains were recovered from within the auto.

While the authorities worked to identify the decedent from personal effects and to determine the circumstances of the death, the remains were brought to the Physical Anthropology Laboratory at California State University (CSU), Chico, to be examined. Beyond the usual forensic anthropological attempt to assist in identifying a decedent by suggesting his probable sex, age, race, stature, and any uniqueness, in this case the authorities were particularly interested in assistance in determining a possible time and cause of death.

BEARS

The last documented case of a grizzly bear in California was in 1922.[1] Today the only bears remaining in California are those commonly known as the black bear. The genus and species *Ursus americanus* is represented in California by two subspecies: *U. a. altifrontalis* and *U. a. californiensis*. The *altifrontalis* variety ranges from British Columbia in the north to the Coastal Range in the northwest portion of California in the south. The *californiensis* variety is found from south-central Oregon and the Cascade Mountains along the eastern side of California in the Sierra Mountains to as far south as the southern end of the San Joaquin Valley. Indeed, because either variety may be found in the area where this incident occurred, it would be difficult to determine which was responsible.

Both are omnivorous, feeding off vegetation, berries, insects, honey, carrion, fish, frogs, fruit, and nuts,[2] all of which are generally passed approximately one day after eating.[3] It is said that as carrion eaters, bears
aid in clearing their range of dead animals and that such activity is likely
to occur after a harsh winter.[4]

While bears are generally considered harmless, information provided
by the Big Game Division of the California Department of Fish and
Game suggests that black bears are notorious for scavenging trash cans,
Dumpsters, and campsites and occasionally break into cabins and mobile homes in their pursuit of a preferred food, such as bacon. Such incidents, if repeated, may require that rangers trap and relocate the
offending animals.[5] Although encounters that require relocation are seldom seen as threatening to human life, authorities suggest that the bears
will attack if provoked. A situation involving a female bear with cubs or
a human withholding food from a bear is considered particularly dangerous. According to Mr. D. Cook, the Department of Fish and Game's
district authority on bears, during the period from 1977 to 1986 there
has been only one potentially life-threatening incident, and it occurred
when a lone camper in Trinity County slept on top of his bacon in a
foolhardy attempt to protect it from animals. The camper survived a
mauling to his lower extremities by climbing a tree, and he was later capable of walking to safety.[6] It would appear that unless the bear or bears
had been provoked, the automobile in this case was approached and attacked as if it were a large Dumpster or small mobile home.

CIRCUMSTANCES OF DEATH

It is difficult to determine the time since death from skeletal remains
alone,[7] and an estimate is usually little more than an educated guess.[8] The
difficulties are in part due to the fact that those agents that affect skele-
tonization, such as temperature, humidity, and the presence or absence of
necrophagous insects and carnivores, are themselves quite variable.[9] However, a positive identification or unusual circumstances may assist in determining an exact time of death, as in a case discussed by Perzigian.[10]
Following the identification of the decedent in this case, it was determined
that he was last seen alive by a sheriff's deputy on November 19, 1984,

when he was discovered in a parking lot asleep in his automobile. When the authorities next discovered the vehicle it was at the evidence scene on July 9, 1985, although it apparently was seen from afar two months earlier by a passing motorcyclist who was riding a dirt bike through the area. The cyclist reports that he had approached the automobile close enough to notice it was badly damaged but did not investigate it further, nor did he detect any emanating odor. Thus the time of death can be narrowed to between November 19, 1984 and early May 1985.

Although a serious explanation for the cause of death cannot be offered, it should be pointed out that the decedent was medically diagnosed as being crippled and requiring a cane to walk. Under the circumstances it may be that the victim found himself in the position where he felt he could not trek out, and, rather, decided to spend the night in his automobile with hope that he would soon be discovered. Such a decision would doom an unprepared person to certain death from exposure, if not from bears, since at this time of the year the elevation of this location would have insured harsh winter storms and nighttime temperatures well below freezing.

Also, although it may be tempting to suggest that the victim provoked a bear attack, it is not likely since bears in this area of northern California hibernate through the winter months from approximately early to mid-October until early April.[11] Furthermore, the condition of the recovered feces and the dried muddy tracks at the scene suggests that the victim was eaten during the spring.

Therefore, based on our knowledge of personal encounters with the decedent, we can only narrow the time of death to between November 19, 1984 and mid-May 1985. Knowledge of the weather conditions for northern California during this period along with knowledge of bear behavior leads us to suggest that the victim probably died early during that period only to be frozen and discovered later during the spring thaw by carrion-seeking bears.

SUMMARY

By the use of various physical anthropological techniques developed both inside and outside forensic science circumstances, it was suggested that human skeletal remains recovered from northern California were those of a male Caucasoid who was approximately forty-five to fifty-five years of age at death. Moreover, the person, who had at one time undergone skull surgery, was believed to have stood between 5ft 8 in. and 6ft 2 in. (171 and 189 cm).

Upon identification of the individual by means of personal effects, dental records, and evidence of skull surgery, it was learned that he was indeed a male Caucasoid approximately forty-six years old at death and that he had undergone cranial surgery twenty years earlier for a hematoma produced by an automobile accident. Furthermore, it was determined that although the victim walked with a cane, he was actually 6 ft (183 cm) tall.

Although the circumstances of the death will never be made clear, we are certain that the individual was eaten by a large carnivore, probably a bear, and that the attack likely occurred during the spring following the victim's death.

<hr/>

NOTES

The authors wish to express their appreciation to those of the Shasta County Sheriff's Department, Redding, CA, and the California Department of Fish and Game, Sacramento, CA, who graciously provided the information used in preparing portions of this report.

1. See B. D. Haynes and E. Haynes, eds., *The Grizzly Bear: Portraits from Life* (Norman: University of Oklahoma Press, 1966).
2. W. P. Dasmann, *Big Game of California* (Sacramento: California Department of Fish and Game, 1975).
3. D. Cook, California Department of Fish and Game, Big Game Division, Sacramento, CA, personal communication, September 3, 1986.
4. See Dasmann; also see J. B. Schoen, S. D. Miller, and H. V. Reynolds III, "Last Stronghold of the Grizzly," *Natural History,* 96: January 1, 1987, 50–60.
5. J. Vencenti, California Department of Fish and Game, Sacramento, CA, personal communication, September 3, 1986.
6. Cook, personal communication.
7. W. M. Bass, "The Time Interval Since Death: A Difficult Decision," in T. A. Rathbun and J. E. Buikstra, eds., *Human Identification: Case Studies in Forensic Anthropology* (Springfield, IL: Charles C. Thomas, 1985).
8. T. D. Stewart, *Essentials of Forensic Anthropology: Especially as Developed in the United States* (Springfield, IL: Charles C. Thomas, 1985).

9. W. C. Rodriguez and W. M. Bass, "Insect Activity and Its Relationship to Decay Rates of Human Cadavers in East Tennessee," *Journal of Forensic Sciences* 28:2, April 1983, 423–432, and "Decomposition of Buried Bodies and Methods That May Aid in Their Location," *Journal of Forensic Sciences,* 30:3, July 1985, 836–852.

10. A. J. Perzigian, "A Dantean Death: Submergence in Molten Salt," paper presented at the thirty-seventh annual meeting of the American Academy of Forensic Sciences, Las Vegas, NV, February 1985.

11. Cook, personal communication.

TWELVE

HIGHWAY TO HELL

THE STORY OF CALIFORNIA'S FREEWAY KILLER

MICHAEL NEWTON

MAKE NO MISTAKE ABOUT IT: CALIFORNIANS LOVE THEIR CARS. They also love their freeways, and they are in love with speed. The Golden State is almost single-handedly responsible for giving us the modern blight or blessing that is drive-by, drive-through culture. It's no coincidence that in California, a driving license acts as the only form of identity document—in fact, nondrivers often find themselves obliged to acquire one simply to have proof of their identity. Nor is it any surprise that 10 percent of all the road rage deaths reported since 1990 happened in California, which has more vehicles on the road than any other state. In California, driving is an integral part of everyday life. And as California goes on wheels, so goes the nation—and it goes all out, ignoring the cautionary signposts along the way.

The southern Californian freeways that began this trend were built by a homicidal sadist named Mack Edwards. Mack drove bulldozers by day and murdered children for the fun of it at night, planting their corpses in the soft earth he would pave the next morning. Finally convicted for a string of homicides in 1970, he asked the jury for a death sentence and got his wish. Still, those appeals take time, and Mack was disinclined to wait. To hell with that, he thought, and hanged himself in jail.

Fair warning: Certain Californians harbor an impatient streak.

Old Mack was gone, but coming up behind him in the fast lane, pedal to the metal, was a convoy of enthusiastic imitators. Their ranks included Freeway Killers, Trashbag Killers, Night Stalkers, sundry Slashers and Slayers, Hillside Stranglers, a prolific Scorecard Killer, and at least two I-5 Killers, christened for their activities along the mother of all freeways, running north from San Diego through three states to a dead-end in Vancouver, B.C. Some of the latter-day practitioners have been more vicious than others; their body counts vary widely.

But none approached the killing game with the enthusiasm of a not-so-gentle giant named Edmund Emil Kemper III.

Big Ed was born in Burbank, at the very heart of freeway country, on December 18, 1948. He was the middle of three children and the only son of Edmund Kemper II and wife, Clarnell. His destiny was written in his genes, with both parents large and heavyset. Clarnell stood six feet tall, her husband six foot eight, and Edmund—known to relatives as Guy—would top his father by an inch when he was grown. The Kempers were loud too, in keeping with their size. Domestic quarrels were frequent, sometimes violent. By age four, Guy already wished his parents were "normal," more quiet and loving.

Strike one.

That same year, 1952, Guy's father shipped out to help the military with its A-bomb tests in the South Pacific. He was gone for two years and returned to a home front in turmoil. Clarnell was never satisfied, nagging incessantly about his "menial" electrician's trade. The aggression between the Kempers grew increasingly strident, often physical.

Growing up in that strife-torn household, Guy developed strange games to amuse himself. One of his favorites was "gas chamber." Kemper would sit poised on a chair, then writhe in mock death throes as sister Allyn "threw the switch." In other games, Guy was the executioner, severing the head and hands of Allyn's dolls. His first real victim was the family cat, buried alive, then exhumed and beheaded, Guy mounting the head on a spindle and praying to it for the death of everyone on earth except himself.

In Kemper's mind, the facts of life became entangled with the rituals of death. He was, in fact, a budding necrophile, though no one recognized the warning signs. At age eight, in second grade, he had a school-boy crush on his teacher, confiding to Allyn that he longed to kiss the older woman. "Why don't you do it?" she teased. Kemper replied, dead serious, "If I kiss her, I would have to kill her first."

The crush on teachers would become a passion, Kemper sometimes sneaking out at night to loiter near the home of his latest flame, hoping for a quick glimpse through a window. As he waited in the dark, his fantasies were more concerned with blood and death than any adolescent voyeurism. To achieve climax with any woman, Guy suspected, he would have to kill.

Guy's parents divorced in 1957, Clarnell moving the children to her native Montana, where she was employed as a bank teller. By then she had already branded her son "a real weirdo," worried about his aberrant behavior. On one hand, she feared that coddling Guy might "turn him gay"; conversely, she worked overtime to suppress his precocious sexuality by any means available. When he was ten, she started fretting over Guy's proximity to his sister Allyn, in adjoining bedrooms, so she moved his sleeping quarters to the basement. Better safe than sorry, thought Clarnell. The darkness and creeping spiders terrified young Guy, but his pleas for mercy fell on deaf ears. Clarnell cared nothing for his sudden rash of nightmares or his strange sleepwalking episodes. The move was final.

And Kemper got nothing but worse. By age thirteen he was dismembering neighborhood pets, stashing favorite bits in his closet. He had also started rough rehearsals for his mother's murder, entering her room at night to stand beside her bed, a knife or hammer in his hand. Once he designed a special "mother-killing weapon," consisting of a spike on a stick, and proudly showed it to Clarnell. "She gave me a very strange look," Guy recalled. In the family's backyard he dug multiple graves, intended for his mother's head, torso, and severed limbs.

From an early age, the automobile seemed to represent freedom to Kemper—freedom from the constraining restrictions of his mother, in particular. Clarnell remarried twice in Montana, and while neither marriage lasted long, one stepfather taught Guy the joys of hunting with guns. From the age of about twelve, he began to associate cars with murder. He fantasized about killing his maternal grandfather and stealing the old man's car, fleeing to find his father in Los Angeles. He did run away at thirteen and made it to L.A. without killing anyone, but Guy's father sent him straight back to Montana. A year later, at Thanksgiving 1963, he tried again. This time he was allowed to stay briefly, despite complaints from Kemper's new stepmother than the hulking youth gave her the creeps. At Christmas, Guy's new family went to visit his paternal grandparents on their farm near remote North Fork, California. Only on arrival did they drop the bomb: The farm would be Guy's new, permanent home.

Strike two.

Clarnell was skeptical about the move. "You're taking a chance, leaving him with your parents," she told her ex-husband. "You might be surprised to wake up some morning to learn they've been killed." Kemper hated the farm. His seventy-two-year-old grandfather was nice enough, but Guy's sixty-six-year-old grandmother ruled the roost, a strict disciplinarian who brooked no nonsense. Infuriated by her criticism and the endless chores she assigned, Kemper later told psychiatrists that the old woman believed herself superior to any man "and was constantly emasculating me and my grandfather to prove it." His only relief was the .22 caliber rifle his grandfather gave him, and he took special delight in shooting the songbirds his grandma adored. "My grandmother loved her feathered friends," he said. "You never saw so many birds disappear so fast."

Kemper was briefly reunited with his mother in June 1964, but she sent him back to the North Fork farm in August. After the short respite, Guy hated the place more than ever. "My grandmother was riding me," he later said. "She never rode me that bad before." Unable to please her, his efforts to become "the perfect boy" shriveled under constant carping. "One night she blew it, screamed at me, said I'd tried to scare her to get her to have a heart attack and kill her."

It sounded like a good idea to Kemper, but he wasn't the kind to rely on fear as a weapon.

On August 27, 1964, Kemper was sitting in the kitchen with his grandmother, watching her work, when she ordered him to stop staring at her. He rose, as if to leave the room, then grabbed his .22 and shot her three times. "There was blood from the right nostril like a faucet," he said. "One eye was open, one shut. I wrapped her head with a towel and put her down. I dragged her into the bedroom." Kemper thought of stripping her corpse but refrained. Instead, he fetched a kitchen knife and stabbed the body repeatedly with force enough to bend the blade.

Moments later his grandfather returned from grocery shopping in town. Kemper met him outside and shot him once in the back of the head. "I did it out of love," he said, to spare the man from seeing his wife's bloody corpse. At the same time, he recalled, "I was like a runaway plane, no control, such a rage."

Kemper telephoned his mother to report the shootings, calling them "accidents," but Clarnell didn't buy it. To the police, he said, "I just wondered how it would feel to shoot grandma." A psychiatrist examined Kemper, calling him "psychotic at this time, confused and unable to function. Has paranoid ideation, growing more and more bizarre. It is noteworthy that he is more paranoid towards women, all except his mother, who is the real culprit. He is a psychotic and a danger to himself and others. He may well be a long-term problem."

Amen.

Deemed insane, Kemper was sent to Atascadero State Hospital, the youngest of 1,500 inmates confined to California's treatment center for sex offenders and the criminally insane. The young giant pumped iron to beef up and worked in Atascadero's psychology lab, where he memorized answers to twenty-eight standardized diagnostic tests, a trick that helped him beat the system. Over time, he was seen by his keepers to "improve." As Kemper explained his situation in psych-speak, "I found out that I really killed my grandmother because I wanted to kill my mother. I had this love-hate complex with my mother that is very hard for me to handle, and I was very withdrawn from reality because of it. I couldn't handle the hate, and the love was actually forced upon me, you know. It was a very strong family-tie type of love."

It sounded like a sketch of Norman Bates from *Psycho,* but Kemper's great "insight" secured his release in November 1969. He would later say that he was "born" at Atascadero, learning details of sex crimes from veteran practitioners, refining and elaborating his own morbid fantasies. When Kemper hit the streets, he was anything but cured. He spent three months in a halfway house, before he was paroled to his mother's custody—in direct defiance of warnings from the Atascadero analysis.

Strike three.

12.1   Head severed in car crash. © Feral House

Lately divorced from her third husband, Clarnell now lived in Aptos, a suburb of picturesque Santa Cruz. On one side, the Pacific breaks against dramatic cliffs; on the other, Route 1 winds through massive redwood forests cloaking the Santa Cruz mountains. Both features beckoned tourists to the region, some of whom decided to put down roots.

There is another side to Santa Cruz, of course. It's a thriving college town, home to the University of California at Santa Cruz, which sprawls over 2,000 hilltop acres on an old ranch site. Students, many of them nubile coeds, are found on the streets at all hours. During the 1960s, they thought nothing of hitchhiking around the web of freeways linking Santa Cruz, San Jose, and San Francisco, avidly pursuing the bright promise of their lives.

They were entirely unprepared to meet big Ed.

Clarnell had found work at UCSC. Guy ogled the coeds hitchhiking up and down Route 1 and dreamed of joining the State Highway Patrol. Aside from the roadblock of his murder record, however, his six-foot-

12.2   Body decapitated in car crash. © Feral House

nine physique also exceeded height limits for the local police department as well as the California Highway Patrol. Frustrated, he hung out with off-duty policemen instead, at cop bars like the Jury Room. Kemper enjoyed shop talk, and picked up souvenirs—including handcuffs and trainee's badges—from the police academy.

Guy's first vehicle was not a car but a motorcycle. However, he couldn't seem to keep it on the road. His first major crash, in November 1970, knocked him cold and left him with a fractured face. He sued the driver of the vehicle that hit him and settled for $15,000. He used part of this payoff to buy his first car, a Ford Galaxie, with a two-way radio and whip antennae, resembling an unmarked police car.

Released from parole and into his mother's custody in July 1971, Kemper found himself an apartment in Alameda, near Oakland, and went to work for the California State Highway department—the same department that had once harbored child killer Mack Edwards. Still, he spent much of his time with Clarnell, who continued to nag him about his laziness and slovenly habits. It was Kemper's fault she had no social life, Clarnell declared, blaming "you, my murderous son" for five years without sex. She constantly regaled him with descriptions of the pretty coeds she met at work, tormenting him. "She's holding up these girls as too good for me even to get to know," Kemper said. "I'm saying, 'Well, why don't you introduce me to some of these girls and quit telling me about them?' She says, 'You don't deserve to know girls like that.' She's foisting me off on these ugly turkeys."

He *would* meet these pretty girls, however, and he would do it with help from Clarnell. Despite her apparent hatred of Guy, she helped him to obtain a UCSC parking sticker for the window of his Ford Galaxie, allowing him to visit her on campus. This same sticker would make hitchhiking coeds believe he was a fellow student, which made them feel perfectly comfortable about getting into his car.

In his spare time, Kemper started cruising around the network of freeways surrounding San Francisco—Route 880, Route 280, and Route 580. Whenever he could, he picked up female hitchhikers, rehearsing various kinds of conversational styles to discover the best ways to put them at ease. It was all practice for the main event. Guy also began stocking his car with knives, blankets, and plastic bags. And he also jammed the latch on the passenger door, so it couldn't be opened from the inside.

On May 7, 1972, while cruising up and down the Eastshore Freeway in the Berkeley area, Kemper picked up Fresno college roommates Anita Luchese and Mary Ann Pesce, both eighteen. The girls were hitchhiking along the freeway to Stanford University, but Guy had other plans. Driving down Route 580, winding through the hills near Livermore, he drew a pistol borrowed from his boss, and told the hitchhikers that he wanted sex.

Mary Pesce tried to talk him out of it. "I was really quite struck by her personality and good looks," Kemper later recalled. "There was almost a reverence there. I made it sound like I was gonna play a few games, and they knew what I meant by that. Pulling over, he handcuffed Pesce, then ordered Luchese to climb into the car's trunk. Returning to Pesce, he slipped a plastic bag over her head and tried to strangle her, then stabbed her repeatedly and cut her throat. Ironically, at one point during the assault Guy stopped and apologized for accidentally touching her breast. He would later tell the police that "There was absolutely no contact with improper areas."

Next, Kemper opened the trunk of his car and attacked Anita Luchese with a Bowie knife; the girl, struggling to defend herself, sustained gashes on her arms and hands. When she began to scream, Guy stabbed her in the face and shoved his fingers in her mouth, to silence her. "I think at that point," Kemper said, "She started dying. She went semiconscious or delirious, moaning and waving her arms around, fending off an imaginary assailant who wasn't there any more."

When Luchese lay still, he slammed the trunk shut and drove home, parking the car with its grisly load in the garage of his apartment house. After dark, he carried the bodies upstairs, placed them in his bathtub, and beheaded them. "There was almost a climax to it," he recalled. "It was kind of an exalted, triumphlike thing, like taking the head of a deer or elk or something else would be to a hunter." Kemper kept these and later heads until they decomposed and used them in sexual games that also included occasional cannibalism.

"I needed to have a particular experience with a person," Kemper said, "and to possess them in the way I wanted to, I had to evict them from their human bodies." He also observed, "If I killed them, they couldn't reject me as a man. It was more or less making a doll out of a human being, carrying out my fantasies with a doll, a living human doll. What I wanted to see was the death, and I wanted to see the triumph, the exultation over the death. It was like eating, or a narcotic, something that drove me more and more and more."

On the May 8, 1972, Kemper took a drive up Highway 1, turning off into the Santa Cruz Mountains, and found a remote site some distance from the highway, where he buried his mutilated victims. Mary Pesce's head was found by mountain hikers three months later, and identified from dental records. When her parents were named in newspaper reports, Guy headed down I-5 in his Ford Galaxie and drove into Los Angeles to skulk around their affluent neighborhood, thrilled anew by confirmation that he had claimed one of the untouchable "rich girls."

In June Kemper met a teenage girl from Turlock, visiting relatives in Santa Cruz. They began to date on weekends, and he often visited her home, staying overnight in the guest room. Guy would describe her as his fiancée; the girl called him a "perfect gentleman," unaware that he was incapable of having sex with living women. June also witnessed Kemper's second road accident, another motorcycle crash, one that caused him to wear a cast on his left arm for nine months. It was an inconvenience, but it would not stop the hulking necrophile from stalking his human prey.

Fifteen-year-old Aiko Koo was hitchhiking down Highway I-80 from her mother's home in Berkeley to a dance class in San Francisco when Kemper picked her up on September 14, 1972. She had money for the bus but preferred to save it and regularly hitchhiked down the highway. As Kemper headed beyond San Francisco and down toward Santa Cruz, he pulled out a borrowed .357 Magnum and told Koo, "I'm afraid you're not going to make your class tonight." Winding up Highway 1 into the Santa Cruz Mountains where he had buried the bodies of his first two victims, he found a remote place to park and ordered Koo to climb into the backseat. As he stepped out of the car to get in the back and join her, however, Kemper accidentally locked both his gun and his keys inside. Embarrassed, he knocked on the car windows and motioned for Koo to let him in; her instant obedience sealed her fate.

In the backseat, Kemper tried a new method of murder with Koo, taping her mouth, then pinching her nostrils shut, finally strangling her with a scarf when suffocation failed to do the job. He lifted her body out of the car and put it in the trunk, then drove back down Highway 1 to his mother's apartment in Aptos, "just passing the time" with Clarnell for a while before he went home to Alameda. That night Koo's corpse shared his bed, beheaded and dismembered after sex. Next morning, Kemper retraced his route down the freeway toward Santa Cruz and buried Aiko Koo's remains in the forest, once again keeping the head as a souvenir.

While out hunting humans on the highways, Kemper for some reason decided that he ought to join the military. Toward that end, he hired a lawyer to have his juvenile record expunged. The procedure required cer-

tification of Kemper's improved mental health, and he met with two psychiatrists in Fresno on September 16, 1972. The doctors were impressed,
one reporting that Kemper "showed no evidence of any tendency toward
antisocial behavior, and there is a total absence of any stored-up anger,
bitterness or resentment that one would expect if some antisocial behavior pattern was manifest. In effect, we are dealing with two different people when we talk about the 15-year-old boy and the 23-year-old man
before us now." The other analyst blamed Kemper's teenage crimes on a
"split" between his emotional and rational mind. "He appears to be functioning in one piece now, directing his feelings toward verbalization,
work, sports, and not neurotic buildup within himself."

Of course, the doctors didn't know their "healthy" visitor was laughing at them, thinking of the severed head concealed behind his sofa in a
paper bag. Psychiatrists are only human, after all.

Guy's petition was granted, his juvenile record sealed by court order,
but he never followed through on his impulse to join the army. Instead,
in January 1973 he left his apartment and went home to mother, moving in with Clarnell in Aptos. Around the same time he bought a .22 caliber pistol and continued scouring the network of quiet interstate
highways in the mountains around Santa Cruz for pretty hitchhikers.
However, the freeways were perhaps not as quiet as Kemper would have
liked them to be—he spared his next three potential victims because he
feared too many people had seen them get into his car.

On January 8, 1972, he picked up a young hitchhiker named Cynthia Schall, a coed at nearby Cabrillo College. Kemper came off the
highway and parked in a secluded place just on the outskirts of Santa
Cruz, drew his gun, and ordered her to climb into the trunk of his car.
Schall was shifting his stuff around in order to make room for herself
when he shot her in the head. "Her eyes didn't even shut," Kemper recalled. "Nothing flexed or moved. It amazed me so much, because one
second she's animated and the next she's not, and there was absolutely
nothing in between, just a noise and absolute, absolute stillness."

With Schall's body in the trunk of his car, Kemper drove back down
Route 1 to Aptos. His mother was out when he got home, so he carried
the corpse upstairs and hid it in a closet. The next day, when his mother
was at work, Guy spent the day raping Schall's body, then dismembered

it with a knife and an ax and bagged up the remains. He then got back into his car and followed Route 1 all the way down the coast, finally coming off the freeway just south of Monterey, where he tossed Schall's remains over a 400-foot cliff into the sea. The severed legs fell short and were found on January 10; other parts washed up along the coast after several weeks. After a surfer came across a severed hand, Kemper said to his fiancée, "Wouldn't it be weird to be swimming along and have it touch you?"

The girl's head, however, remained in a box in Kemper's room. "I talked to it," he admitted. "I said affectionate things, like you would to a girlfriend or wife." Finally he buried it outside facing toward his bedroom window, occasionally offering cryptic remarks to his mother, such as "People really look up to you around here."

On February 5, Kemper hit the freeways again after a fierce argument with Clarnell. His plan: "The first girl that's halfway decent that I pick up, I'm gonna blow her brains out." Prowling around the UCSC campus on the edges of Route 1, he found two victims, twenty-three-year-old Rosalind Thorpe and twenty-year-old Alice Liu, who were hitchhiking separately down the highway. They were barely settled in the car when Kemper drew his gun and shot Thorpe in the face. "She had rather a large forehead," he said, "and I was imagining what her brain looked like inside, and I just wanted to put it right in the middle of that." Turning to Liu in the back, he fired three shots, the first two missing before a bullet drilled into her head.

Driving past a campus police checkpoint, Kemper heard Liu moaning in the backseat. It was "very disconcerting," he said, but he took no further action until he could get off Route 1 to find a secluded spot near the beach, where he shot her again and lifted both bodies into the trunk of his car. At home, he talked briefly to his mother, then went back to the car with a butcher knife and beheaded both corpses in the garage, while they still lay in the car's trunk. The next day, alone with his "dolls," Guy used them for sex, severed their hands, and dug the mutilated bullet out of Thorpe's brain. Late that night he scattered the limbs and torsos along a small road off Route 101 in Alameda County, driving on as far as Devil's Slide before he ditched the heads and hands. Kemper had to use bleach to clean the bloodstains from the cast on his arm.

Meanwhile, the grisly murders were inciting local panic. Cindy Schall had been identified in January, and Thorpe and Liu were discovered on February 15. The press speculated on cults and killers driven by the phases of the moon, but coeds continued to hitchhike around the inter-linked web of freeways connecting the cities of northern California. Kemper sometimes discussed the murders with those he picked up. "They'd be telling me about this guy, comparing notes, speculating on what he looks like, how he carries himself, why he's doing this stuff. Telling me about it." Strangely, he was unable to kill those who spoke of his crimes. "The second they started talking about that," he said, "they didn't realize it, but they were getting a free ride."

Kemper's fantasies grew increasingly morbid and melodramatic. He imagined dropping heads outside the Santa Cruz police station or killing every person on his mother's street as "a demonstration to the authori-ties." He also planned to take his freeway killing act "on the road," to a different set of highways, "as soon as this area dried up." Clarnell and sis-ter Allyn both asked him point-blank if he was the "Coed Killer," but each time Guy laughed and denied it.

In April 1973 Kemper had a near miss with the law. He had pur-chased a .44 revolver, neglecting to mention his murder convictions, and, while the records were sealed, the Santa Cruz sheriff still found a brief computerized reference to the double slaying. Possession of a hand-gun by convicted felons is illegal, and deputies were sent to confiscate the .44. They searched Kemper's Ford Galaxie in the process, and while they found nothing unusual, the experience spooked him.

"I felt that I was going to be caught pretty soon for the killing of these girls," he said, "or I was going to blow up and do something very open and get myself caught. A long time ago I had thought about what I was going to do in the event of being caught for other crimes, and the only choices I had were just to accept it and go to jail, and let my mother carry the load and let the whole thing fall into her hands, like what happened the last time with my grandparents, or I could take her life." Driving two more coeds past the point on the highway where he had killed Pesce and Luchese, Kemper felt the urge again but managed to control himself. "I said she's gotta die and I've gotta die, or girls like this are gonna die. And that's when I decided to murder my mother."

Despite years of bitter hatred, Kemper said, "I certainly wanted for my mother a nice, quiet, easy death, like I guess everyone wants." At 5:15 A.M. on Saturday, April 21, he entered Clarnell's bedroom, slugged her with a hammer, then severed her head. Apparently giving up on the "nice, quiet" death, Kemper jammed her larynx down the garbage disposal, later telling police it "seemed appropriate" after years of nagging. He handcuffed her corpse and raped it. "I came out of her vagina, you see. I came out of my mother, and in a rage, I went back in." Then, after smashing her nose with his fist, Guy propped Clarnell's head on the mantel and used it as a dartboard. Finally, he stated, he put Clarnell in a closet and cleaned up the mess.

That afternoon, in order to buy some time, Kemper hatched a plot to make it seem as if his mother had embarked on a weekend trip. To that end, he called Clarnell's friend and coworker, Sally Hallet, inviting her over for dinner that night. When she arrived at 8:00 P.M., her first remark was "Let's sit down. I'm dead."

"I kind of took her at her word there," Kemper recalled. After punching and strangling the woman, he stripped and raped her corpse before he went out for beers at the local bar, the Jury Room. At 10:15 on Easter morning he loaded a small arsenal of guns into Hallet's car and drove eastward, leaving behind a note that read:

> Approx. 5:15 A.M. Saturday. No need for her to suffer any more at the hands of this horrible "murderous butcher." It was quick—asleep—the way I wanted it.

Kemper headed away from California on I-80, following the highway through California and Nevada into Colorado. Stopped for speeding near Cimarron, Colorado, Kemper fully expected to be jailed, but the state trooper released him after he paid a $25 on-the-spot fine. Surprised and rather disappointed that there was no sweeping manhunt under way, he found a pay phone and called one of his friends in the Santa Cruz Police Department. "I just wanted to stay where I was and see what I could arrange as far as surrender," Guy said, "and if it wasn't satisfactory, then I would continue on."

It took several attempts to persuade authorities that his confession was serious, but a visit to Clarnell's home removed all doubt, and Colorado officers were dispatched to arrest Kemper while he waited passively. Detectives flew east to Colorado to record his statement; Kemper waived extradition, and was arraigned in Santa Cruz on April 30, 1973. His public defender harked back to psychiatric tests from 1964, pleading that Kemper was not guilty by reason of insanity.

At the trial, the Freeway Killer wept openly on the witness stand, describing his bitter childhood. A series of doctors pronounced him legally sane and the jury agreed, convicting him of eight counts of first-degree murder. The next day Judge Harry Brauer asked Kemper's opinion of an appropriate sentence, and while Kemper suggested "death by torture," he received a sentence of life imprisonment. Brauer voiced his intent to warn authorities "in the most persuasive language that I know that you must never be released at any time in your natural life. May God have mercy on your soul, but I must protect the rest of the people from people like you."

Nodding, Kemper told the judge, "Yes, sir. I understand."

Dispatched to the California Medical Facility at Vacaville, the soft-spoken serial killer found a new pastime, recording books on audiotape for the blind. By January 1987 he had spent more than five thousand hours in the recording booth, producing more audio books than any other inmate in history. For his efforts, Kemper is paid $36 per month. Parole has been denied repeatedly, though theoretically he remains eligible for release at any time.

CAR CRASH CONSPIRACIES

CAR CRASH COVER-UPS

THE DEATHS OF PRINCESS DIANA
AND MARY JO KOPECHNE

PHILIP L. SIMPSON

ONCE UPON A TIME, THIS TRAGIC FAIRY TALE BEGINS, there were two fatal car crashes on two separate summer nights. The first took place on a dark road on Chappaquidick Island in Massachusetts on July 18, 1969, and involved a powerful United States senator from a legendary political family and a younger female veteran of his brother's 1968 presidential campaign. The crash happened after the two left a small party where alcohol was allegedly present and then, somehow, drove off a bridge into Poucha Pond. Only the senator and driver, Edward Kennedy, escaped the car and survived the crash. The second of these two crashes, on August 31, 1997, fatally struck down the playboy son of an Egyptian millionaire and the divorced Princess of Wales in a dark Parisian tunnel. Their death car, a high-powered Mercedes, was driven by a man apparently under the influence of alcohol and drugs, their deaths attended by a train of the infamously zealous photographers known as paparazzi. So how can these two separate car crashes be part of the same bleak fairy tale, chronicled repeatedly by widely different media sources both contemporaneously and in the years to follow? The deaths of Diana Windsor, the princess, and Mary Jo Kopechne, the political functionary, are separated by nearly thirty years and two continents. There is no literal connection between the principal characters of each tragedy. Nevertheless, the similarities between these two high-profile automobile accidents and their subsequent cultural repercussions are striking.

Both crashes forever altered the destinies of famous members of two privileged classes—the British royalty and its American equivalent, the Kennedy dynasty. Both crashes drew an enormous amount of media attention and public interest because of the social status of those involved. Both brought allegations of irresponsible and drunken behavior on the part of the drivers. Both initiated official investigations to uncover any possible wrongdoing—and, despite the formal conclusions of these investigations, both generated endless speculation as to what "really happened that night." Both quickly became surrounded in mystery and an obfuscating haze of proliferating conspiracy theories, all of which foregrounded the cultural anxieties and tensions peculiar to the time and place in which both crashes occurred. And with the recent death of John F. Kennedy Jr. in a private airplane crash near the Chappaquidick accident site and the subsequent worldwide outpouring of media-sanctioned grief so reminiscent of Princess Diana's death, the circle connecting the two seemingly disparate events has finally closed.

Automobile crashes involving "royal" or celebrity classes always attract an enormous amount of attention because they allow a voyeuristic public to indulge two different but parallel impulses. The first of these is the sentimental need for communal grief over the loss of a culture's "best and brightest"; the second is an equally compelling desire to see the powerful and privileged karmically brought down by their own incestuous foibles in a cleansing and apocalyptic comeuppance. This second impulse feeds on the natural confusion and unresolved questions surrounding any tragic event, and invariably cooks up a heady broth of folklore, paranoid innuendo, unsubstantiated rumor, sexual fetishism, political intrigue, official malfeasance, xenophobia, and class prejudice.

From this perspective, even the most apparently unconnected events suddenly suggest a sinister design at work, allegedly patterned by a "shadow" government or "rogue" cabal that ruthlessly slaughters threats to its power structure in what appear to be random accidents. The heroic

martyrs and triumphant villains differ from case to case, but a commonly
accepted narrative governing each event is quickly scripted and dissemi
nated by the instruments of the mass media as well as by tabloid newspapers and the alternative outlets of subculture, such as Internet user
groups. When Princess Diana is not lamented as the victim of relentless
paparazzi or a drunken driver, for example, she is seen as the flawed but
relatively innocent victim of a conspiracy involving British intelligence,
supposedly targeted for death mainly because of her growing romantic
relationship with an Islamic man. In the same way, Mary Jo Kopechne is
generally viewed as the hapless proletarian victim of bourgeois Senator
Ted Kennedy's supposed drunken and adulterous appetites, her lonely
death compelling the powerful Kennedy clan and its governmental syco-
phants to close rank against those who would bring her posthumous justice. In relation to the Kopechne crash, moreover, a second scenario has
been advanced by those who either support Senator Kennedy or hold a
more generalized belief in personal redemption. According to this scenario, Kennedy's individual tragedy has compelled him—at least in part
out of guilt—to become in his official life a tireless champion of the
downtrodden and disenfranchised. Any one of these narratives constructs a larger meaning out of a pair of otherwise banal and all-too-
ordinary deaths by automobile.

In the case of Mary Jo Kopechne, initial uncertainty about the circumstances of the midnight crash was exaggerated by Kennedy's failure
to report to the authorities until well into the following morning. Although rumors of a body having been found in Senator Kennedy's submerged car were spreading quickly through Martha's Vineyard that
morning, it was not until Kennedy confessed to driving the car that the
full implications of the crash became known. Kennedy himself claimed
he had been giving Kopechne a ride to the Edgartown ferry, took a
wrong turn, and drove off the bridge. He said he was not drunk at the
time of the accident. He said he had tried to rescue Kopechne but injury
and shock disoriented him, and it was not until the following morning
that he came to his senses and realized he had to report the accident.

Later that afternoon Edgartown police chief Dominick Arena held a
press conference and read out Kennedy's vague statement about the crash.
This meeting provoked a media furor that was only slightly overshadowed

by the first manned moon landing, which happened to be taking place at the same time. By the Tuesday after the accident, many media voices, led by *Newsweek,* began an overtly hostile campaign against the still-silent Kennedy. Over the decades the intensity of media skepticism regarding Kennedy's account of the accident has lessened, but he still remains mute on the subject, and certain persistent doubts about his story remain to this day, any one of which provides fertile ground for conspiracy theorists to work their dark magic.

A by-no-means-exhaustive rundown of questions surrounding the incidents of that night would result in the following, rather lengthy list. What was the nature of the party that Kennedy and Mary Jo Kopechne attended earlier that evening at the Lawrence cottage on Chappaquidick? How much alcohol was consumed? Was Kennedy drunk when he drove away from the party with Kopechne? Can Kennedy's description of taking a wrong turn at the intersection be believed, since he had been to the very small island a number of times before? After his alleged rescue attempt, did Kennedy really swim back across the channel between Chappaquidick and Edgartown and return to his hotel room?

Why was Kennedy's demeanor the next morning so calm, according to witnesses? Was he even driving the car? If not, why in the world would he falsely confess to it? Why was no autopsy performed on Kopechne? Why was Chief Arena so solicitous and polite toward Kennedy, a suspect in a criminal case? Why was Kennedy allowed to leave the island that same day even as an investigation that could have resulted in criminal charges was under way? Why was Kennedy quickly allowed to plead to a traffic misdemeanor—"leaving the scene of an accident"—rather than face manslaughter charges?

Why have the other attendees at the party had so little to say, other than at the official inquest? Why was the inquest closed to the public, and why was it so perfunctory? Why did the presiding judge retire immediately afterward, and why, in spite of his own beliefs, did he not recommend to the investigating grand jury that a criminal indictment be returned against Kennedy? And perhaps the supreme question out of which all the others rise: Was Kennedy, because of his wealth and name, afforded special privileges that the average citizen, faced with such evidence of wrongdoing, would certainly not have enjoyed?

Columnist Jack Anderson was one of the first to propose a scenario at odds with Kennedy's. In Anderson's version of events, a panicked Kennedy came to Joe Gargan and Paul Markham for the express purpose of convincing his cousin Gargan to take the blame for the accident, but changed his mind in the light of day. Another writer, Jack Olsen, proposed a scenario in which Kennedy and Kopechne were spooked by an off-duty police officer who approached their parked car by the side of the road. Kennedy hopped out of the car, intending to meet up with Mary Jo later on the beach, while Kopechne drove Kennedy's car down a road unfamiliar to her and ended up driving off the bridge.

Robert Sherrill outlines some of the most popular alternate theories. In one story, Kennedy knew his car and Kopechne were missing, but was as surprised as anyone to learn that his car was wrecked and Kopechne dead.[1] Of course, many believe that a drunken Kennedy, driving Kopechne (who herself had a blood alcohol level of .09) away from the party to the secluded beach for a sexual liaison, recklessly drove off the bridge and escaped from the car, leaving Kopechne to drown. According to this popular belief, the senator then simply hid for several hours until his blood alcohol level diminished enough for him to report the accident without facing criminal charges for negligence or drunken driving.

Other scenarios crop up periodically, as new writers examine old evidence. Kenneth Kappel, for one, hypothesizes that Kennedy and some of his fellow partygoers *pushed* the car, with an apparently dead Kopechne inside, off the bridge in an attempt to disguise an accident earlier that night in which Kennedy had lost control of the car and careened into a ditch.[2] Kappel further argues that Kopechne did not actually die until the senator pushed the car into the water. Kappel's hypothesis is one of the darkest and most damning ones yet proposed, and has been vehemently denied by a spokesperson for the Kennedy family. It parallels Leo Damore's charge that the "Kennedy compound at Hyannis Port was mobilizing for action" the morning of the accident and has been protecting Kennedy ever since, through political power and financial influence.[3]

This mysterious car crash, which claimed one person's life and severely damaged—if not destroyed—another's presidential aspirations, was the latest tragic development in the public myth surrounding the Kennedys. Yet even at the time of the accident, as suspicions about

Kennedy's behavior mounted, there was hope that the strength of the myth, which had turned so horribly dark since 1963, could preserve this last brother. "Played properly, the tragic drowning of a Kennedy loyalist . . . might even be woven into the fabric of the legend," argued Joe McGinniss. "No one was quite sure how, but with proper handling by the press Teddy might yet be made to seem a victim of the same deadly fates that had haunted his family for twenty-five years."[4]

Interestingly, this is a theme that Kennedy himself touched on in his televised mea culpa a week after the crash. Did an awful curse hang over the heads of the Kennedys? Essentially, this argument was special pleading on behalf of Senator Kennedy. He should be spared further punishment for the death of Mary Jo Kopechne, went the argument, not only because this most public of all American families had suffered enough, but because the senator himself had somehow been destined to drive his car off that dark bridge into that cold water. Another type of special pleading came from those who saw Kopechne and Kennedy not as human beings but as symbolic functionaries in a larger metaphysical scheme that obviously trumped the death of a young woman and any possible blame for that death. "The girl was dead, which was sad," writes Joe McGinniss. "But there were many other girls. And only one Teddy, only one last male Kennedy of the glory generation. It was his reputation, however hollow and even rotten the man himself might be, that would have to be salvaged if the legend was to be preserved at all, if the myth was to retain even a fraction of its power."[5] From this point of view, the Kennedy legend had to be preserved at all costs, and this meant downplaying (or covering up, depending on one's perspective) what had "really happened" on the bridge that night.

Yet there were those who fought just as hard to destroy the myth surrounding the Kennedys, and the Chappaquidick crash and resulting "cover-up" gave them the perfect excuse to do so. Innuendo and half accusations proliferated. Just what was Kennedy doing on that road in the middle of the night with an attractive young woman who was not his wife? Just how much did Kennedy have to drink at that party? Just why did he so fiercely resist an autopsy for Kopechne? The Kennedy myth-destroyers often seemed just as indifferent as the mythmakers about the reality of a dead young woman named Mary Jo Kopechne. She was merely a justification, a toehold for those determined to investigate a very different subject. Even those who explicitly spoke for Kopechne, such as Kenneth Kappel, did so in grandiose terms that implied she was a counter in a larger morality play pitting evil against crusading justice: "Mary Jo Kopechne was an innocent, a true believer. . . . She gave her life. Rather, it was taken from her. She deserved more; and now her tormented spirit deserves a champion."[6]

In death, Kopechne was an idealized symbol of virtue for some, making the allegedly lecherous and drunken Kennedy appear all the more degraded by comparison: a beast who planned to take sexual advantage of an innocent young maiden and then, through his recklessness, accidentally killed her. Since Kopechne's only function in this mythic narrative was to be killed, the spectacle of her drowned corpse yanked from Kennedy's death car was heavily fetishized. The archetype of the dead maiden plays a foundational role in such media flights of rhetorical fancy as this one from a *Medical World News* report: "[Her body] was foam-flecked at the mouth . . . with blonde hair plastered to her head, like some Persephone risen from the sea."[7] One writer who is highly critical of Kennedy nevertheless accurately diagnoses the early tendency in media coverage to idealize Kopechne:

> To read the newspapers in the early days of the case, one would have easily come to the conclusion that a nice Catholic girl of twenty-eight would never, never think of belting a few with a U.S. senator and then going for a roll in the sand. The valedictory phrases that the press baptized the corpse with (by interviewing friends of hers) made one feel nasty indeed to even suspect that this graduate of Our Lady of the Valley High School might entertain carnal thoughts.[8]

Significantly, the Kennedy legend did not begin as a tragic one, though it quickly turned so. The myth had originally been created by the wealthy Kennedy patriarch himself, Joseph Sr., in collusion with a media intent on presenting his three surviving sons to the American public as political saviors who happened to be more glamorous and sexy than film stars. (The eldest and heir apparent, Joe Jr., had been killed in a flying accident in the course of military duty at the end of World War II.) It was the power of this myth that led to the election of John Kennedy as president, and his assassination in 1963 sanctified the myth with the sacrificial blood of martyrdom. The lost Camelot of the Kennedy presidency was on the verge of redemption by Robert Kennedy in 1968 when he too was killed by yet another assassin on the night of his victory in the California presidential primary. The youngest son, Edward Kennedy, then inherited the hopes of those who longed for Camelot renascent. Joe McGinniss explains how inadequate the reality behind that myth truly was. "For the rest of [Edward Kennedy's] life he would wander the country and circle the globe, bearing the burden of legend, eventually drained by the unrealistic demands of the myth, eventually crushed by the incessant pressure to be more than he had the capacity to become."[9]

According to McGinniss, this pressure led to various manifestations of increasingly self-destructive behavior on the part of the overwhelmed Kennedy, culminating in the crash at Chappaquidick. "Even as America yearned to see in him the best of Jack and Bobby," writes McGinniss, "Teddy seemed to need to prove, first to himself and then to the nation, that he was unworthy to carry the torch, unworthy to even bear the family name."[10] Here, McGinniss gives voice to one overriding theme in the attempt to invest a random death by car crash with profound significance— that the fatality was a direct result of a deeply flawed young man's inability to live up to the burden of his mythic family name. Viewed through McGinniss's interpretive framework, Kennedy can be seen as a thoroughly modern, even debased type of Greek antihero: one destined by larger forces to kill an innocent for inexcusable reasons; one who lacks the sympathetic intellectual depth and metaphysical grandeur of the classic tragic hero.

For other writers such as Lester David, who are at least partially intent on rehabilitating Kennedy's public image, a slightly more sympathetic villain—redeemed primarily by his public good works—is responsible for the accidental death of Mary Jo Kopechne. David's thesis postulates the coexistence of "two Teddys"—a good senator and a bad man:

> Ted Kennedy is the Dr. Jekyll and Mr. Hyde of American politics, a complex amalgam of good and bad, one side of his personality seeming to have no command of, or relationship with, the other. He is a good, some say superb senator; but in the quarter-century after the murder of Bobby he has also exhibited a dark side. Judging by his public behavior, which

he has made little effort to conceal, he has been an uninhibited pleasure-seeker, driving too fast, drinking too much, and wenching whenever the mood struck, which was often.[11]

For David, what spared Kennedy from post-Chappaquidick electoral defeat in 1970 (and in every senatorial race since) is the public's ability to separate personal behavior from public performance. Thus, as David notes, the media pundits who almost universally predicted the end of Kennedy's career in 1969 were woefully premature in their judgment. They were also narrow-minded in their reading of the public's willingness to accept personal misconduct as long as it was balanced by professional competence—the "bad Teddy" was offset by the "good Teddy." The Kennedy myth still also had (and still has) a powerful grip on the public imagination, and was instrumental in sparing Ted Kennedy from voter sanctions, as McGinniss observes: " . . . he remained a Kennedy: the last link we'd ever have to Jack and Bobby. We did not want to sever that. We wanted to believe the best . . . He was the last Kennedy we would ever have."[12]

In light of this widespread sentiment and general willingness to overlook the death of Mary Jo Kopechne, Kennedy's chances at being elected president remained viable at least until 1972. In that year, Richard Nixon considered him the gravest threat to a Nixon reelection and consequently embarked on an absurdly Byzantine "dirty tricks" campaign to unearth more damning evidence about the events at Chappaquidick. Kennedy was a strong contender for the presidency again in 1976 but passed up the nomination, suggesting to observers that he really didn't want the job. His embarrassingly halfhearted and failed attempt to run for the Democratic presidential nomination in 1980 served to confirm his apparent lack of presidential ambitions. However, through all the waxing and waning of his career, Kennedy has remained an active force in the Senate and is today considered to be one of the elder statesmen of the centrist-liberals, fighting tirelessly for civil and women's rights as well as the rights of the economically disenfranchised. One might say that this is the "good Teddy," ironically made even better by the Chappaquidick tragedy. Even so hostile a writer as Robert Sherrill admits that the car wreck may have rescued Kennedy "from the burden of . . . expectations . . . and, giving him the recklessness of despair, turned him into a superior senator."[13]

Yet the haunting presence of the "bad Teddy" continues to cripple Kennedy at key moments, such as the 1991 senatorial grilling of Anita Hill during the Judge Clarence Thomas confirmation hearings. During this now-infamous trial, Kennedy remained conspicuously silent, perhaps because he knew only too well that his speaking out would boomerang against Anita Hill. As a figure of dubious honesty himself, writes Sherrill, Kennedy didn't have the credentials to defend Hill against the senators who were attacking her testimony.[14] In another highly publicized 1991 media event stemming from a poolside incident at the Kennedy mansion in Palm Beach—the rape trial of William Kennedy Smith—memories of Chappaquidick were resurrected. Although William Kennedy Smith was not convicted, the media made much of the revelation that Senator Kennedy, his son Patrick, and the defendant had all been out drinking together the night of the alleged rape.

Here again was a salacious story involving a young Kennedy and a hapless female victim. The presence in that narrative of the elder Kennedy, who might be said to have set the standard for such incidents, could only provoke new accusations of a cover-up and charges of privileged treatment for a powerful individual. This negative publicity compelled Kennedy to make a public apology for his personal life before a Harvard audience just before the start of the rape trial. Ultimately, then, for commentators such as Lester David, the paradoxical nature of the surviving Kennedy brother's character is cruelly ironic. The crises of Chappaquidick and Palm Beach—the death of Mary Jo Kopechne and the alleged rape of Patricia Bowman—all too clearly foreground the fact that the "bad Teddy" is capable of enough recklessness to cause great suffering to the very women he so staunchly defends in his senatorial role as the "good Teddy." And the erotic-thanatological icon at the center of this paradox—the image through which Kennedy is either damned or redeemed—is the body of a dead girl, drowned in the backseat of a wrecked and sunken car.

Another dead blonde in a crashed car has set off an even more far-ranging cultural shock wave with more than a hint of vicarious media-enabled necrophilia providing its endless fascination. It is not an exaggeration to say that the death of the beautiful Princess Diana became one of those key historical moments in the late twentieth century (like the President Kennedy assassination, the explosion of the space shuttle *Challenger,* and the O. J. Simpson verdict) that the media, through minute-by-minute coverage, has fixed into our personal memory.

According to Joan Bridgman, the BBC had even practiced coverage of such an event (the death of a royal in a car accident on foreign soil) and was thus instantly prepared to transmit the story to the public.[15] Adding to the crystallization of Diana's death within the public psyche, dozens of conspiracy theories were disseminated on the Internet within days and even hours following the princess's death. Michael Shermer catalogs some of these theories, including ones that named the British royal family, the pope, the DuPont family, British intelligence services, the arms industry (supposedly outraged by Diana's work to ban the use of land mines), the Rockefeller family, and even Bill Clinton. Some argue that the driver Henri Paul, a former military man with at least some connections to French and possibly British intelligence agencies, may have carried out a "suicide mission" under orders.[16]

Even before her death, Diana was often described as the most photographed person of the twentieth century. Whether this claim is true or not, it is certainly accurate to say that the life of the former Diana Spencer, at least from her entrance into consciousness as the Prince of Wales's virginal fiancée in 1980, was a series of narrative paradigms carefully constructed by the media. First, it was an antifeminist fairy tale, capped by the 1981 wedding between Diana and Prince Charles. Next it was a modern-day tale of captivity (or what Julie Burchill calls a fairy tale "scripted by the Brothers Grimm"[17]), in which a beautiful young woman suffers physical and psychological torture at the hands of an evil and perverse family. Finally, following the inevitable divorce, it was a postfeminist tale of personal liberation and redemption that ended tragically in Paris in 1997.

In each of these narratives, Diana's representational status as an iconic figure in a public fairy tale invests her with a singular hollowness or negativity of character—a felt absence, rather than a presence. Even Diana herself seemed aware of this absence, as indicated by her complex reinventions of herself through the complicity of the media. According to Mark Honigsbaum, Diana was quite adept at colluding with the tabloids to manipulate her own image.[18] Donna Cox points out the emptiness behind Diana's various iconographic portrayals: "Diana's designated place becomes fragmented into one of multiple proliferation. 'She' is no thing but a text without an original, a self which comes to believe in itself as a text, i.e., a radically alienating and poignant investment in the performative power of representation in all its multitudinous forms."[19]

Whatever narrative paradigms are applied to the various phases of Diana's life, one motif remains constant—that of Diana as hunted victim, who nevertheless managed to transcend suffering and regain personal integrity and public adoration. Donald Spoto identifies the essence of Diana's appeal during her public life. "Paradoxically," he writes, "she also became more and more beautiful, more and more triumphant over the various systems that so often conspire to crush sensitive spirits."[20] But for this public victim, the specter of tragedy was never very far away.

According to at least one writer, fate had stacked the deck against Diana that night in Paris. "Diana was riding in a car that had once been stolen and shipped for parts and whose warning lights were flashing, with an improperly licensed driver under the deadly influence of alcohol *and* drugs [and] a boyfriend who often ordered his drivers to push the envelope."[21] The same writer refers elsewhere to the cosmic forces arrayed against Diana. "[S]he was sucked up by forces which, tide-like, came to overwhelm her . . . some accidents have a force that feels like fate."[22] And so Diana, always more symbol than real person—at least, according to her representation in the media—achieved her ultimate martyrdom, and the final obliteration of her identity as a living human being, in her decisive role as helpless car crash victim in August 1997.

Yet in the peculiar sense of doubleness that's so much a part of the way we identify with the known and yet unknown celebrity, people quickly realized that behind the icon, a vibrant and attractive woman had died accidentally. Writers immediately began trying to invest the accident with some larger significance so as to ease the public grief. Paul Johnson sought to reassure and also to identify the villains who brought Diana down. "Her death, far from being meaningless, was full of meaning, even symbolic. She was a martyr to a combination of evils: the coldness of royalty, the prurience of the public in demanding even the most intimate secrets of the heart, and the cruelty of the media in providing them."[23]

As such sentiments illustrate, her death would attain meaning only if it could somehow lead to the identification and reformation of those who played a part in the tragedy. It was not enough to criticize French emergency medical procedures, which—according to some—did not transport Diana to the hospital operating room in enough time to save her life. In the early days of the extraordinary public grieving over Diana's frighteningly senseless death, this search for meaning led to a relentless demonizing of the paparazzi—not just those who had supposedly pursued her through the Parisian streets, but all those journalists and photographers whose subsistence depended on the public appetite for celebrity images.

Initial news reports from Paris in the early morning hours of August 31, 1997, emphasized the prominent role that the paparazzi were believed to have played in the fatal accident, and were quick to mention that several of the photographers still in the tunnel when police arrived to investigate had been arrested. Charles Spencer, Diana's brother, himself a frequent victim of the tabloid press, was quick to publicly vent his hostility to the very media he so despised. "I always believed the press would kill her in the end," he claimed bitterly. "Not even I could imagine that they would take such a direct hand in her death, as seems to be the case. . . . It would appear that every proprietor and editor of every publication that has paid for intrusive and exploitative photographs of her, encouraging greedy and ruthless individuals to risk everything in pursuit of Diana's image, has blood on his hands today."[24]

In his eulogy to Diana at her funeral service in Westminster Abbey, viewed by millions via media technology, Spencer again lashed out at those he perceived as Diana's tormentors—including the royal family, but primarily the paparazzi. "I don't think Diana ever understood why her genuinely good intentions were sneered at by the media, why there appeared to be a permanent quest on their behalf to bring her down," he claimed. "It is baffling. My own, and only, explanation, is that genuine goodness is threatening to those at the opposite end of the moral spectrum. . . . A girl given the name of the ancient goddess of hunting was, in the end, the most hunted person of the modern age."

The grieving brother's angry hyperbole aside, the relationship between Diana and the tabloid press was much more complicated—and complicit—than Spencer would have his audience of hundreds of millions believe. Donald Spoto accurately diagnoses the mutual dependency between Diana and the media. "[Diana] was a young woman who desperately needed to feel wanted," writes Spoto. "[A]nd according to the ethos of modern life, nothing so confirms self-esteem as media attention. Diana Spencer was receiving, in other words, the attention from the press that she needed in order to feel alive and valuable. . . . The blunt, unapologetic intrusiveness of the media frightened her, but she needed it."[25] Nevertheless, the paparazzi made convenient villains of first resort for the public, gripped by a need to apportion blame and to find a larger meaning in the sudden death of a popular young celebrity—a princess, no less.

In light of the facts that gradually emerged in the aftermath of the crash, however, the ferocious scapegoating of the paparazzi could no longer continue or, at least, had to assume a secondary role. Donald Spoto sets the record straight. "[I]t is important to add that all police and official investigations discounted the proximity of paparazzi with blinding flashbulbs, on motorcycles."[26] Instead, investigators began focusing on two factors: the degree of driver Henri Paul's intoxication and the presence in the tunnel's left lane of a slower second car, perhaps a Fiat, around which Paul had apparently tried to swerve before losing control. Even these relatively mundane matters took on an air of mystery, however, with some speculating that Paul had been "programmed" to wreck the car and others wondering just where the presumably damaged Fiat had been hidden, or disposed of.

But perhaps the most sinister of the alleged conspiracies surrounding the death of the princess involves the romance she had begun in her last few months of life with Emad ("Dodi") Mohammed Al Fayed. According to conspiracy buffs, the House of Windsor, acting through British, French, or U.S. intelligence services (or perhaps all three), engineered the wreck to prevent the possibility of an interracial and cross-cultural marriage between Dodi and Diana.

Thomas Sancton and Scott McLeod note that rumors of Diana's pregnancy during her romance with Fayed may be significant in this context.

CAR CRASH COVER-UPS   137

"[T]he question of whether or not [Diana] was pregnant," they write, "is potentially one of the most explosive elements in the investigation, because a pregnancy would give greater credence to the assassination plot theories that began in the Middle East and soon proliferated around the globe."[27] These authors further observe that an Egyptian book called *Who Killed Diana?* appeared in Egyptian markets within ten days of the funeral and became a best-seller in the Middle East. The book argued that the British royal family assassinated Diana and Dodi.[28]

Tyrone Yarborough writes that such conspiracy theories appeared on Internet sites literally within minutes of the first media reports of Diana's death. Now there are literally thousands of Internet references to conspiracies involving the death of Diana. In such a paranoid context, it perhaps becomes significant that no autopsy was performed on, or blood samples taken from, Diana's body. These procedures would have eliminated the possibility of Diana's pregnancy. Conspiracy theorists in search of a happier ending literally wish Diana alive again, saying that Diana "was fed up with the intrusions on her private life, and used the resources of the Fayed family to fake her own death."[29]

The traditional publishing world, although moving at a glacial pace compared to the virtual reality of the Internet, has kept the conspiracy mills churning over the past four years since the accident. Typical of the nonfiction "conspiracy" books are Isaac Omoike's *The Murder of a Princess: An Investigational Analysis of the Death of Princess Diana* (1998) and John King and John Beverige's *Princess Diana: The Hidden Evidence* (2001). Undoubtedly the most fascinating of the conspiracy books, however, is Aaron McCallum Becker's novel *Whose Death in the Tunnel?: The Tale of a Princess* (1999). Crafting a fictional narrative based on the facts of the case and using public figures as characters, much like Oliver Stone did with his 1991 film *JFK* or David Bender with his 1997 novel *The Confession of O. J. Simpson,* Becker presents a truly fairy-tale scenario in which Diana, with the aid of sympathetic intelligence agents, fakes her own death, takes on a new identity, and lives a private life far from the demonic reach of the royals and the paparazzi.

In some ways, this alleged international conspiracy is a logical narrative outgrowth of the widespread belief that Diana, a symbol of radical liberation from stuffy English tradition, was targeted for public humiliation and discredit by a House of Windsor desperately struggling to preserve the monarchy. According to at least one source (one of Diana's many spiritual advisors), Diana herself believed that certain representatives of the royal family were out not only to persecute her but actually to kill her. "There is an awful irony in the fact that while she died with an Arab, Dodi Fayed, she had for years believed there was an Arab conspiracy to kill her. She felt that friends of the royal family, notably their rich allies in the Gulf States, would take out a contract on her life. . . . She lived in a state of agitation, convinced that her phone was bugged . . . In fact, Diana did fear that GCHQ, the government intelligence-gathering operation, was keeping an eye on her."[30]

Diana's fears have been posthumously given voice by Dodi's father, Mohammed Al Fayed, who, in August of 2000, announced his intentions to file a lawsuit to force the U.S. Central Intelligence Agency to disclose documents that supposedly reveal the role of the British Secret Service in causing the car crash. Back in 1998, the London *Mirror* reported that Mohammed Al Fayed had his representatives meet with an intermediary (later arrested), who allegedly offered to sell such incriminating CIA documents to Al Fayed. Al Fayed summarizes his theory of the case thus: "[Diana and Dodi's relationship] was a very serious matter. . . . Maybe the future king is going to have a half-brother who is a 'nigger,' and Mohammed Al Fayed is going to be the step-grandfather of the future king. This is how they think, this Establishment."[31] Despite (or because of) the fact that the elder Fayed owns Harrods department store in London, he was a controversial figure in Britain long before the deaths of Diana and Dodi. According to Donald Spoto:

> Fayed had consistently failed in his bid for British citizenship after the Department of Trade and Industry questioned his business dealings and credibility. Regarded in Britain as the vulgar, *arriviste* Egyptian and briber of members of parliament, Fayed was the object of considerable slander among the English—and most particularly among both aristocrats and royals. . . . In Fayed's favor, however, it must be said that the government's case against him has always seemed, to some, manufactured—and perhaps based on a resentment that an Egyptian family had taken over that most cherished institution, Harrods.[32]

In addition to Harrods, the "phony pharaoh" also owned the Ritz Hotel in Paris, from where his son and Diana were sped to their deaths by his own employee, Henri Paul. According to Martyn Gregory, Fayed has chosen to shift attention away from his own culpability in his son's death by widely publicizing his suspicions of a cover-up by the House of Windsor.[33] Thus, in yet another variation on the narrative, Fayed himself—whose activities to inveigle himself into the British establishment may indirectly have brought about the death of his own son—becomes a villain, although a tragic one.

How much more comforting it is to believe that the deaths of these two women, one an unknown functionary and the other a fairy-tale princess, must somehow embody significantly more than what is obvious—the fragility of a human life thrown in the path of the brutal, stupid, and ultimately meaningless force of the car crash. All of these narratives try to make sense of the senseless and transform something that is ultimately banal into something that is suddenly significant. The untimely deaths of two young women in two car crashes under mysterious circumstances is an unhappy affair. What makes the deaths of these women finally significant, however, is their connection to the patriarchal world of power, wealth, and privilege.

Through their involvement with older and wealthier men from established families, however direct or oblique that involvement, these two young women became pawns on the chessboard of male political power. Their connection to these men, in the end, brought them not pleasure and respect but rather lonely and painful deaths. The temptation to read morality plays into these two random car accidents is virtually irresistible. One of the most dramatically satisfying of such narratives tells of a patriarchal conspiracy among the rich and powerful—and the wider ranging that conspiracy, the more fascinating the story. In the case of Kopechne, her death put whatever was left of the Kennedy dynasty under a permanent cloud of suspicion. Diana's death in the age of twenty-four-hour-a-day media has stirred up similar tales of nefarious cabals and cryptic conspiracies, most of them global in nature.

Everyone brings their private vices and personal melodramas with them into their deceptively self-contained vehicles. When cars conveying powerful people careen out of control, we are uncomfortably reminded that the convenience of vehicular transportation comes with a terrible price that is paid every year in battered, bruised, and mutilated flesh. When that traumatized flesh happens to belong to a princess or even a publicly unknown acquaintance of a wealthy United States senator from a famous family, the common but essentially private tragedy suddenly impacts us all. As media spectators of these most public of car crashes, we feel all at once shock, sorrow, voyeuristic titillation, a need to fix blame on the culpable, and an unspoken satisfaction to discover that such powerful people bleed and die in accidents just like we do. The car crashes of the rich and famous allow us to participate vicariously in their last public spectacle and to join, even at a distance, the inevitable investigations into any high-profile accidental death. Perhaps the "real" conspiracy here is our collective need to elevate the public car crash—the price of automobile culture—into a public melodrama of martyrs, victims, and villains.

NOTES

1. Robert Sherrill, *The Last Kennedy* (New York: The Dial Press, 1976), 68–69.
2. Kenneth Kappel, *Chappaquiddick Revealed* (New York: St. Martin's Paperbacks, 1991).
3. Leo Damore, *Senatorial Privilege: The Chappaquiddick Cover-Up* (New York: Dell, 1989), 46.
4. Joe McGinniss, *The Last Brother* (New York: Simon & Schuster, 1993), 553.
5. Ibid., 566.
6. Kappel, 8.
7. Cited in Sherrill, 81.
8. Sherrill, 86.
9. McGinniss, 348.
10. Ibid., 598.
11. Lester David, *Good Ted/Bad Ted, The Two Faces of Edward M. Kennedy* (New York: Birch Lane Press, 1993), 15.
12. McGinniss, 589.
13. Sherrill, 227.
14. Ibid., 222.
15. Joan Bridgman, "Diana's Country," *Contemporary Review* 274, January 1999, 19.
16. Michael Shermer, "The Knowledge Filter: Reality Must Take Precedence in the Search for Truth," *Skeptic* 7:1, 1999, 64–65.
17. Julie Burchill, "A Glorious Force for Republicanism," in Brian McArthur, ed., *Requiem: Diana, Princess of Wales 1961–1997* (New York: Arcade, 1997), 153.

18. Mark Honigsbaum, "Diana and the Tabloids: The Real Story," www.pbs. org./wgbh/pages/frontline/shows/royals/readings/tabloids.html.
19. Donna Cox, "Diana: Her True Story: Post-Modern Transgressions in Identity," *Journal of Gender Studies* 99:8, November 1999, 328.
20. Donald Spoto, *Diana: The Last Year* (New York: Harmony Books, 1997), 101–102.
21. Christopher Anderson, *The Day Diana Died* (New York: William Morrow & Company, 1998), 39.
22. Christopher Anderson, "The Beauty Who Couldn't Tame the Beast," in McArthur, ed., *Requiem,* 32.
23. Paul Johnson, "The Two Dianas," in McArthur, ed., *Requiem,* 149.
24. Cited in Howard Chua-Eoan, et al., "Death of a Princess," *Time,* September 5, 1997, 33.
25. Spoto, 57.
26. Ibid., 175.
27. Thomas Sancton and Scott MacLeod, *Death of a Princess: The Investigation* (New York: St. Martin's Press, 1998), 43.
28. Russell Watson, "Calling Oliver Stone," *Newsweek,* October 27, 1997, 40.
29. Tyrone Yarborough, "Consider the Source: Conspiracy Theories, Narrative, Belief," www.temple.edu/isllc/newfolk/consider1.html.
30. Simone Simmons with Susan Hill, *Diana: The Secret Years* (New York: Ballantine Books, 1998), 170.
31. Cited in Sancton and MacLeod, 108.
32. Spoto, 149–150.
33. Martyn Gregory, *The Diana Conspiracy Exposed: The Definitive Account* (Chicago: Olmstead Press, 2000).

FOURTEEN

WHY DON'T WE MAKE BELIEVE IT HAPPENED IN THE ROAD?

THE MANY DEATHS AND REBIRTHS OF PAUL MCCARTNEY

JERRY GLOVER

At 5:00 A.M. one Wednesday morning in November 1966, Paul McCartney was driving his car in London. Stopping at a set of traffic lights, he turned to look at a meter maid. He didn't see the lights change ahead of him and another vehicle collided with his car, which burst into flames. Crowds of people gathered around the site of the accident. The person inside was badly mangled and hard to identify. He'd suffered severe head injuries and his teeth were knocked out, so he couldn't be identified by dental records. All anyone knew was that he was a young man with dark hair. Shortly after the crash, a Paul McCartney look-alike contest was held. The winner was William Campbell, a police officer from Toronto. Campbell underwent plastic surgery and filled in for McCartney, appearing in all the subsequent Beatles' photo shoots. Right from the beginning the Beatles began putting clues into their songs to tell their fans of Paul's death.

THE MYTH OF THE DEATH OF PAUL MCCARTNEY in a car accident, and its subsequent cover-up, displays many elements common to a clear-cut, skeptical, near-paranoid belief system, a "conspiracy theory" impenetrable to contrary facts and ordinary common sense. The very idea that the Beatles and their management were so mired in their own growing legend that the death of one of their number could be successfully covered up is as scandalous as it is ridiculous.

So why did a rumor, which began with one man writing in a college newspaper in the American Midwest, blossom into a worldwide news story so strong, so impervious to basic common sense, that the Beatles press officer, Derek Taylor, was forced to issue the following statement: "Even if he appeared in public just to deny rumors it wouldn't do any good. If people want to believe he's dead, then they'll believe it. The truth is not at all persuasive." The rumor showed no signs of abating, not until the man at the center of the controversy appeared on camera to affirm that he was very much alive and well. Yet even this was not enough to kill the story.

In the fall of 1966, Paul McCartney took a motoring vacation across Europe. With his Super–8 movie camera and disguise packed (glasses, mustache, overcoat, hair gel), McCartney set out across France in his brand-new Aston Martin DB5. He'd first hit on the idea of going about in disguise to evade the fans during the filming of *A Hard Day's Night*. He'd enjoyed "freaking out" George Harrison and manager Brian Epstein, play-acting an overbearing press photographer to see if he could trick them (which he could). At Bordeaux he rendezvoused with Mal Evans, the Beatles' road manager, and together the pair flew to Kenya to go on safari.

The feeling of freedom was intoxicating to McCartney. The Beatles had played their last concert at Candlestick Park in San Francisco at the end of August. Jaded from the pressures of near-constant touring and recording, the four were reaching the point of burnout. The Beatle image, so carefully cultivated in the preceding years, had reached phantasmagoric heights. 'Who needs this?' they asked each other as another hotel loomed. While it was certain what they *didn't* need—screaming fans, record-burning Jesus bigots, the creepy cripple-stroking and schmoozing of local dignitaries and the press before and after each and every gig—what they *did* need was more of a puzzle. That they wanted to continue recording was in no doubt, but they needed somehow to keep doing that and *stop being Beatles.* McCartney spoke for the whole group when he said that they were "fed up with being Beatles." They "fucking hated" the besuited, compliant mop-top image, feeling it was juvenile and rapidly becoming shop-worn. Plus, they had received death threats on their last American tour. Innocuous noises became gunshots in their imaginations; according to Barry Miles, Lennon later spoke of actually recoiling onstage when he heard a sound he took to be a gun report.

While Lennon went off to Spain and ended up being killed onscreen in *How I Won the War* (1966), McCartney watched the wildlife and luxuriated in that most epicene of celebrity pleasures: anonymity. He made home movies, for once the watched playing at being the watcher. Being nobody was good fun, normal, *novel.* On the return flight from Africa, and with his mind turning again toward work, these experiences formed a new inspiration: "I thought, let's not be ourselves. Let's develop alter egos so we're not having to project an image which we know. It would be much more free. What would be really interesting would be to actually take on the personas of this different band. . . . I thought we can run this philosophy through the whole album: with this alter ego band, it won't be us making all that sound, it won't be the Beatles, it'll be this other band, so we'll be able to lose our identities in this."[1]

Thus, on a flight between continents came the genesis of *Sergeant Pepper's Lonely Hearts Club Band.* Paul quickly convinced the other Beatles of his plan, and they immediately set about spicing up their wardrobes, growing handlebar mustaches, and working deep into the winter nights to reinvent their popular sound with producer George Martin.

Conceptwise, *Sergeant Pepper* was quintessentially McCartney, the sublimated result of projecting alternate personalities for the greater part of his childhood and adult life. From his formative years, McCartney was accustomed to generally hoisting his thumbs and being the "nice-n'-approachable" one—whether charming the press, smoothing over Lennon's acid comments, or having tea with fans who came to call at his St. John's Wood house. He was the most versatile musician, the one most open to alternative musical styles, often shaping his songs to tell the stories of invented people: Eleanor Rigby, Lovely Rita, Desmond and Molly, Rose and Valerie screaming from the gallery. . . . While Lennon's canon formed, for the greater part, a self-centric journal of his own, often very personal, experiences, McCartney excelled at the creation of masks to hide behind, with agile musical pastiches and songs populated by the Lennon-mocked "Beatle people." This method of creativity earned its share of criticism and accusations of superficiality and cuteness from a media more comfortable with singular, "mono-celebric" egocentricity than with multiplicitous, eclectic diversity; easier to dismiss shape-shifting, multifold qualities in an industry nourished on the myth of Dionysian appetite and excess. But McCartney, in his own way, was doing exactly the same as Lennon: plumbing the childhood core of his imagination and filtering it through the kaleidoscopic gauze of psychotropic and psychedelic chemicals. Wearing the faces he kept in a jar by the side of the door . . .

The release of *Sergeant Pepper's Lonely Hearts Club Band* on June 1, 1967, caused nothing less than a cinematic dissolve from one zeitgeist to another. The four young musicians were no longer pop superstars. They were artists, sages even, musical prophets. Brian Wilson reputedly shelved his intended masterpiece, *Smile,* so crushed was he by the Beatles' latest achievement. Other intellectuals took note, and the nonhallucinating generation paid its respects. Comparisons were made in the English broadsheet press between T. S. Eliot's *The Waste Land* and "A Day in the Life." The Beatles were about as far up as they could go. From here on in the only way to go was down. But, as Philip Larkin later observed when the group's dynamic first began to sour, the Beatles could not *get* down. So they explored Eastern philosophies and continued to work. More albums, more singles, a couple of films, solo projects. The gradual and glorious comedown.

Meanwhile . . .

Across Britain and the United States a joke was evolving into a Chinese whisper, thence into a full-fledged rumor. The precise origin of the rumor is not certain. Perhaps it originated in California, perhaps London.[2] Wherever it started, it probably took shape over two or three years, emerging in print for the first time on September 17, 1969, in a Drake University (Iowa) newspaper article written by Tim Harper. This article contained the first published examination of the so-called clues pointing to the death of McCartney in a car crash. The writer didn't claim to have invented the story, having simply compiled information given to him by a friend, who in turn references (never discovered) underground newspapers and friends of friends. Within a week the *Northern Star,* the newspaper of Northern Illinois University, had "borrowed" Harper's article. Less than a month later, a disc jockey and his crew at a Detroit[3] radio station began riffing off one or both of the articles, inventing new Paul Is Dead clues live on air and inviting listeners to call in with their own. Fred LaBour, a reviewer on *The Michigan Daily* student paper, heard the broadcast and was inspired to incorporate a few of his own clues into a review of *Abbey Road,* which, fortunately for clue-seekers, had just been released.

This article, published under the headline "McCartney Dead; New Evidence Brought to Light," brought the story—hitherto confined to campus dorm rooms—to a critical mass. The paper's editors received calls from journalists across and beyond America. Scores of people were now scrying their Beatles album covers for visual clues about the accident, scratching their records backward and forward in the hope of finding concealed audio "evidence" to prove the tragedy. What began as a joke was now an international news event. Derek Taylor, the Beatles' press officer, denied the story to no avail. *LIFE* magazine sent photographers to McCartney's Scottish farm retreat and earned a cold-water soaking from a bucket thrown by a decidedly living McCartney. "The rumors of my death have been greatly exaggerated," he told the drenched representatives. "However, if I was dead I'm sure I'd be the last to know."[4]

The first appearance of the man who was supposed to have replaced McCartney after his accident, a Canadian police officer named William Campbell, is on the Sergeant Pepper cover. "Campbell" has his back to the camera on the reverse cover shot (supposedly because his plastic surgery had not healed, I think the legend has it). The front cover allegedly depicts McCartney's funeral: He is the only one holding a black instrument, the flowers in the dirt spell "Paul is dead," a toy car is present in the composition, and details of the accident are sprinkled throughout the lyrics, revealing how he "blew his mind out in a car" because he "didn't notice that the lights had changed." In the hands of dedicated seekers, the album's design and content became a veritable codex brimming with signs and cryptic meanings. The *Magical Mystery Tour* packaging went even further—every page of the book that came with the record was allegedly encrusted with meaning. By the time the *Abbey Road* album came out in 1969, practically everything the Beatles recorded or displayed on their album covers could, with a sprinkling of imagination (or grains of hash, perhaps), be assimilated to bolster the myth. It would have taken a French philosopher to extract Paul Is Dead inferences from McCartney appearing on live television in front of a sports stadium crowd saying "Yes, I am alive," but I don't think it is overly wild to suppose some would have taken a crack at doing so.

In the space of a few weeks, a ridiculous story about a fatal car crash, supported by nothing more than creative interpretation, went from publication in a small Midwestern newspaper to being publicly denied by McCartney in person. The same rumor in today's networked society would proliferate within hours, but somehow I can't see it reaching such intensity, certainly not to the point where McCartney or his publicists would have to start issuing denials. The myth began as a slow burn, simmered for a time, then suddenly mushroomed, accelerating like a capsule on a slingshot trajectory when the mass media tuned in and compounded its strength. The rumor followed a fractal sequence: from frat-party gossip, to radio studio in-joke, to newsmen's liars' club, to a kind of international parlor game. In this way it resembles a several-times-removed grandchild of *The Protocols of the Elders of Zion*—impossible to trace back to a positive primary source, and therefore impervious to culpability (and journalistic standards) because the source-chain fragments and vanishes into the past.[5]

The theory that the narrative aspect of the rumor—the urbanesque, almost balladic tale of the car crash—may have started in England is very possible, even if the majority of the clue-hunting was a Stateside phenomenon. Tara Browne, the twenty-one-year-old heir to the Guinness brewing fortune and a friend of the Beatles, *was* killed in a car crash in Chelsea's Redcliffe Gardens in the early hours of December 18, 1966.[6] In a curious—possibly significant—coincidence, Browne was with McCartney when the Beatle crashed his moped a few weeks prior to this tragedy, on November 9, 1966. McCartney is also supposed to have crashed his moped on another occasion before this, in Cheshire on December 26, 1965. This crash is more verifiable, as McCartney sustained a chipped tooth and a scar on his upper lip, both visible in the "Paperback Writer/Rain" promo films and the notorious *Yesterday and Today* "butcher" album cover. Predictably, these facts were later to become ominous "clues."

I have not discovered if either of these accidents surfaced in the press. If so, it isn't difficult to imagine the story crossing the Atlantic, changing and expanding, as the rumor grew, from minor moped accident to full-blown car crash (although the story must surely have survived its crossing to America intact, with the U.S. media reporting identical facts). If not, if McCartney's moped accidents were not publicly aired until much later in biographies, then we are left with the ironic possibility that the myth originated within the Beatles' circle itself. Throughout the latter half of 1967, the subject of McCartney's "double" was making the rounds in London. Considering the story's macabre surreality, could it perhaps have been a jest made in jealousy, the usurped leader aiming an off-the-cuff snipe against the main architect of the triumphant *Pepper?*

Does the root of the Paul Is Dead myth dust for Lennon's fingerprints?

The song "Glass Onion," with its lyric "And here's another clue for you all / The walrus was Paul," was written by Lennon and was recorded for inclusion on *The Beatles* album on September 11, 1968. This was just over a year before the publication of Tim Harper's article, so the Beatles could easily have been aware of the rumors. It isn't clear whether the other Lennon "clue" on the same album, the backward "Paul is dead now, miss him, miss him" at the end of "I'm So Tired" is intentional or synchronicitous. The same goes for the quasi-holographic skull just visible on the back of the *Abbey Road* cover between the letters D and N. The skull is there, but is it an intentional clue or merely a printing quirk?

The subject of death and death-related imagery crops up in other Lennon-driven songs, not just "A Day in the Life." Listen closely to *Beatles For Sale, Rubber Soul, Revolver* (from the pre–Paul Is Dead period) where the experience or threat of being dead haunts a number of Lennon's compositions.[7] While McCartney might have been a little accident prone on his moped, Lennon was in another league where misfortune with vehicles was concerned. His mother was run down by a car and killed when he was seventeen. He suffered a serious accident while out driving with Yoko Ono and his son, Julian, in the summer of 1969, resulting in hospitalization. He was shot moments after leaving a car and died in an ambulance.

There is nothing folkloric about this. The theory that the rumor started with Lennon is impossible to verify. Yet I would suggest that a binary polarity exists between him and McCartney: identical prodigies who are two sides of the same person. Without this polarity, this creative supersymmetry, the Paul Is Dead myth would have fewer unconscious resonances. We are now moving into an area where the objective "falseness" of the story is irrelevant. It is true in that it is "successful"—it "works," on a symbolic level. In the same way, the Beatles worked so well in public offstage because they projected an image of one being with four natures: John the "tough one," Paul "the obliging one," George "the shy one," Ringo "the lovable one." As pop critic Nik Cohn observed, "it all made for a comforting sense of completeness."[8] The original title of the *Help!* movie was *Eight Arms to Hold You,* and the Beatles' next planned feature, what came to be titled *Up Against It* by playwright Joe Orton, developed this concept of the four-in-one. Orton wrote: "Like the idea. Basically it is that there aren't four young men. Just four aspects of one man. Sounds dreary, but as I thought about it realised what wonderful opportunities it would give. . . . Already have the idea that the ending should be a church with four bridegrooms and one bride. THE HOME-COMING in fact, but alibied in such a way that no one could object."[9]

The theme of the four sons traces back much further than the Pinter play cited by Orton. Although the Beatles passed on the *Up Against It* screenplay (too rude), the film they made instead, the much-criticized *Magical Mystery Tour,* delved much deeper into unconscious territory, even to the extent of providing strange links between the Beatles and ancient Egyptian myth and ritual. The animal-costumed Beatles are alleged to parallel the four sons of Horus: the man-headed Hesti, the ape-headed Hapi, the jackal-headed Tuamutef, and the falcon Qebhsennuf. (Only the man-headed Hesti is out of place, as one of the Beatles was wearing a walrus mask, but the others fit very well.) In one particularly strange *Magical Mystery Tour* sequence, a drunken singalong on the bus is intercut with a scene of McCartney on the beach at Falmouth. The little photographer, George Claydon, is lying on the sand. Standing at Claydon's head, McCartney raises his arms above his head, pivots left toward the sea, and bows. He then walks backward to Claydon's feet, pivots again toward the sea, and performs the same gesture.[10] As he turns back to face Claydon, the camera pans up and away into the sky. In taking their magical mystery tour, the Beatles touched on depths far beyond the childhood memory-strata from which they—like the first exponents of the Paul Is Dead myth—were drawing much inspiration.

This is not as spurious as it might at first seem. Every act of creation has an antecedent, and before we write off the power of allusion as a vaporous notion, we should recall an obscure drifter and sometime songwriter called Charles Manson who saw the Beatles as another mythic foursome, the Four Horsemen of the Apocalypse—a vision that was powerful enough to inspire murder. By inventing the Sergeant Pepper band, McCartney enabled the Beatles to step sideways into a fictional world housed within a kaleidoscopic, Technicolor reality of fairgrounds and carnival (also recovering a glimmer of the circumstances of McCartney's first meeting with Lennon at a fete). The love and playfulness invoked by these allusions are balanced against the horrors of Manson's Helter Skelter—in his imagination a call to rise up, in reality an English fairground ride where the rider climbs to the top of a conical tower, then slides down a gully that winds around the outside. It harks back to English summer festivals and maypoles and further back down a long, long chain of half-forgotten associations with helixes, serpents, knowledge, DNA, fertility, life, and death. As in so many other songs of this period, McCartney says more than he consciously knows, more even than he intends to express. As designer David Vaughan perceived: "A lot of people thought Paul McCartney was shallow. I didn't see him as that at all, I saw him as very very deep. . . . Because he could absorb a lot without encountering any mental block, he could express that Machiavellian, European horror."[11]

Surely he doesn't mean the man who wrote "Michelle"?

McCartney first met David Vaughan through Tara Browne, and at Vaughan's suggestion he encouraged the other Beatles to whip up the legendary "Carnival of Light" composition for a media event held on January 28 and February 4, 1967, at the Roundhouse Theatre in Camden Town, London. The fourteen-minute result of this collaboration—recorded in the midst of the Pepper sessions—is the only major Beatles piece not to have been commercially released to date, and few have even heard it. Tara Browne, then, the man who "blew his mind out in a car," is the hidden inspiration for two major Beatles myths, Paul Is Dead and the coveted "missing track," as well as what is arguably the most daring and mysterious composition in modern popular music, "A Day in the Life." George Martin, Neil Aspinal, and Stu Sutcliffe all have good claim to be the Fifth Beatle, but only Browne is their shadow muse, a "Beatle person" existing in a domain that lies between the memories of history and the shadows of myth.

It would be inappropriate to use the word "resurrection" in the context of the Paul Is Dead myth, as some have done. McCartney does not "live again" in the myth, the lore of which acknowledges without a doubt that the "genuine" McCartney is positively six feet under (the car crash references, the Pepper "funeral," the Abbey Road "procession," John's "I buried Paul"—actually "cranberry sauce"—in the fade-out to "Strawberry Fields Forever"). It's McCartney's bodily *image* that lives on, a curiously tangible illustration of the widespread notion that everyone has an identical double somewhere in the world. For a short time, almost any young man in the Western world could theoretically have been a Beatle. And who would have refused that chance?

Thus, the story of the Man in the Iron Mask is updated to the Man in the Pepper Mustache. The story is an inversion of the Elvis Is Alive myth, a useful contrast. The Elvis Is Alive narrative is genuinely Dionysic/Osiric in its framing of a king/god who, following his death in a weakened state, regenerates in a more vigorous (albeit pot-bellied) form. In Paul Is Dead, however, the replacement continues the looks and spirit of the deceased, a story structure more closely related to shadows and doppelgangers (William Wilson, Dr. Jekyll and Mr. Hyde, Elizabethan drama) and, beyond that, folk and fairy tales of changelings, one or two of which may have been spun to the young McCartney by his mother, a domiciliary midwife.

Where the Paul Is Dead myth develops existing stories is in its embellishment of the double—the snapshotting and continuation of the image. The first junction between the myth and the invention of Sergeant Pepper's Band is in the summoning of an invented person, a perfect doppelganger to replace the "dead" McCartney. His name is

Campbell, aptly evoking Warhol's screen-print soup cans, where a near-worthless, indistinguishable commodity (an unremarkable nobody) becomes a framed and admired work of art (a famous Beatle). He is a policeman and therefore suspect, one of "Them," perhaps a malignant twin in the classic mode. The conspiracy is set. Those Beatles are a clever lot really. There *has* to be more to those songs than falling in love.

Day by day, word by word, these tiny submyths and suppositions aggregate and before you can sing "you were in a car crash and you lost your hair," an internally consistent and generally plausible narrative has developed. Minute details swell into dogmatic assumptions, sculpted and given credence and velocity through a mass media already practiced in the creation of Beatle sublore: the "Fifth Beatle"; the allegedly crime-free State of New York during the Beatles' performance on the *Ed Sullivan Show;* the mobbish miscontextualizing of Lennon's comments on religion.[12] This clue-hunting game unites a like-minded class of fans, providing a platform on which they can test their Beatle knowledge. It also comfortingly boosts their heroes' cleverness for being able to plant these signs so adroitly, infusing the group with an attractively sinister aspect, like that of the stereotypical master criminal who deliberately leaves a cryptic trail for the police to puzzle over.

Significantly, Paul Is Dead lore allows for little discussion of the fearsome practicalities required to cover up the death and maintain the group, the main one being that someone—Lennon working double time, presumably—goes on to write most of the best songs of the Beatles' remaining years together (even "The Long and Winding Road"). Such is the confidence of the Beatle mythologists in their heroes' powers, perhaps. In a way, the myth also supports an opinion held by many of the previous generation that members of pop groups were nodding, miming dolls, golems created by the invisible wizards of Tin Pan Alley—the *real* talents behind popular music. After all, the Beatles "only" ever played songs we already seemed to know—even McCartney first thought "Yesterday" was an old tune. Perhaps if the rumor had started earlier these issues of authorship would be a stronger part of it, but by the second half of the 1960s it was obvious that these four musically untutored young men could be capable of the most intense musical creativity.

Before we complete this long and winding road, we will venture down an off ramp that leads to an appropriate final twist to the story . . .

In July 1964, the science-fiction novelist Philip K. Dick and his close friend Grania Davidson suffered a fairly serious motor accident while driving in Oakland, San Francisco. Grania escaped unhurt, while Dick was consigned to a body cast and arm sling for two months, a disaster for his writing productivity and for his mental state, which plumbed suicidal depths in the following weeks.[13] The car Dick overturned was a Volkswagen bug, better known in England as a Beetle.

Philip K. Dick is a writer whose tales of flanged reality (to borrow a Lennonism) chime most uncannily with the creation and inner workings of the Paul Is Dead myth. The parallels between classic Dick fiction structure and the Paul Is Dead narrative lie broadly in a supposition about the fundamentals of reality—fundamentals that, upon the unveiling of a greater reality, prove to be false, mere subsets concerned only with containment and gratification. The new overreality, however, farther down the path, is *also* seen to be false, just another layer of the onion.

Along the way there has been tragedy and ecstasy, concluding in a redemption of sorts. Our protagonist has undergone a modicum of "evolution" or is transmogrified somehow at the tale's end. (Cue Phil Spector's heavenly choirs on "Let It Be.") Just as simple cause-and-effect patterns collapse and liquefy in Dick's imaginary future empires so too, in the creation of Paul Is Dead consensus, Aristotelean "objects" melt in the petroleum inferno surrounding McCartney's fictional accident. And out of these mythical flames emerges a fresh working of an old, old story, a clue to the nature of which can be found in the spooky, fathom-deep composition "Blackbird"—a song that can be read as much as a nursery-school reworking of the legend of the bird that dies in order to arise as the political allegory discovered by other interpretators (such as Nik Cohn).

The main question raised by the Paul Is Dead myth can be summarized as "When do inert contradictions become living paradoxes?" In other words, and if we are agreed upon the essential value of such a task, how can we define, observe, and even participate in the process that spins myth from mere reportage? The answer lies in the physical conveyance, the writing and (especially) the telling the daisy-chain whispering of word into sound. An authentic myth, to embrace an oxymoron, is benchmarked against its very absurdities and hence the creative pleasures to be had from being a participant in its blooming. The myth's paradoxes are what make it credible—that is, credible to imaginative, as opposed to rational, instincts. Add common sense plausibility, and the paradoxes and symmetries we find so appealing begin to topple. Or put another way, why not Ringo Is Dead? Somehow it doesn't quite work . . .

NOTES

1. Barry Miles, *Many Years from Now* (London: Vintage, 1998), 39.
2. Most of the information contained within this paragraph is taken from an exhaustive investigation made by Jim Kendall, Robert Pietkivitch, Joel Hurmence, Jay Smith, Jean Gerencer, Charles McGrew, J. Gray, and Saki, who wrote up the results. The full text can be found at rmb.simplenet.com/public/files/faqs/pid.html. The final quote and the amusing detail about the bucket of water is from Peter Brown and Steven Gaines's *The Love You Make* (London: Pan Books, 1984).
3. Oddly enough, this was the same city where Lennon's "we're bigger than Jesus" comments sparked a "Stamp Out The Beatles" movement. Hearing of it prompted McCartney's comment "We're going to start a campaign to stamp out Detroit."
4. Or so the story goes. Richard Di Lello's excellent account of life inside the Beatles' Savile Row offices, *The Longest Cocktail Party,* confirms that the idea to plagiarize Mark Twain happened back at Apple. Yet with the extra knowledge of the Beatles' fragile state at that time, in both creative and business contexts, it is even more appropriate. See Richard Di Lello, *The Longest Cocktail Party* (London: Popular Culture Ink, 1997).
5. Although having said that, Jim Yoakum makes a fascinating case for the rumor's true origin in "The Man Who Killed Paul McCartney," *Gadfly,* May-June 2000. Yoakum contends that the myth began with a friend of McCartney's, who suffered a serious accident on the M1 while delivering drugs to Keith Richard's Sussex house on January 7, 1967. This friend was driving McCartney's distinctively customized Mini Cooper that night and is said to have held enough passing resemblance to the artist to have been mistaken for him by spectators at the scene of the crash.
6. He is said to be the one who "blew his mind out in a car, he didn't notice that the lights had changed" from "A Day in the Life." McCartney denies being conscious of it but Lennon was explicit about Browne's connection to the lyric.

7. "Baby's In Black," "Run for Your Life," "Girl," "Rain," "She Said She Said."

8. Ian Macdonald, *Revolution in the Head* (London: Pimlico, 1994), 21.

9. Joe Orton, *Up Against It, a screenplay for the Beatles* (London: Eyre Methuen, 1979), 7.

10. There is more prescience embedded in this than in all the "raised hand above McCartney's head" clues, which misrepresent the gesture as a Hindu symbol of death. The raised right hand is in actual fact a gesture meaning "fear-not" (abhaya-mudrā) and bestows protection.

11. Cited in Miles, 15.

12. A concise guide to other Beatles submyths can be found at www.getback.org/bmyths.html.

13. Lawrence Sutin, *Divine Invasions, A Life of Philip K. Dick* (New York: HarperCollins, 1994), 53.

PAPAL CONVEYANCE

DAVID KEREKES

AS CELEBRITIES GO, THEY DON'T GET MUCH MORE FAMOUS than the head of the Roman Catholic Church. Indeed, the pope is so great a figure of universal worship and love that the British comedy film *The Pope Must Die* had to have its title changed to *The Pope Must Diet* for its U.S. release for fear of causing offense to a huge Roman Catholic community.[1] Or, at least, more offense than insinuating that the pope was overweight.

The current pope, John Paul II—born Karol Wojtyla—grew up in a pious family in Poland, was religious as a child, and joined the priesthood despite the difficulties he encountered doing so under Polish communism. He later became a bishop at a very young age (thirty-eight) and was the first non-Italian to accept the papal role in over four hundred years. For a pope, he has always been unusually gregarious. His desire to travel around the world, meeting and speaking to his beloved flock, has changed the rules of normal papal engagement. The first "touring pope," John Paul II has visited well over one hundred countries and every continent except for Antarctica.

To travel, John Paul II needed transport. As a young priest, all his traveling had been done on foot, trudging from one parishioner's home to the next. Later he got hold of a bicycle, and when he became a bishop, he was driven around in an ancient chauffeured car. A workaholic who hated wasting time, Wojtyla had a table and light fitted into the car so he could carry on with his work while traveling.[2] As pope, however, in order to "travel the pathways of the world,"[3] he was driven around in a white Jeep, now commonly known as the Popemobile, in which he took his place on a raised seat and spoke to the masses. Described as "an open vehicle resembling a racing hot rod with an elevated roll cage that the Pope could hang on to while standing,"[4] the wonderful Popemobile was far removed from the more traditional, somber papal conveyance of limousines, and immediately helped to galvanize the public image of John Paul II.

Western culture does not connect the godly very naturally with automobiles and is more comfortable with the humble English archetype of a bicycle-riding vicar—tea-drinking and buck-toothed.[5] Nuns and priests at the wheel are considered suitable only as characters for jokes (the nun arrested on suspicion of drunk driving appears in the punch line of numerous comedy sketches). Similarly, to most people, the Popemobile will always seem a little ridiculous, partly because of the way it looks and partly because it marries these elements of godliness and vehicular transportation that Western society is so unsure about. It is certainly bereft of the nobility and elegance of transport typically befitting a pope. An earlier conveyance for the current pope, for example, was a 1966 Mercedes-Benz convertible limousine, customized with white leather and mobile phones, the delivery of which prompted His Holiness to remark "Finally, a new car!"[6]

The "papal conveyance" also sets the current pope apart from his predecessors and affords him a kind of movie or rock star sensibility.[7] John Paul II would not attract the countless millions who regularly flock to see him "live" if not for the terrible curiosity and peculiar reverence people feel toward this public man and his public presence. He also conveys a certain "credibility," evidenced recently in his refusal to be photographed wearing a pair of fancy sunglasses offered to him (for "world peace") by the singer of a successful Irish pop band, but he had no qualms about donning a cowboy hat of his own volition for a ride on a motorcade through Mexico some years earlier.[8] The Popemobile is symbolic, then, in that it represents the vehicle by which a man of the people can get closer to those people. And yet, at the same time, this proximity places him in tremendous potential danger. Indeed, in 1981 the Popemobile was at the center of a major accident—not a wreck, or a pileup, or a head-on collision, but an assassination attempt.

The pope had recently returned from a visit to Turkey, where he was discussing the historical links between Islam and Christianity. Evidently unimpressed, one young Turkish Muslim by the name of Mehmet Ali Agca told the press of his intention "to murder this 'Christian crusader.'" Until the bullets started to fly, however, nobody took Agca's threat seriously⁹—despite the fact that only a few months before John Paul II's visit, Agca had assassinated a "prominent Istanbul newspaper editor" whose campaigns for a modern, westernized Islam conflicted with the young man's nationalist political views.¹⁰

It happened on Wednesday, May 13, 1981, in a crowded St. Peter's Square, Vatican City. At 5:19 P.M., as the Popemobile moved slowly through the crowd, and the pope was talking and blessing, two gunshots suddenly rang out. Wojtyla collapsed with blood seeping through his robes from wounds in his stomach and on his arm. Close by was Mehmet Ali Agca clutching a gun. Following the shots, and hanging on to Agca, was a small nun by the name of Sister Letizia, who diligently prevented the would-be assassin from escaping the approaching guards. Contrary to Agca's protestations, Sister Letizia repeated at the top of her voice, "Yes, you! It was you!"¹¹ Following two operations, the pope recovered. When he returned on August 26 to his regular Wednesday audiences, he supposedly opened in good humor and with the statement, "When I was so rudely interrupted. . . ."¹²

This attempted assassination was not John Paul II's first brush with automobile-related trouble. During the German occupation of Poland, the young Wojtyla was hospitalized on two separate occasions—once after an accident with a streetcar and once after an incident with a German army truck in February 1944. Apparently, the German truck struck him from behind as he was walking home after a double shift in a factory. The truck didn't stop; it just drove off into the night. The future pope awoke in a hospital bed, his head in a bandage and a cast on his arm, and he remained there for three weeks.¹³ Many years later Marvel Comics would publish a one-shot comic title devoted to the enigmatic leader of the Catholic church—*The Life of Pope John Paul II*, dynamically subtitled *The Entire Story! From his childhood in Poland to the assassination attempt.* In the comic, Wojtyla's run-in with the German truck is depicted as an act of cold-bloodedness by the German officers, who shout at the stricken pedestrian "Off the road, pig" and "Hey, it's *only* a Pole! Too many of them as it is."[14]

The assassination attempt on Pope John Paul II echoes other more successful vehicular assassinations, the best known, of course, being the murder of John F. Kennedy, who was shot by rifle fire in 1963. Almost as high profile was the murder of Archduke Franz Ferdinand and his wife, shot in a car in Sarajevo in 1914. This incident—as anyone who has ever studied twentieth-century history will know—is cited as one of the prime causes of World War I. Others famous personages murdered in their vehicles include Rafael Trujillo Monina, dictator of the Dominican Republic, who was machine-gunned to death in his limousine in 1959. Several British members of Parliament and spokespeople have been blown up in their cars by IRA bombs and landmines. These include Christopher Ewart Biggs, the British ambassador to the Republic of Ireland; Airey Neave, Tory MP and spokesperson for Northern Ireland; and Ian Gow, also a Tory MP, who was killed by an IRA car bomb in 1990.[15]

One of the many important similarities between the killing of John F. Kennedy and the attempted assassination of John Paul II is the fact that both are widely thought to have been the result of conspiracies rather than being the work of a lone gunman. In both cases, moreover, the Vatican has been named as the source of the conspiracy. Whether Agca's assassination attempt on John Paul II had anything to do with insiders or not, there was certainly a shift in the balance of power at the Vatican during the four months that the pope spent recovering.[16] It has also been claimed there was a Vatican-based plot to kill the pope during his visit to Manila in 1995[17]; others believe that such rumors of sinister goings-on in the Vatican are regularly concocted by the KGB.[18]

Moving further into the realm of the speculative and metaphysical, recent links between the pope's attempted assassination and the shrine at Fatima have come to light. On May 13, 1917, and over a period of several months, three shepherd children in Fatima, Portugal, claimed that they had seen the Virgin Mary, who bestowed upon them three prophesies. Despite the precise wording remaining a closely guarded secret, the

Vatican has long since made public the essence of the First and Second Secrets ("a harrowing vision of hell" interpreted as a prediction of the end of World War I and the outbreak of World War II). The Third Secret of Fatima—a "deadline of doom" said to have caused Pope John XXIII to tremble with fear and almost faint with horror—was only revealed on May 13, 2000, to mark the end of the millennium.

Five days before his eightieth birthday, Pope John Paul II announced that the gist of the Third Secret of Fatima was a prediction of his own assassination attempt. The pope attributed his survival of the assassination—which took place on the anniversary of the children's first vision—to the intercession of Our Lady of Fatima. Wojtyla claims to have seen a poster of Our Lady in the crowd as he was being shot and believes that the Third Secret's reference to a Holy Father dressed in white, passing through a big city, and being killed by soldiers firing bullets and arrows, does in fact relate to him. That a pope should give credence to a private revelation is not without precedent, but commentators have noted that "a Pope who recognises himself in a private revelation is something really unusual."[19] The nature of the Third Secret had hitherto caused much consternation, leading some to speculate that it heralded Armageddon or the collapse of the church. In 1980 a former priest had made an attempt on the life of John Paul II in Fatima, and the following year a former Trappist monk had hijacked a plane, demanding that the Vatican make public the Third Secret.[20]

With the exception of John F. Kennedy, others who have been killed or have had attempts made on their lives while "behind the wheel" have not attracted the same kind of public attention as Agca's attack on the pope. Frequently, as seems to have been the case with the IRA-related killings, the fact that the assassination occurs while the victim is in a moving vehicle has less to do with public attention than with mere pragmatics—it's easy to hide bombs under cars. For a more ostentatious gesture, however, there is nothing more shocking than to see someone in the full glare of media publicity suddenly collapse because of the actions of one person in the crowd of alleged supporters. If the function of the papal conveyance is to bring His Holiness to the people, then it seems appropriate that this "mutated racing hot rod" should be the location of an assassination attempt by a frustrated member of the multitude.

Public visibility reinforces the performance, makes it real, makes it "legitimate." By its very nature, the assassination is a public act. The same cannot be said for the observance of Catholic worship. John Paul II's need to be conveyed amid his adoring millions could be interpreted as an unseemly interest in the trappings of modernity on the part of a pope who likes to travel and "make show" like none before him, perhaps representing a serious weakness in the Catholic church itself. Agca's bullet, had it hit home, could well have been a consecration, a "crash" whose impact would transcend not only time and place but also belief.

NOTES

With thanks to Sun Paige and Mikita Brottman.

1. *The Pope Must Die,* dir. Peter Richardson (1991), starring Robbie Coltrane.
2. See Joan Collins, *His Holiness Pope John Paul II* (Loughborough: Ladybird, 1982).
3. Ibid., 23.
4. Jonathan Kwitny, *Man of the Century: The Life and Times of Pope John Paul II* (London: Little, Brown, 1997), 51.
5. Pope John Paul I had to make an important trip during a time of gasoline shortage. He could have used his position for a special dispensation but instead chose to travel by train and borrow a bicycle, which he rode while wearing his scarlet papal robes.
6. See *Imperial Web Pages,* www.imperialclub.com/Varieties/Special/Celebrities/popemobile/index.htm (webpage discontinued).
7. As a young man Karol Wojtyla trained as an actor, and as pope in 1995 was said to have completed a screenplay for *Brother of Our God,* a film about a man who becomes a saint.
8. See Collins.
9. Peter Hebblethwaite, *In the Vatican* (London: Sidgwick & Jackson, 1986).
10. See Kwitny.
11. See Claire Sterling, *The Time of the Assassins* (London: Angus & Robertson, 1984). As an aside, the word "assassin" is also of Muslim origin. The *Hutchinson Encyclopedia* (Oxford: Helicon, 1995) describes it as "murder, usually of a political, royal or public person. The term derives from a sect of Muslim fanatics in the 11th and 12th centuries known as *hashshashin* ("takers of hashish"). They were reputed to either smoke cannabis before they went out to murder, or to receive hashish as payment.
12. See Collins.
13. See Kwitny.
14. *The Life of Pope John Paul II: The Entire Story! From his childhood in Poland to the assassination attempt.* Single issue. Marvel Comics, 1983.
15. *Hutchinson Encyclopedia* (Oxford: Helicon, 1995).

16. See Robert Hutchison, *Their Kingdom Come: Inside the Secret World of Opus Dei* (London: Corgi, 1997).
17. See ibid.
18. John Cornwell, *A Thief in the Night: The Death of Pope John Paul I* (London: Viking, 1989).
19. Cited in the *Daily Express* (London), June 27, 2000.
20. "Third Secret of Fatima Revealed," *Fortean Times,* no. 136, July 2000.

SS-100-X

PAMELA MCELWAIN-BROWN

LONG BEFORE THE PUBLIC WAS ALLOWED TO VIEW the Zapruder film, I sat expectantly in the front row of a tiny movie theater on the Lower East Side of Manhattan, impatiently watching the black-and-white David Wolper film of the Kennedy assassination called *1000 Days*. At its end, there was silence and a blank screen, and then the clear, color Zapruder film began. The first thing I noticed was the elegant midnight-blue Lincoln Continental limousine, with its stylish chrome grille, the red parade lights blinking and the presidential and American flags flapping in the wind. Then I saw the president, hand raised, smiling, tanned and relaxed. In the seconds that followed, I saw the president grab at his throat as the first shot hit, then turn to his wife, voiceless, motionless, for what seemed an eternity, and then I saw the president's body thrown back, debris flying up and backward from the fatal head shot.

Although I had seen the few stills *LIFE* had published,[1] I was unprepared for seeing the entire film on a movie screen. At the center of the transition from life to death of the most famous man on earth was this extraordinary vehicle, which, rather than protecting him, had held him captive. I had nightmares for months. I felt as though I'd been there. I still do. And so began my personal odyssey to try to solve the murder and the start of my ongoing obsession with SS-100-X—the presidential limousine.

What did President Kennedy think about the car he was riding in—the car that was designed for him and Jackie by the Ford Motor Company and Hess & Eisenhardt, custom automobile builders of Cincinnati, Ohio; the car that had been their transportation in so many motorcades in the United States and in Europe and in South America? Did JFK care about cars? Did Jackie? Or were they basically oblivious to the vehicles supplied to transport them? Did President Kennedy, with his keen Irish intuition, have any idea of the importance this car would play in his last moments? The rebuilt Kennedy Limousine, now on display at the Henry Ford museum in Dearborn, Michigan, attracts the most attention of any vehicle there. Visitors are drawn to it, stand beside it, gaze at it, and ask questions about it—they seem to sense that in some way this vehicle is a tangible connection to the assassination. They seem to sense that the presidential limousine is indeed a car of mystery and a car of destiny.

Is it possible to look at the assassination from the perspective of the car? Can we consider the assassination of President Kennedy as a car crash? How about a downhill motor race? Writer J. G. Ballard did both. Fascinated both by the assassination and the vehicle, Ballard called the assassination "a special kind of car crash."[2] Ballard's name must be included in the list of those puzzled and perhaps obsessed by the assassination, and especially the part played by the car. How is it that such a terrible event—where one person is killed and another almost killed—could take place in a moving vehicle that escapes unscathed? Why did the government treat the car as if it had experienced a mild fender-bender, readying it for the road and shipping it back to Ford as quickly as possible, to be stripped and rebuilt? Could this paradox contain the ultimate enigma of the JFK assassination? Could the story of the car give us clear evidence of the conspiracy and cover-up that took place? Let's place this specially built presidential limousine at the center of our focus and see if we can find answers to some of these questions.

Looking back, we can see portents of the events that occurred on November 22, 1963. These portents are not as cataclysmic, perhaps, as those depicted in Shakespeare's version of the murder of Julius Caesar—no animal entrails lacking a heart—but the exhilarating anticipation of the successful trip to Dallas was mixed with glimpses of the oncoming horror. First, a full-page ad in the *Dallas Morning News* "welcoming"

President Kennedy to Dallas with questions about his lack of support for oil barons elicited the response that "we're really in nut country now." A flyer, which he did not see, accused the president of treason. Just before the assassination, JFK reputedly stated—as he had done earlier—that anyone "perched above the crowd" could easily kill him with a rifle aimed from a tall building.[3]

There was thunder, rain, and lightening early in the day. Psychic Jeanne Dixon, who had been burdened for some time, saw a "shroud" hanging above the White House when she drove by, and contacted a radio station in alarm.[4] And everything that day seemed to be running late. Jackie was late getting ready for breakfast at the Texas Hotel in Fort Worth. Once *Air Force One* had flown the couple the short hop to Love Field in Dallas, the Kennedys were late getting into the presidential limousine because they took so much time shaking hands with people squeezed along the fence. And though the motorcade had gained a minute or two as it passed through downtown Dallas, the Kennedys were still going to be about five minutes late for their lunch at the Trade Mart. In addition, although there were enough yellow roses—the state flower—for Mrs. Connally, wife of the Texas governor, Jackie was presented with a bouquet of red ones. Was this a symbol that the Kennedys did not "fit" in Texas, though the Connallys did? A nosegay of pale lavender asters was also given to Jackie as the walked along the fence with her husband, shaking hands with well-wishers.

It's a windy, surprisingly warm late-November noon. There's a sense of anticipation as the sparse crowd begins to form into lines on Houston Street and around the corner onto Elm, and a sense of accomplishment in the motorcade, which has wound its way from Love Field, through the streets of Dallas, to this capless, pyramid-shape memorial called Dealey Plaza.

"You can't say Dallas doesn't love you today," comments Nellie Connally to President Kennedy.[5] The president and his wife wave to the crowds—Jackie to the left, JFK to the right, so the experience of seeing these two stunning people together would not be too overwhelming for the citizens. Nellie looks toward the Triple Underpass where Elm, Main, and Commerce streets momentarily converge, thinking that it would be cool for a moment in the tunnel under the railroad tracks. Jackie wonders again why she's chosen the shocking pink wool Chanel suit and matching pillbox hat for a day that has become so warm. The president, to her right, is waving, and she can hear him whispering "thank you, thank you" to the crowds who've come to cheer them through Dallas. Tanned, eyes the color of cornflowers, the wide grin—the most recognizable man on earth raises his arm. Gold from a cuff link glints in the sun.

The right tire of the 8,000-pound presidential limousine scrapes the curb in front of the Texas School Book Depository as the limousine turns from Houston on to Elm. The 180-degree dogleg turn is more than even the limousine can handle, observes Bill Greer, driver of the car. Who in the Secret Service had approved of this turn? Greer is simply following the lead car—he's never driven this route before. The other Secret Service agent, Roy Kellerman, is in charge of this trip; it's his first time in the spot, and he warily checks the crowds, not even noticing the turn.

Suddenly a sound, like a firecracker, pierces the air, and a small funnel of sand spurts up next to the curb. The president listens, arm frozen at the start of a wave. He has sensed—if not heard—the shot. The Secret Service men start to look around, and look to their right. So does the president. Jackie turns as well.

The car is almost completely open that day; the Plexiglas roof is in the trunk and can't give them any protection. Secret Service (SS) car 100-X inches into the descent down Elm Street. The cab area of the extended limo isolates the passengers in back from the front section, where Greer and Kellerman sit. It was Kennedy friend and advisor Ken O'Donnell who'd given the final order regarding the configuration of 100-X that day. "If the weather is clear and it's not raining," he said, "have that bubble top off."[6]

The president continues to stare to his right, as if trying to focus on something. His arm jerks upward and he gasps in surprise as a bullet tears into his throat. He raises his arms slowly and struggles to turn toward his wife. He can't speak.

Hearing a shot, Connally turns to his right, then back toward his wife, Nellie; a bullet rips through his back and into his lung. "My God, they're going to kill us all!" he cries. Nellie instinctively grabs him as he starts to fall into her lap. Another shot hits the president in the back—the first decoy shot from a sharpshooter using the faulty Mannlicher-

Carcano carbine in the sixth floor of the Texas School Book Depository at the corner of Elm and Houston. Yet another shot hits Connally in the wrist and slams into his thigh. Connally lies back in his wife's arms, and she looks helplessly at the growing pool of blood on his white shirt.

Jackie looks around, surprised and bewildered, and places her hands on her husband's left arm, hoping to draw him down into safety. She pulls her face toward his; she can't see into his eyes; he can't speak. The driver, Greer, turns to stare at the president and the car slows almost to a stop.

In an instant, white, gray, and crimson matter sprays upward and backward, all over the car, from the windshield to the trunk, as the right side of the president's head explodes. Did something fly backward? Did a shot come from the front? With an animal energy, Jackie pushes herself on to the trunk of the car. Another shot smashes into the curb of Main Street next to the Triple Underpass. Bits of cement fly into the cheek of a bystander, James Tague, and onto the limousine.

Lee Harvey Oswald, after taking a look at the motorcade from the front door of the Texas School Book Depository, ambles casually into the lunchroom to buy a bottle of Coke. He's waiting for a telephone call that never comes.

The brake lights blink red again as the presidential limousine slows for a second time. Clint Hill, his calf bruised from the bumper of the Secret Service car driving behind—a 1956 Cadillac affectionately called the Queen Mary II—grabs on to a handle and pulls himself on to the trunk. He wants Jackie to stay in the car. She turns and slides back on to the seat, her knees landing in the growing pool of blood under the president's head. Blood and debris, staining her suit and stockings, drip down the backseat and on to the carpet, mixing with the bouquets of red and yellow roses now lying on the floor. She pulls her husband's head into her lap, mumbling "They've killed him, oh, Jack, Jack."

"Move out, we've been hit!" Kellerman shouts to Greer. The car suddenly roars into life. In a second or two the 350-horsepower V-8 engine of SS-100-X easily overtakes the lead car as it exits the Triple Underpass.

Moans and muffled sobs now fill the back of the car. Connally, losing consciousness, can no longer call out.

"Help, please, they've killed him," Jackie calls to Kellerman, but he can't hear her—not because the privacy window is up,[7] but because he's speaking into a microphone. There's just too much space between them, and with the sirens of the follow-up and the lead car wailing, SS-100-X races down Stemmons Freeway, its passengers huddled helplessly in the back. Clint Hill manages a precarious hold, lying across the trunk; he tries not to look down at Jackie and her husband, but he can't help it. He notices a piece of skull on the carpet.

"He's dead, he's dead," he thinks. "It should have been me, not him." He pounds his free hand against the car's trunk. Jackie is safe, but the Secret Service, whose job it is to protect the president, have lost their man.

The presidential limousine turns into the emergency entrance of Parkland Hospital and screeches to a halt. For a moment, no one in front of the hospital moves. The hushed and awed stillness is testament to the dreadful honor of their being the first to look at the car's passengers in their abattoir. The onlookers and Dallas Police Department motorcycle officers, who moments before had proudly escorted the limousine, stare silently at the scene. Then, in a flurry of activity, two gurneys are rolled out of the hospital. A Secret Service agent opens the suicide doors of SS-100-X on the passenger side. Orderlies hold Connally by the arms; he bravely tries to stand, but they insist on carrying him, and place him carefully on a stretcher. Kellerman folds down the jump seat to provide access to the president.

"Get up!" Agent Emory Roberts yells to Jackie, but she doesn't move. Hill leans into the car; Jackie stares up at him.

"Let us be. You know he's dead," she whispers to her agent and friend, tears mixing with blood in rivulets on her cheek. She looks up at him helplessly.

"We must take him to a doctor," Hill whispers, and as her chin starts to quiver, he quickly removes his jacket and places it over the president's head. Only then does she let him go. She follows them into the emergency area, fearful yet with stubborn courage, looking like a forlorn and abandoned child.

While Greer and Kellerman race indoors with the president and Governor Connally, Kinney and Hickey climb quickly from the Queen Mary II and walk over to SS-100-X. The car is in full view of the bystanders.

"We've got to get the top up," Kinney yells at Hickey. "There's blood everywhere. We need a bucket of water."

Quickly, an orderly runs back into the hospital to find one.

"Get these people away from the cars!" Hickey yells to the nearest DPD officer. A perimeter is rapidly formed. As other officers join in, a young man, starting to film the scene, suddenly has his camera ripped away from him, the film tossed carelessly onto the ground.

But there are other curious citizens observing the presidential limousine, and whether cued by a rumor initiated by the Secret Service or by their own observation, one by one they start to point to the windshield. Dallas Police Department motorcycle officer Stavis Ellis, who had ridden ahead of 100-X through Dallas, notices a hole on the driver's side of the windshield.[8] So does his partner, Freeman. *St. Louis Post Dispatch* reporter Richard Dudman notices a hole high in the windshield.[9] And nursing student Evangelea Glanges notices a hole as well, just prior to the limousine being driven away.[10] Although each witness recalls a slightly different location, each recollects a similar description of what they saw—a round hole, small enough for you to put your finger through. Later that day another witness, United States Park Police motorcycle officer Nick Prencipe—a late emerger to the research community—will corroborate this description of a hole in the windshield.

The Secret Service could have called for a tarp to cover the car at Parkland Hospital, or asked for portable room dividers, or requested a flatbed truck to take it from the hospital to wherever the Dallas Police Department (DPD) forensic unit wanted to run tests on it. There was a discussion between Special Agent Emory Roberts—who took control of the agents, since Kellerman had gone inside with the president—and Agent Lem Jones about what the DPD's intentions were. However, Agent Sam Kinney requested permission from Kellerman to put the car's top up, and received it. Soon he and Agent George W. Hickey, with the help of the mysterious bucket of water, had the plastic roof and leatherette cover installed on the car, blocking public's view.[11]

A few minutes after 1:00 P.M., even before President Kennedy has been declared dead, Agent Hickey, driving SS-100-X, and Kinney, driving SS-679-X—the follow-up car—are escorted by DPD officers back to Love Field, where they are sequestered on the C-130 for transport back to Washington, D.C. The plane does not leave until 3:30 P.M., about half an hour after *Air Force One*. Interviews with Kinney and communication with a member of the crew of the C-130 indicate that the agents first began examining 100-X when it was on the ground. A piece of skull, first spotted by Clint Hill when he lay prone over the back of 100-X on its way to Parkland, was also noted by Kinney. Why did the Secret Service rush to sift through the gore in the backseat? What were they looking for? What were they afraid of?

The Secret Service, which had been in charge of SS-100-X from the moment it arrived at Love Field the previous day, had now managed to escape the tentacles of the Dallas Police Department, who would soon realize that 100-X was evidence in the state of Texas. By the time the DPD had sent a forensic unit to examine and perhaps impound the vehicle, SS-100-X was in the air.[12] And, in time, the Secret Service had turned everything to its advantage; they had absconded with the limousine and with the President's body as well.[13] In addition, if there had been a bullet strike to the windshield that didn't fit into the agreed-on agenda, as some would later argue, there's reason to believe the Secret Service would have had time to have the windshield repaired before leaving Love Field, had they so desired.

With this sequence of events, the fate of SS-100-X was forever thrust into the mystery and myth of American culture.

MOTORCADE FROM ANDREWS AIR FORCE BASE TO THE WHITE HOUSE GARAGE

The C-130 carrying SS-100-X and SS-679-X landed at Andrews Air Force Base at 8:00 P.M. EST. The cars were offloaded, and an escort was provided by motorcycle officers of the D.C. Police and the U.S. Park Police (USPP).[14] The USPP officers were in radio contact with a colleague stationed outside the White House. Although it was dark and there was a light mist, the officers could not take their eyes off the presidential limousine. This was the car in which the president had been killed. In the dark, the blood and debris were hardly visible. Special Agent Kinney, accompanied by Protective Research Section Agent Charles Taylor, drove SS-100-X and Agent Hickey drove SS-679-X. They arrived at the White House Garage at 22nd and M streets NW an hour later. At that point, they turned the presidential limousine over to Agent Morgan I. Gies, who was in charge of the White House Garage cars. Gies ordered that the car be covered and guarded. However, at this point, the Secret Service may have done another informal examination of the car. Two policemen and a Secret Service agent were assigned to guard the vehicles, and a log was instituted to track those entering the White House Garage who did not have credentials.

THE WHITE HOUSE GARAGE AND A NEW WITNESS—NICK PRENCIPE

USPP Motorcycle Officer Nick Prencipe states that he drove to the White House Garage during the evening after having a conversation with the driver, Bill Greer, at the West Executive entrance to the White House, where Nick was stationed on November 22, 1963, in charge of assigning escorts to different groups of people during a very busy evening. It looked to Nick as if there were cocktail parties going on in the hulking Executive Office Building across the street; in fact, LBJ's people were gathering there, trying to decide if their meetings with the new president would take place there or at the White House. According to Nick, Greer was quite distressed that evening. "We really missed you guys today," he said, mentioning one of the Dallas Police Department Motorcycle Officers who wouldn't speed up. In this discussion, Greer stated that there were "shots coming from every direction," adding that "one of them came right through the windshield."[15]

Nick states that he walked into the White House Garage that evening without being questioned, although he didn't recognize anyone there. He stated he didn't see any army presence or any guards around the car.[16] The limo was not in a bay along the side of the Garage but was sitting in the center. Nick says he is familiar with both SS-100-X and SS-679-X, the follow-up car, and is certain the car he saw was the presidential limousine.[17] The roof of the vehicle was up, and a tarp covered the windows. Nick states that he walked over and lifted the tarp. He noticed a hole in the windshield, low on the passenger side. He saw no damage near the rearview mirror.[18] How shall we weigh this report? Will it be substantiated or contradicted by the statements of two men who had reason to be with SS-100-X that night—the FBI agent who was in charge of the forensic exam and a witness from the Ford Motor Company?

Analyzing the existing documentation of that evening, it appears that, if Nick's recollections are accurate, he was in the Garage prior to the exams that later took place on the vehicle around 9:00 P.M. Also at around that time, the roof was removed, and the second informal examination of the limousine began. This exam was conducted by Secret Service Deputy Chief Paterni and Sam Kinney. Two bullet fragments were recovered and quickly turned over to the FBI. They were later determined to be of composition consistent with the nearly complete bullet[19] found at Parkland Hospital. Some claim, however, that all this evidence was planted by the Secret Service. The bullet fragments are conveniently small—just enough to tie damage to the president to the rifle found in the Texas School Book Depository. This is evidence upon which the Warren Commission bases the ballistic part of their conclusions.

At 10:00 P.M., according to Secret Service Chief James J. Rowley, the "plastic cover" was removed from the limousine. At that time, a three-inch section of skull was apparently removed from the car, along with a "quantity of brain tissue." Secret Service Deputy Chief Paul Paterni found a bullet fragment in the front seat, and Agent Mills found a fragment on the right front floor.[20] The Secret Service took no notes of their examinations, drew no diagrams, and took no photographs of the car at this time. (Why not?) However, at sometime before 1:00 A.M., Deputy Chief Paterni arranged for FBI agents to examine the limousine for evidence.

NOVEMBER 23, 1963—THE FBI EXAMINATION OF THE PRESIDENTIAL LIMOUSINE

FBI Agent Robert Frazier, a ballistics expert to whom all the bullet fragments had been presented earlier in the FBI lab, logged into the Garage at 1:00 A.M. along with Secret Service/FBI liaison Orrin Bartlett, who drove SS-100-X out from its bay. During the FBI exam, notes were made, diagrams were drawn, and photographs were taken.[21] At that time, the FBI pulled up the back carpeting and pulled out the backseat,

16.1   An FBI photograph of SS-100-X, taken during their forensic exam, November 23, 1963. © National Archives and Records Administration

looking for fragments. They found only three, under a jump seat,[22] and they also scraped the metallic residue off the inside surface of the windshield.[23] In addition, they noted damage to the chrome frame over the rearview mirror. Interestingly, Willard Hess, of automobile builders Hess & Eisenhardt, stated that his mechanics noticed the dent in the chrome molding when the limousine was delivered to them sometime in December for rebuild, and their impression was that this dent had come from the sort of mallet used in replacing a windshield. Mr. Hess was unaware that the photo that became CE 349 was taken during the FBI exam and that the windshield would have had to be made prior the assassination.[24]

The Secret Service had just created a second window of opportunity—of nearly two hours—between the recovery of the piece of bone and the FBI exam, in which they could have altered the car's condition to suit their needs, including having the windshield replaced. Ironically, the Secret Service was said to have ordered a number of windshields from the

Ford Motor Company for some sort of "target practice" prior to the assassination. One of those, with an acceptable defect, could easily have been used to replace the windshield of the presidential limousine.

Robert Frazier decided that the dent in the chrome molding had come from a bullet fragment. He also observed that there was debris all over the car, including the windshield and the visors.[25] FBI photos now show that there was mud on the tires; this could have come from the drive back from Andrews Air Force Base to the White House Garage. In the FBI's photographs, it is evident that the bouquets of roses are no longer in the car, although petals are scattered over the backseat and floor; the small, limp bouquet of asters is still there, however.[26] The seat and carpet below it are covered with blood that extends even to the metal doorframe on the passenger side. (See the FBI photograph.) Despite poor lighting and lack of color, these black-and-white photographs still show how devastating the murder was. And there was another witness to the FBI exam—one who stayed with the car day and night during the next few days—a man from the Ford Motor Company.

THE MOST SIGNIFICANT LIMOUSINE WITNESS TO EMERGE YET— FORD MOTOR COMPANY EMPLOYEE VAUGHN FERGUSON

Ford Motor Company liaison to the White House Garage, Vaughn Ferguson, was responsible for SS-100-X and was first called to the White House Garage immediately after the assassination. Mr. Ferguson was allowed to observe the FBI exam. He comments that the FBI agents "had ripped the leather seats and dismantled parts of the car."[27] Although he had been instructed to put the car into driving condition, he was not allowed to touch it. On Saturday morning, the limousine was still under guard, covered with a "canvas" tarp. At that point Ferguson was only allowed to look at the windshield, as the rest of the car remained covered. He acknowledged that there was damage to the windshield, and found "no perforation, but substantial cracks radiating a couple of inches from the center of the windshield to [starting from] a point directly beneath the mirror." At this time, Agent Morgan Geis asked him to make arrangements to have the windshield replaced.[28] Ferguson, however, did nothing about the windshield replacement at this time. The Ferguson memo, taken in context with other documentation, provides new insight into the mystery surrounding the presidential limousine.

Calling Ferguson into the White House Garage brings into focus the final aspect of the Secret Service agenda—to get SS-100-X ready for the road. Who made this decision? Ferguson believed it was made because President Johnson might want to use the car during Kennedy's funeral.[29] Chief Rowley later claims that Geis made this decision on his own initiative, but that was not likely. How high up would this decision have to be made? Would it have to be made by Robert McNamara, the secretary of defense? Or by LBJ? The car should have been made available for any future reenactments of the assassination that might take place. In fact, as it turned out, the follow-up car, which had been sequestered with SS-100-X but of which no photographs were ever taken, was used in the reenactment.

The Protective Research Section (PRS) of the Secret Service was typically involved in checking on suspects in a city the president was about to visit, looking for those who might present a threat. However, in this case, Mssrs. Fox and Norton of the PRS arrived at the White House Garage at 4:00 P.M. on November 23 for the purpose of photographing SS-100-X. Their color photographs, although taken over twenty-four hours after the assassination, were horrific, even though most of the debris had dried up and much of the blood had soaked into the carpet.

Immediately after the PRS photographed SS-100-X, Agents Geis and Bouck asked Deputy Chief Paterni that the car be cleaned out, as the stench had become unbearable. The FBI quickly granted clearance to do this. At this point, the torn pieces of paper, petals, and other miscellaneous debris were removed from the floor of the limousine and taken to the Secret Service's Washington Field Office. At that point, it appears that the special detail for the limousine and follow-up car was discontinued.[30]

Whatever agenda the Secret Service had for SS-100-X had been completed, with two points of exception. Vaughn Ferguson was unable to remove the stains from the backseat rug with baking soda and water, so he had to order new carpeting from Hess & Eisenhardt, and wait for it to arrive, to be fitted into its frame. Also, the windshield needed to be replaced. This was done on November 26, by Bill Ashby and Bert Marlow from the Arlington Glass Company, who pushed the windshield out with their feet, creating significant spider cracking.[31] Mr. Ferguson's confusion regarding the exact date may well have been as a result of his working the car day and night throughout Saturday, Sunday, and Monday.[32] The windshield was then taken by the Secret Service and used as evidence in the Warren Commission, and also by the House Select Committee on Assassinations. It remains in the National Archives today.[33] There have been various theories about the windshield being switched one or many times. However, Robert Frazier insists that this windshield, which he later examined in the FBI lab, is the same one he photographed, examined, and measured on the night of November 23.[34]

According to the Ferguson memo, the new carpeting was installed in SS-100-X in early December. At this point, there is some conflict as to exactly when the limousine was moved out of Washington, D.C.[35] The conflict in dates probably arises out of the need to have the Warren Commission justify the removal of the car for its rebuild as a bulletproof vehicle. One way or another, during the month of December 1963, the presidential limousine was taken out of the scene as evidence in the assassination. It was then gutted completely and stripped down to metal at the Experimental Garage in the Ford Proving Grounds at Dearborn, Michigan.

Eventually, it was shipped to Hess & Eisenhardt, where it was rebuilt with water-white bulletproof glass that sandwiched polycarbonite vinyl between five layers of plate glass, and armored with titanium steel and even with bulletproof tires. A permanent top was added, a new hand-built high-compression engine was installed, a second air-conditioning unit was added, and communications devices were updated. The bulletproof glass was provided by Pittsburgh Plate Glass. This process is called the "D2" or "Quick Fix." It wasn't really that "quick," however, as SS-100-X wasn't returned to the White House Garage until June 11, 1964.[36] Of course, it was conveniently unavailable for the Warren Commission reenactment of the assassination, which took place in May. The follow-up car, SS-679-X, was used in its place. To the Warren Commission, apparently, all seven-passenger limousines looked the same.

THE LATEST LIMO RESEARCH

Newly released documents confirm that a privacy window was installed in SS-100-X upon its delivery to the White House Garage prior to the assassination, and that the window was removed three months later.[37] It has also been confirmed by FBI Special Agent and ballistics expert Robert Frazier that the group of black-and-white photographs of the limousine were taken during the FBI exam on November 23, 1963, and precede the Secret Service color photographs taken that afternoon.[38] The Vaughn Ferguson memo of December 18, 1963, describes in detail the activities that took place involving the presidential limousine from the day after the assassination until early December.[39] This document is substantiated by numerous other Secret Service reports and Hess & Eisenhardt and Ford Motor Company documents as well as by the statements of Willard Hess of Hess & Eisenhardt.[40]

LIMO MYTHS AND UNPROVEN THEORIES

Immediately after the assassination, rumors about the presidential limousine began to fly. This was understandable; it was proof of the fact that although the Warren Commission did everything within its power to convince people that Dealey Plaza was the crime scene, it was SS-100-X that held everyone's fascination and generated a great amount of mystery. Willard Hess told a number of people that SS-100-X was delivered to Hess & Eisenhardt just a few days after the assassination for rebuild. No one asked for additional information to substantiate this, and Hess never provided any. There is no substantiation for this statement, and yet it continues to circulate even today. Carl Renas said that he drove SS-100-X to Dearborn a few days after the assassination. However, he makes no mention of odor or debris, and does not take into account any of the photographs and statements that indicate the car was in the process of being cleaned by Mr. Ferguson and put into driving condition during that time.[41] This is another unsubstantiated story.

Since the limousine was the actual crime scene, and since the Secret Service did everything possible to hide this fact, we have to ask if some or all of these rumors were deliberately started by the Secret Service to create confusion. The purpose of these rumors seems to be to create the impression of physical damage to the car as well as to negate the value of the car as evidence, since it was supposedly sighted in so many different places soon after the assassination and in so many different conditions.

Another purpose for the rumors could have been to protect the fact that the Secret Service had an agenda for SS-100-X right from the start—to treat the car as nonevidentiary, to get it into driving condition as quickly as possible, and to get it out of town. Possible evidence of this is the fact that the National Archives sent me a copy of the Ferguson memo while it was still in "postponed" status and not available to the public. I posted it on my website and not long afterward was attacked furiously by another "researcher," who claimed that the document was forged and worthless. After inquiries to the National Archives and Record Administration (NARA) by a third researcher, the memo was formally released. It presents a considerable amount of detailed information about what happened to the presidential limousine after the assassination. Apparently this is information the government does not want us to know.

One wishful researcher has speculated that if witnesses saw "holes" in different locations on the windshield (top/bottom, passenger/driver side) they were all talking about the *same* hole. This hole-is-a-hole theory is also intended to bolster another speculation—that the throat shot was intentionally fired through the windshield from a storm drain on the south knoll, causing a "hole" a few inches to the right of the rearview mirror. (This theory has been disproved by aerial photographs of Dealey Plaza that show no such drain existed in 1963).[42] This is tied in with the existence of a lone mystery witness who claims to have watched a windshield on the presidential limousine being switched three days after the assassination at the Ford Motor Company River Rouge Complex Final Assembly building in Dearborn, Michigan. This "witness" also claims that the limousine was "stripped down to metal" at that time.[43] However, documents and photographs clearly indicate that this apocryphal event could not have taken place, since at that time SS-100-X was being readied for the road by Mr. Ferguson in the White House Garage. The information provided by this questionable witness is sketchy and contains numerous conflicts, and thus, fortunately, remains at the level of myth.

In addition, there has been ongoing controversy as to whether the windshield currently in storage in the National Archives is really the windshield that was in the presidential limousine during the assassination. Because different people reported a different quality to the surfaces of the windshield, and because there are large spider cracks on the removed windshield, it has been easy for a few researchers to claim that this indicates a windshield switch. However, there is another explanation. The documented time line that we now have of the limousine after the assassination increases the likelihood that this is, at least, the windshield in the limousine during the FBI exam and probably the windshield present during the assassination.

For one thing, Robert Frazier found dried blood and brain matter on the windshield[44]; anyone replacing it would have to have been bright enough to splatter it with debris. Second, the parade sticker "7" is present in all photos of SS-100-X taken in the White House Garage after the assassination, so those replacing it would have had to be smart enough to replace the sticker too.[45] Third, many people touched the windshield—most of them without any experience with safety glass. This not only removed evidence but actually altered the windshield. Finally, prior to the presentation of the Ferguson memo, there was no documentation regarding the windshield being pushed out by the feet of the Arlington Glass representatives, providing an explanation for the long spider cracks. So this myth can be attributed to researchers jumping to conclusions based on a lack of information or their unwillingness to take the time to analyze this information when it was present.

CONCLUSIONS

Today, we tend to see President Kennedy in a gentle light. He was, after all, a human being like each of us, with strengths and failings, with wife and children. His assassination in broad daylight only adds to his humanity. The limousine in which he died is a common denominator linking us to the president—a traumatic event involving an automobile is something that has affected most of us, at some time in our lives. In the JFK Exhibit in St. Petersburg, Florida, the replica of the presidential limousine sits in the middle of a room in which countless pictures of the president's visits are displayed, reminding us that all through his administration, he was connected to this car.

Those born after the assassination in particular may be unaware of what it was like when Kennedy was president. It is easy to be misled by the classically stylish clothes and hair, his razor wit and quick smile; in truth, however, this man was very outspoken and generated either enormous warmth or intense hostility. At the critical juncture in American history when he came into office, he had the power to see the world as we know it destroyed or see it come to peace. Kennedy was not a warrior like President Eisenhower, even though he was a decorated World War II veteran. He was a man of reason and a man of thought. During his administration he came to realize that war of any sort would inevitably effect us all and lessen the quality of our lives. He came to understand that "we all inhabit this same small planet, we all breathe the same air."[46]

This philosophy of diplomatically negotiated peace and understanding was very new in 1963. It was terrifying to many in the government. In addition, JFK's brother Bobby, attorney general during the Kennedy administration, waited in the wings—as did younger brother Teddy—to continue what could only become a dynasty. After the assassination, Bobby tried to stay within the system, hoping that, by becoming president himself, he might unlock the secrets of his brother's death. But this was not allowed to happen.

There were other specific areas of conflict too, such as JFK's desire to end American involvement in Vietnam, his attempts to negotiate with the Soviet Union, and personal issues for which Secret Service men were required to violate their oaths. President Kennedy also managed to outrage the South because of his views on civil rights. He offended the oil barons because he moved against the lucrative oil depletion allowance, the steel magnates because he tried to regulate the price of steel, and the pro-Israeli faction because he insisted on inspecting the Dimona nuclear "power" complex—which the Israelis insisted was merely for energy production, but which Kennedy correctly assessed to be the beginning of Israel's threat as a nuclear power.[47]

Throughout the Kennedy administration, however, one refrain kept returning, one problem that symbolized the issues of the early 1960s, and that was Cuba. When President Kennedy refused to permit air cover during the Bay of Pigs invasion, he lost the respect of the CIA. Many thousands of Cuban American soldiers were left stranded on the island and later killed or imprisoned. Kennedy subsequently fired both Allan Dulles, director of the CIA, and General Charles Cabell, indicating that they should bear responsibility for the failed invasion. Similarly, during the Cuban Missile Crisis, JFK insisted on a blockade rather than an invasion of Cuba, resulting again in further fury throughout CIA circles. The CIA never forgave Kennedy for betraying them by withholding critical support, and Kennedy threatened to break the CIA into "a thousand pieces."

Was President Kennedy killed as a result of a conspiracy? Could one person have committed the deed alone? What part did Lee Harvey Oswald play? The Warren Commission went to a great deal of trouble to begin and end with one thesis—that Oswald committed the crime alone. Lee Harvey Oswald was dead and unable to defend himself. Why would the government go to such lengths to violate the main axiom of the American legal system—that a person is innocent until proven guilty—unless it had something to hide?

Some conspiracy theorists believe Oswald was the Rosetta Stone of the assassination, perhaps because he had ties to the intelligence community; others believe he was a red herring. Perhaps he was what he said he was—"a patsy." Was there a cover-up after the assassination? Allegedly, Alan Dulles illegally denied the Warren Commission access to secret CIA files demonstrating repeated attempts to assassinate Cuban dictator Fidel Castro. That alone indicates a cover-up at a very high level. But this is only the tip of the iceberg.

Did the cover-up include the handling of the presidential limousine? Is it possible for a lone gunman, using a faulty Mannlicher-Carcano rifle, with its sight out of balance, to have murdered one person and nearly murdered a second without damaging the car? Is it not more likely that trained sharpshooters were instructed to shoot specifically at the president without damaging the vehicle, so it could not be used as evidence in the assassination? Secret Service Chief Rowley went to great lengths to minimize the small amount of damage that did occur—including making the claim that the dent in the chrome molding was made prior to the assassination. Why?

Was the Secret Service involved in this cover-up? Agents Kellerman and Roberts, at least, seemed to be cognizant of whatever actions were needed to keep the car out of the hands of the Dallas Police Department and to take charge of the evidence that it would produce. The FBI did not ask any questions about the state of the limousine, even though the Secret Service had control of it for twelve hours before inviting them in. By wearing blinders and doing only what they were asked to do, the FBI enabled the Secret Service agenda to succeed. The quick rebuild of the car is proof that it was vital to the success of the Warren Commission's agenda[48] that this vehicle be treated as an ordinary car rather than evidence in a crime scene, and that it not be used for their reenactment.

THE CONTINUING MYSTERY

Additional changes were made to SS-100-X after the "Quick Fix" immediately following the assassination. The "R2" fix involved updating the air-conditioning system, strengthening the rear deck lid with fiberglass to accommodate LBJ's jumping or sitting on it, removing all dents and repainting the vehicle from Kennedy's midnight blue to black. President Nixon used SS-100-X in his 1968 inaugural ceremony and on other occasions as well. The limousine was kept in service until the Carter administration. It was retired in 1977, but, out of respect to the Kennedy family, was not displayed until John Jr. turned twenty-one in 1983. And so President Kennedy's two archrivals—Nixon, whom he had narrowly beaten in 1960, and LBJ, who might have been replaced on the ticket in 1964—each had the opportunity to ride as president in the limousine in which Kennedy was killed.

We can only imagine what they were thinking.

Not long ago I had the opportunity to spend a week in the research room of the Henry Ford Museum in Dearborn, Michigan, where the presidential limousine is on display. During my first break from the hot, crowded room, I tore off my rubber gloves—issued to those examining photographs—and walked through the halls to the central area of the museum, where the limousine stands in the middle of the line of presidential Lincolns.

At first glance, there seems to be little resemblance to the configuration of the car as it was on November 22, 1963. It is completely covered; the permanent privacy window is visible from all angles. Still, the presence of this vehicle is remarkable. As time went on, I found myself returning to the car whenever I took a break, sitting on a bench next to it, photographing it, and talking to the people who were drawn to it—many unaware of its history until they read the plaque beside it. And they had so many questions. Why had the car been rebuilt? Had it really been used again? Shouldn't it have been preserved as evidence? I gradually became aware that the car had an undeniable presence to it. It was something quite different from the feeling I had experienced when I insisted on standing in the middle of Elm Street in Dallas, at the point where—the government tells us—the fatal shot hit.

Some of us cannot forget. We are condemned or blessed, depending on one's perspective, to continue the race that began in Dallas. It has partly become a race to find answers, as invisible forces continue to block our efforts, send in agent provocateurs to distract attention from the real issues, and attempt to discredit those who get too close to the truth. We also race against time, as witnesses continue to die—either mysteriously or through old age. We have no choice but to allow our lives to be defined by Kennedy's. It's the least we can do.

Although it has been rebuilt down to everything but the frame, a sense of awe and of dread surrounds the limousine in the museum. However much it may have changed, it still remains, for all time, the car in which President Kennedy took his last breath, in which he smiled and waved and thanked the citizens of Dallas.

Copy of F. Vaughn Ferguson's internal memo to Rod M. Marklel of the Ford
D.C. Office, December 18, 1963.

Ford Motor Company   WASHINGTON OFFICE

Intra-Company Communication   December 18, 1963

TO: R. W. Markley, Jr.

FROM: F. Vaughn Ferguson

RE: Changes in White House "Bubbletop"

On November 23rd, the day following the President's assassination, I went to the White House garage in response to a
telephone call to my home from the Secret Service. When I arrived about 10:00 A.M., the White House "Bubbletop" was in a
stall in the garage with two Secret Service men detailed to
guard it. A canvas cover was over the unit. I was permitted
only to see the windshield of the car and then only after the
guards had received permission from higher ranking Secret Service personnel. Examination of the windshield disclosed no
perforation, but substantial cracks radiating a couple of
inches from the center of the windshield at a point directly
beneath the mirror.

I was at the garage only about one hour that day, but while
I was there Morgan Geis contacted the Secret Service and told
them to have me make arrangements to replace the windshield.

The following day, when I returned to the garage, the unit
was no longer under guard. The Secret Service had cleaned the
leather upholstery the day before, but underneath the upholstery buttons dried blood was still in evidence. On my own
initiative, I pulled up these upholstery buttons and with a
knife removed the caked blood around them. At this time, there
was a heavy odor of dried blood still noticeable. There was
a large blood spot on the floor covering which the Secret Service had not been able to remove, but I did nothing further
about it that day.

In response to my call of November 25, personnel from Arlington Glass came to the White House garage that same day to
replace the windshield. The Arlington Glass personnel advised
Morgan Geis and me that removal would cause additional dam-

age to the windshield but Geis told them to go ahead and remove it anyway. The Arlington Glass personnel did remove it
by putting their feet against the inside of the windshield
and pushing it out. In doing so, additional cracks formed
(downward to the bottom of the windshield). A Mr. Davis of
the Secret Service then took the windshield and put it in the
stockroom under lock and key and I have not seen it since.

That same day, November 25, I tried to clean the blood spot
on the carpet with baking soda with only moderate success.
Late that afternoon I called Hess and Eisenhardt who agreed
to send new carpeting including masking and binding. It was
also that day that Morgan Geis called my attention to a dent
in the chrome topping of the windshield at a point just above
the rear view mirror and asked why I hadn't fixed it while I
was at it. I told him that my experience with chrome had been
that in trying to remove a dent of that size lead only to additional marks that further marred the trim. In addition, the
dent is not visible when the top is on the unit.

On November 26th, late in the afternoon after I had left, the
carpet, masking and binding arrived at the garage from Hess
and Eisenhardt. When I got to the garage on the 27th and was
told that the carpeting material was in, I contacted Morgan
Geis who arranged with the White House upholstery man to receive the metal piece containing the carpet, remove the old
carpeting, replace it with the new carpet, and return the
piece to me for reinstallation in the "Bubbletop." This up-
holsterer did not complete the job until late Friday afternoon the 29th.

On the morning of December 2nd, the re-carpeted piece was delivered to me by a Secret Service agent named Davis and I then
reinstalled it. Also on the 2nd of December I noticed that
the two lap robes had a few blood spots on them but, more than
that, were soiled from handling and required cleaning. Two
White House chauffeurs were detailed to take the lap robes to
Fort Myer for cleaning. These persons remained with the lap
robes until they were cleaned and returned the same day.

I think this represents a complete account of changes made in
the "Bubbletop" since November 22.

                                        F. V. Ferguson

NOTES

1. *LIFE,* October 3, 1964
2. J. G. Ballard, *Crash* (New York: Farrar, Strauss & Giroux, 1994), 130.
3. Jim Bishop, *The Day Kennedy Was Shot* (New York: Funk & Wagnalls, 1968), 19–23.
4. Denis Brian and Jeanne Dixon, *The Witnesses* (New York: Warner Books, 1976), 200.
5. Bishop, 133.
6. Warren Commission testimony of Roy Kellerman, 2H67 (Warren Commission Hearings and Exhibits, volume 2 of the 26 volumes of hearings and exhibits accompanying the report itself), page 67.
7. NARA #1800–10120–10021, Lincoln Continental Modification, September 31, 1961.
8. Larry Sneed, *No More Silence: An Oral History of the Assassination of President Kennedy* (Dallas: Three Forks Press, 1998), 147.
9. James Fetzer, ed., *Assassination Science: Experts Speak Out on the Death of JFK* (Chicago: Open Court Press, 1997) 166.
10. Charles A. Crenshaw, Jens Hansen, and J. Gary Shaw, *JFK: Conspiracy of Silence* (New York: Signet, 1992), 105.
11. Richard B. Trask, *That Day in Dallas: Three Photographers Capture on Film the Day President Kennedy Died* (Danvers, MA: Yeoman Press, 2000) 37 (Cecil Stoughton photos of 100-X at Parkland Hospital).
12. 17H485.
13. 2H97.
14. CD (Warren Commission Document) 80, Secret Service "Report on Handling of Presidential Car since November 22, 1963," Taylor/Geiglein report. The Commission Documents were the documents from which the Warren Commission Document was originally derived. Some of this information was included in the Warren Commission Hearings & Exhibits; the rest was not, but is available through the CD identification.
15. Existing documentation so far places Greer at Bethesda during the autopsy and embalming. There's a time conflict here that hasn't been resolved. In addition, no other documentation to date confirms that Greer discussed damage to the windshield with anyone, much less a shot coming through it. The Zapruder film does show Greer and Kellerman ducking after the fatal head shot however, and Kellerman did reference a "flurry of shots" in his Warren Commission testimony (2H77), so there's a possibility that Nick has information that Greer didn't feel comfortable communicating to higher authorities. As a result, research is ongoing in this area.
16. According to the White House garage log—kept by the Secret Service after the assassination, others were required to log in to see Sergeant Aleskowitz of the U.S. Army, from Fort Meyers, VA; also, per the SS duty roster, the automobiles were kept under guard until the afternoon of November 23, 1963.

17. Documentation does show that SS-679-X was said to have been sequestered and guarded along with 100-X, but there is virtually no detailed information about this mystery car, presenting another area for further research.
18. Nick Prencipe, audiotaped interview with Pamela McElwain-Brown, March 2000. Mr. Prencipe passed away in June, 2001.
19. CE (Warren Commission Exhibit) 399, also called the "Magic Bullet" because it is nearly intact. It is now in the National Archives and Records Administration (NARA).
20. CE 567 and CE 569, the "front seat bullets."
21. Robert Frazier, written interview with Pamela McElwain-Brown, November 1999.
22. CE 840.
23. CE 841.
24. Willard Hess, videotaped interview with D. Weldon, August 1999.
25. 5H66.
26. FBI photographs (also called "bulky" photographs) taken November 23, 1963 during FBI exam, part of FBI document 62–109060–8307.
27. Mr. Ferguson was the Ford Motor Company liaison to the White House Garage from the Truman administration until the Nixon administration. He usually traveled with the presidential limousine, and remained in Washington D.C., instead of traveling to Texas only in order to prepare for the anticipated trip to Philadelphia for the Army-Navy game the following weekend. (Cited in interview with Peter Dobens, Venice, Florida *Herald-Tribune,* November 1983.)
28. F. Vaughn Ferguson, December 18, 1963, NARA #180–10105–10086, "Changes in the White House Bubbletop," internal Ford memo to Rod W. Markley (of the Ford D.C. Office).
29. Dobens, *Herald-Tribune* interview.
30. Although there is conflicting information, the Secret Service duty roster ends at this time; this is confirmed by the Ferguson memo.
31. Ferguson memo.
32. Dobens, *Herald-Tribune* interview.
33. CE 351.
34. Robert Frazier interview.
35. CD 3. Rowley report states the car was driven out on December 20; Hess & Eisenhardt records apparently show SS-100-X there on December 13. CD 3 is the two-volume Secret Service report submitted December 18, 1963.
36. "Three Special Lincolns," *Ford Museum Herald,* 11.1, 1982, 43.
37. NARA #180–10120–10021. Documents and information on the "second windshield" are available at www.jfk100x.com (first sub-section, "Prior to 11/22/63"), as is the Ferguson Memo and copies of the FBI bulkies; all of this new research is presented by Pamela McElwain-Brown.
38. CE 352 and CE 353.
39. Ferguson memo.
40. Willard Hess interview.

41. Crenshaw, Hansen, and Shaw, 106.
42. Longtime JFK assassination researcher Gery Mack examined first-generation contact prints made from the original negatives taken by Squire Haskins a day or two after the assassination. Several of them are very clear and no storm drains appear near the south end of the triple underpass.
43. James Fetzer, ed., *Murder in Dealey Plaza* (Chicago: Catfeet Press, 2000), 12.
44. Robert Frazier interview.
45. FBI photographs taken November 23, 1963 during FBI exam, part of FBI document 8307.
46. John F. Kennedy, Speech at the American University, September 1963.
47. Andrew and Leslie Cockburn, *Dangerous Liaisons* (New York: Harper-Collins, 1991), 89–92.
48. HSCA documents show that the Warren Commission "released" 100-X on December 20, 1964. To date, no additional information is available.

CAR CRASH CINEMA

SEVENTEEN

MACHINE DREAMS

HARVEY ROY GREENBERG

SCIENCE FICTION CINEMA HAS CONSISTENTLY, if unconsciously, manifested an intriguing split in its attitude toward the machine, treating it unabashedly as a dehumanizing oppressor while lovingly lingering over its gleaming gizmos. *Crash,* scripted nearly faithfully by David Cronenberg from English sci-fi writer J. G. Ballard's 1973 cult novel, knowingly interrogates this ambivalence in a harrowing exploration of the human/machine symbiosis—specifically the human automotive interface. (Note that the director himself has been an amateur racer and car enthusiast.)

The film/book's jaded antihero is yuppie television commercial producer James Ballard. (The real-life Ballard claims the novel is an autobiography of his imaginary life, supplying no further details.) The fictive Ballard lives with his stunning wife, Catherine, in a sterile luxury apartment perched at a dizzy height above a serpentine grid of arterials feeding the huge airport complex of an anonymous first world city.

Crash virtually eschews biographical detail. The Ballards, like the film's other characters, float in an eternal anomic present. Lacking nothing materially, awash in entitlement, they seem totally oblivious to their good fortune. Shorn of children, family, or friends, they express little interest in work, play, art. Their central preoccupation is copulation, anywhere, at any time, with each other or with anyone else—described afterward in exhaustive clinical detail to one's partner. Away from sex, their contact is as tenuous as ghosts trying to touch. Catherine's eyes forever slip languorously away from her husband's searching gaze. Discourse is equally tentative, elliptical.

Their intercourse—and coitus elsewhere in the film—frequently occurs *a tergo* (often implicitly anal), staged to elicit hard-core pornography's effect of depersonalized manipulation. At the supposed moment of greatest intimacy, the impression instead is of narcissistic privatism, of being ceaselessly turned on a wheel of unslaked desire. ("Did you come?" Catherine asks James, fresh from his frenetic coupling with an assistant, at the film's opening. "I was interrupted" is his signatory diffident reply.)

One errs if one makes a facile clinical assumption that the Ballards are trying to pump life into a moribund marriage through adultery. It is more likely that an exuberant promiscuity, little touched by tender regard, has always hallmarked their relationship—indeed, may have drawn them together. Cronenberg implies that their compulsive carnality is a fallout of the pervasive alienation wrought by a relentlessly sensation-seeking consumerist culture. In this anhedonic milieu, one just as easily may employ orgasm as the spectacle of televisual/cinematic violence for anodyne against a profound inner deadening. Either cure serves only to entrench the core malaise.

James's complacent modus vivendi is demolished by a head-on collision on his way home from work. The other car's driver is instantly slaughtered. Across exploded windshields, the eyes of the deceased's wife, Dr. Helen Remington, lock with James's in a concussed libidinous stare. After recovering from their injuries, the two are drawn to the police pound where their wrecked vehicles have been stored. A chill passion is consummated in his car, then other automotive habitats: in dark garages, by noisy roadways, the lovers' pumping limbs are shoved painfully against gearshift and steering column.

Remington reintroduces James to Vaughan, a forbidding yet strangely attractive character who had avidly inventoried his wounds and braces in the hospital. James had supposed him then to be a doctor, but he is actually a former computer researcher and media-conscious science popularizer. After a near-fatal motorcycle accident (genital injury is intimated), he has reinvented himself as a crash scholar/connoisseur,

guru to an outlaw culture of fellow survivor addicts. James joins the
weird band and quickly becomes Vaughan's apprentice.

Vaughan haunts accident sites, takes grisly photos that he prizes like
holy relics; stages alarming performances of fatal celebrity collisions; pursues automotive sex with the same maniac intensity as his quest after
some desperate truth amid the broken bits and bodies. With James's
prompting, Catherine falls under his sway. Vaughan takes her violently
in his car (the model in which Kennedy was assassinated) while it glides
through the fecund lather of a car wash as James looks on through the
front driving mirror—the sequence a elegant paradigm of voyeuristic obsession. Later Vaughan seduces Ballard—arguably his design from the
first—in another gritty jam of body against mechanism.

Vaughan's lunatic "research" spins increasingly out of control; he becomes a suspect in several hit-and-run deaths. Coupling with Ballard
provides the terminal thrust to his escalating aggression. Thanatos over-
balances Eros: In an intricate superhighway sarabande, Vaughan attempts to run Catherine's vehicle off the road, is himself rear-ended by
Ballard (!), and dies in flames.

Flash forward to an eerie Hitchcockian crossing: James has assumed
Vaughan's mantle, hungrily cruising after Catherine. Her car hurtles over
an embankment; she tumbles upon the grass and James anxiously cradles
her in his arms. "I think I'm all right," she murmurs, dazed, a single tear
coursing down her cheek. Ballard moves upon her splayed body, whispering "maybe the next one, darling . . . maybe the next one . . ." In a
morbid epiphany characteristic of Cronenberg's endings, the camera
pulls back and ascends, tracking from the Ballard's lovemaking to the
nearby highway, with its hectic pour of traffic.

Crash's scandalous transgressiveness—of which its incessant anal pen-
etrations constitute a prime example—has predictably drawn fire even
from Cronenberg fans. (At the Cannes festival, it had the signal distinction of being simultaneously reviled and granted a special commenda-
tion "For Originality, For Daring, and For Audacity.") Upon repeated
viewing, one's initial resistance—indeed, repugnance—gives way to respect for the unsalacious seriousness of the director's enterprise.

One particularly admires how Cronenberg has transformed the glacial
precision of J. G. Ballard's style into an austere visual beauty. For instance,

through James's eyes, the novel dwells on the elegant designs constructed by the chance juxtaposition of body part against car part or against some other chunk of the inanimate environment. *Crash* translates this hybrid aesthetic, essential to Ballard's subversive purposes, into hieratic, immensely resonant compositions. Picked out with a seeming artless randomness by Cronenberg's laconic camera, many of these frames could be lifted from context and hung on a museum wall.[1]

Crash pointedly refuses the glib excitement of action cinema and the porn flick's crude enticements. Its wrecks are utterly devoid of conventional Hollywood slo-mo pyrotechnics, occurring in a shattered instant, or off-screen. The director focuses instead on the raw aftermath of collision, pervaded by the curious aura of stunned sensuality cited above. The coital sequences are dankly antierotic, emphasizing the participants' driven, stymied desire. (One recalls the robotic sexual rituals in de Sade's cruel fictions.)

Vaughan leads his posttraumatic collective in an odyssey to heal catastrophic injury by actively seeking to harness the machine's dark creative potential rather than enduring its assaults as a passive victim. Accident is transmuted into eroticized performance art, the wounding of celebrities restaged in aid of mastery, thereby also endowing one's own wounds with a narcissistic shimmer. In an ultimate identification with the aggressor, Vaughan and James go forth as automotive marauders, steering wheels tattooed into their bodies, harbingers of the death both have narrowly escaped. Inevitably they are drawn back into its embrace.

The demonic Vaughan[2] dies, seduced by machine dreams of depraved, absolute power pitched at redeeming his damaged state.[3] In a valid supplement to the novel, Cronenberg assigns a more ambivalent fate to James and Catherine, holding out a faint intimation of redemption from their sordid self-absorption. Catherine's poignant tear could speak to her awakening from emotional anesthesia. Recognizing the harm his armored reveries have wrought upon her vulnerable flesh, James displays a moving tenderness, arguably for the first time in their relationship. His ambiguous last words—"perhaps the next one, darling"—could allude to the elusive orgasm attendant upon genuine intimacy.

But James might just as well be anticipating another turn on the ceaseless whirligig of his dispirited lust or even the definitive crash that would liberate them both from their torment into the grave, into the big sleep for which they both have been yearning all along. Cronenberg leaves us thus exquisitely suspended between hope and despair, life and death.

NOTES

1. See J. G. Ballard, *Crash* (New York: Farrar, Straus, and Giroux, 1994). Cronenberg/Ballard's fusion of the human and the inanimate/mechanical has numerous precedents in early twentieth- century painting and theater that address a wide spectrum of ideological positions. The unabashed machine idolatry of many Futurists and Vorticists was informed by a prefascist sensibility. Russian Constructivism often valorized the human/machine interface in the name of the proletarian revolution. The leftist-inflected theatrical projects of Meyerhold in Russia, of Ernst Toller and Georg Kaiser in Germany inter alia prominently featured "biomechanical" tropes in script, acting, and set design. For an extensive discussion, see Oscar G. Brockett, *The History of Theater* (Boston: Allyn and Bacon, 1974).

2. Vaughan is described by J. G. Ballard as a homoerotic icon encased in leather, possessing "a hard mutilated beauty" (171). The novel and film intimate intriguing analogies between Vaughan's implicit "hardbody" fantasies and fascism's collective machine dreams—blitzkrieg and panzers, blood and iron—as well as the dire toll these exacted on their fictive and actual dreamers.

3. The seminal reference in this regard is Klaus Theweleit's studies of the Freikorps, a loosely knit fellowship of disaffiliated young men, many former soldiers, who gathered together after World War I to redeem the Fatherland's savaged honor in the context of what they perceived as the debasements of the Weimar Republic and the rising tide of Bolshevism. Klaus Theweleit, *Male Fantasies: Volume l: Women, Floods, Bodies, History,* trans. Erica Carter, Chris Turner, and Steven Conway (Minneapolis: University of Minnesota Press, 1987); *Male Fantasies: Volume 2: Male Bodies: Psychoanalyzing the White Terror,* trans. Steven Conway, Erica Carter and Chris Turner (Minneapolis: University of Minnesota Press, 1989). Theweleit uses Freikorps mores and costumes as a springboard for a masterful analysis of masculine anxiety regarding castration and impotence, attendant terror of the feminine, and compensatory homosocial/homoerotic visions of male purity. This work has obvious, ominous currency regarding the contemporary American militia movement as well as other renascent fascist movements abroad. Recent studies extending Thewelheit's interrogations of the "armored body" include Scott Bukatman's *Terminal Identity: The Virtual Subject in Postmodern Science Fiction* (Durham, NC: Duke University Press, 1993) and Christopher Sharrett's "The Horror Film in Neoconservative Culture," in Barry Keith Grant, ed., *The Dread of Difference: Gender and the Horror Film* (Austin: University of Texas Press, 1996).

EIGHTEEN

THE END OF THE ROAD

DAVID CRONENBERG'S *CRASH*
AND THE FADING OF THE WEST

MIKITA BROTTMAN
AND CHRISTOPHER SHARRETT

. . . a point is that which hath no parts, or which hath no magnitude

—Euclid

. . . shall he drive
his horses upward, bring again the day?
it will but rise to die

—Seneca, Thyestes

IN *CRASH,* DAVID CRONENBERG NEGOTIATES OUR AMBIVALENT attitudes toward death and destruction on the roads as well as the attractions of car
crashes, using the car and the architecture of contemporary road systems
as symbols of the convergence between humanity's unconscious desires
and its technological artifacts. Cronenberg's film, like Ballard's novel, is
an exploration of the ambiguous fascination and excitement of the car

crash and the latent identity of the machine. This exploration, in the film and the novel, reexamines the contentions of some basic genres. It is a "road film" in the sense that it is an eccentric examination of the cult of adventure, journey, and discovery that has animated that form. Ballard is British and Cronenberg Canadian, but *Crash* seems peculiarly American since its narrative deals with the exhaustion of the civilizing process and the final expenditures of the horizontal, forward-moving momentum that drove this enterprise. It is energy incipient to the western, the biker film, and all manner of male-oriented identity that affirms the potency of a burgeoning society. In *Crash,* the traditional journey of discovery becomes a downward spiral, a frustrated, ever-circling implosion of the defeated bourgeois self at the end of the millennium.

Although the film was condemned in England as "a movie beyond the bounds of depravity,"[1] Cronenberg's film does not fit well within the traditions of pornography. Clearly, sexual arousal in its audience is not the primary motive of the film, and, more significantly, none of the characters seems able to relate to one another in an emotional way. For this reason, in part, Cronenberg himself has described the film as "anti-pornographic."[2] Arousal can hardly be on the agenda since Ballard, faithfully adapted here, has long been concerned with the "death of affect," a concept now basic to postmodernity that Ballard has applied various locations to describe, rather moralistically, the depletion of bourgeois life. Cronenberg's evocation of sex seems iconic; Catherine Ballard (Deborah Kara Unger) leans on a balcony, pulling aside her gown to expose her bare buttocks as if to quote fashion photography or Dali's *Young Virgin Auto-Sodomized by Her Own Chastity.* Pornography is employed here as the end product of the culture of representation that has dissolved all lived experience through filters of mediation.

Other critics, picking up on the film's sense of surgical precision and its fascination with technology, attempted to locate Cronenberg's *Crash* in the tradition of science fiction. Many of Ballard's novels, including *Crash,* certainly adopt a number of sci-fi formations, including the metaphysics and biophysics of time and space-time paradigms and the ontologies of psychic realities. Unlike Ballard's novel, however, Cronenberg's *Crash* deals with the technology of the present rather than that of the future and, in fact, is interested in the future only as a perspective from which to understand the current moment. It has been observed that the movie "looks and feels as if it were made long, long ago in a parallel universe,"[3] a reference to its *mise-en-scène* of pillars and pylons, crash barriers, disused hangars and gas stations, dumped cars and derelict parking lots. This is no sci-fi dystopia but a coruscating vision of the horror that is to be found in the bleak everyday of contemporary life.

Indeed, if Cronenberg's *Crash* fits into a tradition at all, it is that of the road movie—albeit in the form of a hardcore, apocalyptic, end-time variant. As Cronenberg makes explicit, the car crash is to the traditional road movie what the sex scene is to the classical romantic comedy—the unspoken culmination, the hidden act toward which all others tend, the secret, implicit, concealed finale. In effect, Cronenberg's *Crash* is the terminal form of the genre. Its obsession with the aftermath of car accidents vivifies the pathological truth of all previous road movie cycles—that our obsession with the automobile is, in fact, an obsession with atrocity and disaster.

As in all road movies, the road in *Crash* functions on many different levels. Among other things, it serves as a metaphor for the cultural condition of Western civilization—in this case, a bleak, gaping expanse of vacancy. This is explicit in scenes where James Spader—the actor who represents blank yuppiedom par excellence—surveys traffic-clogged highway webworks from his terrace. A representative of "spectator culture," Spader muses anxiously about the increased number of vehicles on the roads, which would serve to disturb him after a disabling car crash, yet he and his wife yearn for "the next time," as their dream of perfect orgasm is conflated with death in the final fusion of Eros and Thanatos. The character is still able to enjoy orgasm even as his emotional life is arid, evidenced best by the chill gray-blue and amber twilight that saturates the film.

Sex is arousing in *Crash* chiefly because it becomes associated with self-annihilation and with the urban-primitive cultism, replete with tattoos and talismans, of the crash reenactors organized by renegade researcher Vaughan (Elias Koteas). The cult recapitulates a humanist theme that Cronenberg asserts, albeit halfheartedly, in all of his major works, as characters' panicked pursuit of meaning and coherence tends to recoup dead belief systems that ultimately hasten dystopia and provoke the holocaust. As in Freud's *Beyond the Pleasure Principle*, the pursuit of the death wish has reduced the self to the base material of the repetition compulsion. In *Crash,* as in Scorsese's *Taxi Driver,* this repetition compulsion takes the form of an inability to be still, a kind of circling insomnia reminiscent of Spengler's "organicist" view of a "denatured" culture gradually winding itself down. Of course, as Freud reminds us, the repetition compulsion is essentially a means of both repeating and avoiding the initial trauma—which, in the case of *Crash,* is bourgeois life itself. In this way, perhaps, Cronenberg's film can be regarded as a mournful, antiillusionist, antiBrechtian version of Godard's bourgeois road fantasy, *Weekend.*

Those who choose to defend Cronenberg against the charge of nihilism do so by drawing attention to the way in which he often attempts to uncover new unifying principles, new myths in the modern technological landscape. It has been argued that the fetishization of the car accident in *Crash* triggers the emergence of both a new sexuality and a new form of creativity and imagination. In other words—for all its dangers—the techno-sex of *Crash* bestows a certain radical potential on humanity by allowing us to jettison bourgeois notions of "appropriate" sexual encounters.[4] In Cronenberg's script, for example, the renegade scientist Vaughan—in a line straight out of Ballard—claims that the car crash should be seen as a "fertilizing event," not a destructive one. By describing the car crash as "the marriage between sex, the human organism and technology,"[5] Ballard seems to be suggesting that such "fertilizing events" can provide people with some kind of collective liberation from their repressed existences. Yet the notion of the car crash—and sexual pathologies in general—as liberatory seems undercut by the gloom of the film, especially in the primal moment when the Spader and Unger characters couple on a piece of roadside wasteland after a near-deadly car crash.

Cronenberg's new unifying myths seem peculiarly appropriate to the postmodern scene. His earlier films have often been analyzed in terms of their presentation of a series of irresistible transformations, wherein the boundaries between Self and Other dissolve, annexing identity. Sometimes this transformation takes the form of the abandonment of self to a collective urge or gestalt (*Shivers, Rabid*); sometimes it takes the form of a merging between two beings (*Dead Ringers, The Fly, M. Butterfly*); sometimes in the surrender of independence to enlistment in conspiracies almost beyond human comprehension (*Scanners, Videodrome, Naked Lunch*).[6]

Like *Scanners* and *Videodrome, Crash* contains a cultlike group that attempts to reinvigorate society (or, at least, a marginal sector of society, since in Cronenberg larger social transformation seems impossible) through the creation of a new mythology appropriate to a secular, postindustrial environment. As noted, it becomes clear that the group's plan is bankrupt and speaks merely to the panic of a postmodern setting that has exhausted all belief systems. Yet Cronenberg's narratives involve a traditional sacrificial ritual with propitiatory victims (Vale and Revok in *Scanners,* Max Renn in *Videodrome,* Vaughan and possibly the main character in *Crash*). This radical, futuristic construction of Self and Other in these films has been read in relation to Richard Slotkin's concept of "regeneration through violence," the magic potential of destruction and the will-to-myth (the will to read experience mythically through the apparatus of victimization), reviving old mythologies or creating new ones more befitting to the contemporary wasteland.[7]

In *Crash,* however, none of these previous models or paradigms has any real application. Something of a departure for Cronenberg, *Crash* is a film whose apocalypticism is conservative rather than regenerative. This is a film in which the symbiosis and dispersal of self produce a terminal, degenerative state of isolation and estrangement. In effect, the destruction in *Crash* is not magical nor sacrificial nor regenerative, but pure suicidal immolation in the failure of collective philosophies. The protagonists of *Crash* lack any sustaining faith in mythical or spiritual belief systems previously supplying consensus to society. The film's apocalyptic spirit is profoundly secular and pessimistic, reflecting the postmodern refusal of both sacred and ideological conceptions of reality, depicting a culture totally cut off from its mythic past. *Crash* is a film about the impulses of Western consciousness toward the worship of catastrophe and self-annihilation. It is a disaster story, though with none of the frantic, panicky overtones of the usual disaster story, since the catastrophe needed to provoke revelation never comes.

Instead, the audience's attention is focused on a small group of rather calm, detached, sexually promiscuous though emotionally barren people,

James Ballard (Spader), his wife Catherine (Unger), and the defiant, compulsive Vaughan (Koteas). As in much self-consciously decadent art, the sexuality of the protagonists is closely bound up with the notion of surplus violence—the need to prove one is alive by lacerating the flesh. And, as René Girard explains, "violence, if left unappeased, will accumulate until it overflows and contaminates the surrounding area."[8] Moreover, in relation to the sexual violence and promiscuity of this distant triad, Cronenberg himself has pointed out that the film's showcasing of rear-entry and anal sex is meant to express its practitioners' disconnectedness from and defiance of the world,[9] evoking Puritan notions of anality as death, waste, the cul de sac of experience. As an act of paraphilia, anal sex is a metaphor for a profoundly degenerate attitude toward human life. The pursuit of satisfactions in *Crash* is the pursuit of a Sadean void; as in Pasolini's *Salo*, anality becomes an emblem of the transmogrification of transgressive sexuality. Although *Crash*, unlike *Salo*, doesn't associate anal sex with tyranny and sadism, it does liken this taboo—almost as a pun—to the dead end of human experience. Anal sex also suggests the peculiar paucity of accumulation and violation of taboos, a succinct summation of bourgeois life.

In the traditional road movie, the road functions as a metaphor for the path of history, the impetus and trajectory of human civilization. In his 1895 work *The Law of Civilization and Decay*, historian Brooks Adams analyzed the relationship between intellectual tendencies and the economic laws governing the movements of the material universe, concluding that human society must pass through a number of distinct intellectual phases in its oscillations between barbarism and civilization. According to Adams, when any human race reaches the limit of its material energy, that energy becomes surplus and needs to be dissipated through economic competition. When surplus energy accumulates in such bulk as to preponderate over productive energy, it becomes the controlling social force, "and energy vents itself through those organisms best fitted to give expression to the power of capital."[10]

    In such highly civilized and centralized societies, according to Adams, the imagination slowly fades and eventually falls into contempt, whereas "the economic intellect" grows gradually "less tolerant of any departure from those representations of nature which have appealed to the highly gifted of the monied type among successive generations."[11] In the end, this loss of energy is manifested by a gradual dissipation of capital, which, at last, leads to disintegration: The pressure of economic capitalism has exhausted the energy of the race. "Consequently," writes Adams, "the survivors of such a race lack the power necessary for renewed concentration, and must probably remain inert, until supplied with fresh energetic material by the infusion of barbarian blood."[12]

Adams's doleful, apocalyptic interpretation of history is an interesting way of making sense of the entropy and mythic dysfunction of Cronenberg's *Crash*—an elliptical, interiorized film with no final narrative release, only dissolution and disintegration. Here the recognizably postmodern (yet actually rather Puritan) theme of the downfall of civilization lacks any restorative mythic dimension. James, Catherine, and Vaughan are the survivors of a declining civilization in the decadent stages of late capitalism, whose excess economic energy has been sublimated into a universalizing death drive. Their descent into barbarism is willed, either consciously or unconsciously, by each of them, suggesting an acknowledgment of the failure of myth to revitalize society, to generate consensus, and to give energy to the construction of a new order. These are characters who do not hesitate to embrace the revelations about themselves and their sexuality that technology has made possible. Cronenberg argues that the Darwinian version of evolution having to do with survival is anachronistic within a capitalist society:

> What I think has happened is that we have seized control of evolution without being aware of it. Survival of the fittest as a principle—one now has to say, what does "fittest" mean? . . . It might be the guy who makes money the best in a capitalist society. There are cultures which embody the notion of suicide within them. . . . [I]f you can get enough people to will it along with you, it *is* the reality. . . . [13]

The logic of the film unfolds in accordance with the economic system that makes such a narrative possible, vivified most clearly by the alienating effect of its depicted technology (the camera gazes fetishistically over bent fenders, crutches, stretchers, the brushes and levers of the car wash), the lifeless intensity of its *mise-en-scène* (streetlights are reflected hazily in windshields, wet roads, and the hoods of cars). The dolorous, liturgical tone of the film and the distant, laconic interactions of its characters are Cronenberg's attempt to depict the dehumanized eroticism of late capitalism, the failure of the imagination characterized by Adams.

A movie about the end of the historical road, *Crash* is set on the downward edge of the historical cycle. The film explores the contradictions of a decadent capitalist system out of control as well as the psychological consequences of this superproductive consumer society. These consequences include not only the descent into barbarism, obsession, pathology, and collective rage suggested by Adams but also the forceful desire to tear society apart, to "throw stones at the Crystal Palace," as Dostoyevsky puts it. As a consequence, the destroyed commodity becomes part of a nostalgic reliquary for lost ritual and consensus built around shared myth and language systems. In *Crash,* the particular commodity facing ritualized destruction is that most symbolic artifact of American consumer culture—that wasteful, aggressive, violent totem of Western civilization, the car.

The obsession with technology in *Crash* is not—as it is elsewhere in Cronenberg—an attempt to create new meanings from the minglings of flesh and machine, but to reflect an increasing preoccupation among commercial designers and architects with the relationship between the technological environment and the design, gestures, and contours of the human body. This commercial relationship between human and machine reaches a perverse fruition in the car crash, with its "blood-soaked instrument panels, seat-belts smeared with excrement, sun-visors lined with brain tissue. . . . The intimate time and space of a human being . . . fossilized forever in this web of chromium knives and frosted glass."[14] Ballard's perception that "the precise make and model-year of my car could have been reconstructed by an automobile engineer from the pattern of my wounds"[15] has nothing to do with what *Videodrome* describes as the "new flesh" but is rather a symptom of immanent apocalypse. It is a symbolic representation of a society obsessed with violence, brand names, destruction, machines, time, boredom, and repetitive sex, a society on the cusp of collapse into nihilistic dereliction and disaster.

One of the most symbolic constructions of capitalism is the notion of celebrity. Celebrity is possible only within the framework of a consumer culture, which provides the economic forces necessary for the formation of the public relations and the motion picture industries. Writer Jay McInerney claims that one of the most significant indications of a collapsed value system is the fact that we have come to define ourselves by our distance from these empty luminaries or our connection to them, however vague. This is because the celebrity is, essentially, an ego ideal. Our fascination with celebrity death is a vicarious extension of our own death drive and its endless cycle of repetition compulsion. The dead celebrity stands for the surrogate propitiatory victim, the "mirror image" whose failed sacrifice serves only to highlight the miserable charade of commodity culture. Consequently, the public death of a celebrity has become one of the most horrifying and fascinating taboos that can be transgressed in our time.

Part of the horror of such a death is the body's sudden loss of revelatory power. The celebrity body, once so expressive and so intensely scrutinized, is abruptly transformed into a limp marionette, the strings suddenly cut that once attached it to the complex and hidden mechanisms of media relations and industrial investment. If death itself has become fetishized within capitalism, the celebrity death has become so much more symbolic, the object of so much violent eroticism, voyeurism, and obsessive curiosity. This notion of the celebrity death is always present in the background of Cronenberg's *Crash,* whose clinical atmosphere evokes the tone of news reports and other accounts of disasters. In the film's cold landscape, private terrors merge with public possibilities, personal nightmares with the nightmare of history, and the inner spaces of psychosis with imaginable large-scale disasters.

In Ballard's novel, Vaughan becomes obsessed with the death of Elizabeth Taylor and takes to following her home from the film studios, hoping to engage her in a violent, frenzied, sexual collision. In his attempts to induce the actress's death by automobile, Vaughan himself is finally killed—"his only true accident"—while Elizabeth Taylor escapes unharmed. Taylor is not mentioned in Cronenberg's film—perhaps for

18.1   James Dean. © Photofest

legal reasons—but other celebrities become similar objects of fixation. Vaughan, who in the novel "dreamed endlessly of the deaths of the famous, inventing imaginary crashes for them,"[16] in Cronenberg's film becomes a crazed impresario, restaging his own performances of such celebrity accidents as James Dean's "death by Porsche." In the small, floodlit stadium, Vaughan relates all the details of the crash to his audience of midnight connoisseurs, including the date (September 9, 1955) and the "performance cast." Dean, played by the psychotic stuntman Seagrave, will slam his new Porsche Spyder into the side of the Ford driven by college student Donald Turnupseed, who, according to Vaughan, was very important. "The two would meet for a moment," Vaughan shouts gleefully to his fans on the bleachers, "a moment that created a Hollywood legend. I myself will play engineer Rolf Wutherich from Zuffenhausen, Germany."

In Cronenberg's film, Seagrave meets his end by reenacting, in drag, Jayne Mansfield's fatal crash of 1967, around which he has built "an abbatoir of sexual mutilation."[17] Seagrave's highly detailed and authentic reenactment disregards the claim that the truck under which Mansfield's car was steered decapitated her. After the crash, Seagrave's wig is stuck on the same door as had been Mansfield's, which—some claim—led the first eyewitnesses to the crash to conclude that the actress had been decapitated.[18]

This connection among death, celebrity, and the automobile embodies the totemic iconography of all crash vehicles and other dysfunctional commodities in Cronenberg's *mise-en-scène* and is reinforced by the fact that Vaughan himself roams the freeways in a car that itself has mythic dimensions—a black 1963 Lincoln Continental convertible, the model in which Kennedy was assassinated. Indeed, in a piece of dialogue taken directly from the novel, Vaughan proposes the Kennedy assassination as "a special kind of car crash."[19] In the novel, James Ballard, confined to his apartment, fantasizes about the injuries of film actresses and television personalities, "whose bodies would flower into dozens of auxiliary artifices, points of sexual conjunction with their audiences formed by the swerving technology of the automobile."[20] If the obsession with celebrity is a by-product of capitalism, then the obsession with the celebrity car crash is a fantasy of literalization: the final and much longed-for union between the celebrity and members of their audience.

The traditional road movie is often regarded in psychoanalytic terms as a story of birth and regeneration. The car can easily be read as a symbol of a claustral (womblike) environment within which its driver feels safe and secure, and from which at the same time he or she experiences an ambivalent urge to escape. If the classical road movie deals with birth and regeneration, however, then *Crash* is a narrative of abortion.

In psychoanalytic terms, the car accidents depicted by Cronenberg (both "live" and televised in the Swedish crash-test films screened by Vaughan)—especially those in which a figure is projected through the windshield—suggest a number of parallels with the forcible expulsion from the womb and the anxiety associated with birth trauma, or still-birth. The obsession with car accidents shared by the characters in *Crash* suggests the death wish underneath much apocalyptic thought and resonates closely with a number of psychodynamic constructs that psychoanalyst Henry Murray describes as "anti-claustral complexes." These include "cathection of claustra" (strong emotional investment in claustral enclosures such as the car), feelings of chaos and lack of control, and a violent terror of suffocation and confinement.[21]

Sexuality in *Crash* does not lead to birth and renewal but instead represents an emblem of chaos and alienation. Vaughan and Seagrave's compulsive sexual desire to both observe and reenact crashes in which a figure is forcibly ejected from the car seem to suggest, among other things, an "egression complex"—an anticlaustral tendency associated with active attempts to separate from the mother's body. In most cases, this yearning to escape from the womb is associated with strong desires for autonomy and the establishment of an independent identity. Birth traumas are usually reenacted in order to master the anxieties associated with the birth process. In the case of *Crash,* however, the magic of birth no longer has any regenerative function, because what is at stake here is stillbirth. No creation comes out of this chaos. In the crashes enacted by Vaughan and Seagrave, the forced ejection of a body from the car results not in the establishment of an independent identity but in sudden, violent, and premature death.

"In *Crash*," writes Fritz Leiber in his review of Ballard's novel, "geometry is king." Leiber argues that in this novel, "Ballard is seeking to satisfy a compulsion or an imperative" that manifests itself in the form of "a delirium of Euclidian eroticism."[22] In his film of Ballard's novel, Cronenberg realizes this imperative by configuring the traditional horizon of the classical road movie as circular, leading endlessly back on itself, as empty and as meaningless as a Euclidean dot. The horizon in *Crash* is like Vaughan's ill-lit, clandestine racetrack where cars pile into one another pointlessly, chaotically—as Ballard puts it, "cars meeting head-on in complex collisions endlessly repeated in slow-motion films."[23]

Consequently, unlike most road movies, there is no real sense of narrative form in *Crash;* the plot is merely a gateway to a certain cultural, historical, and psychological locale in which the power of myth has given way to a barbarism whose violence lacks any restorative or regenerative function. Repetitive and insistent, Cronenberg's film is like a piece of newsreel footage being played over and over again, a circular rerun of obsessions, a pointless, elliptical quest to find interconnections between apparently inexplicable phenomena. Where the traditional road movie follows a linear horizon, Cronenberg's regressive fantasy is vertiginous and entropic, giving its audience a sense of queasy dislocation and foreboding.

Crash is a compulsive nightmare, a film about the end of culture and of history, the road movie of the apocalypse. It is full of those "premonitions of disaster" that James Ballard senses as he sits at home on his veranda, watching through his binoculars the traffic move along the motorway, "determined to spot the first signs of the end of the world by automobile."[24]

NOTES

1. Alexander Walker, in *The London Evening Standard* (June 3, 1996), describes the film as containing "some of the most perverted acts and theories of sexual deviance I have ever seen propagated in mainstream cinema." In the November 9 issue of the 1996 *Daily Mail,* critic Christopher Tookey added his voice to the outrage, declaring that Cronenberg's film promulgates "the morality of the satyr, the nymphomaniac, the rapist, the pedophile, the danger to society," and marks "the point at which even a liberal society should draw the line." As evidence of the director's allegedly perverted morality, the reader's attention is drawn to the fact that "the initially heterosexual characters lose their inhibitions [and] they experiment pleasurably with gay sex, lesbian sex, and sex with cripples."

2. Cited in Xavier Mendik, "Logic, Creativity and Critical Misinterpretations: An Interview with David Cronenberg," unpublished, 1999, 17.

3. Chris Rodley, "*Crash:* An Interview with David Cronenberg," *Sight and Sound,* June 1996, 6.

4. Roy Grundmann, "Plight of the Crash Fest Mummies: David Cronenberg's *Crash,*" *Cineaste* 22:4, March 1997, 24–27. Grundmann points out that the sexual encounters featured in *Crash* "challenge notions of who has sex with whom, in what kind of environment, in what manner, and for what purpose."

5. David Pringle, *J. G. Ballard: A Primary and Secondary Bibliography* (Boston: G. K. Hall & Co., 1994), xxix.

6. Gavin Smith, "Mind Over Matter: Canada's Radical Director Interviewed," *Film Comment,* March/April 1997, 14.

7. See Richard Slotkin, *Regeneration Through Violence: The Mythology of the American Frontier 1600 - 1860* (Middletown, CT: Wesleyan University Press, 1973).

8. René Girard, *Violence and the Sacred,* trans. Patrick Gregory (Baltimore: Johns Hopkins University Press, 1977), 10.

9. See Grundmann, 27. He goes on to point out that "[t]hey don't seem to fuck each other so much as they fuck the world from which they're alienated. As rear-entry sex involves a refusal to face the sex partner and to confront his or her humanity, the film uses it as a close analogy to the cult members' practice of crashing one another's cars. This practice, too, involves a calculated refusal to see the crash partner as a human being."

10. Brooks Adams, *The Law of Civilization and Decay* (New York: Sonnenschein & Co., 1895), viii.

11. Ibid., 294.

12. Ibid.

13. David Cronenberg, cited in Smith, 18.

14. J. G. Ballard, *Crash* (New York: Farrar, Strauss & Giroux, 1973), 12.

15. Ibid., 28.

16. Ibid., 15.

17. Ibid., 135.

18. See Grundmann, 25. He points out that "[t]he lowly Seagrave is to Vaughan what Renfield is to Dracula. Seagrave is Vaughan's assistant in all important affairs." He also discusses "the Dean intertext of Fifties drag strip races, teen rebellion and car sex," which "suggests the close link between the sexual revolution and the car culture," giving "the fetishistic techno-play" of the film's characters some historical grounding. See also the introduction to this volume and chapter 1 by Kenneth Anger for more about the Jayne Mansfield decapitation debate.

19. Ballard, 183. In the novel, Vaughan also refers to "[t]he special involvement of at least two of the Kennedys with the automobile." (See chapters 13 and 16 in this volume).

20. Ballard, 180.

21. See Henry Murray et al., *Explorations in Personality* (New York: Oxford University Press, 1947).
22. Fritz Leiber, "Fantasy Books," *Fantastic Stories*, 26:1 (February): 129–30.
23. Ballard, 8.
24. Ibid., 50.

HEART LIKE A WHEEL

TONY WILLIAMS

A lot of people watching for wrecks and roaring for blood. All they
want to see is a car turn over so they can hold their breath. And, in the
end, when they remove what's left of you, they point to it and say, "Oh,
they've taken him away!"

—Lee, in Howard Hawks's *The Crowd Roars* (1932)

The whole experience is somewhere between an orgasm and a glimpse
of Armageddon. It is l-o-u-d. It is primal. It is ferocious. . . . I have
been fascinated with the machinations of nitromethane and its incum-
bent pyromania for quite some time. I am also fascinated with women
who harness, finesse, dominate, and control the fierce, unwieldy machines of drag racing.

—Cole Coonce: "Drag Strip Blast Off Girls:
Shirley Muldowney and Stacy 'the Femme Fatale' Paul"

APPROXIMATELY SEVENTY MINUTES INTO THE RUNNING of Jonathan Kaplan's *Heart Like a Wheel* (1983)—the story of female drag racer Shirley
Muldowney—there comes a point at which the style and imagery radically differ from the preceding and succeeding narrative sequences.
While the film in general appears to reinvent the racing movie genre in
favor of a female heroine, this brief three-minute sequence depicts an en-

tirely different set of values. Rather than appearing human, the figure of Bonnie Bedelia's Shirley Muldowney now appears like something resembling a mechanized image in a science fiction movie. She seems almost robotic. Dialogue becomes suspended. An eerie moog synthesizer dominates the soundtrack, contrasting with the basic aural representation employed in this film, and Shirley's body becomes suddenly objectified. Her living personality is reduced the level of the mechanized objects in the world of drag racing.

Helmet, androgynous overalls, and vehicle all dominate her identity. She is now part of her car. Only her eyes remind us of a human personality. She begins her race, but her vehicle suddenly catches fire. She drives along the track, lost within the flames of the burning car, before stumbling out like a lighted torch. The safety team arrives. Shirley's son John (Anthony Edwards) immediately runs to the scene and takes control, as Shirley's crew chief-lover Connie Kalitta (Beau Bridges) can only stare in dumb amazement. The sequence ends with a tracking shot into one of Shirley's eyes—the only remnant of humanity remaining in her charred body.

This striking scene depicts the worst accident out of four that the real-life Shirley Muldowney experienced during the three years she drove her competitive vehicle. The sequence could have formed the stylistic whole of any contemporary apocalyptic narrative, such as Cronenberg's *Crash* (1996), in which the human body becomes objectified and damaged by the camera's gaze. In *Heart Like a Wheel*, however—a film dealing with the attempts of working-class heroine Shirley Muldowney to prove her prowess in a male-dominated sport—the sequence has a rather different function. Shirley has long ago left her husband to become a contender. By doing so, she is challenging those patriarchal dictates about a woman's place that still exist in the film's fictional world of the early 1970s, and, as a result, she is presented as the sacrificial victim demanded by the bloodthirsty spectators.

In this important sequence, Kaplan's Shirley becomes dehumanized for the first and only time in the film. Her status and fate evoke suggestions of those unfortunate women burned at the stake during paranoid male reaction to femininity in earlier times. This suggestion is not without foundation in terms of the film's narrative structure. The most significant merit of *Heart Like a Wheel* is its revelation of the presence of hidden but still-powerful forces operating within the context of Western civilization and always ready to threaten any interloper. The quotations introducing this chapter represent two diverse perspectives governing female representation in the sports movie. The first comes from an earlier era where women are passive spectators, not participants. But even if barred from competing, the female is able to understand the animal roar of the crowd, like that inspired by the gladiatorial combats of the Roman Empire. The second quotation emerges from a different generation, which sees women now participating in a formerly male-dominated sport. Here male writer Cole Coonce ecstatically indulges in postapocalyptic language, depicting the female body both as an image of orgasmic pleasure and an object of potential sexually charged fiery dismemberment. Burn baby burn.

> The sound of a dragster is nothing if not the sound of destruction. Every time a valve opens in the combustion chamber of a supercharged Top Fuel motor—an action taking place as many as 8 times a second per valve—it allows a highly volatile mixture of oxygen and nitromethane (a fuel developed by Third Reich scientists as a rocket propellant during World War II) to *penetrate* the cylinder. This incendiary cocktail then awaits a high amperage spark so it can EXPLODE. Not burn like the gasoline in yer grocery-getter, but detonate like the Manhattan project in miniutia.[1]

After opening his article with this phallic image, however, Coonce then interviews a woman who is known as the "suffragette" of dragster racing and whose achievements are still ignored by the "billionaires boys and girls club that depends on corporate financing for its existence." Although disappointed that her skill has not done anything to secure her future, the real-life Shirley Muldowney still asserts her independence as well as criticizing certain other female drivers who are "glorified trophy girls" living off corporate bankrolls and dependent on their crew chiefs for success. Both the real-life Shirley Muldowney and her cinematic counterpart in Kaplan's film have achieved great things. But they are both wary of destructive males who eagerly anticipate their demise in a spectacular car crash climax.

Jonathan Kaplan's *Heart Like a Wheel* stands midway between an earlier heroic tradition best represented by Howard Hawks's *The Crowd*

Roars (1932) and the same director's *Red Line 7000* (1965) and later apocalyptic depictions of a society fascinated by death and technology, such as Cronenberg's *Crash* (1996).

Hawks's *Red Line 7000*, for example, begins with a deadly drag-strip car racing sequence showing a speedometer reach the red-line danger level of 7000 before a car crashes and bursts into flames. This inferno is taken from actual documentary footage shot at a real racetrack. If we imagine Shirley Muldowney as a cinematic development of Laura Devon's Julie Kazarian in *Red Line 7000*, a kid sister who can never compete in a male-dominated sport, *Heart's* position between an older and a later tradition becomes apparent. As Robin Wood points out, although *Red Line 7000* ends with a race in which all three heroes overcome the difficulties they encounter, the last shot is of a blazing car that the women spectators, startled, leap to their feet to see. It is not the car of any of the characters we know, but "the image fixes in our minds, the sense that it might have been any of them . . . and may be in the next race."[2] The same holds true of Shirley Muldowney's near incineration described above. Next time, perhaps?

While Hawks's brief crash sequence anticipates the context of Cronenberg's *Crash, Heart Like a Wheel* leads in a different direction. Kaplan's film seems to focus deliberately on the celebration of female autonomy, although this may be because the film appeared at a time before the cultural consequences of Reaganism made independent female characters much less common. However, as the film makes clear, Shirley's autonomy is threatened by the nihilistic apocalypticism of her celebrated 1973 crash, in which her vehicle caught fire during the U.S. Nationals Race in Indianapolis. The depiction of this violent crash in Kaplan's film positions Muldowney as a sacrificial victim of a culture fascinated by celebrity and violence and of a male-dominated sport that attempts to punish outsiders who dare to compete within it.

Although car crashes form a minor part of *Heart Like a Wheel*, their echoes dominate the narrative. Shirley and her fellow competitors strive for fame and fortune in a combative arena, one whose hazards may prove deadly at any moment. The pleasures of spectator participation involve cheering on the winner and also finding a sadistic enjoyment in the spectacle of violent crashes and the incineration of competitors. Ironically, a year after the film's release, the real Shirley Muldowney sustained near-fatal injuries during a race in Montreal. A high-speed crash at 250 miles an hour almost caused her death, leaving her with broken bones in all her fingers, a broken pelvis, and mangled legs. After enduring major surgery five times, she went through eighteen months of physical therapy, and returned to race a car at 280 miles an hour.

Although it depicts only one of Shirley's most violent crashes, a specific type of sadistic voyeurism can be found in *Heart Like a Wheel.* This involves the operation of an implicit master narrative highly relevant to the film's historical and narrative construction. By daring to compete in a male-dominated sport, Shirley fulfills the earlier desires of Hawks' females Julie Kazarian (Laura Devon) and Gaby (Marianna Hill) in *Red Line 7000,* but she also provokes a great deal of male resentment. Shirley's husband Jack (Leo Rossi) and her boyfriend Connie Kalitta (Beau Bridges) both attempt to assert ownership over her body, and both express anger over their inability to exercise control. This male anger and frustration is a part of the dominant patriarchal values structuring both society in general and the racetrack in particular.

As Steve Jenkins has noted, *Heart Like a Wheel* is a film marked by the presence of several gazes, mostly male, but also significantly female.[3] For example, one takes place at a birthday party Shirley has arranged for her son John (Anthony Edwards). In the middle of posing for a family photo with his mother and sister, John immediately leaves the room when he hears the phone ringing to answer a call from his father. Despite living and working with his mother, John still responds to his father's voice. Towards the end of this scene, moreover, Shirley's mother gazes ruefully at the embrace between Shirley and her secret lover, Connie. The violent crash sequence that follows is thus not simply a celebration of catastrophe and self-annihilation characteristic of Cronenberg's *Crash,* but functions as punishment for Shirley's illegal desires as a competitor, as a mother, and as a woman. The crash operates as part of a narrative fully conscious of the conservative issues of class and sexuality that threaten its heroine.

Consequently, the film functions oppositionally in relation to earlier structures of classical Hollywood cinema and anticipates features of the future discourse of Cronenberg's crash culture. In other words, it stands at a midpoint between the heroic tradition of the classical sports film and the later, nihilistic dimensions of postmodernism. As Daniel Lopez points out, most drag racing films are "boring and repetitive." They share "a race as the basis for a challenge to man and machine" and suggest that "all other happenings, such as romance, comic relief, musical interlude, or grief, are secondary to the real business of the racers—to compete and win the race."[4] However, Lopez finds that an occasional above-average film appears to validate the genre. These exceptions ironically raise the "secondary" levels to key features of the text, as *Heart Like a Wheel* shows.

Heart begins with a black-and-white sequence showing Shirley's father, Tex Roque (Hoyt Axton), driving recklessly along a country road. As Shirley's voiceover expresses her fear ("I wanted him to slow down but he drove so fast"), an accompanying shot shows the young Shirley sitting in the passenger seat clutching a teddy bear. Next Tex lifts her on to his lap and moves her hands to the wheel. Bereft of her cuddly toy, Shirley begins the first stage of her personal odyssey. But despite the presence of a reassuring father who encourages her to be self-sufficient, she also has to fight the restrictive customs of the 1950s and beyond. These are represented in the film by the implication that a woman's place should be at home with her family and by the sense that an apocalyptic incineration lies in wait for this most excessive of gender transgressors.

During the first "chicken run" sequence, which is introduced by the romantic lullaby "I Only Have Eyes for You," Shirley finds herself gazed at by the figure of Sonny Rigotti (Dean Paul Martin, son of the famous singer). The song stipulates the woman's place in 1956: to be looked at. In this sequence, Shirley reprises the role of Natalie Wood in *Rebel Without a Cause* by starting the race but not taking part in it. In the following sequence, however, she successfully persuades her reluctant husband, Jack, to let her to take his place in a second contest with Sonny, who sneeringly remarks, "If I beat her, do I get to keep her?" This time Shirley wins while Jack looks on in a manner that suggests the female role in a typical sports movie. The sequence concludes with a dissolve of the "chicken run" road mixed with her memory of Jack waving, backed by a reprise of "I Only Have Eyes for You." This sequence of music and imagery suggests not only the poignancy of her parting from

Jack and her farewell to the world of 1956 but also the dangers she will face in the future.

The "chicken run" sequences comprise no mere postmodernist pastiche but have an important rationale of their own. In *Rebel Without a Cause* (1955), the "chicken run" gained its share of morbid notoriety due to the death of its star, James Dean, in a road accident almost immediately following the film's release. Although Dean Paul Martin never achieved any form of stardom, posthumous or otherwise, his presence gives the film an unintentionally ironic nuance. Martin's big break occurred in *Players* (1979), but the film's disastrous reception meant that thereafter he was offered only minor roles in film and television. He eventually perished in an "aerogeddon" scenario when the Phantom F-4 jet he was piloting as captain in the Californian Air National Guard crashed into a mountain during a routine training mission in 1987. Although he never achieved the posthumous fame of James Dean, the death of Dean Paul Martin led to the spiritual death of his better-known father, who drifted away after falling into alcoholic oblivion, ill health, and depression.

When Shirley later visits the racetrack, she meets Don "Big Daddy" Garlits (Bill McKinney) who will act as mentor in providing the first signature she needs to become a competitor, and with whom she will later compete in good-humored gender rivalry. She persists in her efforts, despite Jack's warning—"[t]hey're looking for a guy to push their product"—which also articulates the past and present difficulties facing the real-life Muldowney in her attempts to gain corporate sponsorship. But the way Jack gazes at her when she first sits in Garlits's car represents the first of many aggressive looks that she will encounter throughout the course of the film.

Connie eyes her as a future sexual conquest. When Shirley rebuffs his first attempt at seduction by slapping his face ("[t]he only thing I do fast is drive," she counters), Connie responds with the exclamation "Cha Cha Cha!" This line evokes the period before 1973 when Shirley was known as "Cha Cha Muldowney." Following her separation from Jack, Shirley appeared dressed in hot pants, go-go boots, and halter top. This was not just an attempt to gain the sponsorship that so often eluded her, but also represented the trappings of a "star" image imposed on her by her lover, Connie, who later lays claim to making Shirley a "champ." At this time, Shirley allowed herself to be marketed in terms of an image that she later rejected. "There's no room for bimboism in drag racing," she later claimed.

Shirley's 1973 crash therefore may be seen as a punishment for her complicit participation in her stage persona as well as for the gender threat she offers to a traditionally male-dominated sport. She has not only rejected domestic constraints, like her male counterparts within the genre, but has even reconstituted a new type of family by having her son John as a crew member. Like Huckleberry Finn, she lights off alone to the territory, moving from her former East Coast location of New York State to California. The film concludes with a freeze frame of mother and son united after Shirley's 1980 victory over former lover and competitor Connie Kalitta.

Ironically, the position of Shirley's husband, Jack, parallels that of the female in earlier sports movies. He is a spectator rather than participant, in a manner paralleling the women in *Red Line 7000,* who watch rather than joining in. When Jack dismisses Shirley's competitive aspirations earlier in the film, he asks her, "You think *you're* Big Daddy?" while passively watching baseball hero Mickey Mantle on television. Shirley later counters Connie's first overture to her in 1968 by asserting ownership of her vehicle and her personal autonomy ("It's not my husband's. It's *my* car. He's the mechanic"). Jack's final appearance in the film shows him watching Shirley's victory in the 1980 race on television. His separation from the action parallels the female's position in most similar movies.

In fact, gender is inverted in several ways in *Heart Like a Wheel.* For example, Connie's wife, Marianne Kalitta (Ellen Geer), ages prematurely, in very much the same manner as Maureen O'Hara in her final appearance in John Ford's *The Long Gray Line* (1955). Like O'Hara, Geer looks much older than her husband, stressing the tolls patriarchy inflicts on the domesticated woman. (Marianne Kalitta believes that a woman's role is in the home.) Shirley escapes this particular fate, but she has to pay an even steeper price in *Heart's* car crash sequence by undergoing the same fiery torment once inflicted on independent women in the form of witch trials.

However, despite the camera's sadistic gaze at Shirley's burned body in this unnerving sequence, the film does conclude with some positive reverberations. While Connie stands dumbfounded, John takes control and does everything possible to help his mother survive and compete again. The following sequence shows Kaplan's understanding of the relevance of the car crash scene to the rest of the film. First, we see the television in Shirley's hospital room showing ABC TV's coverage of Billie Jean King on the tennis court. Before the camera pans to Shirley, the caption "Battle of the Sexes" appears. When Shirley later returns to visit Connie, she finds the track dominated by Chrysler car exhibits. Her lover resents the way in which the media now dominates the sport that, he complains, is becoming "all image." "Television, that's what it's all about," Connie comments. After he is suspended for giving the sport "a bad image" following a fight at the track, Shirley offers him a position as her crew chief. But Connie accepts the offer only after becoming jealous when he sees Shirley embracing an old friend.

After this sequence, Shirley appears on a television program to promote her image. This time, however, she openly rejects Connie's designated nickname, "Cha Cha Muldowney," and now wishes to be called by her real name, a wish that is ignored. Later, after winning the 1977 National Hot Rod Association Top Fuel Championship, Shirley finds herself relegated to the background while Connie claims credit for her success. Shirley's dissolution of their partnership is introduced by a scene showing a magazine cover stating "He Made Shirley the Champ." The breakup of their relationship leads Connie to use physical violence against both Shirley and her son, the latter appearing more like a defending lover. Shirley also defends her autonomy ("Do you want to take credit for everything?" she asks him). The film concludes with Shirley again on the track competing against Connie for the 1980 championship, enduring his sarcastic gaze both before and during the race, and finally generously embracing her former lover and defeated rival.

However, Connie still asserts his proprietary ownership of Shirley ("You had a good teacher," he claims), and vows revenge ("I'm going to get you next time"). Although the film ends with the victorious Shirley together with her son, Connie's threat remains in mind, along with the earlier disturbing image of Shirley's incineration. Despite surviving a dangerous car crash following the film's release, she may still face many others. Her position is as precarious as that one facing the various characters in *Red Line 7000*.

In a 1995 interview, Muldowney faced her future realistically. If she doesn't die in action, she feels, her prospects are grim. "I've been at this a long time," she says. "I've worked hard at it. I'm disappointed that it hasn't done anything to secure my future. I'm pretty sure that once I'm out of the race car, there won't be a place for me in this sport."[5] While other car racing movies, such as *The Crowd Roars, Red Line 7000,* and *The Last American Hero* (1973), usually arrive at a successful resolution of the hero's competitive and domestic problems, *Heart Like a Wheel* ends in freeze frame. Shirley may have finally won a victory over her former lover and self-styled teacher Connie Kalita, but she still faces continuing attempts at domination by the men around her as well as the danger of another violent smash-up. However, by revealing these warning signs, *Heart Like a Wheel* does offer the possibility of moving beyond the death drive if the danger signs are heeded.

NOTES

1. Cole Coonce, "Drag Strip Blast Off Girls: Shirley Muldowney and Stacy 'The Femme Fatale' Paul," www.nitronic.com/research/bog.html.
2. Robin Wood, *Howard Hawks* (London: BFI, 1968), 148–149.
3. Steve Jenkins, *"Heart Like a Wheel," Monthly Film Bulletin,* 51: 603, 1984, 106.
4. Daniel Lopez, *Films by Genre* (Jefferson, NC: McFarland & Co., 1993), 185.
5. Cited in Coonce, 1.

TWENTY

THANATOS EX MACHINA

GODARD CARESSES THE DEAD

DAVID STERRITT

CARS AND CAR CRASHES ARE RUNNING THEMES in the cinema of Jean-Luc Godard, appearing most notably during the 1960s era that produced several of the classics upon which his reputation primarily rests. His first feature, the 1960 crime romance *Breathless,* begins with Jean-Paul Belmondo's anarchic antihero, Michel, stealing a car for a joyride during which he plays pop tunes on the radio, fiddles with a gun he finds in the glove compartment, cheerfully chatters to himself, and breaks the rules of commercial film by talking directly to the camera. His advice to us spectators is direct: We should go fuck ourselves if we don't appreciate the pleasures of the everyday world as much as he and Godard evidently do.

Moments later Michel shoots a cop who chases him down the highway, initiating an association between automobiles and death that will continue in Godard films as different as *My Life to Live,* where the prostitute Nana dies alongside the car her psychopathic pimp has parked in front of the ironically named Restaurant des Studios; *Pierrot le Fou,* where the protagonists use a car for their transition from incipient social misfits to full-scale cultural outlaws; and most famously *Weekend,* a crash-ridden extravaganza in which the uproariously alienated main characters propel their battered convertible through a surrealistic traffic

20.1   *Contempt.* © Strand Releasing

jam caused by a deadly accident complete with shattered corpses and blood-smeared pavement.

Godard depicts this *Weekend* episode in a heroically long tracking shot whose leisurely rhythm provides a conspicuously lyrical contrast to the grotesquerie of the images on display. Attraction and repulsion vie for first place in his implicit attitude here—attraction toward the gleaming techno-possibilities of a mechanized civilization that gives us horrific road accidents and exhilarating road movies with equal munificence, and repulsion toward the money-driven forces of materialism, dehumanization, and spiritual decay of which the automobile is the most obvious symbol and ubiquitous embodiment. Godard's political sensibility deplores the metaphysical degeneration induced by the ability of late capitalist society to transform people into mind-numbed automatons. Yet his camera portrays its exanimate victims with the gentleness of one who understands and perhaps envies the escape they have made from a world that traps the mind in stultifying dead ends as readily as it frees the body for meaningless voyages to nowhere. Godard has been called a misanthrope and worse, and *Weekend* could be Exhibit A if he were prosecuted on this charge in a courtroom. Yet here, as elsewhere in his work, he compassionately caresses the dead at the side of the road.

The uncanny mixture of Eros and Thanatos that courses through the car-conscious facet of Godard's career reaches one of its most expressive peaks in the 1963 masterpiece *Contempt,* made less than a decade after his mother was killed in a Swiss traffic accident that appears to have made a searing and lasting impression on her second-eldest child, then in his middle twenties. *Contempt* met with critical skepticism and general audience bewilderment when first released in the United States, where its producers (including Carlo Ponti and Joseph E. Levine, no strangers to the mass-market exploitation of art-film cachet) had hoped to score a commercial success via the presence of Hollywood actor Jack Palance and French actress Brigitte Bardot, then at the peak of her international popularity.

No aspect of the film was more pointedly censured than Godard's decision to resolve its plot through an out-of-the-blue automobile accident that reviewers found at best an arbitrary trick, at worst a desperate act of narrative capriciousness by a lazy storyteller who had tired of his own tale and did not particularly care how he extricated himself from it. The movie's reputation has skyrocketed since then—critic Colin MacCabe deemed it not just the finest film but "the greatest work of art produced in post-war Europe" when it was reissued in 1996—and the critical obtuseness of early commentators is hard to fathom today. This is especially true of the scorn that greeted its car-crash climax, an instance of profoundly inventive and deeply moving cinema that stands with the most inspired moments in all of Godard's work.

Contempt centers on Paul Javal, a French screenwriter (played by Michel Piccoli in one of his subtlest performances) who agrees to rewrite the screenplay of an Italian film production based on *The Odyssey* in order to pay for the Rome apartment where he and his wife (Bardot) want to settle down. Paul is troubled by taking a motion picture assignment, since he sees himself as a serious writer more interested in high-flown theater than lowbrow movies. His intellectual side is soothed by the idea of working with legendary German filmmaker Fritz Lang, played in *Contempt* by Lang himself, one of Godard's longtime heroes. But he also has to work with Jerry Prokosch, a Hollywood producer (Palance) who is less interested in Homeric poetry than in the naked women he gets to ogle when viewing the daily rushes. Jerry is instantly smitten with Paul's wife, Camille, and flirts with her from their first moments together. When he invites the couple for a drink in his villa, Paul unhesitatingly agrees to let Camille ride in Jerry's two-passenger roadster while he finds a taxi for the trip. Camille takes this as a sign of Paul's decreasing commitment to their marriage—she gathers that he is indulging the producer's lust as a way of currying his favor—and begins to reveal her own anxieties and insecurities about their future.

The situation grows more complicated as it proceeds, especially when the threesome move to an exotic villa on Capri, where the *Odyssey* production is being filmed. Camille endures and even encourages Jerry's continuing flirtation; Paul shows a casual romantic interest in Jerry's attractive assistant; and Lang maintains a philosophical air while trying to keep his movie on a reasonably high plane despite Jerry's crassly commercial interventions. At one point, Paul places a loaded pistol into his pocket, clearly intended for use on Jerry and/or Camille if her growing contempt for him (hence the film's title) erupts into a full-fledged refutation of their marriage. But fate intervenes before he can fire it, assuming that he could actually have brought himself to do so. Camille leaves Paul for a new life with Jerry; the producer's luxurious Alfa-Romeo is crushed in a crash that kills both him and Camille instantly; and Paul prepares for his departure from Capri, as Lang films a sweeping ocean-side shot that concludes *Contempt* on a note of intricately blended lyricism, melancholy, and resignation.

After constructing a narrative setup that could compete with most Hollywood stories for conventional romance and suspense—Will Camille stay with Jerry? Will Paul chase after them? Will he regain his errant wife or murder his ruthless rival?—why did Godard choose not to resolve it in a conventional manner, opting instead for a climax that seems to deliberately court accusations of arbitrariness and caprice? To understand this aspect of *Contempt* one must comprehend the film as a whole, with special attention to at least two related moments that come before and after the scene in question.

An early clue is given at the film's beginning, since *Contempt* starts with an evocation of movement—not a car traveling down a highway, but a camera traveling down a track, prefiguring the story's ultimate resolution in its very first shot. This opening scene takes place at Cinecittà, the fabled Italian studio. A camera track stretches into the distance, perpendicular to the camera that is filming the image we see, and a visible camera is gradually wheeling along this track toward our vantage point. In this moment we have one of Godard's most ingenious statements about the meaning(s) of movement in cinema. The tracking of the on-screen camera is steady in its course, carefully guided by the technicians at its controls, and imperturbably composed in its implicit attitude toward whatever vicissitudes of life may come within its purview. The cool, collected nature of this visible camera's motion is underscored further by the unseen camera that is providing this image to us, as it calmly reframes the shot, adjusting its angle until the gazes of the two cameras meet. Our camera looks upward at a slight angle while the on-screen camera looks imperiously down at our own lens, as if inviting our eyes to worship at an altar of cinema. Considered in retrospect, every aspect of this shot establishes a brilliant counterpoint with the deadly convulsion that will erupt at the film's climax.

An additional counterpoint comes from the voiceover narration that we hear during this scene: "'The cinema,' André Bazin said, 'substitutes for our gaze a world that corresponds to our desires.' *Contempt* is the story of this world." Film critic Jonathan Rosenbaum has noted that Bazin is probably not the actual source of this quotation, which most likely comes from a writer less prominent and influential than the renowned theorist, and that the quotation itself is probably inaccurate. Rosenbaum also notes, quite rightly, that this does not matter. The idea expressed by the quote is perfectly in sync with the philosophy of *Contempt* in particular, and Godardian cinema in general. We watch the spectacle of Paul the wanderer, Camille the not-quite-fathomable wife, and Jerry the self-absorbed suitor because it brings to us a concatenation of notions and emotions that conform to the world of our own desires, and because one of humanity's most longstanding desires is to gain some shred of understanding vis-à-vis the deep-rooted tension between order and chaos in human experience.

Godard begins *Contempt* with a vision of *cinema* as *movement* as *order*, and he climaxes the film with a vision of *life* as *stasis* as *disorder*. This may seem like an unhappy trajectory, yet the message underlying it is paradoxically reassuring, since the vision of Camille and Jerry in their wrecked automobile conveys a sense of calmness and restraint that counteracts the horror we might feel if we were watching this in the world that *is*, rather than in a world that *corresponds to our desires*. We never see the crash that kills them; we only hear it on the sound track (like the alleged Bazin quotation at the beginning) while the written word "adieu," penned by Camille in her farewell letter to Paul, fills the screen. When we do see the dead couple, they are in a state of peacefulness and repose. Their car stands motionless, crushed incongruously between the tail ends of two oil trucks that are as enormous as they are symbolic, suggesting that capitalism has taken a rage-filled revenge on Jerry for trying to choose the excitement of romance over the drone of money-spinning commerce. The lovers are equally still and silent, each lifeless head echoed by the empty hole it punched in the windshield during its catastrophic impact just an instant earlier. The few traces of their scarlet-red blood are less jolting to our eyes than the matching orange-red of Jerry's sweater, the Alfa-Romeo's paint, and the fire extinguisher rudely protruding from one of the murderous trucks. Most tellingly, the couple's faces are turned in opposite directions, reaffirming in death the many forms of miscommunication and noncommunication—linguistic, social, spiritual—that marred their relationship from its first moments and would surely have doomed it if they had lived. Their final nonembrace is auto/erotic in more than one sense, and the grotesquerie of this cinematic pun is well suited to the futility of the romantic fling they vainly tried to pursue.

Godard is not mocking this unhappy pair, however. He is mourning them. In his book *The Lives of a Cell*, biologist Lewis Thomas observes that although everything in the world dies, plants do it so gracefully that we hardly think of the process as death. Something similar happens with animals, he adds, since they have "an instinct for performing death alone, hidden," dying within the reach of human eyes so infrequently that we feel a "queer shock" when we pass a huddled piece of roadkill on a highway.[1] Human deaths are far more visible, in the movies at least, and Camille and Jerry are made quite a spectacle of, captured by a lens as imperious and implacable as that of the camera we saw in their story's opening shot. Yet here, as in other films, Godard chooses to caress the vulnerable corpses, comforting their invisible souls and cushioning our queer spectatorial shock with the gentle motion of his camera, the soothing texture of Georges Delerue's rich musical refrain, and the calm precision of a *mise-en-scène* as eloquently arranged as a still life in a gracefully shifting frame.

Godard's serene depiction of this chthonic scene echoes another of Thomas's insights into the meanings and mechanisms of death: that dying "is not such a bad thing to do," notwithstanding the aversion to it that we acquire through our attachment to the "long habit" of living. Thomas cites the experience of a nineteenth-century explorer saved by a companion just as a lion's jaws had begun to crush his chest. Recalling the experience later, the near-victim was "amazed by the extraordinary sense of peace, calm, and total painlessness associated with being killed."[2] He concluded that the coming of death is as benign as it is inevitable, marked not by agony and anxiety but by quietude, equanimity, and an easeful "haze of tranquillity" that envelops consciousness as it gracefully glides into its opposite.

Godard agrees in *Contempt,* which culminates in imagery that indeed corresponds to our desires—our desires for untroubled sleep, peaceful death, and the termination of all tension that psychoanalysis identifies as a fundamental human drive. The climax of *Contempt* has been attacked as a deus ex machina device, but how could that time-honored trope be considered offensive in a film whose narrative makes constant reference to the Homeric world, whose themes are animated by thoughts of fate, destiny, and the enigmatic actions of ancient and modern gods? This profoundly moving scene is precisely a deus ex machina, and its deus has been selected with exquisite care. It is Thanatos, the urge toward a calming death that drowns all care, sorrow, useless striving, and bitter hopefulness.

Confirming this god's melancholy yet comforting message, Godard ends *Contempt* with a final scene at the Capri villa, where Paul is bidding farewell to Lang and his *Odyssey* dreams. Lang is filming a valedictory shot on the roof of the ocean-bathed building, and again we see an on-screen camera in motion, this time not coming assertively toward us but sliding elusively to the side. The camera that shows us this image moves as well, outpacing both Lang's lens and the sword-wielding actor who is the ostensible focus of his shot. In mere moments, the *Contempt* camera has found its true destination: the sea, blue and swelling beneath the sun, empty of detail yet teeming with significance as a deeply expressive symbol of the final, all-absorbing domain into which every road and river of life must flow.

"Silence!" cries Lang's assistant, played by Godard himself. Fittingly, this word (with an echoing Italian translation called into the air) is the final sound of both the film that Lang is making and the film that Godard has made. The sea and the screen will now be as silent as the ill-starred lovers whom a thundering Thanatos ex cinema has ushered into a quieter, calmer realm.

NOTES

1. Lewis Thomas, "Death in the Open," in *The Lives of a Cell: Notes of a Biology Watcher* (New York: Penguin, 1974), 96.
2. Lewis Thomas, "The Long Habit," in ibid., 47–52.

SIGNAL 30

MIKITA BROTTMAN

AN INTERESTING SYMPTOM OF OUR OBSESSION with traumatic encounter and violent death is the current popularity on the home video mail-order market of the driver's education "scare films" that were made in the late 1950s and early 1960s by the National Highway Traffic Safety Administration. Originally given titles like *Signal 30, Death on the Highway,* and *Highways of Blood,* these films are now marketed in compilation or outtake form, and advertised as "Real-Life Traffic Splatter," "Mechanized Death!" or "Highway Safety Films—Two Hours of Blood and Bone-Crunching Horror!" The most frequently compiled footage comes from *Signal 30,* a reference to the police call-out code for a serious road accident. In this movie, the camera follows various police officers to a series of car accident scenes. Each scenario is a grim narrative vignette, given form by editing, camerawork, and voiceover techniques. The emphasis of these moral tales is authenticity. Over and over again we are reminded that these are *real* accidents involving *real* people. "Most of the actors in these movies . . . received top billing only on a tombstone," begins *Signal 30.* "They paid a terrific price to be in these movies—they paid with their lives."

Poor film quality is offered as an index of "truth." "This is not a Hollywood production, as can readily be seen," the narrator intones, proudly. "The quality is well below their standards. However, most of these scenes were taken immediately after the accident occurred." This ingenuous disclaimer detracts attention from the fact that the film is, in effect, carefully shot and edited to create a deliberate and specific effect. Camera movements are sometimes loose and jerky, in the best traditions of cinema verité, and sometimes they are much smoother, particularly when the camera glides easily over piles of twisted metal, panning for mangled body parts. In other scenes, close-ups lit by the flashing blue light of a police car reveal mutilated limbs trapped in a tangled mass of glass and steel. Long shots lingering over wrecked vehicles are occasionally juxtaposed with stills of dead bodies, sometimes slumped over the steering column or sometimes extricated from their respective wreckage, inert and bleeding by the side of the road.

In theory, *Signal 30* invites us to take our place in the passenger seat of the cop car as we join a team of Highway Patrol Officers on their daily rounds, although it soon becomes pretty obvious that the film has been compiled over a long stretch of time. But never mind these inconsistencies—look, here comes the "signal 30"! "Will we find a minor mishap," speculates the lascivious narrator, "or will we look upon the stark face of death?" No prizes for guessing the right answer to this one. Those of us hoping for a "minor mishap" will be gravely disappointed as our cop car sets off on cruise control to oblivion. A loud series of drum rolls announces our entrance into the inferno of autogeddon, and the quivering camera leads us through an orgy of major collisions. We are about to encounter fatal pileups filled with "bodies burned beyond recognition," "parts of mangled corpses," "horrible wrecks," and other "images of death" "sprawled across the highway of blood." The libidinous excess of this language and imagery brings to mind J. G. Ballard's conviction that the car crash forms a powerful imaginative link between the nexus of sex, love, eroticism, and death. The heart of the automobile, contends Ballard, is wired into the central nervous system of all human beings.[1]

When the garrulous narrator is silent, the film's soundtrack consists of haunting and ghoulish musical sounds—either solemn single drum beats or eerie, shrieking violins that are barely distinguishable from the ambulance sirens. At other times, and always emphasized by the narrator, the soundtrack becomes part of the narrative, featuring groans, shouts, screams, and the distracting static of the police radio. "These," we are informed, "are the sounds of excruciating agony. There are no words to describe them. . . . [T]he cries and moans of the maimed are a grim accompaniment to the tragedy." "Death," we are told somberly, "sometimes plays an overture of torture." Cue the screams of another injured victim. "Here," continues our droll narrator, "the cries of the maimed are heard, cries of suffering and pain."

This wry voiceover has an exaggerated solemnity that at times seems almost malicious in its grandiloquence. A car crash is never simply a car crash but "an apocalyptic flight into oblivion," a "carnage of twisted metal and destroyed flesh"; lives are never simply lost, they are "erased in an instant by vehicular destruction." The rhetoric is grotesquely overblown, often ghoulishly so. "Her features were so distorted that this woman was virtually unidentifiable," we learn as the camera zooms in on a huge mass of guts being scraped off the road and shaken into a plastic bag. During a similarly cheerful scene, we are invited to consider "the nauseating task" of "removing the shattered hulk of a life that had been lived so little." The "finale to the tragedy" comes when "the body of the lad is placed in a rubber sack—a gift offering to the great God Speed."

Sometimes the narrator takes off on flights of fancy that are dubiously speculative, to say the least. One grisly vignette involves the death of a baby (cue the inevitable close-up of a baby bottle lying by the side of the road beside some blood-splattered children's toys). "The officer was heartbroken," apparently. "His heart," although broken, "rushed to his own home, and his own three little ones." Elsewhere, the mangled fusion of car and body makes it hard to see how the cause of the crash could be even vaguely determined. Yet each accident is attributed unequivocally to a specific cause: "the tragic effects of the tired mind," "fatigue," "speed," "drinking," "a moment of inattention," or the failure to wear a safety belt (yes, "a mere web of fabric could have preserved the fiber of life").

The more dreadful the accident scenes, the more baroque the rhetoric that accompanies them. In one sequence, the camera zooms in to scrutinize the tangled recesses of a shattered car, then offers a series of close-up shots of the ambulance crew trying to pry flesh from metal. Dismal music accompanies the news that this particular young man "was dead before the collision dust had settled on the street," and "the autopsy revealed enough physical injury to kill three people." In

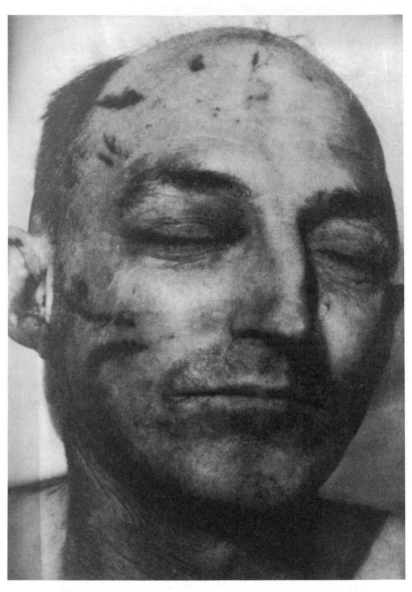

21.1   Car Crash Victim. © Feral House

another scene, the camera moves in excitedly on the oblivious faces of two dead bodies that have been thrown from their car like the predictable "rag dolls." "Their staring eyes still seem to hold the horror they saw a second or two before death," we are informed delightedly. When two huge trucks plow into one another on an interstate highway, the camera loiters pruriently over the harrowing result. "You have seen the blackened body of a dead man in a horrible wreck, far from family and friends," we are told, in case we are unable to identify the showcased pile of roadside remains.

Details about individual accidents in this eerie parade of crashes are given only when they are informed by a bleak irony in keeping with the narrator's morbid rhetoric. One man and his wife were in town to attend his mother's funeral the following day. "Less than twenty-four hours before the said ceremony," however, "death occurs." A sudden drum roll accompanies a close-up of the poor man's corpse, "sprawled on the ground, already showing the pallor the doomed assume." Another poor man and his wife end up in a "mechanized catastrophe" despite (or because of?) the fact that they were "preparing for a party the following day—a party that would celebrate their young son's first birthday." Another unlucky young man sets off toward obliteration "on his first trip for his new company in a brand-new job," only to end up "crawling out of a tangled mass of metal . . . his life having only beating hours to run."

At its most excessive, the narrative rhetoric sounds almost Elizabethan in its melodramatic archaisms: "Mark well these few words"; "His remains were interred with the blessing of his church"; "Death had visited both vehicles"; "think again, friend, think again." Elsewhere, the narrator comes across as righteously indignant, tut-tutting that we mere mortals should even so much as consider pitting ourselves against the power of the great automobile: "We have fallen into the trap of our own technology, as we discover that the human body is no match for a powerful engine, and the mass of steel housing it. As long as people continue to drive, there will be death on the highways."

It's almost as if this exaggerated language is an attempt to make the film's basic appeal to voyeurism appear more lofty and important, perhaps in order as to excuse and justify the creepy litany of graphic horrors being shown to us.

In other places, the voice-over takes on a wryly sardonic tone. "Speed is a relative matter," we are told. "How would your relatives feel if you were killed by speed?" Later we are shown the wreckage of a vehicle whose driver apparently had "too flippant an attitude" and, as a result, smashed headfirst into an exit sign. "It was *his* exit also," the narrator comments, flippantly. Perhaps the deliberate bad taste of these ironic asides is a way of helping the audience deal with the horrors of death, encouraging fantasies of immortality. But although it may venture into the realms of irony, the tone never becomes overtly mocking or deliberately comic. Again and again this violent imagery is justified by laconic repudiations on the part of the spectacularly deadpan narrator who reminds us that, while these shocking images might be disturbing, they are being shown for our own good. "We are cruel, cold, and harsh, you say?" inquires our host, as the camera shows a dying woman being pried out of the wreck of her car. "You shouldn't have to see this? . . . This is not a pretty motion picture. It is not supposed to be. It has only one purpose—to cause you to take time to *think.*"

The question remains, however: To think about *what?*

One especially interesting feature of *Signal 30* is the filmmakers' attempts to shape each gruesome little vignette into some form of coherent narrative. For example, many scenes open with the type of mythical formula typical of a ghost story or urban legend. "More than one hundred persons die on our highways every day," begins one segment, "but I doubt there was a stranger accident that January day than the one you're about to see." This heightened, literary style of discourse seems to conflict with the cinema verité camera style and promises of urgent and spontaneous police action. Even more confusingly, openings to other segments stress the everyday nature of the episode: "It was eleven o'clock on a Friday night, and the trio was out on the town"; "A high school football star drives down a winding road late at night." Victims become ciphers, anonymous spirits from Hades, distinguished by mere formulaic markers of identity—"a visitor from a neighboring state" or "a hard-of-hearing farmer." Generally, however, they are acknowledged to be significant only in relation to their role in the accident, the part they play in their own particular morbid sideshow: "the driver of the flat-bed semi"; "the twisted body of a two-year-old child." Finally, to the strains of a maudlin violin, each scene ends with a grim coda of ironic warning or morbid speculation: "That must have been his last thought"; "Imagine yourself in this position. Believe me, it could happen to you"; "There were many nights when he screamed in pain"; "The family will miss him in their new life."

These conflicting modes of discourse in *Signal 30* seem symptomatic of a more fundamental instability in the presentation of this grim parade of accidents. Are they a result of careless driving (the discourse of "needless slaughter"), or are they something that could happen to any one of us, at any time (the discourse of "grim destiny")? On one hand, the movie's fables of drunken fathers, speeding high school football stars, and other somber examples of overconfidence suggest that the car accident is something that the cautious driver can avoid. This rhetoric of blame and attribution is a form of social scapegoating, an attempt to reinforce the laws of the community and to unite its members by reminding us of the "gruesome tragedies" that can ensue whenever these laws are broken. On the other hand, however, the discourse of Death visiting "out of the blue" and innocent victims "meeting their destinies" on the lonely highway implies that the accident is something that *cannot*, in fact, be avoided.

Perhaps this instability is itself symptomatic of a wider cultural confusion, because, after all, one man's act of negligence is another man's accident. Consider the semantic distinction between a car "accident" and a car "crash," words used interchangeably in *Signal 30*. A "crash" is not necessarily inevitable, and usually occurs as a result of human or mechanical error. An "accident," on the other hand, denies all responsibility, separating the car from the actions of the driver involved, suggesting an implicit fatalism—an unlucky conflation of circumstances that is nobody's fault and could not have been avoided.

Apparently intended to shock youngsters into safer driving habits, movies like *Signal 30* clearly have a long and lasting appeal far beyond their original audience. This is partly because the accidents featured are all especially nasty. A massive truck slams into the midsection of a car, sending it on a "wild, hurling dance of death"; a pickup truck and a flat-bed semi meet head-on, giving the truck driver "a ringside seat at the slaughter." The more violent the accident, the more fascinating the ensuing carnage. Our appetite for destruction has long been testified; all children and many adults seem to find great pleasure in smashing and breaking things, or watching things being smashed and broken. "The death instinct turns into the destructive instinct if . . . it is directed outwards, on to objects," explains Sigmund Freud.[2] But *Signal 30* seems to appeal to a more complicated nexus of appetites than the mere instinct for triumphant destruction.

Consider the crowd that gathers at the scene of any accident. People have always been fascinated by the sight of the opened body, the collapse of fleshly boundaries, and the visible evidence of trauma and the wound.[3] And while we might mourn the victims of the car accident and perhaps even identify with them to a certain extent, there's always a sense of vicarious relief—even a thrill—that the crash has happened to somebody else and not to us. This way of thinking is sometimes known as the triumphalism of the survivor.[4] And there is something especially appealing about a series of accidents (or their aftermaths) released on home video, as in the case of *Signal 30*.

In Ballard's *Crash,* the character Vaughan is obsessed with photographs and reenactments of the celebrated deaths of James Dean and Jayne Mansfield. He knows that photography, like reenactment, gives us control over time, "freezing the moment when the mortal being becomes Other, fully transformed into pure image."[5] The photographic image of the fatal accident is both the testament made by the dead to the living and a sacred talisman to ward off the ghosts that we fear may survive when both body and mind have disintegrated. In *Signal 30,* our ability to rewind and replay the aftermath of accidents—to watch bodies collapse and disintegrate before our eyes, again and again—essentially puts us in control of the accident, which then ceases to be an accident and becomes instead an act of deliberate motivation. In other words, these powerful images protect us from the terrors of contingency.

It is pretty clear that *Signal 30* goes way beyond driver's education. Those who remember being forced to watch such films as teenagers often confess to being terrified even to *look* at another automobile, to say nothing of actually getting in one. As a result, "atrocity exhibitions" like *Signal 30* stopped being shown in schools in the early 1970s, and were soon replaced by less traumatizing material. Nevertheless, the enormous popularity of *Signal 30* on the home video mail-order circuit suggests that it clearly satisfies some important social and cultural imperatives.

One of the most vital of these imperatives is the way the film fulfills the repetition compulsion. To sit through a series of violent car crashes, one after another after another, is a way of integrating the trauma into a psychic economy, thereby attaining some level of mastery over it. In other words, repetition of the trauma produces two conflicting attitudes toward death: that which acknowledges it as traumatic and that which denies its power to harm.[6] This is not to say that these graphic images of road accidents ever cease to be shocking, but rather that they end up producing a generalized feeling of shock that can not be located precisely in any one single image or accident. Perhaps this is because the original trauma, by definition, can not be represented. It can only be repeated, and repetition is not reproduction.[7] As Freud explains, "it takes two traumas to make a trauma."[8] What is more, *Signal 30* recalls Freud's belief that the "accident" is governed by the unconscious motivation of the death drive: Accidents repeated over and over again stop looking like accidents and start to seem repetitive, automatic, deliberate, and technological.

Another deeply appealing aspect of *Signal 30* is the way the film hypnotizes spectators with a spell cast using the power of "negative magic." Negative magic is a response to the superstitious guilty implication that the observer may feel in relation to an accident—that, as a spectator, we have dictated the event or even indirectly caused it.[9] This exaggerated and compulsive expression of the observer's own conscience can be countered only by a repetition of the traumatic event, leading to a reaction formation: The accident is repeated in order to magically undo what has been done. As Freud explains, negative magic endeavors, "by means of motor symbolism, to 'blow away' not merely the *consequences* of some event (or experience or impression), but the event itself."[10] As a function of popular customs and religious ceremonies as well as obsessional neurosis, "negative magic" compels the repetition of the accident in order to make it "not have happened"—a defense against something that should have been done the first time but was forgotten or inhibited.

In short, the crashes obsessively showcased in *Signal 30* are compelling because they partake of the magic nature of the ceremonial, whose function is to ward off suffering through ritualized repetition. Ballard makes a similar point about the "sacramental aspect" of the car accidents featured in *Crash:* "The compulsive rehearsal of the same scenario—these endless crashes being planned and executed—is in fact no more than the sort of repetitions you find in religious observance. The same mantras are recited, the same knees are bent before the same bleeding Christ upon his cross."[11]

Perhaps there are other reasons why *Signal 30* seems so compelling to some of us and so disturbing to others. One of these could be that the movie's emphasis on unexpected, premature deaths is a way of preserving our own existence intact. As Freud explains, by repeatedly stressing the fortuitous causes of death, we are really trying to modify its significance from a necessity to a mere accident.[12] Another reason could be because the film actually reduces the mystery and superstition surrounding the dying process, thereby—in total contrast to the film's explicit intentions—actually helping to prepare us for death by making us think very carefully about our own mortality.

"Death is forever," intones the narrator of *Signal 30* excitedly. "Take time to think."

"If you would endure life," advises Freud, "be prepared for death."[13]

NOTES

1. See J. G. Ballard, *Crash* (London: Cape, 1973); also Iain Sinclair, *Crash* (London: BFI, 1999), 80.
2. Sigmund Freud, *Civilization and Culture* (New York: Collier, 1963). "The living creature preserves its own life, so to say, by destroying an extraneous one," continues Freud. "Some portion of the death instinct, however, remains operative *within* the living being, and we have sought to trace quite a number of normal and pathological phenomena to the internalization of the destructive instinct" (143).

3. For further discussion of this appeal, see Mark Seltzer, "Wound Culture: Trauma in the Pathological Public Sphere," *October*, 80, spring 1997, 3–26, and Mikita Brottman, "Carnivalizing the Taboo: The Mondo Film and the Opened Body," *Cineaction*, 38, fall 1994, 25–38.

4. Hal Foster, "Death in America," *October*, 75, winter 1996, 37.

5. Barbara Creed, "The *Crash* Debate: Anal Wounds, Metallic Kisses," *Screen*, 39:2, summer 1998, 145.

6. Freud, 131.

7. See Jacques Lacan, *Four Fundamental Concepts of Psychoanalysis*, trans. Alan Sheridan (New York: W. W. Norton, 1978), 50.

8. Freud, 131.

9. For some interesting examples of negative magic, see Foster, 55, n. 54.

10. Freud, 33.

11. Ralph Rugoff, "Dangerous Driving" (interview with J. G. Ballard), *Freize*, 34, May 1997, 50.

12. Freud, 112. "A multitude of simultaneous deaths appears to us exceedingly terrible," Freud continues. "Towards the dead person himself we take up a special attitude, something like admiration for one who has accomplished a very difficult task."

13. Ibid., 133.

THE DEATH DRIVE

ELEVEN DEAD CADDIES AND ONE DEAD PUNK

JEFF FERRELL

A WHILE BACK I HOOKED UP WITH A NAVAJO MAN, maybe forty years old, shivering cold on a late-winter afternoon in Flagstaff, Arizona. He'd left the nearby Navajo Rez a couple of days before, hitchhiking down notorious Highway 89, a concussive mix of two-lane curves, gawking Grand Canyon tourists, late-for-the-weekend Lake Powell junkies jerking big ski boats along behind overpowered SUVs, and Rez residents driving old pickups back and forth to Flagstaff. As a result, Highway 89 is known for something else too: all those white roadside crosses, here marking one of the highway's countless head-on collisions, there pinning down some deadly moment when a car cartwheeled off 89 and out into the surrounding sandstone.

At any rate, my new acquaintance had made it past the calvacade of crosses, safely down the death march of 89 to Flagstaff, on his way to Phoenix, 150 miles south. Already picked up once by the police since his arrival in town the night before, he and I both knew he didn't have much chance of making it further on foot through the cold and past the police patrols to his intermediate destination: the warmth of the Flagstaff bus station. Besides, he reminded me, "They won't let you stay in the bus station without a ticket." So, gathering up a blanket and old coat for him,

I loaded him into a car, drove to the bus station, bought him a ticket for the next Phoenix bus, and sat down to get warm and talk for a while (mostly about Jesus, as it turned out—maybe all those white crosses got to him on the way down).

A few months later, this time myself hopping an early-morning bus to Albuquerque, I remember his claim and decide to ask about it. No, an employee behind the counter assures me, it's not a problem for folks to hang out in the bus station without a ticket, "as long as they're not causing trouble." Walking back to my seat in the waiting area, curious as to what might constitute "trouble" and on whose terms, I'm just awake enough to realize that the bus station's all of a sudden become *Apocalypse Now*. The prerecorded, computer-simulated sounds of punches and pain have begun to fill the small waiting area as a gangly twelve-year-old kid—in camouflage shirt and camouflage shorts—jams quarters into a combination combat/kick-boxing video game. With little brother watching attentively from just off his left elbow, he leans in, pumping the joystick and talking loudly back to the game. I can almost catch the smell of napalm in the morning. And I wonder: Does he have a ticket? And who's causing trouble?

I also wonder whether all this video violence portends some sort of automotive apocalypse on my bus ride down I-40 to Albuquerque—but of course I know that it does. See, the thing is, 89's not the only roadway decorated with the detritus of automotive death. Throughout the southwestern United States, generations of residents have built roadside shrines to friends and family members killed in auto accidents; and, over the last decade or so, as the number of such shrines has increased dramatically so has their dispersion into areas beyond the Southwest. Growing out of the Latino/a and Native American tradition of *descansos* ("resting places") designed to mark and memorialize the place of death, these shrines typically center on a small cross constructed of wood, stone, or rock, and decorated with flowers and other memorabilia.[1] In my decades of living and wandering in Texas, Colorado, Arizona, and New Mexico, I've seen many hundreds, maybe thousands of such shrines, approaching them with reverence and a certain inquisitive embarrassment, and recording and photographing those I thought appropriate. Now, riding the Greyhound from Flagstaff to Albuquerque, I watch them come

22.1   Highway 60, West Central Mexico. © Jeff Ferrell

into view once again, strung out along the interstate like some busted
string of prayer beads: two little white crosses in the median, one with
pink plastic flowers, the other with purple. A white cross wrapped with
red plastic roses; another ringed by luminarias. An old cowboy hat af-
fixed to a cross on a little hill just off the south side of the highway; and

22.2   Route 66 Shrine. © Jeff Ferrell

beyond, a second cross, purple and white flowers encircling it, yellow flowers atop.

You don't have to ride the interstate to find these shrines, though; they're just as common along the smaller rivulets of automotive destruction that feed into it, along those little two-lane backroads that punctuate the Southwest's open spaces. East of Muleshoe, Texas, twin crosses rest under a lonesome shade tree, top heavy with plastic flower bouquets. On Highway 6 through central New Mexico, another set of twin crosses writes a message almost unbearable in its sadness. Draped in plastic flowers and rosaries, the crosses for "Dad" and "Mom" support a broken car mirror, and next to them a pinwheel flutters in the wind, "we-love-you-forever" written on its blades. In fact, rosary beads hang from many of the crosses that I find in New Mexico, and shattered car parts, physical reminders of the fatal crash, are often collected at or near a cross's base. West of Willard, New Mexico, a cross constructed from silver iron tubing features at its base a sturdier reminder: a rough rock headstone with the deceased's name and dates of birth and death carefully carved. And along a long-abandoned stretch of old Route 66, paralleling I-40 near

Mesita, New Mexico, sits a shrine that I have visited many times, amazed by all it seems to embody. There, along a forgotten remnant of the very "Mother Road" that carried the Dust Bowlers all the way to Barstow and San Berdoo, that opened the American West to automotive touring, a forgotten cross hangs on, its broken, white-painted wood charred by brushfire, its uneven lettering composed from old upholstery tacks pressed into the wood one by one.

In marking the deaths and commemorating the lives of those they honor, these folk shrines accomplish something else as well: the transformation of the roadsides on which they are erected. Working with little more than wood, stone, and plastic flowers, families and friends affix identity, celebrate meaning, in locations that otherwise would remain empty, transitory, anonymous. In so doing, they remake the roadside as memorial, salvaging the sacred from the everyday profanity of speed, death, exhaust fumes, litter. Sociologist Clifton Bryant argues that families and friends who build such shrines create an "anchor in space," because for them "the place of death is as important as the time and cause" and because "the anonymity of modern life is frightening."[2] The poet Carl Sandburg said it better. Recalling the countless forgotten battlefield dead at Austerlitz and Waterloo, Gettysburg and Verdun, he wrote, "Two years, ten years, and the passengers ask the conductor: What place is this? Where are we now?"[3] Each roadside shrine answers these questions, forcing us to confront the lives and deaths of those who travel with us, to remember, glimpsing a cross and flowers, what place this is and where we are now. Taken as a whole, encountered mile after mile and one after another, these shrines accumulate into a collective condemnation and remembrance of ongoing automotive carnage; they commemorate a mass battlefield and graveyard, as deadly as Gettysburg and Verdun, strung out along the open road.

Of course, city streets constitute a similar battlefield—and graveyard. In fact, Ken Kelton believes that, in the same way rural highways constitute mass killing fields, urban streets harbor a sort of automotive "serial killer." Outraged about the way in which "automobiles seem to have taken over the streets and society," Kelton travels the streets of San Francisco map in hand, searching for sites at which pedestrians have been killed by cars. Once a site is located, Kelton lays a life-size body stencil

on the pavement, outlines it with white spray paint, and writes an asphalt epitaph: "5–15–99 Nameless Man Killed Here By Traffic";
"4–15–99 Woman 71 Killed Here By Traffic." Although police officials
confirm that Kelton risks citation for public vandalism, he continues to
consecrate city streets because, as he says, "There's something wrong with
the whole traffic layout, the whole system." Kelton's more intimate concerns reflect the work of those who erect crosses on rural highways. A
pedestrian death "doesn't seem to matter. It doesn't even make the
paper," he says. "I'm trying to underscore that this is life and death."[4]

For bike messengers in San Francisco and other cities, the streets also
cough up life and death. Weaving around cars and buses, earning their
living along traffic-choked avenues, they face one of the highest death
and injury rates afforded by any occupation. The zines and websites produced by various bike messenger communities in the United States and
Canada catalog this ongoing encounter with street violence and death; as
Gary Genosko notes darkly, "Perhaps this makes the obituary the stylistic model of messenger writing."[5] But like those who erect roadside
crosses, like Ken Kelton and his body stencils, bike messengers also commemorate life and death directly in the streets they ride. The day after
San Francisco bike messenger Thomas Meredith was run over and killed,
bike messengers blocked a major thoroughfare, with fifteen of those
present arrested. In the following weeks messengers and friends main-
tained flowers at the street site of his death. And at the next Critical Mass
event—a collectively "disorganized" bicycle ride held monthly in San
Francisco and other cities—1,200 bicyclists took to the streets of the city,
dedicating their ride to the memory of Thomas Meredith.

If you leave behind the streets of San Francisco and the memory of
Thomas Meredith, get back on that east-bound bus with me, roll on
down I-40 to Albuquerque, and then continue on past Santa Rosa and
Tucumcari, you hit yet another sort of roadside shrine, an hour or so after
crossing the line into Texas. Coming into Amarillo from the west, cutting
through the monotony of the West Texas flatlands and the stench of cattle feed lots, an automotive shrine—hell, an automotive apparition—rises
just south of the interstate: wealthy eccentric Stanley Marsh III's famous
Cadillac Ranch. A collection of ten old Cadillacs, planted all in a row, east
to west, fins up, the ranch sits at the end of smooth dirt path worn into

the West Texas sod over the years by all the foreign tourists and fat-ass families drawn to this strange Stonehenge of Modernity.

A little farther down the road, rolling into what passes for downtown Amarillo, you come to the little Amarillo bus station. I came to it one night about 3 A.M., riding yet another bus out of Flagstaff, this time hoping to catch a connecting bus to Fort Worth. Waiting the remainder of the night for my delayed connection, jammed shoulder to shoulder with a hundred or so other bus station down-and-outers lost in the inefficiency of America's nonautomotive mass transit, trading that open-road feed-lot stench for a claustrophobic waiting room cloud of cigarette smoke and bus fumes, I swore I once again caught the smell of napalm in the morning. And sitting there I thought of another video game, much like the one the kid was humping back in the Flagstaff bus station. Except in this one, there's no doubt at all as to who's causing trouble.

Among the many currently popular video games that reduce life and death to a touch of the reset button, one in particular displays its automotive politics with all the subtlety of a head-on collision. *Carmageddon* and subsequent versions like *Carmageddon High Octane* and *Carmageddon 2 Carpocalypse Now* offer a driving game in which players race their cars against each other, or against the computer, in a variety of virtual environments. But *Carmageddon* comes with a homicidal twist: Players earn points, and eventually win, not just by completing the racecourse but by killing pedestrians. And it's this twist that has online reviewers raving. One, who lists his interests as "technology, cars, anything fast," offers a sanguine summary: "The point of the game is simple, drive over pedestrians, farm animals, and destroy other cars, or race them. . . . To put it in a simple way, drive and kill, and you will win!" "*Carmageddon* captures a feeling of power behind the wheel," adds another reviewer, "leaving only your wheels on the road and the screams of anyone who falls between them. . . . In addition to the graphic presentation of splattered pedestrians, players are also treated to extremely colorful language." A third reviewer is moved to a more descriptive account. "Fleeing, screaming pedestrians . . . aren't safe from your raging red death mobile as you can run, skid, back up, and land on them creating bloody messes you can later run over with squishy, slippery results. And best of all," he notes helpfully, "you get bonus points for causing all this havoc."

Interestingly, these reviewers link *Carmageddon* to the everyday realities of an autocentric death world, while at the same time denying any
such link. One player, who describes his interests as "classic automobiles,
muscle cars, wrestling," points out that he wouldn't recommend the game
for "people who take things way to [*sic*] seriously," but also allows that
"*Carmageddon* is wonderful stress relief for those days you feel like chok-
ing someone." Another writes that the game is "not for the weak of stomach," but that, on the other hand, "if this [game] doesn't get rid of any
amount of road rage you might have, I have no idea what would!" And
"Kfgecko," a reviewer of *Carmageddon High Octane*, echoes this idea:
"After a hard day's work and stressful commute in traffic home, I'd say a
lot of people need this game to release their tension so they can lead
peaceful lives and keep their sanity. *Carmageddon* is a smash 'em bash 'em
race 'em crazy game that is truck loads (pun intended) of fun. This game
let's [*sic*] you do everything in a car that you wouldn't, shouldn't, and can't
do in real life." He goes on to enumerate the types of pedestrian victims
the game offers up for stress-relieving virtual slaughter—"business men in
suits, regular men and women, old grandma's [*sic*] with walkers, grandpa's
[*sic*] with canes, cows, policemen, punks"—but adds: "Just remember that
this is a game and isn't training grounds for the real world."[6]

Were he still alive, Brian Deneke might disagree. Until his death in
1997, Deneke had spent most of his nineteen years in Amarillo. And, for
whatever else he experienced there, his last Amarillo memory was a
Cadillac—not one of Cadillac Ranch's upturned models, but the one
that secured his place on Kfgecko's list of (virtual) victims. A high-profile
figure in Amarillo's small punk community, organizer of underground
concerts and the force behind other alternative projects, Deneke enjoyed
the adulation of younger kids in the community, and at one point even
ended up employed by Stanley Marsh III to paint illicit road signs
around town. Like other members of Amarillo's punk scene, though,
Deneke paid a heavy price for his public identity. Regularly harassed
while traveling around town by foot, often targeted for assault as the perceived leader of the local scene, he earned an all-too-descriptive nickname: Fist Magnet. Most prominent among those throwing beer bottles
and throwing fists at Deneke and other punks was a single group, themselves identifiable by their ritually white baseball caps. These were the

rich boys from Amarillo's Tascosa High School, football and baseball players, student council representatives, and future oil company executives. "Those guys have a real big issue with pride," said one Tascosa student. "That's why all their cars are so big."[7]

This ongoing conflict came to a head in December of 1997. Looking to settle scores from an incident the week before, punks and white caps had come together to brawl in a mall parking lot across from the local IHOP hangout. It was already violent enough—fists, beer bottles, baseball bats, batons, and by most accounts "a shitload of guys" ganging up on Brian Deneke—when Dustin Camp rolled up. Member of Tascosa's white cap elite and junior varsity football player, Camp was driving two friends to the brawl in his big beige Cadillac. Arriving at the scene, caught up in all that aggressive adrenaline, he didn't even bother to get out of the car. Camp first spotted local punk Chris Oles, swerving toward him and bouncing him off the hood of the Caddy. Then he gunned it for Brian Deneke. The Cadillac "looked like a monster, like this metal monster coming after him," Oles remembers thinking as he climbed up off the pavement. Indeed it was. Camp hit Deneke full speed, rolling him under the wheels of the Cadillac and killing him instantly. Deneke's punk friends rushed to him; the crowd of white caps cheered; and inside the Cadillac, according to testimony at the subsequent trial, Camp found himself playing his own game of Carmageddon. "I'm a ninja in my Caddy," he said. "I bet he liked that one."[8]

At that trial in late August 1999—Camp's trial for the murder of Brian Deneke—Camp's defense attorney argued that in reality the case was not about Dustin Camp but about Brian Deneke and "a gang of young men who chose a lifestyle . . . designed to intimidate those around them, to challenge authority, and to provoke reactions from others." "The lesson of this case," he added, is that the punks' aggressive lifestyle "has consequences." And to emphasize the aggressive disregard that punks like Brian Deneke had for authority, automotive and otherwise, he displayed Deneke's favorite T-shirt in court, its motto there for all to see: "Destroy Everything." With all this in mind, the jury retired for deliberation and returned with its verdict on the first day of September. Dustin Camp was guilty not of murder but of manslaughter. He would not be put in prison, but on probation. And he would be fined $10,000—not even the price of a good used Caddy.[9]

But Stanley Marsh III can afford the price of a good used Caddy. And since he was Brian Deneke's friend and employer for a while, he ought to buy one, drive it out to Cadillac Ranch, and add it, fins up, to the row of Caddies that is already there. That would make eleven, and with eleven, he could create the biggest, baddest roadside shrine yet. He'd just need to gloss over all the graffiti that has accumulated on the Caddies over the years, and in its place paint a big black block letter on the tail fin of each one, like this:

B R I A N D E N E K E

Better yet, more broadly, he could paint a tribute to automotive death itself, to all the splattered urban pedestrians, to all the roadside shrines strung out across the Southwest, a tribute to the eleven dead Caddies and the one dead punk:

C A R M A G E D D O N

NOTES

This chapter has been adapted from Jeff Ferrell, *Tearing Down the Streets: Adventures in Urban Anarchy* (New York: St. Martin's/Palgrave, 2001).
1. See, for example, Andy Steiner, "Highway to Heaven," *Utne Reader,* 99, May-June 2000, 28–29; Laura Trujillo, "Place of Tragedy, Place of Rest," *Arizona Republic,* March 12, 2000, F1, F4.
2. Cited in Trujillo, F4.
3. Carl Sandburg, "Grass," *The Complete Poems of Carl Sandburg* (New York: Harcourt Brace Jovanovich, 1969), 136.
4. Cited in Harry Mok, "California Man Draws Attention to Pedestrian Deaths," *Denver Rocky Mountain News,* June 27, 1999, 59A. See the website www.pedsafe.org. See also Anna Sojourner, "Walk!" *Bike Summer,* 1999, 5.
5. Gary Genosko, "Dispatched," *Borderlines,* 44, 1997, 13–15. See Howard Williams, "Bike Messengers Struggle for Union," *Bike Summer,* 1999, 15.
6. All of the cited review quotations are from www.epinions.com, ca. summer/fall 2000.
7. Chris Ziegler, "Death in Texas," *Punk Planet,* 36, March/April 2000, 68–81. Quotation p71. See Pamela Colloff, "The Outsiders," *Texas Monthly,* No-

vember 1999, 118–122, 144–153, who likewise quotes a local Amarillo mother: "Teenagers here pay a lot of attention to . . . what kind of car you drive. If you can't compete, you're an outcast" (122). For more information on this case, see also www.briandeneke.org.

8. Ziegler, 73–74; Colloff, 121.
9. Ziegler, 76–79.

VIOLENCE AND VINYL

CAR CRASHES IN 1960S POP

JACK SARGEANT

> We affirm that the world's magnificence has been enriched by a new beauty: the beauty of speed.
>
> —Marinetti, *The Futurist Manifesto* (1909)

AN IMPORTANT PART OF THE POWER OF POP SONGS is in their ability to evoke an emotional response that is both personal and universal. As a result, there are a vast number of songs about love, especially failed or lost love. Many of the most successful of these songs were written in the 1960s and marketed to emotional teenage consumers whose lives they seemed to describe so perfectly. In among these songs of first love and heartbreak are songs in which the agony of lost love is made the worse by the death of the lover. These songs include several in which death occurs as the result of a crash—a common tragedy among reckless teenage drivers—and the death is detailed with an explicitness largely unimaginable in most pop lyrics. The following is a tip-of-the-iceberg exploration of pop-song crashes: three cars and one motorcycle. It is not a chronology so much as an examination of a small number of 1960s pop songs.[1]

Cars, trucks, and motorcycles have often been a thematic focus in popular music. Automotive vehicles are, of course, the clearest manifestation of the theme of travel in songs, a theme that is especially prevalent in American blues and folk traditions, where the idea of migration forms the culture's most potent mythologies. Moreover, with the postwar consumer boom, car ownership in the United States grew dramatically and by the mid-1950s was running at an unprecedented peak. And if car ownership was increasing in the United States in general, in Los Angeles having a car rapidly became essential. With its permanent summer climate and its cultural importance as the home of the entertainment industries, Los Angeles—a city designed specifically for the booming car culture—came to represent economic optimism and the (supposed) realization of the mythic American Way.

During the 1950s and 1960s, California also became the particular home to various growing youth crazes, most notably the surf and drag culture that celebrated the twin obsessions of beach sports and hot rods. The music of groups like the Beach Boys and Jan and Dean was specifically marketed to teenage fans of the surf and drag culture, whose carefree and reckless lifestyle was immortalized in their lyrics. In 1964, for example, Jan and Dean acknowledged the danger of the teenager's inherent fascination with speed with the release of "Dead Man's Curve." This song details a late night-race through L.A. that culminates in a high-speed accident at the notorious locale of the title. However, if this song seems brutal, it nevertheless detailed a common aspect (and risk) of the speed- and drag-obsessed teenager's life. And it was a life that the singers lived themselves—Dean and Dennis Wilson of the Beach Boys once held a notorious grudge race. And in April 1966, Jan Berry suffered a horrific accident, crashing his new Corvette into the back of a truck on Whittier Boulevard, just below Sunset, in Beverly Hills. The extent of his injuries was so severe that the paramedics at the crash scene initially believed the singer was dead. Cut from the ruins of his car, Berry was rushed to hospital. He was unable to fully return to his music career for more than a decade.

Ray Peterson's maudlin ballad "Tell Laura I Love Her" (1959) is ostensibly a crass, cheesy love song whose lyrics detail the relationship between young lovers Tommy and Laura. Tommy enters a stock car race in the hope of winning a thousand dollars in order to buy his girl-friend a wedding ring. However, unable to speak to Laura, Tommy leaves the eponymous message with her mother. During the race, his car crashes. The song's lyrics detail the disaster, noting that the car "overturns" in "flames."

Not only is Tommy killed in the violence of the car crash, but his hero's dying phrase—"tell Laura I love her"—is uttered while he's being pulled from the "flaming wreck." Tommy's gory death is articulated with a surprising clarity. The final verse describes Laura's vigil in the chapel, praying for her dead lover "alone." But if "Tell Laura I Love Her" appears violent, with its "flaming wreck" and overtly emotional (and ultimately kitsch) chorus, it nevertheless suggests that successful popular songs are permitted not merely to allude to lost love but to describe the visceral brutality of that loss in vivid detail.

Out of the fire, and into the grime.

—liner note on *Dirtdish* by Wiseblood (1986)

It was four girls—two pairs of sisters—from Queens, New York, whose singing group ultimately became synonymous with the car crash pop song.[2] As the Shangri-Las, Betty and Mary Weiss and Marge and Mary Ann Ganser largely specialized in songs of doomed and/or tragic love composed by songwriters George Morton, Ellie Greenwich, and Jeff Barry. Their numerous pop hits between 1964 and 1966 included the first-love memoir of their single "Remember (Walkin' in the Sand)" and the absurdly militaristic pro-Vietnam pop song "Long Live Our Love." However, the heartbreaking excesses of romantic anxiety are most clearly manifest in their two classic crash songs, "Leader of the Pack" (the group's second single) and "Give Us Your Blessings."

"Leader of the Pack," released in 1965, is an extreme manifestation of the teenage doomed-love crash theme. The song plays almost as a form of pop theater, with the vocalists performing distinctive roles within the extended narrative. It opens with the girls discussing Jimmy, the rebel motorcyclist of the title, who, as the generic representation of the rebel demands, comes from the "wrong side of the tracks" and is consequently misunderstood by society.[3] When the father of Jimmy's girlfriend Betty tells her she can no longer see him, she kisses the outlaw good-bye and he rides off into the rain. Jimmy's fate is vertiginously transparent. "I begged him to go slow," sings Betty, but Jimmy, of course, skids, crashes his rebel's motorcycle, and dies. This timely accident not only affirms the notion of true love but also, with a brutal narrative convenience, eradicates the rebellious and misunderstood boyfriend, thereby avoiding a more complex resolution (extramarital sex or marriage before emotional maturity).

As in "Tell Laura I Love Her," the relationship between the two teenage lovers fuels the narrative drive of "Leader of the Pack," and the song's emotional impact is made more powerful by the first-person narrative and the gossipy conversational structure of the singers' vocal interactions. More significantly, the second half of the song suggests a certain level of emotional cruelty by using the "actual" sounds of the crash within its musical structure, where previously there has been only the periodic roar of the throttle. When Jimmy rides away from Betty's house, the musical arrangement is minimal, mixed low beneath the vocals, until the music explodes into life with the screech of brakes as the girls scream "look out, look out, look out" and the skid ends in an explosive crash of breaking glass. Finally, the closing bars of the song echo the sound of a motorcycle revving, and an extended skid is replayed and faded out. Jimmy's final, fatal moments are drawn out into an eternity. Unlike Tommy, who finds his eternal rest in the chapel—and, one presumes, in the arms of God—Jimmy crashes into a godless oblivion. As the girls repeat the line "now he's gone," the final skid is never allowed to culminate in an impact.

The listening pleasures of this song include all those elements familiar to the genre of classic 1960s girl pop: themes of sexual awakening and romance (Betty, for example, still wears Jimmy's ring), catchy melodies, and the question-and-answer nature of the singers' vocal interactions. However, they also include the pleasure of playing aural witness to the sounds of the crash itself. It is not enough for the songwriting team merely to describe the accident and the death of the protagonist. Instead, the actual crash forms a key section of the song's structure, compelling the listeners to imagine all its horrors for themselves.

As a result, "Leader of the Pack" functions at a variety of levels. Its basic narrative deals with the familiar theme of lost love, but the intense focus on Jimmy's death and the extended fetishization of the crash locate this theme within a maelstrom of psychosexual perversity. The vocalists' perspective shifts from that of innocent teenagers discussing first love to that of a tragic chorus that is part of the song's musical background. On its release in the United States, the song was an immediate hit, reaching number one in the American charts. And although the song was initially banned in England for its "depraved" theme and "poor taste," it quickly became a classic.[4]

The Shangri-Las repeated the crash theme on "Give Us Your Blessings." Opening with the ominous sound of a storm breaking and the chant of "Run, run, run, Mary" and "Run, run, run, Jimmy," the song begins with a vocal narration that describes the young lovers' request for parental blessings on their proposed marriage. When the approval is not forthcoming, however, the couple decide to flee and drive off crying into the night, but the tears in their eyes obscure their vision, and, in the dark, they miss the DETOUR sign. The thunder echoes again, and the tempo increases as we hear how, the following day, the parents kneel over the bodies of their dead children with the request "Give us your blessings" echoing poignantly in their memories.

While this song lacks the sheer impact and inventiveness of "Leader of the Pack," it nevertheless provides a suitably bleak narrative, with its final images of parents standing in the rain over—one presumes—the mangled, bloodied corpses of their teenage children. The appeal to a teen pop audience—whose lives often revolve around melodramatic familial crises—is clear, detailing the archetypal mantra "recognize my desires or be responsible for the outcome," and the song clearly acknowledges these emotions.

Although lacking the visceral crash of the earlier record, the rumble of thunder that appears at key points throughout the song adds to a general atmosphere of foreboding. The noise of the storm is augmented by the sound of a bell that rings initially to emphasize the concept of marriage, ringing after the words "wedding day." However, as the song ends, the sound of these bells returns, thus suggesting that the bells are less about marriage than the certainty of mortality. The bell, it appears, has rung for Mary and Jimmy.

Eros and Thanatos merge in these songs—they are fused together, compacted more thoroughly than a rib cage and a steering column. In the Shangri-Las world, happiness, true love, and desire can only be understood in terms of loneliness, absolute loss, and death. While the links between sex and death are culturally established with a clearly recognized genealogy, it nevertheless seems remarkable that these pop songs, aimed at a teenage audience, maintain such an intense emotional engagement with death as the certain end to forbidden love. In placing the agency of destruction in the automobile, the Shangri-Las (or, rather, their songwriting team) acknowledge the importance of the car and motorcycle in the teenager's life. But these are not the seductive hot rods or thrilling races pragmatically described by Jan and Dean. Rather, these are vehicles of deadly retribution for the transgressions of youthful desire.

In these songs, the car and motorcycle are responsible for narrative closure; further, they are also responsible for freezing the teenage lovers in time, affirming the eternal power and beauty of youth. Like James Dean, these lovers punctuate memory with their youthful beauty, suspended forever in a coital imminence, dead long before the consummation of their relationships.

NOTES

1. It should be noted that there are numerous different kinds of "car crash" songs in American folk traditions. See, for example, country songs such as "Phantom 309," which tells of a truck driver who—when his brakes fail— deliberately swerves, crashing his vehicle and dying rather than plowing into a school bus. In a similar vein is "Tombstone Every Mile," which details the numerous hazards on a treacherous piece of road. Such songs, however, are less about the physical crash than they are about the individual heroism of the narratives' truck-driving protagonists.

2. Subsequent rock and pop songs, especially those written by punk and postpunk bands, have also engaged with the theme of car crashes. These include the Avengers' song "Car Crash," the Birthday Party's "Dead Joe," and Sonic Youth's "In the Kingdom #19." The Normal's "Warm Leatherette," a song subsequently made famous by Grace Jones, does not detail the events of a specific car crash but engages with the literary manifestation of auto death

depicted most explicitly in J. G. Ballard's *Crash*. There are, of course, many others. In a notable twist, Wiseblood produced an album and single that, rather than focusing on car crashes per se, actually used the car as a metaphor for complete apocalypse, as an extension of a predatory, killing male über-phallus, and decorated their albums *Dirtdish* and *Motorslug* with the *mise-en-scène* of high-speed auto destruction. Yet these songs are produced from the gleeful nihilism of punk or the knowing post-Ballardian avant-garde, and their designated audience is older than the teenagers who were the targeted audience of the Shangri-Las' records.

3. The misunderstood outlaw—the rebel whose defiance is covertly existential rather than overtly political (or, as the Shangri-Las put it in "Leader of the Pack," Jimmy is "sad" rather than "bad")—has its pop cultural roots in figures such as Marlon Brando's Johnny in *The Wild One* (dir. Laslo Benedek, 1953), and in the James Dean character of *Rebel Without a Cause* (dir. Nicholas Ray, 1955).

4. "Leader of the Pack" also inspired the British singer Twinkle's pop song "Terry" (1965), which, like the former song, focused its pop tones on a biker whose crash separates him from the song's narrator. In a suitably camp narrative twist, the tale of Terry continues beyond the crash to the (literal) Gates of Heaven. The song is, in the final analysis, more an example of tragic-comedy kitsch than melodramatic violence.

TWENTY-FOUR

DEATH AS ART/THE CAR CRASH AS STATEMENT

THE MYTH OF JACKSON POLLOCK

STEVEN JAY SCHNEIDER

To "die at the top" for being his kind of modern artist was, to many, I think, implicit in [Pollock's] work before he died. It was this bizarre consequence that was so moving. We remembered Van Gogh and Rimbaud. But here it was in our time, in a man some of us knew. This ultimate, sacrificial aspect of being an artist, while not a new idea, seemed, the way Pollock did it, terribly modern, and in him the statement and the ritual were so grand, so authoritative and all-encompassing in its scale and daring, that whatever our private convictions, we could not fail to be affected by its spirit.

—Allan Kaprow, "The Legacy of Jackson Pollock" (1958)

The Pollock myth has the function of diverting our attention from the actual paintings which bear his name. It confers on "mere painting" a status which places it beyond the reach of a criticism which is solely concerned with painting. It insists that Pollock be judged as a cultural hero rather than as the author of certain works of art which may be good or bad, according to the standards one applies in judging them. . . . Pollock's pictures are now a kind of currency used in the commerce of his reputation.

—Hilton Kramer, "Jackson Pollock and Nicholas de Stael: Two Painters and Their Myths" (1959)

WHEN MIGHT A CAR CRASH BE MORE THAN JUST A CAR CRASH? When at least one of the victims is (a) famous, (b) in some sense "important," or (c) when his or her life or work has something tragic pervading it. Jackson Pollock, American painter and one of the founding fathers of Abstract Expressionism, satisfied all three of these conditions. So was the car crash in which he died while speeding along an East Hampton road on the evening of August 11, 1956, more than just a car crash? What else could it have been? A message? A suicide? A work of art in its own right? And to what extent was this "something else" a product of Pollock's own interests, concerns, desires, or, alternatively, those of his family, friends, colleagues, the news media, art historians, or the public at large? It is with this difficult complex of questions that the present chapter is concerned.

There can be no denying the fact that neither the press nor the public was able to resist interpreting Pollock's colorful, violent, random death as an extension of his life's work—a final artistic statement, perhaps. Pollock's colleagues, and those in the art world familiar with his highly original painting techniques, reacted the same way. As friend and fellow painter Allan Kaprow put it in the October 1958 edition of *Art News*, "we . . . could not escape the disturbing itch (metaphysical in nature) that this death was in some way connected with art."[1] In this chapter, I'll endeavor to identify this connection. More important, however, I'll seek to diagnose the multiple (and to some extent conflicting) causes of this "disturbing metaphysical itch" that could be scratched only by looking—and finding—meaning in the most meaningless of accidents. By projecting Pollock the painter on to Pollock the car crash victim, I'll argue, we have consigned Pollock the man to the dustbin of history and fallen victim ourselves to the Pollock myth. It's almost impossible for us to confront the harsh truth that Pollock's untimely death—like the untimely deaths of so many other celebrities—was the least glorious moment of his life.

In what follows, I'll present a detailed account of Pollock's final death drive, paying particularly close attention to those places where gaps in the story exist, as well as those places where the numerous accounts of what transpired contradict one another. It's here, of course, that traces of the normally invisible process of mythmaking are at their most apparent. I'll then go on to examine highlights (to many, lowlights) of the Pollock

legend as manifest across a variety of media. These include a highly controversial (because allegedly manipulated) photograph of the Pollock
death scene that appeared on the front page of the *East Hampton Star* on
August 16, 1956. They also include a kiss-and-tell memoir written by
Ruth Kligman, Pollock's mistress during the last year of his life, and the
only person to survive the crash—the book was entitled *Love Affair,* and
the author was sarcastically referred to by those in the know as "Death
Car Girl." Last, but certainly not least, they include a 1983 television
docudrama on Pollock (the first of a five-part "Strokes of Genius" series
commissioned by the eminently respectable Public Broadcasting System), featuring a B-movie grade reenactment of the events precipitating
and including the fatal accident.

All of this tasteless (yet for a variety of reasons understandable)
dramatization of Pollock's death will lead quite naturally to a consideration of "Car Crash Art" as practiced by such influential figures as Carlos Almaraz, Jim Dine, Robert Ameson, Andy Warhol, and—it can be
argued—Pollock himself in some of his early work. Finally, I'll conclude
with a brief look at the latest attempt to cash in on the Pollock mythos:
a pair of big-budget Hollywood films based on the life and, in some
(sad) sense more important, the death of this controversial artist.

As noted by his most responsible biographer, B. H. Friedman, 1953 was
the first year in almost a decade that Pollock would fail to register even a
single one-man show. Always a fragile personality (in 1939 his psychoanalyst diagnosed him with schizophrenia) and since his youth a notorious
alcoholic, Pollock by the age of forty-one was "tired . . . tense, confused,
desperate, drinking more than ever, under pressure to paint masterpieces,
to maintain the standard of . . . his 1952 show."[2] Although some rather
generous historians have contended that the last three years of his life were
years of "consolidation" and "reinterpretation"—a period in which the
artist was preparing to "harvest all his past and revalidate it for a new beginning"[3]—accepted wisdom has it that Pollock was in a deep funk at the
time, losing his battle with booze and unable to paint to his (or most others') satisfaction. Even Clement Greenberg, the E. F. Hutton of art critics,

who in the early days backed Pollock when just about everyone else was condemning him, wrote in a famous essay that his 1954 show "was the first to contain pictures that were forced, pumped, dressed up . . ."[4]

Most interestingly for our purposes, a retrospective review—more like a eulogy—that appeared in TIME magazine in 1955 claimed that "Pollock's paintings, charged with his personal mythology, remain meaningless to him for whom Pollock himself is not a tangible reality. As Indian sculpture is related to Vedic and Upanishadic thought, exactly so are Pollock's canvases related to his self. Ignore that relation and they remain anonymous and insignificant."[5] Just why Pollock's paintings are "charged with his personal mythology," however, and precisely how his canvases are "related to his self" remained unsaid.

Barroom brawls, minor car accidents, and more or less amusing scrapes with the law were old hat for Pollock, but, as his drinking increased, so did the frequency of such escapades. On September 2, 1954, the *East Hampton Star* reported a collision that had taken place earlier in the week:

> On Tuesday night . . . two cars met head on through the fallen tree in front of Nelson Oshorn's house on Main Street. Lester Hildreth was in a 1950 Chevrolet, on the south side of the tree. He was facing north and waiting to go around the tree. Franz Kline, operating a 1937 Lincoln roadster, was going south and he was unaware of the one lane traffic. He pulled out to pass the cars going south, and crashed through the tree. He met Hildreth head on. Jackson Pollock, a passenger in Kline's car, was the only injured person. He suffered a cut on the lower lip.

A year later, Pollock used an awkward yet evocative automotive metaphor to describe his state of mind (and body) to a friend: "I've gone dead inside, like one of your diesels on a cold morning. I need a booster for the self-starter to get me turning over—a sex-starter, so my sap will flow."[6] That "sex-starter" soon arrived in the form of Ruth Kligman, a voluptuous, twenty-five-year-old brunette from New Jersey who worked primarily as an artist's model and who was intent on meeting one of the "important artists" known to hang out at the infamous Cedar bar in New York. Besides Pollock, other candidates included Franz Kline (one of the drivers in the above collision) and Willem De Kooning, with whom Kligman would take up some time after Pollock's death. While their affair had gathered a great deal of momentum even before Pollock's wife (fellow painter Lee Krasner) left for Europe, her temporary absence made the situation for Pollock and Kligman that much easier to negotiate.[7] And although Pollock was allegedly (and understandably) self-conscious about bringing Ruth with him to social events and other public functions, friends of both parties have testified that the young woman's companionship had a positive effect on the artist, at least between bouts of drinking and depression.

On Friday, August 10, 1956, Kligman called Pollock at his home in East Hampton and asked him to meet her at the train station the next morning, where she would be arriving from Manhattan with a friend, Edith Metzger. Metzger was an attractive, twenty-six-year-old beauty salon manager, who, having never met Pollock before, was reluctant to make the trip. That same evening Pollock remarked prophetically to an acquaintance that while "life is beautiful, the trees are beautiful, the sky is beautiful . . . I only have the image of death."[8] Saturday morning came and, much to Kligman's dismay, Pollock arrived at the train station dirty and disheveled. To make matters worse, instead of taking the young women straight home, he drove them to a nearby bar for some drinks. The afternoon passed awkwardly. They left the bar and Pollock in turn got drunk on gin, pleaded with Ruth to join him upstairs in the bedroom, broke down weeping, cooked some steaks for dinner, and hit the bottle once more. After a great deal of debate over whether to attend a charity concert at The Creeks, home of Pollock's artist friend Alfonso Ossorio, the trio finally went out for the evening.

In keeping with the biographical tradition of presenting Pollock's life as if it were a work of fiction, Jeffrey Potter writes that "the actual sequence of events after this is confused enough, along with multiple retellings by others, to compare with *Rashomon*."[9] For one reason or another, the trio never made it to the concert that night. According to newspaper reports, at approximately 10:15 P.M., while speeding north on Fireplace Road (less than 300 yards from his home), Pollock lost control of his 1950 green Oldsmobile convertible coupe on a sharp curve. The car made a right turn off the road, struck an embankment, spun around, and headed left in the other direction. Plowing more than 175 feet through underbrush on the west side, the car smashed into four white oak trees, flipped end over end, and finally landed upside down a few feet away.

Official police records state that Kligman, who was thrown clear of the Olds, suffered a fractured pelvis and back injuries, as well as numerous cuts and bruises. Though she suffered shock from the trauma and was hospitalized for almost two months, she got off easy. Metzger—who had known Pollock for all of one day—was found dead in the trunk of the car, presumably rammed there by the impact. As for Pollock, he too was jettisoned from the car, but after traveling a good 50 feet in the air ("it was like he was planing . . ." recalled Patrolman Earl Finch, "elevated about ten feet off the ground"[10]), his head hit a mature oak, killing him instantly. The death certificate lists the causes of death as "compound fracture of skull, laceration of brain, laceration of both lungs. Hemothorax—shock." Such a description, though true to the facts, is deceivingly gruesome; eyewitnesses noted that although there was a small amount of blood on his forehead, Pollock looked more or less okay, save for a neck "swollen like a balloon from the oak he hit."[11]

What actually happened that evening to precipitate the crash has, over the years, become less important than what people believe—or at least what they claim—happened to precipitate it. This is because the Pollock legend has been constructed not so much upon truths or facts about the man or his life as upon the often-conflicting perceptions and understandings of this life as mediated through people who used what they (thought they) knew to help fashion their own identities and self-conceptions. Kligman, describing the crash in her book—a mere eighteen years after the fact—provides a textbook example of this mythmaking process:

> We were both standing in the road next to the car. Jackson refused to get out, refused to budge. I finally coaxed Edith to get back in. We started on our way home. Jackson was fully awake, fully conscious. He was angry, annoyed at us, and began to speed.
>
> Edith started screaming, "Stop the car, let me out!" She was pleading with him. Again she screamed, "Let me out, please stop the car! Ruth, do something, I'm scared!"
>
> He put his foot all the way to the floor. He was speeding wildly. "Jackson, slow down! Edith, stop making a fuss. He's fine. Take it easy. Please, Jackson, stop! Jackson, don't do this." I couldn't reach either of them.

Her arms were waving. She was trying to get out of the car.
He started to laugh hysterically.
One curve too fast. The second curve came too quickly. Her scream-
ing. His insane laughter. His eyes lost.
We swerved, skidded to the left out of control—the car lunged into
the trees. We crashed.[12]

In this vivid, frightening, impressionistic yet suspiciously calculating passage, Kligman performs a number of tasks. First, she implicitly
asserts that the crash, if accidental at all, was not merely accidental but
suicidal to a greater or lesser degree depending on how one chooses to
interpret Pollock's "wild speeding" and "insane laughter." Second, she
charges Pollock with sadism, a character trait exacerbated but certainly
not engendered by alcoholism. (It's interesting to note that while Kligman begins her account of the tragic car ride by emphasizing Pollock's
drunkenness, her description of him as "fully awake, fully conscious"
in the above passage would appear to contradict this conclusion.) Finally, she positions herself in the middle, figuratively, if not quite literally, between Edith (sacrificial lamb, hysterical—in the sense of
uncontrollable—female) and Jackson (grim reaper, hysterical—in the
sense of unreachable—male). As the self-described mediator between
innocence and experience, naïveté and cynicism, heaven and hell, Kligman manages to claim for herself equal shares of praise (for being composed and mature) and blame (for being passive and codependent).
Her skewed logic is, of course, infallible—behaving properly in a time
of crisis is admirable but dull; behaving improperly censurable but impossible to forget. Despite her privileged role in the tragedy, not everyone shared Kligman's retrospective take on what took place that
evening. Art critic Ivan Karp, in a *Village Voice* "Memoriam" published
six weeks after the crash, asserted that "Pollock, who generally drank a
great deal, was sober, though fatigued, on the night of his violent
death."[13] Karp's surprising claim was based partly on his belief in the
integrity of Kligman, with whom he discussed the crash soon after it
occurred, and partly on his firsthand knowledge that Pollock often displayed a clarity of mind and behavior even while drinking.[14] But even
leaving aside the question of just how inebriated Pollock actually was
when the car swerved off the road, it's ridiculous to believe he was

sober. What, then, could be the purpose (in Karp's case a somewhat less than conscious one) of such a fantastic reconstruction of events? Besides being a fairly transparent—not to mention futile—attempt at deflecting criticism away from the painter, it allows for a more stark raising of the possibility (present but confused in Kligman's account) that Pollock's "accidental" death was a suicide, a final artistic—or perhaps antiartistic—statement. Karp himself chose the latter interpretation: "We can only speculate whether the pain in him had come to the point where, driving at terrific speed, he had conceived a permanent release from the unrelenting pressure of his art."[15] In the end, such journalistic irresponsibility mattered very little, as the thought that Pollock really wanted to end his life that night became far more interesting and important than the claim that he did so while sober. As one commentator summed things up nearly eight years later, "After his death . . . [Pollock's] keen sense of destruction . . . was now seen to include a final assault upon himself."[16]

As for the various newspaper and magazine accounts of the crash, most walked a fine line between straightforward statement of the facts and more-or-less-subtle innuendo concerning the relationship between Pollock's artwork and his death drive. Although none of the early pieces dared speculate on the role alcohol may have played in what happened, most found a way to juxtapose details of the crash with facile descriptions of the painter's technique, vision, and artistic legacy. So the late edition of the *New York Times* on August 11 quoted an anonymous critic who once "dismissed" Pollock's work as "unorganized explosions of random energy." It is unclear how the author of this article arrived at the conclusion that the above remark was intended as a "dismissal" (as opposed to, say, a compliment), but regardless, the critic in question might as well have been commenting on the aesthetics of automobile accidents.

The August 12 edition of the *Herald Tribune* went even further, including (beneath a late Hans Namuth photo of the artist in which he appears bloated, with full beard, furrowed brow, and cigarette dangling from his lips) a photograph of the overturned Olds. The accompanying article cites Pollock's famous declaration that "my painting does not come from the easel. I need the resistance of a hard surface. . . . When I am in my painting, I am not aware of what I am doing." In conjunction with the still images, these words take on additional and uncanny significance, as it becomes all too easy to imagine the artist a figure in his own, terminal artistic endeavor.

This tradition of conjoining relatively uncontroversial statements about Pollock's fatal accident with rather simple-minded claims about his work continues to the present day, as in a recent Internet essay which claims that the artist "died violently in a car crash that mimicked the elements of chance and chaos visible in his paintings."[17] Although infusing the objective (facts) with the subjective (judgments) in such a manner may look innocent enough, it has the effect of promoting both personal and critical misunderstandings—not least because, as Thomas Hess has astutely observed, "in almost all his mature work, Pollock deliberately pushed violence to the point where it contradicts itself and includes calm. *The painting is made radically stable; its elements are planned and fixed.* The overall activity on the surface leads to poise, rest, even to a sort of incandescent gentleness."[18] The same can hardly be said for the violent, chaotic, radically unstable crash in which Pollock and Metzger lost their lives, not to mention the other two automobile accidents that took place in the Hamptons that same evening and that claimed the lives of a then-record seven people.

If it was not the most egregious media offender when it came to interpreting Pollock's random death as self-conscious work of art, the August 16, 1956, edition of the *East Hampton Star* was certainly the most controversial. This issue of the newspaper featured a photograph called "A Still Life" (the title appearing in bold capital letters just below the newspaper's logo on page 1), credited to one "Dave Edwardes." According to Friedman, Edwardes made it to the scene of the crash not half an hour after it occurred; he was also responsible for the photo of Pollock's upside-down Olds that first turned up in the *Herald Tribune* and which accompanied "A Still Life" in the *Star.*

The photograph in question makes every effort to live up to its title. In a patch of leafy underbrush, appearing out of context in some undisclosed location (but presumably not far from the wreck), a shiny hubcap with the Oldsmobile insignia on it is flanked by two cans of Rheingold

24.1 Artist's rendition of the photograph published in the *East Hampton Star,*
August 16, 1956

beer and what looks to be Pollock's right penny loafer. Situated just beneath the picture is the following caption:

> TRAGIC AFTERMATH of Saturday night's automobile accident on the
> Springs road. The photographer took this picture half an hour after the
> crash. The objects shown were not arranged: that is the way they fell. The
> Star publishes this dramatic picture in the hope that it may further the
> safer driving campaign being carried on by nation and state. Nassau and
> Suffolk counties are among the worst offenders in this state with regard to
> automobile accidents.

Despite the *Star's* obvious efforts at forestalling criticism—first by emphasizing the arbitrary positioning of the objects in the photo and second

by explaining its public service minded rationale for publishing it at all (and on the front page, no less)—the paper still took a great deal of heat for "A Still Life." A neighbor of Pollock's, who allegedly arrived at the accident in time to assist the traumatized Kligman, is quoted by Jeffrey Potter as recalling that "We saw this guy putting the shoe and the wheel cover there—it wasn't an Olds one anyway—and beer cans are all over the roadside down in Bonac. That picture was faked and most knew it."[19] To be fair, there is no hard evidence to corroborate this person's claim concerning the depicted hubcap's actual manufacturer. But it is difficult to imagine what possible motive would have compelled him to lie about the artificial or deceitful nature of the photograph. Viewed in this context, the photo's caption—with its candid acknowledgment of the shot's "dramatic" impact (note that it is referred to as a "picture" only)—seems to be protesting a bit too much.

As reported by Friedman, Lee Krasner Pollock and a number of Jackson's artist friends responded to the publication of "A Still Life" by canceling their subscriptions to the *Star* and by staging an informal boycott of the paper: "They argue[d] that Pollock and the many other artists by then living in the East Hampton area were responsible for its vitality, chic, real estate values, and tourist business and that therefore Pollock deserved thanks rather than that [type of] editorial."[20] While not going so far as to admit to any wrongdoing, the *Star* nevertheless took Krasner and company's criticisms to heart, and soon began treating Pollock, his widow, and the art community in general with "more gentleness and respect."[21]

Without going so far as to levy the paranoid charge that a kind of deal was struck whereby the *Star's* (and Edwardes's) journalistic integrity would be preserved in exchange for a positive shift in editorial policy toward Pollock (such a shift was, after all, part of a far more widespread trend in the mass media[22]), it is worth noting that the crucial issue here was not whether Pollock's death should be treated as an artistic statement in its own right but whether the Pollock myth should be perpetuated in terms that were deconstructive (the artist as pathetic ironist) or reparative (the artist as tragic genius).[23]

As for Ruth Kligman's memoir of her brief but undeniably passionate relationship with Pollock, we have already seen from her description of the crash how she chose to perpetuate an altogether different myth—that of the artist as suicidal (even homicidal) trickster. But what is most interesting and arresting about *Love Affair* is neither Kligman's take on Pollock nor the publication of a book on a famous painter written by someone with little or no insight into his paintings. Rather, it is the extent to which the author attempts to insinuate herself into the Pollock legend. In her "Afterword," Kligman writes that: "[Pollock] captures my imagination and I transmit his energy through that imagination. . . . I feel possessed by his spirit. I feel his words are my words and his feelings have become my feelings. The same thing is happening to me that happened to him. I felt some strong impulse to act out his death, as though I had to in order to be free. One night driving on that road, I felt death driving with me in that car. It was a struggle to get home."[24]

A page or so later, she adds the following: "My existence is related to his dying . . . I became the myth of the Girl in the Car with Jackson, and everyone knew it."[25] Kligman's intense identification with Pollock, understandable enough when he was alive (considering the inherently unbalanced nature of their relationship), takes on a pathological dimension after his death. It is almost as if she felt the only way to preserve Pollock's memory was to conceive of, or at least represent, herself as a mere vessel for the artist's self-destructive spirit, still summoning her from beyond the grave. And this, of course, falls in with the popular tradition of keeping Pollock alive not so much through examination and appreciation of his art as through morbid speculation and a dramatic reenactment of his death drive.

We've so far looked at a number of attempts at interpreting (in some cases, fashioning) Pollock's accidental death as some kind of artistic, or perhaps antiartistic, statement. Although I have been arguing that such attempts say more about their authors than about what "actually happened" the night in question, this is not to deny the aesthetic potential and possibilities of automobile wrecks in general. In fact, a number of artists have explored and exploited the potential and possibilities of car crashes as the subjects of their art. A study of their work will, at the very least, give us some objects of comparison to help us understand how Pollock's own car crash had everything to do with human weakness and nothing whatever to do with art.

Carlos Almaraz (1941–1989), an acclaimed Chicano artist from East Los Angeles, specialized in paintings of spectacular car crashes. As one of "Los Four," the first all-Chicano artists' collective, Almaraz worked primarily using spray cans or house paint, thereby combining the popular folk art of the barrio with what he learned at university.[26] His drawings and large-scale murals of urban fantasies incorporate scathing critiques of existing social or political institutions, and his series of car crash paintings was no exception. By vividly depicting the explosions resulting from multiethnic wrecks, Almaraz imaginatively represented the clash of cultures in California.

Unlike the accident that took the lives of Pollock and Metzger, the aesthetic value of Almaraz's car crash series can hardly be denied. This is because, as L.A. Times art critic Suzanne Muchnic rightly points out, "Almaraz delivers messages of doom without making them seem immediately threatening. He accomplishes this by setting a dreamlike atmosphere and by using ingratiating color. Ghostlike figures arising from mad dogs, bloodless car crashes, and cancer-causing TV sets are observed as if they belong to someone else's universe—or to a nightmare that is, after all, only a dream."[27] No such effort at achieving aesthetic distance is to be found in the reports, descriptions, or reenactments of Pollock's own crash.

At the other end of the spectrum from Almaraz lies Jim Dine's 1960 performance art piece, Car Crash. Visual evidence of the piece's macabre intensity exists in the form of related paintings, lithographs, and drawings, many of which were hung in the entryway of New York's Reuben Gallery, where the actual performances took place.[28] Three actors—Pat Oldenburg, Marc Ratliff, and Judy Tersch—helped Dine act out the disturbing events. His head bandaged, and wearing a silver jumpsuit, Dine would describe the real wreck he was in by drawing the car again and again in a frenetic motion; the feelings of defenselessness and chaos were reinforced by a sign that spelled out the word "Help" over and over. The overall scene was crude, disorderly, and electrifying. Looming overhead was a cemetery cross, and many of the accumulated props were painted white to suggest both the accident and hospital sites.[29]

Not only did Car Crash serve as a cathartic reenactment of Dine's own experience in a real accident, it was "a potent metaphor for the danger, tragedy, and omnipresent specter of death that [the artist] sensed in

American life."[30] What made *Car Crash* so powerful, what provided it with an aesthetic dimension at the same time, was the hyperbolic activity of the performer-victims as well as the creative shorthand Dine used to refer to various elements of the accident. Though hardly anyone who went to see *Car Crash* would be inclined to call Dine's performance "beautiful" (unlike Almaraz's series of car crash paintings), most left with some measure of appreciation for what they had just witnessed. In the case of Pollock, however, there was neither approbation nor appreciation—only sadness, sensationalism, and gossip.

Even Pollock himself, in some of his early works on paper, exhibits something of a fascination with the carnage, chaos, and aesthetic possibilities inherent in the spectacular car crash. As Bernice Rose has astutely observed, "the scene of violence which appears frequently in Pollock's work usually has more to do with tensions *within the work itself* than with socially violent subjects."[31] In pieces such as *War* (1944, subsequently inscribed 1947), however, it is precisely the subject matter—inspired by Picasso's *Guernica*, with its commentary on the horrors of warfare—that conveys a sense of unremitting violence. Despite the drawing's title and totemistic imagery, the brutal pen-and-ink lines depicting what appears to be a pile of skulls, bones, and assorted parts (machine? automotive?) conjure up the aftermath of a devastating head-on collision. But even if Pollock did consciously intend, in some of his early work, to thematize the car crash as symbol of modern man's precarious reliance on technology, this would provide little if any additional evidence for the claim that his own car crash death was meant as an artistic "statement." Instead, the drunk-driving accident that deprived America of one of its most gifted painters was the tragic consequence of a distinctly individual—not social or technological—failing.

The car crash artwork perhaps most relevant to this investigation is the collection of acrylic and silkscreen canvases produced by Andy Warhol in 1963–64 as part of the posthumously titled *Death and Disaster* series. Warhol had no interest in parodying (much less celebrating) the cult of male grandiosity that saw the car crash as transfiguring— macho martyrdom made simple. Warhol's paintings, which sometimes take press photographs for inspiration (thereby reversing the causal chain apparently responsible for Edwardes's "Still Life" photo), depict particularly gruesome deaths with a graphic realism unprecedented outside contemporary mass-media representations. This series culminated in the *Ambulance Disaster* and *Saturday Disaster* pieces of 1964 whose "scale, power, and apparent veracity tend to stun criteria of style, demanding engagement with the image's face value."[32] Commentator Neil Printz continues: "In Warhol's world, there is no subtextual glamour in death by car crash; the very mundaneness of his victims and their grotesque deaths compels viewer empathy."[33]

There is an important lesson here for those who would read Pollock's car crash death as the culmination of a professional career rather than as the accidental, alcohol-related demise of a man who just happened to be a famous artist.[34]

Perhaps unsurprisingly, it is apparent that the lesson implicit in Warhol's car crash paintings has not been heeded: Journalists, biographers, and film-makers continue the tradition of rendering Pollock's death an essential part of the Pollock legend, a tradition that ensures that consideration of the artist's work remains incomplete without reference to his saddest moment.

In the 1999 BBC "Close Up" series documentary, *Jackson Pollock: Love and Death on Long Island* (dir. Teresa Griffiths)—on the whole, a sensitive and extremely polished production—the narrative is framed by an actor wearing a police uniform (shades of Officer Earl Finch) describing the accident in intimate detail. Through interviews with scholars and friends, including Kligman (who remarks, predictably enough, that Pollock's death "was a romantic way to die. If he hadn't met me and died in that car, he would've died a sick man, maybe with an enlarged liver"), plus taped footage of Krasner and Pollock himself, the film succeeds in conveying the artist's expressionist spirit as well as the extent to which his extraordinary popularity was the result of more than just originality and talent—namely, media savvy and plain old good fortune. However, it does not succeed in establishing that Pollock's death had anything whatsoever to do with (his) art. This is not for lack of trying: The obnoxious framing mechanism described above, the numerous point-of-view shots of a car driving down an East Hampton road, and the disturbing fact that Metzger isn't mentioned once, even in passing

282   STEVEN JAY SCHNEIDER

(was her death not "romantic" enough to warrant inclusion?) all signal an effort at presenting Pollock's crash as the key to unraveling the mystery of his abstract and emotionally charged paintings.

Although the Hollywood feature film *Pollock* (produced, directed by, and starring Ed Harris) is in postproduction at the time of this writing,[35] judging from the biography upon which it is based there is every reason to believe that the sensationalization and aesthetic overvaluation of his death will continue. The biography, *Jackson Pollock: An American Saga* (1993), by Steven Naifeh and Gregory White Smith, opens with Pollock telling a friend in 1952, "I'm going to kill myself"; what follows is 900-plus pages of tenuous connections drawn between Pollock's childhood traumas, homosexual inclinations, self-destructive impulses, and (by the way) his art. At one point the authors assert that "drinking alone couldn't explain why . . . Pollock's new Cadillac convertible . . . had [in 1952] skidded off a dry road and wrapped itself around a tree. . . . There was something behind the drinking that was pushing at Jackson from within, tormenting him, even trying to kill him."[36] Perhaps it is true that Pollock's death did not result from "drinking alone"—alcoholism need not be a mere brute fact, unexplainable in terms of deeper psychological conflicts. It is even reasonable to hold that Pollock's addiction to alcohol sprang from the same source as his artistic passion and creativity. But none of this means that the automobile accident in which Pollock—and let us not forget Metzger—died was itself intended as an artistic (or antiartistic) message or statement, that it warrants appraisal aside from any general interest one may have in car crash aesthetics. In short, that it signifies much of anything at all.

It is only by putting Pollock's death in its proper perspective that we will finally be free to focus on his life's work.

NOTES

I would like to extend my sincerest thanks to Mikita Brottman, Cynthia Freeland, Ivan Karp, Owen Perla, and Kirk Varnedoe for their assistance with the writing of this chapter. An earlier version was read (in my absence) by David Sterritt—to whom I also own thanks—at the twenty-sixth annual conference on Literature and Film, held at Florida State University, February 1–2, 2001.

1. Allan Kaprow, "The Legacy of Jackson Pollock," *Art News,* 57, October 1958, 25.

2. B. H. Friedman, *Jackson Pollock: Energy Made Visible* (New York: Da Capo, 1995), 205.
3. Thomas Hess, "Pollock: The Art of a Myth," *Art News*, 62, January 1964, 39.
4. Clement Greenberg, "'American-Type' Painting," in *Art and Culture: Critical Essays* (Boston: Beacon Press, 1961), 228.
5. "The Champ," *TIME*, December 19, 1955, 66.
6. Cited in Jeffrey Potter, *To a Violent Grave: An Oral Biography of Jackson Pollock* (New York: Pushcart Press, 1985), 217.
7. My thanks to Kirk Varnedoe for helping to clarify this point.
8. Friedman, 233.
9. Potter, 240.
10. Cited in Potter, 244.
11. Potter, 245.
12. Ruth Kligman, *Love Affair: A Memoir of Jackson Pollock* (New York: William Morrow & Co., 1974), 201.
13. Ivan Karp, "In Memorium: The Ecstasy and Tragedy of Jackson Pollock, Artist," *Village Voice* (New York), September 26, 1956, 8.
14. My sincerest thanks go to Ivan Karp of the O.K. Harris Gallery in New York City for taking the time to clarify—with remarkable eloquence and grace—his motivations for writing the article in question *forty-five years after the fact*. Telephone interview, February 27, 2001.
15. Karp, 8.
16. Hess, 39.
17. Claire O'Mahoney, "Jack the Dripper," Global Doras: Arts-Visual Arts, March 24, 1999, www.pushie.ie/globaldoras/358489
18. Hess, 64. Emphasis added.
19. Cited in Potter, 256.
20. Friedman, 244.
21. Ibid.
22. Compare the 1997 crash in which Princess Diana lost her life, which led to a similar backlash against the publication of private or intrusive photographs of public figures, especially in the tabloid newspapers.
23. To this day, the *East Hampton Star* evinces a sense of embarrassment, even shame (if not necessarily guilt), concerning Edwardes's "Still Life" photograph. A formal request by the author of this manifestly neutral essay to republish the photo was politely but firmly turned down, at least in part on the grounds that "we are extremely hesitant to add to the debate over its legitimacy. . . . unfortunately, this may be the intent of your contribution." *The Star's* editorial staff went so far as to deny a further request to send out a Xerox copy of the original for private use only—a service normally provided by the paper.
24. Kligman, 217.
25. Ibid., 218.
26. The other members of "Los Four" were Roberto de la Rocha, Gilbert Lujan, and Frank Romero.

27. Myrna Oliver, "C. Almaraz, 48: Chicano Artist of Urban Scene," *L.A. Times*, December 14, 1989, 26.

28. Compare these genuine performances to those of Vaughan in J. G. Ballard's *Crash*, which take place illicitly at a moonlit racetrack and involve similar reenactments of various wrecks within the pantheon of great automobile accidents.

29. Jean Feinberg, *Jim Dine* (New York: Abbeville Press, 1995), 16–17.

30. Ibid., 16.

31. Bernice Rose, *Jackson Pollock: Works on Paper* (New York: Museum of Modern Art, 1969).

32. Neil Printz and Remo Guidieri, *Andy Warhol: Death and Disaster* (Texas: The Menil Collection and Houston Fine Art Press, 1988), 14.

33. Printz, 14.

34. It is worth comparing Warhol's *Death and Disaster* series with the gruesome car crash photography of Mell Kilpatrick, collected in *Car Crashes & Other Sad Stories* (London: Taschen, 2000).

35. In February 2001 the film *Pollock* opened in the United States to great critical acclaim (Harris as Pollock, and Marcia Gay Harden as wife Krasner, were both nominated for Academy Awards). Although the film version of Naifeh and Smith's biography deserves credit for not "aesthetically overvaluing" Pollock's death, it is certainly guilty of playing up the suicide angle, and of perpetuating the myth surrounding the artist's last moments. The final scene of the movie has Pollock driving drunk with Kligman (who, interestingly enough, is portrayed more sympathetically than any of the other central characters) beside him and Metzger in the backseat. Pollock is totally smashed, and refuses to slow down even in the face of Kligman's pleas and Metzger's screams. Nothing objectionable thus far. But in the seconds immediately preceding the crash, Pollock appears sober (in both senses of the term) and seems to acquire an otherworldly prescience of what is to come. Audiovisually speaking, the film encourages this interpretation by muting the women's voices, and by focusing on Harris's eerily calm face. If that isn't enough, Pollock is then shown lifting his head up to the sky, effectively erasing any doubts on the part of the uncritical spectator that his death was, if not wholly premeditated, at the very least pregnant with "meaning."

36. Steven Naifeh and Gregory White Smith, *Jackson Pollock: An American Saga* (New York: C. N. Potter 1989), 3.

TWENTY-FIVE

REBEL WITH A CAUSE

ALBERT CAMUS AND THE POLITICS OF CELEBRITY

DEREK PARKER ROYAL

ALBERT CAMUS OPENS HIS FOUNDATIONAL ESSAY, *The Myth of Sisyphus,* with a challenging and now-famous dictum: "There is but one truly serious philosophical problem, and that is suicide."[1] Almost twenty years after the publication of these words, the author died in a car accident, a death that resulted not from any nihilistic purpose of his own hand but from a fateful combination of uncertain road conditions and questionable automotive circumstances. As the above quotation suggests, death was a thematic cornerstone of Camus's writings, and he spent most of his literary life articulating a moral philosophy surrounding this inevitability. Indeed, his writings, as well as his life, have gained meaning largely within the context of his death.

Camus himself witnessed firsthand the ramifications of death, as his experiences in the French Resistance and the Algerian crisis attest. Even the essence of his literature—the thematic significance of the murder of innocents, the metaphorical uses of the plague, and the symbolic magnitude of human alienation—was founded on issues of dying. What Camus did not anticipate, however, was the weight of his own death in the general literary and political reception of his thoughts. This contextualization was left up to a number of critics who viewed his January

1960 automobile accident as a means to justify—or condemn—the struggles of the West in the years following the end of World War II. Albert Camus's untimely death, as tragic as it was, became for many critics a touchstone with which to gauge the high stakes involved in the cultural Cold War.

For many, Camus's death was the stuff of romantic reverie. A highly popular literary figure, a moralist concerned with issues underlying death and the voice of "the absurd," died in what many viewed as an ironic—and absurd—manner, but one that was filled with enough pathos to engender a devoted and heartfelt following. One reason why Camus's tragedy has assumed romantic overtones stems from the way critics pronounced the death of the "hero of the absurd" as *quintessentially* absurd. The most notable example of this came from Jean-Paul Sartre, who called the accident that killed Camus "shameful, because it revealed the absurdity of our most profound demands within the midst of the human world . . . For those who loved him, there was an unbearable absurdity in his death."[2] Such ways of reading the car death are not only too intellectually tidy, but simplistic in their understandings of Camus's philosophical ideas. His untimely death, like those of the many popular figures trapped within the public gaze, became a focal point of importance. Yet Camus never wanted to be considered a James Dean figure, a celebrity who lived fast and died young. If anything, he abhorred the reckless lifestyle. So why, after his death in 1960, has he been seen and read as one of the twentieth century's tragic celebrities of French literature and philosophy?

Camus's curious position in the intellectual world stems partly from the way his life and work was portrayed in the media. In his own writings, at least according to many journalists, he seems to resemble one of his own subjects, Sisyphus, forever rolling the stone of democratic moral commitment up the slope of a postwar world that had forsaken political moderation. To others he was a bourgeois apologist who made the right much more palatable to the literate masses. Yet regardless of how he was read, it was his death in an automobile that in many ways determined the political significance of his work.

The circumstances surrounding his death are tragically straightforward, containing no overt political or philosophical import. On the morning of Sunday, January 3, 1960, Camus left his home in Lourmarin, a village in the southern French Vaucluse region, to travel north with his close friend and publisher, Michel Gallimard.[3] He had several appointments in Paris and had planned on traveling by train. But Michel, who was driving to Paris for the holidays anyway, convinced Camus to accompany him and his family—his wife, Janine, his daughter Anne, and their dog, a Skye terrier—in their Facel Vega sports car. Michel was at the wheel and Camus was sitting up front in the passenger's seat, while the women were curled up in the back. The trip was intended to be somewhat leisurely, taking two or three days, and was supposed to be occupied with friendly talk and enjoyable meals.

But in the early afternoon of the second day, the Gallimard car skidded off the road and crashed into a row of trees lining the highway, old National 5, stretching from Le Sens north toward Paris. The accident was caused by either a blowout or broken axle—experts are not sure which—and the Facel Vega ended up wrapped around a tree 40 feet from the first tree it initially impacted. Camus's head flew backward against the rear window, resulting in a skull fracture and broken neck, killing him instantly; Michel Gallimard was propelled out of the car, bleeding profusely; Janine and Anne were both thrown clear of the accident, in shock but without any serious injury. Officials noted that the dashboard clock had stopped at 1:54 or 1:55 P.M., taken to be the moment of the accident, and the speedometer was allegedly stuck at 145 kilometers, or approximately 90 miles per hour. Michel eventually died in the hospital, saving him from any personal recriminations concerning his responsibility for the death of the popular Nobel laureate.

Camus's death assumed a cultic significance for several reasons. For one, he died with his final and unfinished manuscript, *Le Premier Homme* (*The First Man*), in his briefcase. Second, he—a man who apparently abhorred reckless driving—was killed in a speeding accident. And finally, he was, at the time, an important political figure as a critic of ideological authoritarianism. The first of these facts proved to be particularly poignant for Camus's literary following. At the time of his death, Camus had written approximately eighty thousand words of *Le Premier Homme,* and he was hoping to finish the novel by summer 1960. This was to be his first major full-length novel, a work vast in scope that would not be a *roman-fleuve*. As Camus explained to his wife shortly before the accident, the novel in progress was largely autobiographical, a sort of *éducation sentimentale* that would highlight the writer's French Algerian past and position himself as the product of a melting pot experience.[4] The book would also emphasize the rootlessness endemic in modern society, which required of the individual the necessity of self-definition through an engagement with the social and political issues of his time.

Camus's life—cut short by a senseless automotive accident—was as incomplete as his work. Like those of other twentieth-century writers such as Nathanael West and Jack Kerouac, Camus's untimely death created a tragic yet romantic sense of the "what if." What would *Le Premier Homme* really have been like? How would the Nobel Prize winner further enhance his place within the literary world? Readers who are familiar with his writings, especially the unfinished novel, may wonder what Camus was ultimately capable of, and if his success as a writer would have surpassed his early critical reception.

Or, one may argue, had Camus survived the crash, his literary reputation might not have enjoyed the security it does today. Although such speculations are, in the end, groundless, they nonetheless resonate in the reader's imagination. Is the heroic standing of the popular French writer and dramatist mainly a result of his early death in a car crash? As this volume suggests, automobile accidents hold a curious place in the popular imagination, especially when they involve public figures. They are the birthplace of rumor, the impetus to myth, and the stuff of legends. Camus's tragedy was no exception, placing him in the pantheon of car crash victims populated by such figures as James Dean, Jayne Mansfield, Jackson Pollock, and Princess Diana.

Yet despite the importance of his unfinished novel and cultic personal status, the main significance of Camus's death is the way that it has been used by critics with their own political agendas. In the decades following World War II, partisans on both ends of the political spectrum sought to discover—or appropriate—literary and intellectual figures that would lend cultural credence to their particular Cold War views. At times, the writers were quite willing participants in this alliance, as in the cases of Jean-Paul Sartre and Lionel Trilling. Others, however, such as George Orwell, found their work and their ideas placed within a political context that was inappropriate at best, at worst manipulatively misleading.[5]

Such appropriations of Camus and his work occurred in various ways. For example, in Simone de Beauvoir's 1954 novel, *The Mandarins,* Camus is represented as the iconoclastic member of the French left who stubbornly refuses to follow the lead of his contemporary intellectuals. By many on the American right, as well by those in what, politically speaking, Arthur Schlesinger Jr. would call the "vital center" of the time, Camus was heralded as the champion of a tireless anti-Marxist sentiment. Yet whether vilified by the left or glorified by the center and the right, Albert Camus's reputation was largely a construction of the various individuals who surrounded him, read his work, and used his writings to support, accurately or inaccurately, particular political agendas.

The public persona of Camus is linked in many significant ways to his untimely death. His car accident brought to the fore the issues that largely defined his life. The cultural publications that highlighted these issues, both before and after his death, present a curious mixture of attitudes—at times ambiguous and at times contradictory. Many of the popular weekly magazines tended to paint a fairly sympathetic picture of Camus, especially in terms of their American readership. For instance, a *Newsweek* piece in 1954 quotes the French writer as saying "If one loves in one's friends only the good qualities, one has no friends. One must also love the faults of friends. I still love America."[6] In a 1957 *LIFE* magazine article, interestingly entitled "Action-Packed Intellectual," popular readers are given one of their first and more intimate images of Camus. The piece was comprised primarily of photographs of the famous author directing a play, fooling around in the rain, addressing Hungarian youth, and enjoying a calm moment with his children. The article shows a warmer and more human side of Camus—one that would go a long way in endearing the atheistic author to the magazine's American readership.[7]

Even his driving preferences were given a romantic gloss. About two weeks after his death, *TIME* quotes Camus as having said "It is wonderful to drive fast . . . when one is not driving oneself."[8] However, later critics and biographers, perhaps with the benefit of hindsight, painted a more tempered picture of the French writer. Donald Lazere argues that, in contrast to the "juvenile delinquent" form of rebellion found in much postwar culture—and embodied by such figures as James Dean, Marlon Brando, Ken Kesey, and J. D. Salinger—Camus possessed a rather tragic vision of life, one preoccupied with fate and death. He also fought against bourgeois self-righteousness, celebrated the individual's harmony with nature, and was keenly aware of the necessity of human solidarity and the personal dilemmas involved in political commitment.[9] Lottman paints a similar portrait in his biography. He writes that Camus was more cautious than he was reckless, and adds that he "didn't like fast driving, except perhaps his own." Whenever the writer was riding with Michel Gallimard, he would say, "Hey, little brother, who's in a hurry?"[10]

Had the critical assessment of Camus stopped at the strictly personal, such uncertain applications of his life and his work might be understandable. After all, the Nobel laureate had become somewhat of a literary celebrity—perhaps not on the scale of an Ernest Hemingway, but nonetheless one whose dramatic, fictional, philosophical, and political writings had acquired international recognition. And it was the political reception of his work during the Cold War that gave his reputation such weightiness. Interpretations of his political ideology were as ambiguous as the descriptions of his personal life. Camus's automobile tragedy only contributed to the appropriation of the ideas that defined his literary output. In the absence of the living author's clarifying voice, speculations over Camus's political philosophy took on a variety of forms, many of them incongruous each with the others.

At the time of his death Camus felt as if he were embarking on a new stage of his work. Not only had he recently won the Nobel Prize for literature, not only was he engaged in writing his full-length novel, but his political attitudes were continuing to evolve. Unfortunately it is impossible to know how his philosophy would ultimately have developed. He was unable to respond to the intellectuals, especially within American circles, who were placing him within particular political categories. As a result, many cultural Cold Warriors with an investment in staking out political territory used Camus for their own agendas—and many did so by referring primarily to Camus's best known political treatise, *The Rebel*.[11]

Neoconservatives, such as those who were associated with *Commentary*, found in Camus a voice whose criticisms of the Soviet Union could be interpreted as anticommunist, if not downright sympathetic to Western capitalistic democracies. One of its most representative figures, Norman Podhoretz, argued that "the truths of *The Rebel* were on the whole the truths of the 'Right,' as that term was understood [during the 1950s]."[12] H. J. Kaplan not only found the French writer a very moving figure—winning him the affectionate label, "Brother Camus"—but praises Podhoretz for his "instinctive grasp" of Camus in his time. Those whose sympathies lay more to the left, such as Conor Cruise O'Brien, took a similar view of Camus, but with a different tone. O'Brien accused Camus of supporting Western colonialism in Algeria and criticized "the increasing right-wing positions of his later years."[13] What's more, O'Brien goes on to condemn Podhoretz's assessment of Camus. "What a pity," he writes, "the novelist did not have a neoconservative father-confessor at his side, to get his penance right for him, and see his books got rewritten."[14]

And such political critiques were not limited to the antithetical "right" and "left." Cold War "centrists"—sympathetic to the "left"[15] yet critical of communism—acknowledged Camus's philosophical indebtedness to Marxist thought but defended him for his moralism and his sense of political moderation. Germaine Brée, for instance, praised Camus's "courageous public stand against communism"[16] and wrote of *The Rebel* that it is, "in effect, the cry of a 'son of' the real Prometheus, protesting against the perversion of the hero."[17] William Barrett argued that the political message underlying *The Rebel* was a plea for a Third Force between the bourgeois West and the communist Soviet Union.[18] Similarly, democratic socialists—such as those associated with *Dissent*—praised Camus's anti-Stalinist attitudes but, in contrast, they highlighted his Marxist/socialist leanings more than those in the democratic center might have done. Michael Harrington argues that "Camus was a man of the Left," then goes on to say that "[p]ositively, he could find nothing more than a romantic syndicalism to counterpose against his own corrosive skepticism."[19]

Before Camus's death, Irving Howe wrote of the author: "One feels about Camus that . . . he is a writer to be trusted to the very end. Because he is a man like all other men, he is also a writer who may mislead; but because he has looked at the face of power and turned away, he will not violate his readers with ideological or spiritual trickery."[20] And, writing almost thirty years after the fatal car crash, Jeffrey C. Isaac emphasized the democratic socialism underlying *The Rebel.* Isaac believed that Camus endorsed Marx's critique of bourgeois mystification yet pointed out that many Cold War critics of the 1950s—both left and right— failed to see Camus's strongest arguments: that communism is important for history because it articulated, then betrayed, human freedom.[21]

It is easy to see why many of Camus's critics, especially in the aftermath of the automobile accident and in the midst of the Cold War, looked to *The Rebel* as one of the most representative works in his political philosophy. Yet perhaps more important, it is the controversy surrounding the publication of this book that helped fuel the passions of the Cold Warriors. This fervor stems primarily from the famous exchange between Camus and his one-time friend Jean-Paul Sartre.

The break between the two men over *The Rebel* is the stuff of French intellectual legend. Because of the highly volatile issues involved—such as Sartre's supposed Stalinism and Camus's assumed apologies for Western bourgeois society—the argument became a rallying point for those on both the left and the right. There have been a number of enlightening studies on the French intellectuals' disagreement, as well as on the effects this had in helping to define Western politics after World War II.[22] The issues at the heart of this disagreement not only help to provide an understanding of Cold War intellectual culture but also allow a glimpse into the political ramifications of Camus's untimely death.

The bitter exchange between Camus and Sartre was to prove a critically defining moment in twentieth-century political thought. Far from being merely a personal squabble based on inconsequential differences, this debate was politically charged with the problems that had so enlivened an entire generation. Such volatile material easily transcended the narrow confines of the Parisian literati and became a beacon for cultural Cold Warriors on both the right and the left. To Germaine Brée, writing in 1963, it stood "as the ideological centerpiece of our time."[23] In fact, the intellectual debate between the two men was founded on the ideological issues that defined much of the last half of the twentieth century.

The actual debate between Sartre and Camus took place in the pages of Sartre's own publication, *Les Temps Modernes,* in August 1952. In this polemic, both men, along with the magazine's manager, Francis Jeanson, debated Jeanson's earlier review of Camus's *The Rebel.*[24] In his review, Jeanson had attacked what he considered the pseudophilosophical underpinnings of the book, particularly Camus's misunderstanding of Marx and what he saw as Camus's rejection of history. The book, he argued, would give comfort to right-wing critics and only serve to stoke the reactionary passions of anticommunism.

Although this review was a catalyst in the break between the increasingly estranged Sartre and Camus, Jeanson's own significance in the polemic was minimal. His review served as a trigger for the release of the tensions that had been slowly mounting between the two men. Camus was not, after all, unfamiliar with criticism, nor was Jeanson's review the first instance in which Camus's work had been condemned as an apology for the bourgeoisie.[25] Likewise, it should have come as no surprise to Sartre that his former friend would have been so offended at the offhand manner in which the review was commissioned. Despite the growing political chasm between the two men, Camus would have assumed that his friendship with Sartre should warrant a personal review from him, the magazine's publisher. The emphatic response of both men—each with its accusatory and combative tone—betrays the deeply personal edge as well as the sheer intellectual urgency behind the exchange.

Camus believed that Jeanson was only a front, a mere "hatchet man" for Sartre, and formally addressed his letter to "Monsieur le Directeur."[26] His "collaborator," Camus charged Sartre, had falsely accused Camus of refusing the role of history in the genesis of revolution.[27] What *The Rebel* had done, in fact, was to criticize the attitude that makes an absolute of history. A Marxist critique of economic and social history was a legitimate enterprise, Camus argued, but that had not been the focus of the book. What he had attempted in *The Rebel,* and what Jeanson had conveniently overlooked, was an examination of the conditions under which rebellion led to repression and terror. Therefore, it was not history that he'd rejected but a particularly dogmatic interpretation of history.

More distressing to Camus was the method in which Jeanson had criticized his book. Defending Marxism as an implicit dogma, Jeanson had refused any attempt to critique this ideology and had pushed to the right all arguments that did so, a tactic that Camus found intellectually dishonest. Faithful to the philosophy of moderation that he espoused in his text, Camus believed that all political constructions were subject to thorough critical examination, regardless of ideological considerations.[28] "One does not judge the truth of a thought according to whether it is on the right or on the left," argued Camus, "still less according to what the right and left wish it to be."[29] He refused to succumb to this form of intellectual blackmail, claiming that if "the truth appeared to me on the right, I would be there."[30] Furthermore, he argued, Jeanson's exclusionary logic restricted the freedom of possibility by leaving no room for a third way: It was either the status quo or Stalinism.

Such arguments, claimed Camus, naturally led to a silence on the evils inherent in authoritarian socialism. While accusing Camus of denying history, Jeanson had in fact turned a blind eye to the Soviet gulags. Such hypocrisy, Camus argued, could find legitimacy only in a political philosophy that "free[d] man from all shackles in order to practically encage him in a historical necessity."[31] This was the main philosophical problem that Camus found in Jeanson's critique, and he addressed it to Sartre point-blank:

> Only the principles of prophetic Marxism (with those of a philosophy of eternity,) can indeed authorize the pure and simple rejection of my thesis. But can such views be definitely maintained in your journal without contradiction? Because, after all, if man has no end that could be taken as a rule of value, how can history have a definite meaning? If it has one, why shouldn't man make of it his end? And if he did that, how could he be in the terrible and unrelenting freedom of which you speak?[32]

The Rebel attempted to reveal the consequences of such a prophetic philosophy. It argued that only a "happy ending" to history could justify the sacrifices of yesterday and today, and such an ending was far from certain. Totalitarian atrocities were the dangers of justifying any violence in the name of ideology. Camus argued that Jeanson had failed to address this central point. To admit that history is in any way meaningful would have shaken the existential foundations on which Jeanson's philosophy rested. Instead, Jeanson had engaged in "skillful distinctions" that lead only to the impasse against which *The Rebel* had warned: "It is not me that he has maligned, but our reasons for living and for struggling, and the legitimate hope that we have of overcoming our contradictions."[33]

Sartre's reply was a vivid display of his polemical powers. In contrast to Camus's indirect accusations, which contained the "nasty smell of wounded vanity,"[34] his was highly personal and to the point. Much in the same way as Camus had indicted Jeanson, Sartre accused Camus of engaging in an unattractive moral absolutism. "You bring a portable altar with you," he argued, to terrorize Jeanson and his like into silence.[35] "But I ask you, Camus, just who *are* you, to stand off at such a distance? And what gives you the right to assume . . . a superiority which nobody accords you?"[36] To Camus's insistence that he was speaking with a passion for the working class and the hopes of all men, Sartre responded in unequivocal terms. Regardless of what Camus may think, claimed Sartre, he was actually working *against* the proletariat by attempting to destroy its only real hope of betterment, the Communist Party. Here Sartre, like Jeanson before him, consigned Camus to the ranks of the reactionary right (a position that some Cold War intellectuals delighted in and others abhorred). The once-admirable man—*resistant*, editor of the clandestine *Combat*, author of *The Stranger*, and hero of the absurd—was nothing more than an apologist for the bourgeoisie. "I am deeply afraid," wrote Sartre, "that you have moved into the camp of the stiflers, and that you are abandoning forever your former friends, the stifled."[37]

What Sartre had found particularly objectionable was the discussion of the Russian gulags. Contrary to Camus's insinuations, Sartre had indeed expressed his alarm at the existence of these camps. He'd committed *Les Temps Modernes* to the issue of the labor camps the moment it hit the French intellectual consciousness. The gulags were a horror, of course, but what was equally inadmissible, according to Sartre, was the exploitation of them by the bourgeois press. One should not take the suffering of those in communist regimes, he argued, and use it to justify the suffering and exploitation caused by capitalism. Sartre reproached Camus for his part in this crime. He too was guilty of exploiting these atrocities by using them to demolish Jeanson's review.

Furthermore, he had used his arguments to justify an acceptance of the status quo that undermined the effectiveness of any progressive politics. By condemning the Communist Party, in Sartre's view the only force capable of effectively mobilizing the masses, Camus had sabotaged such immediate struggles as the peace movement and the emancipation of the Vietnamese and Tunisians. Failing to choose between the effectiveness of the Communists and the tyranny of the Fascists, Sartre told his old friend, "I see only one solution for you, the Galapagos Islands."[38] He then exposed Camus's misguided reading of history: "It is not a question of knowing whether History has a meaning and whether we should deign to participate in it, but to try, from the moment we are in it up to the eyebrows, to give History the meaning which seems best to us, by not refusing our participation, however weak, to any concrete action which may require it.[39]

While Camus had recklessly accused Jeanson of worshiping history, he himself claimed that he could approach the issue only with great trepidation. Such, Sartre asserted, was to be expected from such a "beautiful Soul" who places himself outside history, remaining pure against any contact with reality. What Camus loved was not man, with his hands dirtied by struggle, argued Sartre, but the majestic idea of "man." *The Rebel,* with its blanket condemnation of the Soviet Union and its preaching of bourgeois moderation, was nothing more than a rejection of man's historic project. It was with much indignation that Sartre pronounced in no uncertain terms, "Your book will serve only as a touchstone to reveal the bad faith of the guilty party."[40]

The break between the two men was inevitable. Far from being an issue over contemporary politics, the debate surrounding *The Rebel* was deeply rooted in the philosophical inconsistencies surrounding dialectical history. By the early 1950s, Sartre had begun to reject his earlier existential philosophy and had come to see Marxist thought as the only tenable solution to the growing problems of postwar Europe. As if answering Marx's call to change history, Sartre sought to commit himself to the dialectics of history and create an art of engagement. Camus, on the other hand, condemned the messianic impulse in Marx and relied more on a Nietzschean critique of history. This took form in the character of the Promethean rebel, an ever-critical consciousness that would keep a constant vigil on the safeguard of the present moment. The various essays, dramas, and fictions that would follow from both men would serve as vivid expressions of the philosophies of caution and commitment that underlay their personal politics.

In Camus's case, the works written in the four years following the end of World War II are perhaps the most significant. These works broached many of the vital issues he would later raise in *The Rebel,* particularly that of moderation. For instance, the danger that Camus saw inherent in twentieth-century ideologies, and in messianic Marxism in particular, was a will to abstractions. In *State of Siege,* suffering comes at the hands of the character Plague, a personification of abstraction and morbid efficiency. Diego, a young medical student who confronts Plague, cuts through the bureaucratic fog and refuses to be counted among its victims: "Only masses count with you; it's only when you're dealing with a hundred thousand men or more that you condescend to feel some interest . . . But a single man, that's another story; he can upset your applecart."[41] This, in effect, was precisely the charge that Camus had leveled against the intellectuals of *Les Temps Modernes* in what he saw as their worship of history. By concentrating on the process of history, they had naturally overlooked the individual, or more importantly, the lived moment. Existence, detached from the possibility of the present life experience, became an abstraction and therefore life-denying.

In *The Plague,* Camus again uses the theme of pestilence to reveal this pernicious ideological disease. As long as the citizens of Oran saw the plague in abstract terms—a punishment from God, a series of bureaucratic proclamations, or a collection of funereal statistics—they were destined to remain powerless and ineffectual. The heroes of the novel are those who refuse to submit to the plague and fight it, in all its manifestations, in the trenches of the everyday. They demonstrate the importance of immediate human welfare over any vague and lofty preconceptions.

Rambert, the young journalist accidentally trapped in the quarantined city, protests the governmental decrees that separate him from the wife he dearly loves. After initial thoughts of flight, his rebellion takes the form of solidarity with the sanitation squad in alleviating the suffering brought on by the plague. Another citizen of the town, Dr. Rieux, refuses to take his eyes from the tasks his office requires. When Father Paneloux reminds him that through his medical help he too is working for man's salvation, Rieux responds, "Salvation's much too big a word for me. I don't aim so high. I'm concerned with man's health; and for me his health comes first."[42]

Camus abhorred the idea of history as progress. He likened the dialectic mind to Father Paneloux, who sees in the plague an abstraction of Christian salvation and passively accepts its consequences as a fate ordained by God. In doing so, he thereby neglects the true horrors of the plague and any possibility of overcoming it. Prophetic Marxism, like Christianity, defines the future as a time of heightened judgment and increased objectivity—a philosophy that is life-defying in that it privileges the future at the expense of the present. This Camus could not accept.

Through Tarrou, Camus's alter ego, the plague takes on a more obvious ethical dimension. Much like the city of Oran, he too is infected with a plague, but one of a moral nature. "I had plague already, long before I came to this town and encountered it here," he confides to Dr. Rieux.[43] In his younger days, Tarrou had joined the cause of justice by committing himself to a revolutionary band dedicated to the overthrow of social orders based on the death sentence. Their methods were akin to those of the regimes they sought to defeat, but with a difference. "I knew," Tarrou reveals, "That we, too, on occasion passed sentences of death. But I was told that these few deaths were inevitable for the building up of a new world in which murder would cease to be."[44] But one day, after witnessing a series of executions at the hands of the revolutionary comrades, he grasps the true horror of his commitment: "I came to understand that I, anyhow, had plague through all those long years in which, paradoxically enough, I'd believed with all my soul that I was fighting it."[45] Thus he learned, in a world of pestilences and victims, that he too was infected, and that it was up to him not to submit to and join forces with the pestilences, in whatever forms they may take. Tarrou, as a result, undergoes a change, espousing an ideology of affirmation rather than one based on destruction.

This same outlook formed the moral imperative of *The Rebel*. A cause armed with slogans of justice or cries for a classless society is admirable, but it runs the risk of turning against itself without a sense of moderation. Absolute justice without human roots becomes a dangerous abstraction that can be used to justify the very atrocities against which the individual reacts. The rebel must never lose sight of his fundamental intentions, and he must constantly scrutinize—critique—his methods. This is Camus's "philosophy of limits": "The logic of the rebel is to want to serve justice so as not to add to the injustice of the human condition, to insist on plain language so as not to increase the universal falsehood, and to wager, in spite of human misery, for happiness." In short, "the consequence of rebellion . . . is to refuse to legitimize murder because rebellion, in principle, is a protest against death."[46] When the rebel loses sight of his limits, then Prometheus becomes a Caesar, and a life-affirming impulse turns against itself and becomes life-defying.

Perhaps no other work more candidly elucidates this issue than *The Just Assassins,* a drama in which a young band of Russian terrorists attempts to assassinate the Grand Duke of Russia. Their efforts are initially foiled when one among them, Kaliayev, fails to throw the bomb upon seeing the Grand Duke's two children in the carriage with him. He cannot bring himself to take the lives of innocents, and his actions draw the attention of his comrades Stepan and Dora:

> STEPAN: Not until the day comes when we stop sentimentalizing about children will the revolution triumph, and we be masters of the world.
> DORA: When that day comes, the revolution will be loathed by the whole human race.
> STEPAN: What matter, if we love it enough to force our revolution on it; to rescue humanity from itself and from its bondage? . . . No, don't misunderstand me; I, too, love the people.
> DORA: Love, you call it. That's not how love shows itself . . . Even in destruction there's a right way and a wrong way—and there are limits.[47]

Stepan, blinded by a lust for revolution, lacks what the Camusian rebel must possess, a sense of "la mesure." Legitimizing the murder of

children: Here is the abstraction of ideology taken to its logical conclusion. It is a dangerous man who maintains, as Stepan does, "I do
not love life; I love something higher—and that is justice."[48] This is
what Nietzsche would call one of the dreaded "apologists of history"[49]
who possesses a heightened desire for objectivity and posits his salvation in a future state of justice.

This is not the case with Kaliayev. He has joined the revolution because of his love of life. For all his revolutionary idealism, he nonetheless
understands the true meaning of rebellion. He is Camus's most striking
literary embodiment of the hero defined in *The Rebel*.[50] In a particularly
revealing passage, Kaliayev protests to the stalwart Stepan, in words that
could well have been Camus's to Jeanson and Sartre, "I shall not strike
my brothers in the face for the sake of some far-off city, which, for all I
know, may not exist. I refuse to add to the living injustice all around me
for the sake of a dead justice."[51] For this Camusian hero, political justice
must not be abandoned, but instead tempered, or moderated, with the
immediate human issues that define existence.

Camus's concept of moderation—especially as it was spelled out in
The Rebel, his drama, and his fiction—stands in stark contrast to the fervor surrounding his death. What's more, it inadvertently provided many
intellectuals with a means by which to justify their own Cold War politics. Perhaps this is an inevitable risk for writers highly conscious of their
public significance and so willing to take a chance with their political
voice. But in Camus's case this is particularly unfortunate, for his life was
an unfinished text, a work in the making. It is perhaps ironic that while
working on *The Rebel*, Camus was wary of a linear and messianic philosophy that would threaten the processes of political moderation and
negotiation. After his fatal car crash, however, he was considered to have
reached an endpoint in his own political thought. Such a reading of
Camus's life is problematic and, perhaps more important, incomplete—
just as, by the very nature of his accidental death, it must always be.

While the deaths of such celebrities as James Dean and Princess Diana
created a media storm that reflected the chaos of their own lives, the death
of Camus should have alerted his public to the (absurd) fragility and fluid
nature of one's life and ideas. But even calling his death "absurd" is a form
of Monday morning quarterbacking. Camus's car accident was a tragedy,

but it was a tragedy quite separate from the philosophy and images that make up his reputation. An analysis of this untimely death is both a case study in celebrity politics and, by contrast, a means of fully appreciating Camus's important contributions to Western literature and philosophy.

NOTES

1. Albert Camus, *The Myth of Sisyphus and Other Essays*, trans. Justin O'Brien (New York: Vintage, 1955), 3.
2. Jean-Paul Sartre, "Albert Camus," *Situations*, trans. Benita Eisler (New York: George Brazillier, 1965), 111–112.
3. The following account of Camus's death is taken from Lottman's seminal biography. See Herbert R. Lottman, *Albert Camus* (Garden City, NY: Doubleday, 1979). See also Patrick McCarthy's *Camus* (New York: Random House, 1982).
4. Camus's personal disclosures on his unfinished novel are recounted in Lottman 650–651, and 658–659, and in McCarthy, 318–319.
5. For a fascinating study on the cultural appropriation of Orwell, see John Rodden, *The Politics of Literary Reputation: The Making and Claiming of "St. George" Orwell* (New York: Oxford University Press, 1989).
6. "A Hopeful Frenchman," *Newsweek*, September 22, 1954, 50–51.
7. "Action-Packed Intellectual," *LIFE*, October 14, 1957, 125–128.
8. Bernard Murchland, "The Rebel," *TIME*, January 18, 1960, 28–29.
9. Donald Lazere, *The Unique Creation of Albert Camus* (New Haven, CT: Yale University Press, 1973), 236–237.
10. Lottman, 662–663.
11. Albert Camus, *The Rebel*, trans. Anthony Bower (New York: Vintage, 1956).
12. Norman Podheretz, *The Bloody Crossroads—Where Literature and Politics Meet* (New York: Simon and Schuster, 1986), 12.
13. Conor Cruise O'Brien, *Albert Camus of Europe and Africa* (New York: Viking, 1970), 75.
14. Conor Cruise O'Brien, *Passion and Cunning: Essays on Nationalism, Terrorism and Revolution* (New York: Simon and Schuster, 1988), 250.
15. I'm keeping in mind that labels such as "right," "left," and "centrist" are relative and, in terms of literary and political assessments, are best understood in relationship one to the other.
16. Germaine Brée, *Camus* (New York: Harbinger, 1964), 28.
17. Ibid., 219.
18. William Barrett, *Time of Need: Forms of Imagination in the Twentieth Century* (New York: Harper & Row, 1972), 50.
19. Michael Harrington, *The Accidental Century* (New York: Macmillan, 1965), 167 and 169.
20. Irving Howe, "Between Fact and Fable," *The New Republic*, March 31, 1958, 17–18.

302 DEREK PARKER ROYAL

21. Jeffrey C. Isaac, "On Rebellion and Revolution," *Dissent,* 1989, 377.

22. See, for instance, Robert Greer Cohn, "Sartre-Camus Resartus," *Yale French Studies* 30, University Press of New Haven, 1963 (reprint, Kraus: New York, 1962); Bernard Murchland, "Sartre and Camus: The Anatomy of a Quarrel," in *Choice of Action: The French Existentialists on the Political Front Line,* trans. Michel-Antoine Burnier (New York: Random House, 1968), 175–194; Germaine Brée, *Camus and Sartre: Crisis and Commitment* (New York: Delta-Dell, 1972); and Donald Lazere, "American Criticism of the Sartre-Camus Debate: A Chapter in the Cold War," in Arthur Schilpp, ed., *The Philosophy of Jean-Paul Sartre* (LaSalle, IL: Open Court, 1981). Brée's is perhaps the most extensive study of the intellectual and political differences behind Camus and Sartre. Lazere's, on the other hand, is the most revealing account of the Cold Warriors' use of the debate.

23. Germaine Brée, "Introduction," in Germaine Breé, ed., *A Collection of Critical Essays* (Englewood Cliffs, NJ: Prentice-Hall, 1962), 2.

24. Jeanson's review of *The Rebel,* under the title "Albert Camus or l'âme révoltée," appeared in the May 1952 issue of *Les Temps Modernes.* Camus, although popularly associated with Sartre's intellectual milieu, never joined his friend's magazine. For a detailed account of the history behind Jeanson's review, see Lottman, 500–507.

25. Emmett Parker clearly illustrates that "Neither Victim nor Executioner," not *The Rebel,* was the first of Camus's works to draw serious ideological reaction. See Emmett Parker, *Albert Camus: The Artist in the Arena* (Madison: University of Wisconsin Press, 1965).

26. Camus's reply to Jeanson's review appears as "Révolte et Servitude" in *Actuelles II: Chroniques 1948 - 1953* (Paris: Galllimard, 1963), 86. All translations of this text are mine with the help of a good friend, Claude Chauvigné.

27. Camus, "Révolte," 86.

28. For a brief discussion of Camus's notions surrounding political moderation, especially as they concern postwar dramatic criticism, see my essay "Camusian Existentialism in Arthur Miller's *After the Fall,*" *Modern Drama,* 43, 2000, 192–203.

29. Camus, "Révolte," 86.

30. Ibid.

31. Ibid., 116.

32. Ibid., 115.

33. Ibid., 123.

34. Jean-Paul Sartre, "Reply to Camus," *Situations,* trans. Benita Eisler (New York: George Braziller, 1965), 71.

35. Ibid., 73.

36. Ibid., 79.

37. Ibid., 82.

38. Ibid., 86.

39. Ibid., 104.

40. Ibid., 73.

41. Albert Camus, *State of Siege. Caligula and Three Other Plays*, trans. Stuart Gilbert (New York: Vintage, 1958), 205.
42. Albert Camus, *The Plague*, trans. Stuart Gilbert (New York: Modern Library, 1948), 197.
43. Ibid., 222.
44. Ibid., 226.
45. Ibid., 227.
46. Camus, *The Rebel*, 284.
47. Friedrich Nietzsche, *On the Advantage and Disadvantage of History for Life*, trans. Peter Preuss (Indianapolis, IN: Hackett Publishing, 1980), 48.
48. Ibid., 244.
49. Ibid., 48.
50. In *The Rebel*, Camus expresses his admiration for the historic Kaliayev in his discussion of historical rebellion. Above everything else, Camus feels, Kaliayev and his comrades never lose sight of the human world for which they are fighting. When their terrorist activity called for death, each one of these rebels was willing to pay for that death with his or her own life, as the dramatic Kaliayev does, admirably demonstrating a true understanding of the stakes involved. These "fastidious assassins," as Camus calls them, "while simultaneously affirming the world of men, place themselves above this world, thus demonstrating for the last time in our history that real rebellion is a creator of values" (172).
51. Camus, *The Just Assassins*, 260.

TWENTY-SIX

CAR CRASH CRUCIFIXION CULTURE

JULIAN DARIUS

THE DUAL NATURE OF THE CAR CRASH, automotive accident and fiery wreck, represents the (post)industrial equivalent of the crucifixion. Despite separation through time and culture, the cross and the car, as well as the crucifixion and the car crash, have analogous mythological significance. Cultures have long memories, even if these memories are constantly in the process of revision. As a person's psychology often transfers impressions of one figure onto another, so a culture's mythology often transfers older configurations on to new events. God may be dead, but the geography of his corpse continues to define us.

UNDERSTANDING THE CRUCIFIXION

To track the fascination with the crucifixion, one must track its origins in the Christian zeitgeist in which the West continues to participate, however reluctantly. Christianity transformed a common instrument of public death into a totem of worship and popular fixation; zero period Romans wondered about this cult's strange obsession with a torture implement. Largely forgotten about Christ's crucifixion is its mundane nature—a messiah in a land rife with them, executed in conventional fashion. The dual nature of Christ—both purely human and purely divine—finds ultimate expression in the crucifixion, affirming both human death and divine myth through an act simultaneously dramatic and quotidian. The late Middle Ages brought the fetishization of Christ's body, both in depictions of Christ as hunk and in the Cult of the Wounds. These attributes, of course, belong to an older tradition, and can be witnessed in the cults of pre-Christian (demi-)gods and their deaths, but Christianity coded them at the center of Western cultural myth.

CAR AS CROSS

As the cross provided the central symbol of the Middle Ages, so the car acts as totem for twentieth-century Western civilization. A brief view of the car's symbolic capital through the lens of intellectual history will put this comparison in its proper context. Globalization and technological advance, particularly with the printing press—and, lately, the Internet— have brought a radically new context to the crucifixion myth. As cultural imperialism has replaced military imperialism, so transportation, whether of data, or materials, or ourselves, has replaced physical torture as the means of hegemonic control.

When firms selling everything from pizza to computers advertise their quick delivery, OPEC debates outputs, and nations restrict Internet usage, they affirm the cultural ascent of transportation. Building solvent companies has been subordinated to the transportation of stocks be- tween hands, particularly when those companies are transportation- related, such as Amazon.com, which produces nothing and transports everything. Overt control through torture and execution is passé; passive control through transportation is all the rage. Geographic borders no longer signify military might; they signal the limits of control over the means not of production but of transportation. The age of borders is re- placed by the age of Borders, transporting books to meet Internet orders (transported data) and to stores to which customers drive in order to transport, in turn, these books to their houses (presumably later to auc- tion them online and repeat the process).

Freeways have replaced armies as signs of development, and it's no co- incidence that the Internet is equally well known as the information su- perhighway, while computers are said to "crash." The official demand for public and tortuous execution by means of phallic object is today rather slight. Death is rarely publicly witnessed, violence generally despised, torture internationally condemned, and the cross largely devoid of its original context, more relevant as a footnote symbol or generic (optionally neon) religious logo than a large wooden instrument of cruel and slow death. The cross fundamentally opposes movement, allowing its impaled and displayed victim transportation only to the other side. As its replacement in the age of transportation, oil tankers and computers lack the requisite drama. The car alone serves as the appropriate supplement: phallic symbol publicly displayed, exotic version of the age's mundane type of instrument.

Aldous Huxley saw this, in his way; his *Brave New World* (1932) describes the removal of the tops of crosses so they can become "T"s (as in Model Ts) and the replacing of "our Lord" with "our Ford." And recently, in Colorado Springs, I spied a sign that absolutely astounded me. It was one of three religiously themed word balloons, each perhaps six inches long and hanging from the interior of a car's front window, and it asked, apparently unconscious of irony, "Have You Traveled with the LORD Lately?"—with the word "LORD" stylized to look like the Ford corporate logo.

One of the main distinctions between car and cross is the difference in composition. Updated each year and quickly obsolete, the car is a complex instrument of synthetic metals, streamlined plastic, and sleek glass that embodies our age of mass production, simulacra, malleability, complexity, and rapidity of change. In contrast, the cross was a simple instrument of wood, designed and intended solely as a functional tool in a heinous murder rite, signaling "earthiness" in comparison with the artificial automobile, stoic rigidity over adaptability, pragmatism over appearance.

Both instruments are classic phallic symbols. The cross represents the earthy phallus of agrarian society and of Dionysus (mythological inspiration to Christ), whereas the car is sleeker—the perfect, powerful phallus of the Hollywood sex scene, closer to a stylish vibrator than a human penis, quite appropriate to the age of simulacra.

CAR CRASH AS CRUCIFIXION

As car serves as cross, so too the car crash, deliberate or not, offers a (post-)industrial crucifixion whose victim is impaled on a structure of metal and plastic. Cruciform signs warn drivers of where children or animals cross the road, a clear sign of the relationship between crucifix, automobile, and putative death—and a signal to avoid crucifixion. But the parallel between car crash and crucifixion, besides both being the bloody products of analogous instruments, is best seen in our reactions.

Our response to the car crash is paradoxical, like contemporary responses to the crucifixion. While obviously dramatic (one gleefully imagines exploding windows, crumpled steel, bodies thrown from the car, and blood on the highway), the car crash is not only commonplace but also embodies the futility of a death or injury seemingly without point or poignancy. These two conflicting positions cannot be occupied simultaneously; both are quite potent but unable to confront mutually from a single position, creating an effect like the well-known optical illusion of two faces and a candlestick. We can see either vividly powerful option—automotive accident or fiery wreck—but not both simultaneously. This incongruity duplicates for our time the concurrently dramatic and mundane qualities of the crucifixion. As crucifixion was a common execution method, so the car crash is a simple automotive accident. As crucifixion was a public display of might used for its dramatic potential, so the car crash is a fiery wreck, always remarkable and always "striking."

THE CELEBRITY CAR CRASH

But the car crashes that truly parallel the original role of the crucifixion are those whose victims complement the simultaneously mundane and dramatic means of their death with a life that is concurrently both human and divine. The celebrity car crash offers exactly this in an age when celebrities have their likenesses reproduced as icons for worship, present as posters in nearly every dorm room and as plastic effigies in every toy store. Television offers hours of worship at regular intervals, like the matins and vespers of old.

In the age of simulacra, Madonna has replaced the Madonna. As we observe her and attempt to decipher her ambiguous video mythology, so we once observed Christ and tried to interpret his equivocal textual mythology. Celebrities appear in commercials because their very presence connotes divine blessing. Their fans' fanatical mob enthusiasm shows religious ecstasy of the most intense sort. They attempt their own public miracles and ministries, campaigning to heal the various lepers and outcasts of our day. In recent years Richard Gere has tried to fashion himself into a Buddha and by so doing inevitably acknowledges the dominance of Christianity by providing an alternative still defined in Western culture by its otherness. Objects for meditation, ranging from trading cards and figurines to coins and standing displays, commemorate various moments in celebrities' mythologies as church walls and illuminated books once did for Christ. The Who's rock opera *Tommy* was right on the Tommybuck when it depicted Marilyn Monroe as the religious idol of choice in the age of acid, psychiatry, and pinball—to be replaced by Tommy himself and his messianic cult, who are eager to consume any product bearing his iconic likeness. And Marilyn Monroe is a particularly apt choice, reminding us that the celebrity term "sex goddess" communicates more than we may think.

We try to romance like James Bond, to tantalize or make pithy comments instead of being honest. We imagine ourselves as cool as the leads in *Back to the Future, Pulp Fiction, The Matrix,* or whatever movie seems hip in a particular year. We walk, dress, and speak like our celebrity idols, who, unlike us, inhabit a fast-paced, edited world without traffic jams or self-doubt. The difference between purchasing a line of clothes endorsed by a celebrity and outright stalking is one of degree, not state of mind.

Movie theaters are the new churches, in whose pews we observe a respectful silence, broken only by occasional gasps of shock or sounds of sympathy, providing a liturgical response at preordained places in the sermon. Here we experience mass religious ecstasy, identifying with people and places not physically present. Here we receive an audiovisual sermon that transmutes a dead canvas into a living world we believe to be real—a sermon whose ultimate message is the perpetuation of the cult of celebrity. This is the point of every close-up encouraging our vicarious identification and the obliteration of self. This is the point of every upward shot at the celebrity, which demands our constant supplication in the form of raised eyes and craned necks. This is the point of each godlike celebrity likeness, perfected by airbrushing, editing, cosmetics, and surgery. Even when tabloids reveal less tantalizing images, they still invoke perfection by perfection's startling absence, thereby reenacting the myth of the at-least-temporarily fallen idol.

As celebrities are godlike, so their crucifixion via car crash completes this ascent. Witness James Dean, whose death by car crash created his cult. Such accidents often involve a trade in relics associated with the death, often granted supernatural powers, resembling the medieval relic cults. Parts of Dean's "death car" (a sleek and sexy Porsche) were sold, purchased for reuse in other vehicles. After a series of coincidental, often improbable accidents plagued the parts' buyers, magical powers were ascribed to the car. In the end, like Christ's true cross, Dean's true car is lost to history, probably stolen by a crazed fan obsessed with celebrity relics.[1]

PRINCESS DIANA

The parallel between crucifixion and celebrity car crash is never greater than when the celebrity is a royal one, best replicating for our times the crucifixion of the son of David. Such figures have tensions about their monarchical identity that mirror those of Christ. Royal car crashes fetishize the victim as with the medieval Christ, complete with new cults of wounds. In the aftermath of the royal car crash, the government, like the Romans, receives absolution; Pilate is exonerated (as is often the car's pilot), and the search for Sanhedrin conspirators begins.

Diana, like Christ, existed within the context of a national monarchy, but came to be positioned against that monarchy; both were national figures alienated from the present regime and celebrated by those dissatisfied with it. Both, at least in their mythologies, rejected the earthly kingdom with which they were associated, both came to be loved for their charitable works, which undermined the hierarchical establishment but by changing it, by offering an alternative. Both Christ and Diana were earthly royals who distanced themselves from that royalty, becoming instead monarchs of heaven or spiritual goodness, Prince of Peace and Princess of Hearts. Beyond the simple facts of Diana's life, she was commonly seen to be at odds with the rest of the monarchy; some people explicitly claimed they preferred a "social royal" concerned with land mines and AIDS to the older hierarchy of kings, a preference reflecting Christianity's early appeal to the oppressed.

26.1   James Dean crash. © Photofest

Diana's apparent kindness, patience, social sacrifice, and maternal warmth were all assets in her public persona's accumulation of symbolic holiness, and her manner of controlling and orchestrating her photographs rarely allowed a close examination of this image. Even her well-documented marital infidelities didn't affect her accumulation of spiritual capital even in the more sexually conservative climate of Great Britain. Her marriage to a man who was widely perceived as indifferent or abusive further positioned Diana, in her helplessness, as sensitive and vulnerable in comparison. It also helped cast her sexual adventures as independent quests for self-fulfillment rather than simple adultery. Just as modern depictions of Christ are increasingly human, encouraging identification, so Diana's infidelities made her seem more human and sympathetic in a time when social structures have been dramatically reshaped by the frequency of divorce.

The reverence for Diana's suffering certainly reflects the present tendency to revere and even exalt victims, a cult fundamentally Christian in its anti-Nietzschean praise of the weak. Diana's own pitied history of self-mutilation—including cutting herself with a lemon slicer, using a razor blade on her wrists, throwing herself down stairs, and stabbing herself multiple times with a penknife—recapitulates the lives of the famous Christian martyrs, on whose remains Christianity rose. It also evokes the self-mutilation of the Middle Ages, during which outbreaks of self-flagellation became so extreme that the practice had to be suppressed. The holiness ascribed to her history of often self-imposed suffering has deep Christian roots, merging our modern fetish for victimhood with Christian suffering, the archetype of which is Christ. Supernatural power was even ascribed to Diana during her lifetime. A propaganda piece for a then-fledgling godling, Andrew Morton's *Diana: Her True Story*, the 1992 international best-seller, greatly contributed to the early formation of Diana's mythology. It attributes to Diana a number of prophecies regarding death or illness that materialized soon after, and it does so in a simple style of reporting reminiscent of the gospels' handling of miracles.

This parallel of (perceived) personalities suggests the grafting of the Christian mythos on to the figure of Diana and illustrates how celebrity and royal images act as magnets for floating tensions and symbol systems. Diana's divinely human death via car crash solidified her accumulation of symbolic capital. In retrospect, Diana seems to have been remarkably well poised for deification, but her human foibles were still all too transparent. For all the contortions of her media face, Diana remained a controversial tabloid celebrity well known for her marital problems and often foolish gallivanting with lovers. The holy car crash that took her life acted as a crucible, instantly transforming this transparently flawed human into a divinity mourned in didactic religious rhetoric and widespread histrionics.

This deification took place, of course, by means of the various world media organizations that reported the pitiful story quickly and *ad nauseum*. In the hours following the crash, Diana's death was quickly recast as a tragedy, prefabricated from myth, commercially viable, and comfortably stable. The British monarchy—especially her husband—was placed in the role of villain who had practiced psychological torture, an emotionally and psychologically convenient casting coup. The unappealing parts of her life were quickly forgotten, and Diana became a martyr, constantly depicted as a kind woman, perfect mother, and brave campaigner for justice, known for her charitable works. Martyred Diana was a sad girl trapped in a lonely battle against a cruel monarchy at whose inflexible whims she had endured Christ-like suffering. There, beside her crushed Mercedes, her Cult of Wounds was already forming as photographers allegedly snapped pictures of her body as it lay battered and bleeding in the backseat; within hours these pictures had been sold and circulated throughout the world by means of the Internet.

By the time of her much-publicized funeral, Diana's ascension into divinity was complete, and reporters spoke of her only in terms of her holy myth. The all-consuming rapidity with which this version of events consumed all commentary was remarkable; those who offered any other interpretation faced harsh rebuke. English florists couldn't hope to fill the abundance of orders they received; the streets filled with thousands of mourners, and hysterical grieving was the order of the day. Elton John revised his "Candle in the Wind" for Diana, positioning her as the mythological inheritor of "sex goddess" Marilyn Monroe, by making the song into nothing less than an apostrophe addressed to a newly ascended divinity, "our nation's golden child" whose name "the stars spell out."

Since I began working on this chapter, a graphic novel written by Jamie Delano, the English comic book author noted for his clever and satirical work on the American title *Hellblazer*, was published in four installments. Set in England in 2025, the work partly responds to the deification of Diana. Living "in close proximity to the burial site at Althorp House in Northamptonshire," Delano, according to publicity, "vividly remembers his village filling up with 'weeping pilgrims' during the burial services," and the sky above being "riddled with press and security helicopters." In an interview, he also referred to "the hysterical national overreaction to her death—very 'un-British' wailing and rending of garments, the apparent instantaneous beatification and spontaneous eruption of a 'cult' following (Visions of the Blessed Diana reported by kitchen mystics up and down the country, etc.)."[2]

JFK

Whereas Diana's cult may fade with time, that of John F. Kennedy continues to grow. In fact, his status as deity has become so entrenched that the Republican party uses his image in its promotional materials (including a montage played on the night of George W. Bush's speech at the 2000 Republican National Convention). Like Christ, JFK was seen during his lifetime as a political messiah; since his death, he's become a spiritual messiah instead, one symbolizing national hope, vibrancy, and change—as well as America's failed promise.

If Diana was a tabloid figure before her crucifixion, JFK was a practitioner of *realpolitik*. And, like Diana's, his media face was carefully constructed. His hospitalization prior to his election raised him to national attention, affirming his human frailty and his divine perseverance. His dynamic and idealistic speeches cast him as a national mystic, a religious visionary asking us (in his June 1963 speech at the American University) to "re-examine our own attitudes." His public assumption of the blame for the failed Bay of Pigs invasion showed both his humanity and a divine strength in admitting human weakness. The famous photo of him looking deeply thoughtful through a window during the Cuban missile crisis iconically depicted his sensitivity and concern, while his successful handling of the situation made him seem both humanly capable and divinely blessed. He had become, like Christ, an emissary of peace.

In retrospect, JFK seems, like Diana, to have been well positioned for the ascension his "special kind of car crash" provided. In the decades since his death, his divinity has steadily grown as revelations have gradually expanded both sides of his Christ-like dual nature. His adultery, his use of the Secret Service as procurers of women, his political maneuvering, his alleged overindulgence in prescription drugs, his severe physical ailment and alleged venereal disease have conspired to reaffirm his humanity in the strongest terms possible, while his speeches (which have received much more attention after his death than during his life), his installation of a phone line to the Kremlin, and his ambivalent if not skeptical attitude toward Vietnam have conspired to paint him as a messiah of peace. Even his cavorting with Marilyn Monroe demonstrates both his human weakness and his intimate association with the ultimate sex goddess, a mortal failing that seems poetically appropriate for an Olympian.

Like Diana, JFK is seen as having been opposed to his nation's monarchy or political establishment—primarily a postmortem view. His divine death came just at the right time, cementing his godlike youth and allowing the traumas of Vietnam and Watergate to seem a repercussion of the death of America's Prince of Peace. In the more fervent forms of this mythology, the Bay of Pigs caused a rift between him and the political establishment, leading to tensions, Kennedy's firing of powerful Washington figures, his attempt to destroy the CIA, and possibly to his assassination.

Kennedy's mythmakers came to cast Nixon as the Satan who had opposed him in the 1960 elections. Nixon's exaggerated features and his sweating on camera, as well as his reputation for lying, enforced this connection. As the time was right for Kennedy, so the time was wrong for Nixon, whose impeachment had much more to do with the economy than with the burglary and acted to cement his Satanic role. The Watergate tapes and, more important, the public perception of them further reinforced this role, depicting Nixon as arrogant, racist, and "demonically" fond of cursing. Rumors of his involvement in Kennedy's assassination continue to circulate, and many sources claim that he was in Dallas on November 22. Kennedy and Nixon have become mutually dependent opposites, defined in mythological contrast, a uniquely monotheistic opposition.

The conspiracy theories surrounding Kennedy's death at best recognize that the official version of events was mythological, based on the comfortable tale of the lone nut and of responsible investigators, and that any alternative version is also mythological, based on the intensely dramatic possibilities of cabals and the security that lone men cannot derail history. The American mind recoils from the assassination, choosing one simultaneously comfortable and unsettling mythology or another. The result of the many intense conspiracy theories is that the followers of Kennedy's mythology are split between orthodoxy and multiple heresies, each with firm and sometimes profound credos, a situation much like that of early Christianity. The many deaths of the various witnesses mirror the martyrdom of witnesses for Christ, and the effect seems the same: encouragement, rather than suppression, of the cult.

The strength of Kennedy's mythology has led to a remarkable proliferation of his Cult of Relics. In lieu of the holy lance, we have the magic bullet; in lieu of the Holy Grail, we have the presidential limousine, lost blood receiver sought in religious quests. The labeling of Kennedy's administration as Camelot, which quickly followed the assassination, not only symbolizes a lost golden age extending from a blessed leader but the temptation by the faithful to seek the grail despite adversity. Jackie's pink suit, stained with John's blood, which she refused to change, is preserved in photos as a Shroud of Turin. Oswald's rifle has become a relic for study, as have the famous backyard photographs that publicly sealed Oswald's guilt, their legitimacy called into doubt just like those objects in the medieval Cult of Relics. The bullets and bullet fragments themselves act as talismans, weighed and examined in an attempt to gain enlightenment. Even Kennedy's bullet-torn brain serves as a lost relic, one that reportedly vanished from the National Archives. In the pursuit of evidence for conspiracy, the Zapruder film and virtually every document pertaining to Kennedy have also become relics that might bring worshipers closer to their sacrificial god, and the sealed government files on the assassination seem like secrets kept locked in the basement of the Vatican.

So too has the investigation into Kennedy's assassination produced an obsession with the crucifixion itself, a desire to prove who stood where and when, one mirroring exegetical study of the seemingly conflicting descriptions of the crucifixion in the gospels. Kennedy's Cult of the Wounds has people analyzing the Zapruder film frame by frame and charting the course and exact time not only of the fatal head shot but of the seven wounds attributed to the magic bullet. This same fervor has been extended to Jack Ruby's murder of Lee Harvey Oswald, shot while surrounded by police.

The finest expression of Kennedy's mythology must be Oliver Stone's 1991 film *JFK,* which Stone has explicitly called a "counter-myth" to the mythology of the Warren Report. It features virtually all of these concerns, including rhetoric about how Kennedy's assassination marked the end of a more hopeful era, as if nature itself was responding to the crucifixion. Its courtroom finale features a model of Dealey Plaza and a memorable reenactment of the injuries caused by the magic bullet that comes straight from the Cult of Wounds. As New Orleans District Attorney Jim Garrison plays the Zapruder film's fatal head shot, he repeats words "back and to the right," hammering home his description of the body's response to the grisly wound with late-medieval obsessiveness.

In the mythology on mythology that is *JFK,* Garrison mourns Camelot's loss and acts as a knight pursuing the Holy Grail and the truth it represents. His twelve assistants, complete with one dissenter whom Garrison describes as "Judas," mirror Christ's twelve apostles. His Christ-like sacrifices for a truth he sees but others disdain, as well as the public martyrdom he suffers as a result, demonstrate the power of Kennedy's mythology, in which Garrison acts as a kind of Paul. As controversy surrounding the film escalated to fever pitch, Stone himself was inextricably drawn by the mythmaking media into Kennedy's mythology and characterized just as his Garrison had been, despite Stone's far greater self-consciousness, creating a mythology of Stone containing Stone's mythology of Garrison, who sought the truth behind Kennedy's mythology.

CONCLUSION

Other deaths may bring fond remembrances, but the crucible of the car crash allows the fullest form of deification. Not all deaths bring this level of obsession, compulsive reenactment, conspiracy theory, and cults of wounds; nor do all deaths occur, in a manner combining the dramatic and the mundane, to a person who embodies both the human and the divine. Our fascination with car crashes, particularly those blessed with a celebrity presence, represents an overlaying onto the crucifixion in the cultural consciousness—or an attempt to replace the absent crucifixion, to fill that Nietzschean void with an equally brutal and sacrificial (post-) industrial equivalent.

NOTES

1. Dean's mythology has his "death car" seriously injuring five men, including two deaths. See the introduction to this volume; see also Mikita Brottman, *Hollywood Hex: Death and Destiny in the Dream Factory* (London: Creation, 1999), 27–28.
2. See Jamie Delano, *Hellblazer Special: Bad Blood* #1–4, Vertigo (D.C. Comics), September-December 2000. This publicity text, including Delano's statements, appeared in the "Subculture" page of the Vertigo line of comic books (an imprint of DC Comics) in the month bearing the cover date of September 2000; *Hellblazer* #152 is one example. Delano's graphic story appeared as a "miniseries."

TWENTY-SEVEN

CRASH CULTURE AND AMERICAN BLOOD RITUAL

CHRISTOPHER SHARRETT

THE CAR CRASH IS A COMPONENT OF OUR RUBBERNECKING culture that takes joy in the suffering of others, the new *schaudenfreude* that is the earmark of postmodernity. But this is a pathology with roots deep in American culture, manifest today in the anxiety over the pursuit of a "politic of meaning" that is a fixation for neoliberalism. The fascination with mass death on the highway, with the persecution of people on "real TV" cop shows and the like, is about the bankruptcy of American mass ritual at the end of its road. The endless satisfactions demanded and promoted by late capitalism have reached a point of critical mass, producing a Sadean void where pleasure and pain become nullity. The bourgeois subject is reduced to base matter, and the Freudian death wish is finally actualized on a transpsychical scale. Ballard's *Crash* and *The Atrocity Exhibition*[1] illuminate an important aspect of postmodern death culture: the fixation on details and the fetishization of commodities at a particularly diseased register. The particulars of the commodity, and our absorption in them, represent an almost caricatured alienation, especially as the commodity—the detritus of postindustrial culture—is conflated with death and the cadaver. The anality of commodity culture becomes rather literal, as consumer interest alternates between hysterical consumption of worthless goods and the enthrallment with death, destruction, excrement, disease, the injured body, and holocaustal sites. Never before has the psycho-political association of gold with shit become a commonplace, acted out repeatedly by the promotional culture of the mediascape.

Martha Stewart is an important locus. Her frenetic commodity pre-occupation seems a primer of the denial of death that haunts her every gesture. Neatness, perfection, and the exhausting, inexorable pursuit of nothing become paramount as age and death etch themselves into her face; her constantly working hands and steadily disheveled aspect are somehow iconic. She is, in microcosm, the free-floating anxiety whose fullest expression is the nihilism of daily life, self-absorption turned to self-destruction. But the foundation of crash culture is more basic than the illness of consumer capital. It rests on a great and terrible awakening to the absurdity of sacrificial death and its attendant rituals within the American experience.

Death on the highway becomes a *petit recit,* a small narrative that sub-stitutes for the social revivification once provided by the Alamo, Gettys-burg, Custer's Last Stand, Iwo Jima, and similar sites manipulated by state power to create a bogus consensus supporting the centrality of sac-rificial bloodletting. The sites of restorative meaning, the "sacred ground" formed from the fragments of an ill-remembered past, now have little to do with the commemoration of blood sacrifice in service of na-tion building. Instead, the preoccupation with the Alamo, Civil War bat-tlefields, and similar sites is informed by a kind of tourism characterized by the search for details of slaughter and souvenirs that capture such de-tails in kitsch replication.[2] The tales of body count become all, which is why highway death eventually becomes a satisfactory substitute for the formative massacres of the American conquest.

The ideological and historical contexts of bloodshed are lost, even as archivists and preservationists attempt to rationalize the barbarism of these events, their goal to reinstate public acceptance of blood ritual as the formative component of national identity. Civil War "reenactors" repeat in mime the bloodshed of the American past in an attempt to reinstate the social and political fervor that once (in their fevered imaginations) an-imated it. But in so doing they merely articulate, in their own way, Lévi-Strauss's warning about the transformation of myth into narrative.

The more noticeable crisis reflects René Girard's notion of the failure of ritual to create consensus and thereby ward off all-encompassing social violence. According to Girard, the function of ritual is to dispel violence by locating it in discrete acts that contain and finally expel it.[3] The dependence on such ritual becomes pronounced as consensus fails, as language systems and social contracts come apart. Conflicts of intertribal and intratribal sorts ensue, as the destruction of a new Other is sought to reinstate meaning in a totemic system, to reinvigorate language and a social contract. The difficulty here is the tendency of violence to become widespread, "on all fronts," resulting in a general conflagration. The danger becomes pronounced, as ritual is no longer able to still the tide of violence.

Such is the situation with American historical sites and with the "commemoration culture" that reminds the populace of events, now empty of meaning, reproduced in the hall of mirrors that is simulacra culture. This is a problem that plagues popular culture in general, and art is no longer able to "keep it off the streets." The more often the myths are articulated, the more empty of meaning they become. If postmodernity can be reduced to one essential concept, it is that of a civilization no longer able to believe its informing myths but repeating them anyway.

Ritual processes that previously organized society and contained its violence have been exposed, particularly artistic and religious ritual. Expressions as disparate as born-again Christianity and allusion-stuffed cinema are panicked discourses speaking to the failure of belief systems, burdened with anxious cries of a need to believe (a common refrain in postmodern rock music) and a deeply melancholic nostalgia for lost forms. Other manifestations include unending rituals of nostalgia such as those commemorating World War II and the "greatest" (because the most conservative) generation, the Beatles, Woodstock, the public death of Kennedy, and the crises of capital (the Depression, Vietnam, Watergate). This nostalgia points the public to moments that, however horrid, represent, at least in the politics of media representation, a time of illusory cohesion. This is the "sacrificial crisis" described by Girard, now taking place on a pandemic scale, as panic sets in over the loss of this imagined social cohesion.

The new status of the Other is instructive. For example, one can look at the changing concept of the monstrous within horror fiction. Early in the twentieth century, Frankenstein's monster, the Wolfman, and Dracula suggested the pathos of Otherness, the rage of repression, and the "outside" position of the subject vis-à-vis bourgeois normality. The new monsters—Freddy Krueger, Leatherface, Michael Myers, Jason Vorhees—and their real-life (and equally loved) counterparts—Charles Manson, Jeffrey Dahmer, and Ted Bundy—suggest that life is in chaos, that any "outside" has disappeared, and that the romance of alienation has been replaced by insanity, murder, and suicide.

Or perhaps we should see the serial killer as an extension of the folk heroes of the Old West, those freelance berserkers like Wild Bill Hickok, Billy the Kid, Jesse James, and John Wesley Hardin. These men were the entrepreneurs of blood, whose currency still seems involved in creating for us a mythology of unreason and implacable murder (or, rather, a church of blood-meaning now facing a catastrophic climax in the vacant climate of postmodernity). Expressions of this impulse range from Jonestown—a coda to old-fashioned American charismatic religiosity and apocalypticism—to the Columbine High School massacre, a frenzied, terrified extension of the gunfighter nation going back to Bloody Kansas, Antietam, Tombstone, and Teddy Roosevelt's "big stick."

Similarly, white guilt feelings about the racial Other dissipate as pleasure is taken in the random murder and state-sponsored extermination of blacks and other minorities. This is done in the name of hysterical cries for the preservation of "civilization," the "canon," and "family values," with white propertied America wishing to turn back the clock to a mythical, uncontentious way of life. All of this is motivated by the urge to convince ourselves that our individual and collective existence— so long assured by doctrines like the Manifest Destiny—are still justified. But there are no arenas to test the divine mandate for conquest, no places to regain the old confidence beyond the vacuous barbarism of the mediascape. So with the fading of the nation-state and its associated massed epics of bloodletting, the highway, the fast-food restaurant, the place of employment, and the schoolyard become natural alternatives for blood ritual.

Perhaps such phenomena as "road rage"—the deliberate causing of accidents or the assault by drivers on other drivers with guns and similar weapons—is less about the stress of late-capitalist survival (not to be minimized) than an attempt to recreate meaning by murder, even mass death. The pathos of the situation is in its association not with the re-creation of a new epochal moment, a new Civil War or struggle for lib-eration but with the manifestation of the primeval need to prove one's existence by destroying it, to show one can still feel *something* by shed-ding blood and seeing the pain of the Other.

The oddness of this condition, as Ballard has persuasively claimed, is the fixation on the details—the void, not God, is in them, and, as if to assert the presence of the void, the minute particulars of the crash are keenly observed. The driver approaches a scene of jammed traffic at first with a feeling of exasperation and then a sense of entrapment and the di-minishment of individualism (God forbid in America) in the already overstressed circumstances of the congested, decaying highway system. Then the slow approach. What *is* happening? Anything interesting? The driver must stay focused in the bullying circumstances of the road.

Impatient hands grip the wheel . . . visions of unrestrained horsepower like in car chase movies of the 1970s, when you can plow right through everyone, making use of what's *yours*. After all, history has always allowed for it—like the Cimarron Strip Land Rush, Conestoga wagons crashing on the prairie, hapless people trampled. (Recall those great scenes of Yancey Cravat lighting out for territory in *Cimarron?*) As Burroughs puts it (borrowing from Ronald Reagan regarding the Panama Canal): "We bought it, we built it, we paid for it, we're gonna *keep it!*"

Back to the highway. Patience grows thin . . . the .357 stainless steel. It's handy all right, and thank God for the stainless—no rust. Diastolic pressure goes up several points. A tractor-trailer blocks the view . . . you can't even see what the fuck is *up* there. If it's construction it could be forever, unless they've got the courtesy to halt work periodically to let de-cent people through. Maybe those clouds mean rain . . . those redneck blue-collar types will knock off if it *is* construction. Then . . . a glimpse of flashing colored lights. Cops, or an ambulance, or both? Finally. At least something to *see*.

Inching along, the scene becomes visible and looks downright extrav-agant. A thrill insinuates itself, like a new infection twitching within an old abscess. Now there's something to wait for. On the CD player, in-dustrial sounds, the screams of some repulsive thrashcore singer. Now flicking on the radio—a traffic update that promises delays, remarking on the weather that is "on tap." Some smarmy cunt, a public-relations graduate from some school of "communication." She loves radio. Sinatra's version of "I've Got You Under My Skin." The debauched rogue loving his compulsive behavior. Dreams of analingus with a teenager. The erotic reverie brightens the experience, adds fuel to the fire, makes the whole thing move along a bit better.

The hallucinatory cop car lights fill the horizon but are nearly overpowered by the arc lights left by the workers who have turned the highway into an eviscerated carcass—a boondoggle that will be there for years. There's construction *too!* Goddamn it to fucking hell! A cracked-open overpass that looks like a parapet of a fort, smoke billowing behind it. Steel girders scattered everywhere, like the wreck of something rather than its beginning. Pockmarked chunks of concrete . . . some flannel-shirted construction slob leaning on one, smoking a cigarette. The slow approach.

Now you can get a real good shot at what's going on. An Audi turned fully on its side, the roof sheared away completely. Long pieces of chrome and stainless steel, hundreds of tiny red and amber plastic fragments. Broken glass. EMS workers throwing down flares like darts at a dartboard. *I'd sacrifice anything come what may for the sake of having you near* . . . Coming up around the curve, the front of another vehicle, a new Camry, is visible. The front is caved in, the car apparently somehow spun around on collision. Then a shocker: the remains of the Audi burst into flames. The cops and firemen jump back. More cops halt traffic completely . . . no more inching along.

Somewhere else on the turnpike, a driver suddenly pulls out of his lane and starts going in reverse, then starts driving in violent circles in front of the oncoming traffic. Tires screech as brakes are applied. *That comes in the night, oh it screams how it yells in my ear* . . . The whole scene is visible in the rearview mirror. People give up and decide to run into each other. *Crash the damn thing!* Drivers see their cars as deadly weapons, chariots of those long vanquished. By late in the day, the turnpike is littered with vehicles. Angry quarrels on the side of the road. One man strikes another in the face with The Club, shattering his nose and upper jaw, spraying bones and teeth. A wife scrambles for something in the dashboard. Gunshots make the slowed-down onlookers run into each other. A new Matthew Brady takes pictures. Politicians mourn the event, suggesting its social lessons. Each year new cults arise, T-shirts, commemorations that celebrate more than eulogize, everything with a nudge and wink. Smoke rises.

NOTES

1. J. G. Ballard, *Crash* (New York: Farrar, Strauss & Giroux, 1973); *The Atrocity Exhibition* (San Francisco: V/Search, 1990).
2. A good survey of the American fixation on sites of mass death is Edward Tabor Linenthal, *Sacred Ground: Americans and their Battlefields* (Urbana and Chicago: University of Illinois Press, 1991).
3. See René Girard, *Violence and the Sacred,* trans. Patrick Gregory (Baltimore: Johns Hopkins University Press, 1979).

TRAFFIC OF THE SPHERES

PROTOTYPE FOR A MEMORIAL

GREGORY ULMER

THIS PROPOSAL FOR A NEW KIND OF MEMORIAL (a MEmorial) is addressed to the combined agencies of the National Endowment for the Arts and the National Aeronautics and Space Administration. The proposal is part of an emerAgency (a virtual Internet-based distributed consultancy) consultation on a problem stated by theorists of architecture (among others). This problem states that the entertainment media in general, and television in particular, bear responsibility for the decline of the public sphere in mediating the relationship of private citizens with the State. Monumental architecture once played a large role in maintaining this public sphere, having to do with the forming and preserving of a community. But is it really the case that the electronic excludes monumentality?

The purpose of the experiment proposed here is to explore the possibilities of the monumental electronic, to help invent a role for the electronic in a counterpublic sphere, applied to community formation and identity. The focus is the memorial aspect of monumentality, concerned with the way the rituals of mourning contribute to the formation of a community. Societies from Ancient Egypt to contemporary America have embodied their experience of death, loss, and separation in built constructions, landmarks that provide a referent of unity linking the passing generations to one another. Memory, both collective and individual, is re-organized in an electronic apparatus (electracy). The challenge is to adapt the possibilities of this apparatus to the cultural function of monumentality, producing both individual and collective identity.

REGIONAL CONTEXT

The Gainesville community recently commemorated the tenth anniversary of one of the worst crimes in its history. During the last week of August 1990, five students, in Gainesville for the start of the fall semester at the University of Florida, were murdered in their apartments. First, two women were found stabbed and mutilated. Rumors spread that there were still more bodies. The police denied it. The next day another victim was found, a "petite brunette" like the first two. More rumors, and more denials. The third day, two more victims—a man and a woman this time. Panic. Parents came to take their children out of school; others packed up and left on their own.

The front section of the local newspaper, during the following weeks, was devoted equally to the investigation into the murders and the crisis in the Persian Gulf—the invasion of Kuwait. The two stories were united by the same theme, a shared "mythhistory." The murderer (whose identity had not yet been established at the time) and Saddam Hussein were characterized in similar terms, as being at once crazy and calculating. Although the events were described as the work of these respective individuals, journalists explained that the instability in the Gulf region and the insecurity of local apartment complexes would remain unchanged even if the two villains were eliminated.

The second shared element of the "mythistory" was the declaration that this time of crisis was the finest hour of the respective communities: that the nations of the world and the people of Gainesville had come together in a qualitatively new way in response to the dangerous situation. Phil Donahue brought his TV show to Gainesville in this spirit, he said, to help the community carry out the mourning process (and not to exploit or sensationalize the mutilation murders of coeds). The local and global stories were the same. The new cooperation of the Eastern and Western nations, united in ostracizing Iraq, was repeated locally in the way friends formed groups for mutual protection and comfort and in the joining together of the city and the university in the rituals of mourning. The relationship between disaster and community formation was clearly manifested during those weeks.

How to do something, knowing how to repeat a performance, is a kind of memory, a kind of thinking that takes place in the collective conduct of a ritual. How to stop making mistakes? How to reduce error and eliminate accidents? These are the goals of a certain scientific method incapable of thinking of wreckage as sacrificial ceremony, as the foundation of a national identity. To think of car wrecks as mistakes, as errors, as not knowing how to drive, for example, reflects the Enlightenment's contempt for dreams. Individuals may not want to wreck their cars, but nations do.

PROBLEM/DISASTER

Public discussion remains fixed on the events, rarely reflecting on the frame of the events, never raising the structural questions that might help grasp the cause and function of private and public death. Nonetheless, a certain awareness persists of the relationship of the events to our demand for freedom—that a lifestyle of independence in terms of private cars and apartments carries a price: A price we are willing to pay. But do we know what we're getting for this expenditure?

Why does the community insist on treating public and private crises on a case-by-case, individualized basis? Is it not possible to grasp the frame, to bring into perceptibility and make recognizable for a public consciousness the cumulative significance of a quantity of dispersed, private acts? Georges Bataille pointed out the difficulty of this level of consciousness in his discussion of the General Economy of the movement of energy on the planet: "Man's disregard for the material basis of his life still causes him to err in a serious way. Humanity exploits given material resources, but by restricting them as it does to a resolution of the immediate difficulties it encounters, it assigns to the forces it employs an end which they cannot have. Beyond our immediate ends, man's activity in fact pursues the useless and infinite fulfillment of the universe."[1]

The example Bataille gives for such an unexamined productivity is the manufacture of automobiles in America. Bataille's theory of General

Economy offers an insight into the link between the Gainesville murders and the Gulf crisis, which may be understood as reflecting the possibilities of energy use: Available energy must be spent. "If the excess cannot be completely absorbed in [the system's] growth, it must necessarily be lost without profit."[2] In these terms, the large, anonymous apartment complexes, with each unit supplemented by a mobile room parked in the parking lot, may be seen as the utilitarian side of an energy use whose alternative is a war in the Gulf: The quantity of oil that it would take the mobile rooms to burn in decades may be consumed in a matter of days in a Gulf war. The possibility of consuming a major part of the world's oil reserves all at once is a monumental prospect, whose prospectus was expressed in the oil fields left burning in the wake of the Iraqi retreat from Kuwait.

Automobile production is normally considered within what Bataille calls the Restricted Economy—the conventional capitalist understanding of profit, productivity, expansion, accumulation. In this context, it is possible to understand the difference between emerAgents and normal consultants: EmerAgents consult from the perspective of the General Economy, while consultants work within the Restricted Economy. In terms of the rhetoric and logic of electracy (the name of the digital apparatus that is to new media what literacy is to print), emerAgents transfer the methods of advertising learned in the Restricted Economy to the dynamics of the General Economy.

How to regard this prospect? Automobile accidents are a link between the two options, or crises—between murder and war—according to electrate cognition. The car crash may serve as the material basis, that is, of an electronic monumentality, precisely because of its status as accident. This monumentality performs a certain lap-dissolve shot marking the historical moment in our civilization in which the windshield gives way to the monitor screen as the glass mediating our experience of time and space.

HISTORY

World War I, the Eastern Front. A soldier in the German army named Ludwig Wittgenstein is sitting in a trench. The austerity of the trench suits his mood. Two problems compete in his mind for attention: the nature of the significant proposition; the need for paper to use in the latrine. He finds a magazine. Leafing through it, he comes on a schematic picture illustrating the possible sequence of events in an automobile accident. The metaphor of the car crash as war does not occur to him. Instead, he realizes, in a flush of ecstasy, that the analogy supporting the function of the diagram—the correspondence between the parts of the picture and the event in reality—could be reversed. He realizes that "a proposition serves as a picture, by virtue of a similar correspondence between its parts and the world. The way in which the parts of the proposition are combined—the structure of the proposition—depicts a possible combination of elements in reality, a possible state of affairs."[3] This insight allows Wittgenstein to complete the manuscript of his *Tractatus Logico-Philosophicus*. This invention, bringing together car wrecks, war, and language philosophy, shows an idea (eidos, shape) without speaking of it directly.

How to read the designs made of wreckage? Wreckwork is the materialization of dreamwork in public ceremony, a paradoxical manner of thinking that is at once memory and forgetting. The place of the wreck is cleared, the scene erased, leaving the event to dissipate, dissolve, fade, decay into an outline, a pattern that is learned then all the more easily. The wreck lives on, survives as this abstraction, a transparency consulted ceaselessly by bodies negotiating cultural traffic. Here is the scene of mourning. The curve of a two-lane blacktop highway, narrow shouldered, with tall prairie grasses nearly obscuring two metal crosses posted just beyond the embankment. Along the fence line is posted a series of signs, red with white lettering, faded but still legible:
Around the curve
Lickety split
Beautiful car
Wasn't it.
Burma Shave.

PRINCIPLE (SIC) INVESTIGATOR

Gregory Ulmer
I only took one class in architecture. In a General Education class at the University of Montana I became interested in philosophy after reading something by Heidegger. I went to an academic advisor, a man wearing

a hearing aid that seemed to give him considerable trouble. It functioned less as a prosthesis and more as a sign—"I am deaf." "I'm interested in the notion of *Dasein*," I told him. "Could you recommend a class I might take that would deal with *Dasein* in more detail?" He sent me to a course in architecture, an introduction to *design*.

I have never been able to decide whether the advice was a mistake or not. For one thing, we all pronounce the word "design" incorrectly as "duh-zein," as in "I'm interested in duh-zein. What kinda jobs do duh-zeiners get?" More significantly, the instructor in the architecture class devised design problems based on readings of philosophers. "Draw Kierkegaard's laugh and integrate it into the model of Nietzsche's eternal return that you constructed out of cardboard last week." In fact, I didn't notice the possible error until years later, while reading Barthes's *S/Z* (his poststructuralist text on Balzac's short story): "Z is the letter of mutilation; phonetically, it stings like a chastising lash, an avenging insect; graphically, cast slantwise by the hand, it cuts, slashes. This Z is the letter of deviation: S and Z are in a relation of geographical inversion: the same letter seen from the other side of the mirror."[4]

THEORY

Traffic of the Spheres is a work of chora as elaborated by Jacques Derrida, concerning the three categories of being and discourse: mythos, logos, and genos. Chora, associated with genos, replaces topos as the concept of "place" in electrate design. "The chora seems to be alien to the order of the 'paradigm,' that intelligible and immutable model. And yet, 'invisible' and without sensible form, it 'participates' in the intelligible in a very troublesome and indeed aporetic way."[5] Chora is about the crossing of chance and necessity, whose nature may be discerned only indirectly in the names generated by a puncept rather than as a concept (or paradigm), including the qualities associated with "core" terms: chorus, choreography, chord, cord, corral, coral.

The project suggests the necessity of adding to this series the term "coroner." This consultation is conducted in the spirit of the musical sense of chora—"music" associated with the muses and hence with General (Economy) education, as it was for the ancient Greeks. The signifi-

cance of the patterns and rhythms absorbed unawares through the musi
cal experience by the young were to be made explicit later by means of
philosophy. "Chora"—signifying a space that is sacred in classical
Greek—was used by Plato in *Timaeus* to name the order of genos within
which being and becoming could interact. This dialogue transmitted the
Pythagorean notion of the music of the spheres—the metaphysics of cos-
mological correspondences—to the Christian Middle Ages. The function
of chora in this metaphysics is to sort chaos into kinds (Earth, Air, Fire,
Water). As reactivated in contemporary theory, chora names those places
that reveal the categories (classifying system, metaphysics) of a society.

The musical or formal order of the car crash is noted in the remarks
of a traveling salesman, quoted in a newspaper account of a chain-reac-
tion crash caused by a morning fog covering Interstate 75 over the Hi-
wassee River in Tennessee. Fifteen people were killed in this crash, and
fifty-one more were injured. The salesman pulled off when he noticed
the traffic slowing down. "I started hearing bangs and booms from
everywhere," he said. "Immediately after that there was a truck on fire
from across the road. We started hearing them banging and booming
from over there. Then all of a sudden you started hearing booms from
everywhere." Booms in the fog.

Booms in the fog.

*The wreck is not the "thing itself," in the same way that the dream is the "royal
road to the unconscious." The road is clear, free of wreckage and punctuated
with crosses. Sacrifice is not the thing itself but a mediation, bringing into relation a people with its god. Perhaps the car wreck is to sacrifice what shopping malls are to Christmas—a secular support for a sacred practice.
Wreckwork brings into existence a space for thought, an interface within
which people and machines may communicate. This opportunity is lost if we
only think about eliminating the interface rather than accessing its memory.
What might be recalled by means of wreckage?*

*The least advanced, most neglected area of electronic culture is interface
design. Thinking in this area works only with the economy of savings, con-
ceiving of those who use computers in the way that Buckminster Fuller
thought of drivers: They will never learn to drive safely, so roads must be built
on which it is impossible to get hurt. But what of the economy of expenditure?
Do thoughts need the same protections to which bodies must submit? Should
navigation through a database be restricted by the habits of highway safety?*

METHOD

We now have proof of the compatibility of the ideas of two French post-structuralist theories. Actually, the compatibility exists at the level of metaphor—the key metaphors used in two important theoretical texts. The metaphors model the concept of dissemination or distribution of ideas. Jacques Derrida, in *The Post Card,* developed the image of mail delivery and the whole history of the "post" as a model for a theory of signification. Gilles Deleuze and Felix Guattari introduced in *A Thousand Plateaus* the image of a rhizome as a kind of spreading growth (weeds, crabgrass) that offered an alternative way to think about how ideas spread through cultures and history.

What is the relationship between these two conceptual images? The answer may be found in an article in *Natural History* magazine, describing how some of America's most troublesome weeds were dispersed through the mail, by means of the mail-order seed business. In the late 1840s, when postal rates became affordable, "the mail quickly became an efficient dispenser of plants," such as Johnson grass, sold across the country. "The high forage production of this grass came at a steep price for the farmer. In the course of its vigorous growth, Johnson grass forms tenacious tangles of rhizomes, among which few other plants can grow."[6]

From the old seed catalogs the author draws the following lessons: "how good intentions can go amiss"; never disseminate any wild plant until "we have firm evidence that it is unlikely to become weedy."[7] Ironically, one of the icons of the American frontier—the tumbleweed (also the product of unwanted seeds distributed through the mail)—originated in Russia.

SACRIFICE

Georges Bataille points out that, despite all the discussion over the ages, "there is nothing that permits one to define what is useful to man."[8] The problem is that individuals, and human societies, can have "an interest in considerable losses, in catastrophes that, while conforming to well-defined needs, provoke tumultuous depressions, crises of dread, and in the final analysis, a certain organic state."[9] Bataille distinguishes between the normal practices of production/consumption and unproductive expenditure—"luxury, mourning, war, cults, the construction of sumptu-

ary monuments, games, spectacles, arts, perverse sexual activity." These
are activities with "no end beyond themselves"; not a balanced economy,
but one in which the "loss must be as great as possible in order for that
activity to take on its true meaning."[10]

Expenditure works openly in a community organized around the
practices of sacrifice. "Sacrifice" is one of those concepts, such as "taboo"
and "fetish," translated from the practices of "primitive" civilizations to
the theoretical systems of the human sciences. Bataille extends the concept as a way to understand his own society, considering war as that
which makes social life what it is. The purpose of sacrifice in primitive
societies, according to Bataille's sources, was to reveal this continuity
through the deaths of discontinuous beings (the monumental function).

> If I am to find an answer to the enigma of sacrifice, I must be deliberate
> and shrewd. But I know and have never for an instant doubted that an
> enigma as dangerous as this one lies outside the scope of academic
> method; the sacred mysteries must be approached with craft, with a show
> of boldness and transgression. The enigma's answer must be formulated
> on a level equal to that of its celebrants' performance. It is my wish that
> it become part of the history of sacrifice, not of science. This general wish
> may account for my proposing to solve the enigma—in laughter.[11]

> *These are the things that happen to thought in dreamwork, rendering it
> incoherent: condensation or compression. Every situation in a dream seems to
> be put together out of two or more impressions or experiences. The dreamwork
> then proceeds just as Francis Galton did in constructing his family pho-
> tographs. The photographs of the victims remain in the possession of those who
> remember them. It superimposes the different components upon one another.*

> *The components, as it were, collide. The most convenient way of bringing
> together two dream-thoughts which, to start with, have nothing in common,
> is to alter the verbal form of one of them, and thus bring it half-way to meet
> the other, which may be similarly clothed in a new form of words. A parallel
> process is involved in hammering out a rhyme. How to listen to the hammer-
> ing out in the rhythm of wrecking?*

PROPOSAL

An immense sacrifice is performed annually in the private sphere in
America, occurring at an individual level, unperceived, or, if perceived

statistically, then not experienced and certainly not understood. That sacrifice is the death of nearly 50,000 people each year in automobile crashes in the United States.[12] Death is necessary, Bataille reminds us, and it seems obvious that highway fatalities are an expenditure of fundamental importance to the community's identity. The premise of the MEmorial is that traffic fatalities are not an anomaly in an otherwise rational order, as normal consultants would have it.

Buckminster Fuller remained within the model of individual responsibility for one's actions when he declared drivers to be ineducable, leading to his proposal for the four-lane divided highway, intended to eliminate most collisions. Even Marxist or social-constructionist critics, who shift the frame from ethics to politics to point out that the corporate demand for profits overrides all other considerations in a capitalist culture, still remain within the terms of the Restricted Economy. The design premise, rather, is that traffic fatalities are fundamentally "abject," meaning that they are a sacrifice on behalf of some "value" that is more important to the society than the annual loss of 50,000 citizens. This "value" is not an ideal that may be named in a concept (justice, virtue, freedom) but remains inarticulate, within the bodies and behaviors of individuals in the private sphere, untransformed, nontranscendent, unredeemed (formless).

The goal of Traffic is to make this sacrifice perceptible, thinkable, recognizable as such—to shift it from the private sphere of one-at-a-time individual personal loss to the public sphere of collective identity. Americans: we-who-die-at-the-wheel. The proposal is to launch a satellite—a giant EAR in the sky, equivalent to the eye-in-the-sky weather satellites. In the same way that citizens catch a glimpse of the earth each evening during the weather report on the local news, graphically enhanced to show the activities of clouds, rain, and wind, so too would the ear-in-the-sky make it possible to focus on the sounds significant to our culture. With its sensitive recording capacities, the ear satellite is programmed to pick up the noise made by car crashes all over the country. With computer enhancement, the recorded crashes are replayed at various speeds, compressed in various ways, similar to time-lapse photography, in order to discern the rhythm of the crashes.

It is possible that the accidents produce a specific beat. While this beat should be analyzed scientifically for any patterns that might provide an insight into the enigma of sacrifice, it could also be adapted to performative ends, including the invention of a new musical form. Following the lead of those composers who mix documentary sound with music, and exploiting the technology of sampling, the crash rhythms become danceable. Such a record may lead to better forecasting of crash rates, of the sort already provided before holiday weekends. Reported in their own spot on the evening news, with the help of satellite technology, automobile deaths could take on their proper significance for our society, making clearer than is now possible why we are willing to go to war for Arabian oil. A new national ritual is to be introduced, similar to the one introduced to coincide with the opening of the Columbian exposition in Chicago in 1893—the pledge of allegiance to the flag. The new ritual consists of a moment not of silence but of "noise," played at the end of each school day, as the teenagers prepare to drive home. In this way the disproportionate number of teen lives sacrificed for the car is recognized.

Such a recognition, giving these victims their due, contributes to the mourning process, making available for the first time an appreciation of the community service performed by the lost loved ones. The service could be expanded eventually, with improved technology, to record the cries of victims of other crimes (murder, rape, mugging)—a chorus. The title for the person assigned to organize this service is choroner. Simonides, it should be remembered, invented artificial memory by being able to identify the bodies of those killed when a roof collapsed on a party. (He remembered where each person was seated.) The relationship between death and memory must be reorganized once again for an electronic apparatus, which continues the mnemonic tradition in its own way.

To imagine the future of Traffic as an institution, compare its current embodiment—the video arcades—with the beginnings of cinema, similarly organized originally as a sideshow for the circus or carnival. The games of road-racing (and the inevitable crash) and war-making that tend to dominate the arcades provide a technological and social location for grafting onto current practices the monumental function of Traffic of the Spheres. The new behavior known as "road rage" in this context may be seen for what it is: patriotism.

Psychoanalysis and automobiles were invented at about the same time. In condensation, two strangers travelling at high speed enter one another's vehicles through a mutual windshield. The parts of the vehicles in contact have something in common, forming a composite idea, while indistinct subordinate details correspond to the parts that are scattered about the roadway. If displacement takes place in addition to condensation, what is constructed is an "intermediate common entity," which stands in a relation to the two different cars similar to that in which the resultant in a parallelogram of force stands to its components. At least two wreckers are needed in such a case, if not the "Jaws of Life," for the idea to complete its shape.

PERIPHERAL

While the ear-in-the-sky is a long-range proposal, the MEmorial is to be initiated in a more immediately practical way, by means of a "peripheral" monument. Peripheral monuments, like their computer counterparts, add functionality to an established memorial. The peripheral is a transitional device, relating literate monumentality to its electrate counterpart. An existing memorial, such as the Vietnam Wall on the Mall in Washington, D.C., honors a sacrifice for an acknowledged community value. The peripheral establishes a connection between this acknowledged value and the unacknowledged but lived value of the loss in the private sphere—in this case, traffic fatalities. The juxtaposition creates an analogy for visitors that adds to their tourist practice the status of theoria (witness). The most inspired peripheral to date is the quilt appropriated for the NAMES project (the AIDS Memorial Quilt), which helped shift AIDS-related deaths from individual loss to collective sacrifice. The achievement is especially important as a relay for electronic monumentality, since many of the victims were associated with behaviors that the mainstream society experienced as abject (homosexuality, drug abuse).

The genre of a MEmorial includes the following elements (with the response of Traffic of the Spheres in parentheses):

- Select an existing monument, memorial, celebration to which to attach the peripheral. (Vietnam Memorial)
- Select an organization, agency, or other administrative unit that has some responsibility for policy formation in relation to the disaster,

to be the nominal recipient of the consultation. (Mothers Against Drunk Driving)

- Select a theory as the source of the rationale informing the consultation. (Bataille, *The Accursed Share*)
- Place an (electronic) device at the site, designed to link symbolically the established sacrifice with the unacknowledged sacrifice.

The exemplarity of this case, juxtaposing traffic victims with war dead, is due in part to the controversy surrounding Maya Lin's design for the Wall, which was widely denounced as the "black gash of shame" and, as such, unsuitable for paying respects to our soldiers. An editorial published in the *National Review* during the controversy, prior to the building of the Wall, argued that this black wall listing the names of dead soldiers dishonored their sacrifice for the nation: "They might as well have been traffic accidents," the editorialist complained.[13] The car crash is abject in being a degraded, disavowed, repressed sacrifice. Most deaths in America are assigned to such categories as Natural Causes, Accidents, Disease, Murder, Suicide, to which the MEmorial would add Sacrifice. The soldiers died for the ideal of freedom; they did their duty, in the official story of the nation. And the automobile operators and passengers? They died for a formless value—the behavior that performs freedom: to drive wherever I want, whenever I want, in whatever manner I choose, so help me God.

The Traffic peripheral makes an excellent prototype since it literally is a computer peripheral device—a printer. A computer is set up at the Vietnam memorial to print out the names of victims of crashes as they occur. The total number of Americans killed in Vietnam (58,000+) establishes a threshold for the acceptable annual automobile death rate. Should this number be exceeded, the computer triggers a mechanism in the Sky-Ear satellites that causes all monitors nationwide to blink uncontrollably. The satellites at the same time take over traffic lights nationwide, setting all signals to red. No driving is permitted from that moment on, until the New Year, when the meter returns to zero and the lottery begins again. Meanwhile, citizens visiting the Wall to touch or make rubbings of the names of loved ones lost in the war may at the same time get a copy of the page listing the name or names of loved ones killed in traffic.

The manifest content of wrecks consists for the most part in pictorial situations; and the wreck- thoughts must accordingly be submitted to a treatment that will make them suitable for a representation of this kind. The material will be submitted to a pressure that will condense it greatly, to an internal fragmentation and displacement that will, as it were, create new surfaces, and to a selective operation in favor of those portions of it that are the most appropriate for the construction of situations.

Dreamwork builds with the forces of wreckage a rhetoric governed by the five forces of stress. Compression is the direct expression of gravity pulling everything to the center of the earth. Tension is the opposite of compression; where there is one, there must be the other. The other three forms of stress are based on these two pure forms. Shear is a complex stress. When two forces are thrusting in opposite directions but offset and slide past each other, shear is present. In structural concerns, shear and bending are found between the pulling of tension and the pushing of compression. Torsion is a result of all four of the other forces. Torsion is twist. The dreamers' hands turn the steering wheel, exerting a torsional force that is transferred torsionally to the dream-thoughts. Torsion is actually a specialized bending, a circular bending. With these forces in both harmony and discord the living and the inanimate face the perils of dreaming.

What happens to cars happens to thoughts. The forces of compression, tension, shear, bending, and torsion work upon bodies and minds in the manner of stress. The wreckage—these designs we are reading—presents us with a wish in unrecognizable form. It is interesting to observe that the popular belief that car wrecks foretell the future is confirmed. Actually the future that the wreck shows us is not the one that will occur but the one that we should like to occur. The popular mind is behaving here as it usually does: what it wishes, it believes.

COMMENT

The students who fled Gainesville in their cars to avoid becoming victims of the mad slasher put themselves at greater risk of death, statistically, than if they had stayed at home, taking appropriate precautions by propping shut their sliding glass doors with broom handles.

REFERENCES

Jean-Luc Godard, *Weekend*

Loud music over a shot of wrecked cars blazing on either side of a road. There are bright orange flames, clouds of black smoke; the wrecks crackle and bang as their petrol tanks explode. Camera cranes up as ROLAND and CORINNE limp into view in the background. Roland addressing a corpse lying in the road: "Hey, you, where's the nearest garage?"[14]

Jim Dine, *The Car Crash*

Traffic sounds (crash) for approx. 2 min. Spot on wringer. Car cranks out help, Pat is saying help softly, one white person is banging softly, other is passing out help signs. Pat gets louder, keeps saying help in a drone. Car begins to stutter and draw cars and erase them. Two white people stand and cough, gag, stammer and stutter.[15]

Peter Greenaway, *A Zed and Two Noughts*

The film begins with a car crash. Outside a zoo, a mute swan smashes into the windscreen of a white Ford Mercury, registration number NID 26B/W, driven by a woman wearing white feathers called Alba Bewick. An accident? "Five thousand accidents happen every day—bizarre, tragic, farcical. They are Acts of God, fit only to amaze the survivors and irritate the Insurance Company." This one is different for God's sake. Or Darwin's.[16]

J. G. Ballard, *Crash*

In his vision of a car-crash with the actress, Vaughan was obsessed by many wounds and impacts—by the dying chromium and collapsing bulkheads of their two cars meeting head-on in complex collisions endlessly repeated in slow-motion films, by the identical wounds inflicted on their bodies, by the image of windshield glass frosting around her face as she broke its tinted surface like a death-born Aphrodite, by the compound fractures of their thighs impacted against their handbrake mountings, and above all by the wounds to their genitalia, her uterus pierced by the heraldic beak of the manufacturer's medallion, his semen emptying across the luminescent dials that registered forever the last temperature and fuel levels of the engine.[17]

EQUIPMENT

Communication satellites are microwave relay links in space. Generally, there are [four] types of satellites: weather and observational satellites;

communication satellites; space probes; [and sacrifice frames]. Since the late 1970s, four geostationary satellites have been in orbit for U.S. weather observation. Their viewing areas take in the North and South poles. One satellite covers the area from the Mississippi to New Zealand; the other, from about 500 miles off the California coast to the western coast of Africa. The other two are parked in reserve orbit. The daily task of the satellite service station is the collection and distribution of images. The satellite spins on its axis, and every time the camera comes around facing the earth, it takes one scan line.[18]

A similar arrangement is feasible for the Sky-Ear, using geostationary or synchronous satellites fixed over a particular spot on earth. The orbits for the Sky-Ears, however, would have to be somewhat lower than those for the Sky-Eyes. Three designers—Williams, Rosen, and Hudspeth—working for Hughes Aircraft, invented the geostationary satellite in 1962.[19] Enough progress has been made in surveillance technology to permit low-orbit listening transmission, including relays from ground stations placed at regular intervals relative to the interstate highway system. The advances in global-positioning networks and hand-held devices may support this additional service.

The ceremony of the car includes the design process. Designed for safety more than sacrifice, cars are built as impact cushions, collapsing and folding upon contact, so that even modest fender-benders produce spectacular wreckage. The car as ruin is anticipated in its creation. What of these postcrash designs, the ones we are reading as architecture? Are these the first to rectify the balance of design, mountains of drawings in the production process, and none coming after the catastrophe? The latter lift from the wreck the memories it contains, showing us the writing of the event. It is not so much writing but a score. It is music to be played.

Dawn Gregerson tells her story in an ad for Volvo. "We were laughing because on this desert highway, in the middle of nowhere, in the middle of the road, there was a man painting yellow lines on the road. We never saw it coming. He came out of nowhere. One second we were joking, the next we were flying through space, tumbling and tumbling." Each year there are 34 million traffic accidents in this country, the ad continues. An accident every second. An injury due to traffic accidents every six seconds. A death every twelve minutes. When Dawn Gregerson opened her eyes after the accident, she felt like she had been sleeping for a hundred years. Volvo has been able to develop

*crumple zones that absorb impact energy, steel-reinforced passenger cages, and
a side-impact protection system, the ad declares, so that Dawn did not become
a statistic. She just had a bad dream.*

THE DEATH CAR: URBAN LEGEND

My friend from Los Angeles breathlessly announced that she could pick
up a $5,400 Porsche Targa sports car for only $500. The reason for the
reduced price was that it had sat in the middle of the Mojave Desert for
one week with a dead man in it; consequently, the smell of death could
not be removed from it.[20]

NOTES

1. Georges Bataille, *The Accursed Share: An Essay on General Economy* (New York: Zone, 1998), 21.
2. Ibid.
3. Norman Malcolm, *Ludwig Wittgenstein, A Memoir* (London: Oxford University Press, 1958), 7–8.
4. Roland Barthes, *S/Z*, trans. Richard Miller (New York: Hill and Wang, 1974; translation modified).
5. Jacques Derrida, "Chora," in *Poikilia: Etudes Offertes Jean-Pierre Vernant* (Paris: Ehess, 1987), 265–266.
6. Richard N. Mack, "Catalog of Woes," *Natural History,* March 1990, 51.
7. Ibid., 52.
8. Bataille, *Accursed Share,* 116.
9. Ibid., 117.
10. Ibid., 118.
11. Bataille, *Visions of Excess: Selected Writings, 1927–1939,* ed. and trans. by Alan Stoekl (Minneapolis: Minnesota University Press, 1986), 61.
12. Statistics from MADD.
13. "Stop that Monument," *National Review,* September 18, 1981, 1064.
14. Jean-Luc Godard, *"Weekend" and "Wind From the East,"* (London: Lorrimer, 1972), 54.
15. Jim Dine, "The Car Crash" in Michael Kirby, ed., *Happenings* (New York: Dutton, 1966), 190.
16. Peter Greenaway, *A Zed and Two Noughts* (London: Faber, 1986), 13.
17. J. G. Ballard, *Crash* (New York: Vintage, 1985), 8.
18. Ken Marsh, *The Way the New Technology Works* (New York: Simon and Schuster, 1982), 79–88.
19. Brian Winston, *Misunderstanding Media* (Cambridge, MA: Harvard University Press, 1986), 261.
20. Jan-Harold Brunvand, *The Vanishing Hitchhiker* (New York: Norton, 1981), 20.

CONTRIBUTORS

KENNETH ANGER is an author, artist, filmmaker, magician, collector, and acknowledged expert on subjects ranging from the occult to Hollywood movies. Born in 1930 in Santa Monica, California, he is the creator of such legendary films as *Scorpio Rising, Lucifer Rising,* and *Invocation of My Demon Brother,* and of the infamous *Hollywood Babylon* books. Anger resides in Hollywood, and remains an influential force in the American avant garde and underground film scenes.

STEPHEN BOLESTA, M.D., is Assistant Professor of Pathology at St. Louis University, St. Louis, Missouri and Medical Lab Director at Memorial Hospital, Belleville, Illinois. He has served as Assistant Medical Examiner for Boone and Callaway counties (1984–1988) and as Associate and Deputy Medical Examiner for the Office of the Chief Medical Examiner of New York (1988).

MIKITA BROTTMAN is the author of a number of books on the horror film. She is interested in all kinds of pathologies, and regularly publishes in academic as well as alternative and underground journals. She is currently a Professor in the Department of Liberal Arts at Maryland Institute College of Art in Baltimore and an Associate of the Columbia University Seminar on Film and Interdisciplinary Interpretation.

JULIAN DARIUS is a graduate student in the Department of English at Southern Illinois University, Carbondale.

JAY D. DIX, M.D., is Associate Professor of Pathology at Missouri-Columbia and the Boone and Callaway counties Medical Examiner.

JEFF FERRELL is the author of *Crimes of Style: Urban Graffiti and the Politics of Criminality* and *Tearing Down the Streets,* and co-editor of *Cultural Criminology, Ethnography at the Edge,* and *Making Trouble.*

JOHN R. FINCH, M.D., was a resident in Psychiatry at Baylor College of Medicine in Houston, Texas, from July 1962 to June 1965. He was appointed to the faculty as an Assistant Professor of Psychiatry and remained there until his death on July 23, 1971, when he, his wife, and two sons died in a hotel fire in New Orleans, Louisiana.

JERRY GLOVER is an independent writer-producer for television and film. He has written several novels, and contributes to many publications under various guises. Reach him at jerry@gag.co.uk.

HARVEY ROY GREENBERG, M.D., is Clinical Professor of Psychiatry at the Albert Einstein College of Medicine in New York. He practices psychiatry and psychoanalysis privately and frequently publishes on cinema, media, and popular culture.

TAKESHI IMAJO, M.D., is Deputy Coroner, Cuyahuga County Coroner's Office, Cleveland, Ohio, and Instructor of Forensic Pathology, Case Western Reserve University, School of Medicine, Cleveland, Ohio.

DAVID KEREKES is editor of the underground journal *Headpress*. He is author of *Sex Murder Art: The Films of Jörg Buttgereit* and coauthor of the books *Killing for Culture* and *See No Evil*.

HOWARD LAKE continues to be fascinated, mesmerized, and joyously appalled by post-postmodern society in all its awful hyperreality, a situation only compounded by his regular gig as editor of several prominent U.S. adult magazines. For relaxation he enjoys pro wrestling, religious insanity, and allied pursuits. He can be contacted at howard.lake@virgin.net.

ERIC LAURIER holds an Urban Studies Research Fellowship at the University of Glasgow. During his research career he has looked at driving as a fundamental way of experiencing the city, the improvised making of cars into mobile offices, and how drivers organize "stuff" in their trunks, backseats, and front seats. He has been knocked over and not killed three times by, in order of occurrence, a taxi (at age seven), a retired police officer (at age fifteen), and a large silver Mercedes (at age thirty).

A. LOUDERMILK is a poet with individual publications in *Rhino 2000, The Red Envelope, The James White Review,* and the Academy of American Poets' forthcoming book *New Voices . . . 1989–1998,* edited by Heather McHugh. Loudermilk's first collection of poems is called *Daring Love.*

WILLIAM LUHR is Professor of English at Saint Peter's College, New Jersey, and Co-Chair of the Columbia Seminar on Cinema and Interdisciplinary Interpretation. He is the author of *Raymond Chandler and Film;* editor of *World Cinema Since 1945* and *The Maltese Falcon: John Huston, Director;* and coauthor of *Thinking About Movies: Watching, Questioning, Enjoying* as well as books on Blake Edwards and other topics.

JOHN M. MACDONALD, M.D., is now retired. He was formerly Associate Professor of Psychiatry, University of Colorado School of Medicine, and Associate Director, Inpatient Service, Colorado Psychopathic Hospital, Denver, Colorado. He is the author of numerous articles in the field of crime and psychiatry as well as two full-length volumes, *The Murderer and His Victim* and *Psychiatry and the Criminal.*

PAMELA MCELWAIN-BROWN is a Phi Beta Kappa graduate of Bucknell University. Her area of specialty is the Kennedy Presidential Limousine. She hosts a website at www.jfk100x.com., has been published in journals on both sides of the Atlantic, and was a presenter in 1999 at the JFK-lancer conference in Dallas. Pamela lives in the Twin Cities, where she is a free-lance flute player. She is currently developing a full-length manuscript on the presidential limousine.

TURHON A. MURAD, PH.D., has been a Professor of Anthropology at California State University, Chico, since 1972. He is a Diplomate of the American Board of Forensic Anthropology and Fellow of both the American Academy of Forensic Sciences and the American Association of Physical Anthropology.

MICHAEL NEWTON is a freelance author with 153 books published since 1977 and 14 pending release from various houses through 2002. He is best known for his work in the true-crime genre, including the recent *Encyclopedia of Serial Killers*.

ADAM PARFREY cofounded Amok Press with Ken Swezey and published the early *Amok Dispatch* sourcebooks but split to form his own company, Feral House Publishers. Parfrey is best known for his seminal anthologies *Apocalypse Culture* (1987, 1990) and *Apocalypse Culture II* (2000), hailed by J.G. Ballard as a collection of "the terminal documents of the Twentieth Century."

ALEX D. POKORNY, M.D., is currently an Emeritus Professor of Psychiatry at Baylor College of Medicine in Houston, Texas. He has been a member of the Baylor Psychiatry faculty since 1949. From 1949 to 1973 he was on the staff of the Houston VA Hospital, most of the time as Chief of the Psychiatry Service. At Baylor he has served as Assistant Chairman and Acting Chairman of the Psychiatry Department. He has been active in research and has many publications, especially in the areas of psychopharmacology, alcohol and drug abuse, and suicide and violent behavior.

DEREK PARKER ROYAL is Assistant Professor of English at North Georgia College and State University. He primarily works on American literature and theories of ethnicity but has published on a variety of authors and genres. His writings have covered such figures as Philip Roth, Albert Camus, Mark Twain, Nathaniel Hawthorne, Arthur Miller, Jean-Paul Sartre, John Updike, Cynthia Ozick, Woody Allen, Kenneth Branagh, and Laurence Olivier.

J. C. RUPP, M.D., PH.D., is now retired. He was the medical examiner in Corpus Christi, Texas, from 1970 to 1993. He now does consulting and is an authority on sex crimes and death scene investigation. The last several years have been spent producing a multimedia CD-ROM on the medical and forensic problems related to illegal drug abuse. His website may be visited at www.deep6inc.com.

JACK SARGEANT is author of *Deathtripping: The Cinema of Transgression, Naked Lens: Beat Cinema,* and *Cinema Contra Cinema.* He is editor of the journal *Suture* and contributes to numerous publications including *Headpress, Bizarre,* and *Sleazenation,* among others. His underground film events and tours are legendary, combining academic lectures, screenings, and occasional outbursts of virulent nihilism. He has compiled the first official video release of New York punk cinema *The Cinema of Transgression,* available via www.bfi.org.uk. Sargeant also teaches at the London Institute, London College of Printing. He is thirty-three years old and divides his time between his home in Brighton and traveling. He hates relaxing.

STEVEN JAY SCHNEIDER is a doctoral student in Philosophy at Harvard University and in Cinema Studies at New York University's Tisch School of the Arts. His essays and reviews on the horror film genre have appeared in numerous journals and anthologies. He is currently editing a special issue of *Post Script: Essays in Film and the Humanities* on Realist Horror Cinema as well as a collection entitled *Fear Without Frontiers: Horror Cinema Across the Globe.* Steven is also writing a book on director Wes Craven.

CHRISTOPHER SHARRETT is Professor of Communication at Seton Hall University. He has long been obsessed with violence in culture and has written on such subjects as *The Texas Chainsaw Massacre, Taxi Driver,* David Cronenberg, *Apocalypse Now,* the Mad Max films, Jack the Ripper, *Psycho, The Alamo, Zulu, The Wild Bunch,* Oliver Stone's *JFK* and *Nixon,* and Syberberg's *Our Hitler.* He is on the editorial board of *Cinema Journal.*

PHILIP L. SIMPSON received his undergraduate degree in English from Eastern Illinois University in 1986, his master's degree in English from Eastern Illinois University in 1989, and his doctoral degree in modern American literature from Southern Illinois University in 1996. He currently works as an Associate Professor of Communications and Humanities at the Palm Bay campus of Brevard Community College in Florida in 1997. Dr. Simpson's book, *Psycho Paths: The Serial Killer in Contemporary American Film and Literature,* was published in the fall of 2000 by Southern Illinois University Press.

JAMES PATRICK SMITH, J.D., is an attorney who was on the full-time faculty at Baylor College of Medicine during the course of a study funded by the Department of Transportation that resulted in the publication *Drivers Who Die*. Since then he has primarily been in the private practice of law in Houston, but he has remained on the voluntary faculty in the Department of Psychiatry at Baylor as a Clinical Assistant Professor.

DAVID STERRITT is film critic for *The Christian Science Monitor*, Professor of Theater and Film at Long Island University, adjunct film professor at Columbia University, Co-Chair of the Columbia University Seminar on Cinema and Interdisciplinary Interpretation, and past Chair of The New York Film Critics Circle. He is author of *Mad to Be Saved: The Beats, the '50s, and Film; The Films of Jean-Luc Godard: Seeing the Invisible;* and *The Films of Alfred Hitchcock;* and editor of books on Jean-Luc Godard and Robert Altman. Articles by Dr. Sterritt have appeared in the *Journal of Aesthetics and Art Criticism, Mosaic,* the *New York Times,* the *Chronicle of Higher Education, Film Comment, Cineaste,* the *Quarterly Review of Film and Video,* and many other periodicals. He is a frequent lecturer at universities and museums and a juror at international film festivals.

GREGORY L. ULMER is Professor of English and Media Studies at the University of Florida and is the author of *Heuretics: The Logic of Invention*. His current project, in collaboration with the Florida Research Ensemble, is a chorography of Miami entitled *Miami Miautre*.

TONY WILLIAMS is Professor and Area Head of Film Studies in the Department of English, Southern Illinois University, at Carbondale. His articles have appeared in *Cinema Journal, CineAction, Asian Cinema, Wide Angle, Film History,* and *Jump Cut*. He has recently published *Structures of Desire: British Cinema 1939–1955*.

INDEX